Multicultural
Spanish Dictionary

Multicultural Spanish Dictionary

How Everyday Spanish Differs from
Country to Country

Edited by Agustín Martínez

Schreiber Publishing, Inc.

Multicultural Spanish Dictionary
Edited by Agustín Martínez

Published by:

Schreiber Publishing, Inc.
Post Office Box 4193
Rockville, MD 20849 USA
www.schreibernet.com
spbooks@aol.com

copyright © 1999 Schreiber Publishing, Inc.

First Printing

Library of Congress Cataloging-in-Publication Data

Martinez, Agustín, 1967-
    Multicultural Spanish Dictionary: how everyday Spanish differs from country to country / edited by Agustín Martinez.
        p.   cm.
    "The Spanish companion to The translator's handbook"--Cover.
    ISBN 1-887563-45-8 (pbk : alk. paper)
    1. Spanish language Dictionaries--English. 2. English language Dictionaries--Spanish. 3. Spanish language--Provincialisms--Latin America Dictionaries. I. Title
PC4640.M26 1999
463'.21--DC21

99-22373
CIP

TABLE OF CONTENTS

ACKNOWLEDGEMENTS

The publisher wishes to acknowledge the diligent work of the editors and contributors of this groundbreaking volume. The idea for this kind of innovative Spanish dictionary was born during annual conferences of the American Translators Association, to which most of the contributors belong. It grew out of the practical experience of Spanish translators who have been confronting the daily realities of having to find the right Spanish word for such common things as a flat tire or a bow tie. When called upon to participate in this effort, they all came forward and plunged into this exploratory task with great enthusiasm. Their contributions are greatly appreciated.

LIST OF CONTRIBUTORS

Ana María Berger, *Guatemala*
Teresa María Campero, *Bolivia*
Nefertiti Casado-Hagan, *Dominican Republic*
Milagros Cobos, *Spain*
Enid González, *Puerto Rico*
Andrés Harnecker, *Costa Rica*
Ana Kalnay, *Argentina*
Ana Victoria Krizán, *Ecuador*
Agustín Martínez, *Cuba*
Anamaris Martínez, *Panama*
Arne Myne, *Costa Rica*
Lidia Nazak, *Uruguay*
Ruth Olson, *Venezuela*
Katia Panhans, *Mexico*
Guadalupe Reynolds, *Peru*
Sandra M. Rivera de Aquino, *Puerto Rico*
Teresa Román, *Chile*
Carolina Valencia, *Colombia*

INTRODUCTION

What kind of Spanish do you speak?

This may seem to be an odd question, since Spanish is Spanish is Spanish. Not so. When you go to the grocery store in Uruguay, you go to the *almacén*. In Peru you go to the *bodega*. In Uruguay the *bodega* is a wine cellar. In fact, if you travel to a dozen different Latin American countries, you will find a dozen different names for "grocery store."

There are scores of Spanish-English dictionaries to choose from, but none of them takes cognizance of the variety of everyday Spanish words as used throughout Latin America and in Spain. In fact, if you compare the word "grocery" in a number of widely used Spanish-English dictionaries, you will find that there is little consistency among them as to which Spanish term they list first, and none of them lists them all.

This is where *The Multicultural Spanish Dictionary* comes in. It is not meant to replace the standard Spanish-English dictionaries, but rather to pick up where they leave off. As such, it has many uses. It can serve native speakers of Spanish who are interested in finding out how certain words vary in other parts of the Hispanic world. It can also serve non-native speakers who have dealings with or travel to one or more Spanish-speaking country and need to know how a particular word is rendered in each country. In short, anyone who works with the Spanish language needs to add this book to his or her reference shelf.

Since this small volume is breaking new ground, it is far from being an exhaustive work. The editors have chosen the most common areas of everyday life and have attempted to cover the most commonly used words in each area. To facilitate the use of this book, words are accessible in three ways:

PART I: ENGLISH - SPANISH: words which vary in one or more Spanish speaking countries (e.g., "apple," is not included in this section, since everyone calls it *manzana*; "grapefruit" is included, since most call it *toronja*, yet in Argentina, Chile, Spain, and Uruguay it is called *pomelo).* Each English word is matched with what appears to be the most widely used Spanish equivalent and followed by variations according to country (a key to country abbreviations is provided at the bottom of each page).

PART II: SPANISH - ENGLISH: words which vary in one or more Spanish-speaking countries. Here the most commonly used Spanish word is followed by Pri., for "Primary Term," while variations are given with the country indicator.

PART III: SUBJECT AREAS: This English-into-Spanish section include all the common words in that particular category. Words which vary are bolded.

Each Spanish-speaking country included in this book is represented by a native speaker of the language of that country. One must keep in mind, however, that even within a country—particularly large countries like Mexico or Argentina—there may be more than one way of rendering a common word. In a big city, "grocery store" may be *supermercado,* the free rendition of the American English word "supermarket," while in a smaller town one still goes to the corner grocery, which retains the old name. Language can never be reduced to one absolute term, especially in our fast-changing world. No matter how thoroughly researched, a dictionary is always a working guide rather than a definitive and immutable source. With this in mind, one can put this book to good use without expecting it to always provide the final word.

Some countries are covered more in depth than others. Honduras and El Salvador are not as fully covered as the other Central American countries, and Nicaragua is not dealt with specifically.

Many of the words in Central America, however, are common throughout the region. Similarly, although Paraguay is not dealt with specifically, it shares many words with other countries in southern South America.

At a conference on the Spanish language held in Mexico in the late 1990s, scholars, writers, linguists, and even heads of state (including the king of Spain) discussed the nature and direction of the Spanish language. Is Spain still the standard-bearer of Spanish? Has Latin America, or one particular Latin American country, such as Mexico, taken the lead? Is there a standard Spanish language? These questions sparked much debate but little agreement.

The Varieties of Spanish

There are several reasons for the great variety of common Spanish words. Historically, Spanish originated in the Iberian Peninsula, at the southwestern tip of Europe. It descended directly from the Latin spoken by the Romans who invaded the peninsula around 200 B.C. Three other Latin-based languages which emerged on the peninsula are Portuguese, Catalan, and Galician. In the eighth century, Spain was invaded by the Moors from nearby North Africa, who brought with them their Arabic culture and language. For nearly eight centuries they ruled the peninsula and left their mark on the Spanish language. Many Spanish words, particularly those beginning with *al*, Arabic for "the," are derived from Arabic. These include *almohada* (pillow), *albañil* (mason), and *albaricoque* (apricot). Other linguistic influences in the peninsula predate Latin. For example, the Basque language of northern Spain produced the word *izquierda* (left), derived from the Basque *ezkerra*.

But perhaps the greatest cultural impact on Spanish came after Spain colonized the New World. During the ensuing four centuries, Spanish spread from California in North America to Tierra del Fuego at the southern tip of South America, making Spanish one of the most widely spoken languages in the world. In the New World, the Spanish language was exposed to many indigenous languages and cultural influences. This had an enormous impact on European Spanish, creating in effect multiple varieties of the mother tongue. In Mexico, the Aztec language and culture provided Mexican Spanish with names of flora and fauna and with place names. In Peru, Ecuador, and Bolivia, the Quechua language of the Incas intermingled with Spanish and produced everyday words like *adobe* (sun-baked brick), and *choclo* (corn). In Caribbean countries like Cuba, African slaves gave Spanish words like *marimba* (an African xylophone). Many of Puerto Rico's place names date back to the Taino Indians. In Argentina and Uruguay, significant immigration from Italy greatly influenced the local Spanish, creating an accent which is a mixture of Spanish and Italian, and adding such greetings as *chau* to the local speech.

Another major influence on Spanish is American English. Its impact is felt in the areas of Latin America closest to the United States, such as northern Mexico and Puerto Rico, to a lesser extent in Central America, and much less in South America. In Guatemala, for example, "to park (a car)" is *parquear*, while Argentinians still say *estacionar*. In South America "soccer ball" is *pelota*, whereas in Puerto Rico it is *bola*.

One may wonder why there are so many ways of saying "trunk (of car)" and "flat tire" throughout Latin America. One possible explanation is the following: Unlike the United States, which established a unified economy early on and developed a uniform technical terminology in areas such as the automotive industry, each country or region within a country in Latin America operated within its own local economic and social structure and was compelled to develop its own technical words. Thus, when the first cars arrived in Uruguay with a trunk on the back resembling a large box, Uruguayans called it a *baúl* (storage trunk), a name which has stuck to this day, while in other Latin American countries the word for "car trunk" is of a more recent origin.

In some cases, politics has created a difference in terminology. Just take the Argentinian and Chilean coast guards, which have not always been on good terms. In maritime Spanish, what Chile called *boya* (buoy) Argentina at one point called *baliza* (beacon), and vice versa, just to make sure that their buoys and beacons along the coast were not mixed up.

To quote our Colombian contributor, "Irrational as life itself, Spanish is not cast in stone. It is a constant process of dynamic expressions of people from town and country." Clearly, Spanish speakers worldwide cherish their freedom of expression, and the day when they all will start calling things by the same name is not near.

PART I: ENGLISH - SPANISH

A

abdomen (n) abdomen
Chi. guata
Col. región abdominal, vientre
Dom.R. vientre
Per. barriga
actor (n) actor
Col. artista, galán
actress (n) actriz
Col. artista
Adam's apple (n phr) manzana de Adán
Arg. nuez de Adán
Cub. nuez
Spa. nuez de la garganta
addicted (adj) adicto
Col. narcómano
addiction (n) dependencia
Col. adicción, hábito
Cos.R., Dom.R., Mex., Pan.,
Pue.R. adicción
adult (n) adulto
Col. persona mayor
aerobics (n) aerobismo
Col., Mex. aerobics
Dom.R., ElS., Gua., Hon., Pan.,
Pue.R., Uru. aeróbicos
Spa. aerobic
air conditioning (n phr) aire
acondicionado
Cos.R. airecondicionado
airfare (n) precio del pasaje

Arg., Ecu. tarifa
Col. tarifa aérea
Mex. tarifa de vuelo
Spa. precio del billete de avión
Venz. precio del boleto
airline (n) aerolínea
Col. compañía de aviación,
línea aérea
Dom.R. línea aérea
airplane (n) avión
Col. aeronave
alcoholic beverage (n phr) bebida
alcohólica
Chi. trago
alley (n) callejón
Col. callejuela, pasadizo
Per. pasaje
aluminum foil (n phr) papel de
aluminio
Chi., Pan. papel aluminio
Cos.R., ElS., Gua., Hon., Pan.,
Per. lámina de aluminio
amateur (n) amateur
Col., Mex., Venz. aficionado
Chi. amador
Cub. no profesional
Per. novato
amazing (adj) asombroso
Arg., Chi., Dom.R. increíble
Col. estupendo, fenomenal
anchovy (n) anchoa
Chi. anchoveta
Cos.R., Dom.R., Pue.R.,

---

boquerón
Per. anchoveta, boquerón
angry (adj) enojado
Col., Cub., Venz. bravo
Dom.R. furioso
Ecu. enfurecido
Pue.R. enfogono, molesto
antiperspirant (n) desodorante
Gua., Mex., Pue.R.
antiperspirante
apartment (n) apartamento
Arg., Bol., Chi., Mex.
departamento
Spa. piso
apartment building (n phr) edificio de
apartamentos
Arg., Bol., Mex. edificio de
departamentos
Chi., Col. edificio
Dom.R. torre de apartamentos
Spa. edificio de pisos
Uru. propiedad horizontal
appetizer (n) aperitivo
Arg., Dom.R., Uru. entrada
Cos.R. bocas
Ecu. entrada, primer plato
Pan. abreboca
Per. bocaditos
Spa. tapa
Venz. entremés
apricot (n) albaricoque
Arg., Chi., Uru. damasco
Mex. chabacano
armchair (n) silla de brazos
Arg., Chi., Spa., Uru. sillón
Cub., Pue.R. butaca
Dom.R. butaca, sillón
Mex. silla con coderas
armpit (n) axila
Dom.R. zobaco

Pan. sobaco
arrival (n) llegada
Chi. desembarque
artichoke (n) alcachofa
Arg., Uru. alcaucil
athlete (n) atleta
Pan. deportista
attaché case (n) maletín
Arg. portafolios
Mex. portafolio
automatic transmission (n phr)
transmisión automática
Spa. cambio automático
avocado (n) aguacate
Arg., Bol., Chi., Per., Uru. palta
awful (adj) horrible
Arg., Chi., Col. espantoso
Dom.R. terrible
awl (n) lezna
Bol., Col., Spa., Venz. punzón
Mex. berbiquí

Spanish contains numerous words of Arabic origin adopted over eight centuries of Moorish rule in Spain. Many begin with *al*, meaning "the" in Arabic: *almohada* (pillow), *albaricoque* (apricot), *albornoz* (bathrobe), *alquitrán* (tar), and *albañil* (mason).

B

baby (n) bebé
  Arg., Uru. beba, bebe
  Chi. guagua
babysit (v) hacer de niñero/a
  Arg., Uru. cuidar a un/a beba/
  bebe/chico/chica/nene/nena
  Chi., Col., Ecu., Per., Pue.R.,
  Venz. cuidar niños
  Mex. cuidar a un bebé/niño/niña
babysitter (n) niñero/a
  Arg. babysitter
  Chi. nodriza
  Mex. nana
  Per., Venz. cuidador/a de niños
back (soccer) (n) defensa
  Spa. defensor
backstroke (swimming) (n) estilo
espalda
  Cub. al revés
  Mex. dorso
bagel (n) rosca de pan
  Bol., Col., Pue.R. bagel
baggage (n) equipaje
  Cos.R. maletas
bags (under eyes) (n) ojeras
  Chi. chasquillas
  Dom.R. bolsas
baguette (n) baguette
  Bol., Chi., Col., Dom.R., Venz.
  pan francés
  Pan. pan flauta, pan francés
  Spa. barra de pan
bake (v) hornear
  Spa. cocinar en el horno
bakery (n) panadería
  Chi., Col. pastelería

  Pue.R. repostería
balcony (n) balcón
  Chi. terraza
  Col. balaustrada, balconcillo
ball (soccer) (n) pelota de fútbol
  Col. balón de fútbol
  Pue.R. bola de balompié
  Spa. balón
banana (n) plátano
  Arg., Uru. banana
  Col., Ecu. banano, guineo
  Dom.R., Pan., Pue.R. guineo
  Cos.R. banano
  Venz. cambur
bangs (hair) (n) flequillo
  Col. capul
  Cos.R. pava
  Cub., Ecu., Per. cerquillo
  Dom.R., Venz. pollina
  Mex. fleco
  Pan. gallusa
banjo (n) banjo
  Spa. banyo
banned film (n phr) película prohibida
  Col., Dom.R. película censurada
bar (music) (n) compás
  Col. barra (entre compases)
bar (n) bar
  Col. taberna
  Mex., Pan. cantina
barber (n) barbero
  Arg., Ecu., Mex., Per. peluquero
barracks (n) cuartel
  Pan. barracas
  Pue.R. barraca
barrette (n) broche para el pelo
  Arg., Bol., Col., Cub., Pue.R.
  hebilla
  Chi. traba
  Dom.R., Pan., Per., Spa. gancho

---

para el pelo
  Venz. ganchito de pelo
bartender (n) barman
  Col., Ecu., ElS., Gua., Hon.,
  Mex., Pan., Pue.R. cantinero
  Cub., Dom.R. bartender
basket (basketball) (n) cesta
  Arg., Mex., Pan., Per., Uru.
  canasta
  Bol. cesto
  Dom.R., Pue.R. canasto
basketball (n) baloncesto
  Arg., Per., Uru. basketbol
  Mex., Pan. basketball
bass (stereo) (n) graves
  Col. bajo
bass (voice) (n) bajo
  Col. contrabajo
batch (n) hornada
  Chi. horneada
  Col. tanda
  Cos.R. lote
bathing suit (n phr) traje de baño
  Arg. maya
  Col., Ecu., Pan. vestido de baño
  Cub. trusa
  Spa. bañador
bathrobe (n) bata de baño
  Bol. batón
  Spa. albornoz
bathroom (n) cuarto de baño
  Bol., Chi., Cos.R., Cub., Ecu.,
  Spa., Uru., Venz. baño
bean sprouts (n phr) germinados de
soja
  Arg., Uru. brotes de soja
  ElS., Gua., Hon. retoños de soya
  Pan. frijol nacido
  Pue.R. habichuelas de soya
beans (n) porotos

Col., Cub., Gua., Mex., Pan.
frijoles
Dom.R., Pue. R. habichuelas
Ecu. frejoles
Spa. alubias
Venz. caraotas
beans, black (n phr) frijoles
  Arg., Uru. porotos negros
  Col., Cub., ElS., Gua., Hon.,
  Mex., Pan. frijoles negros
  Pue.R. habichuelas negras
  Spa. alubias negras
  Venz. caraotas negras
beans, broad (n phr) habas
  Arg., Uru. chauchas
  Dom.R. guandules
beans, green (n phr) habichuelas
  Arg., Uru. chauchas
  Dom.R., Ecu., Per., Venz. vainitas
  ElS., Gua., Hon., Mex. ejotes
  Pue.R. habichuelas verdes
  Spa. judías verdes
beans, kidney (n phr) habichuelas
  Cub. frijoles colorados
  Dom.R. habichuelas rojas
  Spa. alubias rojas
beans, lima (n phr) frijoles de media
luna
  Cub. habas limas
  Spa. habas
beautiful (adj) bonito, hermoso
  Arg. lindo, precioso
  Chi., Cos.R., Cub., Dom.R. bello
  Col. bello, lindo, precioso
  Ecu., Pue.R., Venz. lindo
become intoxicated (v phr)
emborracharse
  Chi. embriagarse
  Spa. estar bajo la influencia
  del alcohol o de las drogas

---

bed, double (n phr) cama doble
Gua., Mex. cama matrimonial
Spa. cama de matrimonio
bed, king-sized (n phr) cama grande
Arg. cama camera
Col., Dom.R. cama king size
Mex. cama king-size
Pan., Venz. cama king
bed, queen-sized (n phr) cama doble
Arg. cama camera
Dom.R. cama queen size
Mex. cama queen-size
Pan. cama matrimonial
Venz. cama queen
bed, single (n phr) cama
Chi. cama de soltero
Col., Ecu., Pue.R. cama sencilla
Gua. cama imperial
Pan. cama tres cuartos
Mex., Venz. cama individual
bedroom (n) dormitorio
Arg., Col., Cub., Pue.R. cuarto
Dom.R. aposento, cuarto
Mex. cuarto, recámara
Pan. habitación
beet (n) remolacha
Bol., Chi., Per. beterraga
Mex. betabel
beetle (n) escarabajo
Chi. cucaracha
Dom.R. avejón
bell (bicycle) (n) timbre
Arg., Chi., Dom.R., Uru. bocina
Bol. campanilla
belly (n) barriga
Arg., Cos.R., Dom.R., Mex.,
Uru. panza
Chi. guata
Col. panza, pipa
Venz. estómago

belly button (n phr) ombligo
Chi. pupo
belt (n) cinturón
Col., Dom.R., Pan., Pue.R. correa
Cos.R. faja
bench (n) banco
Arg. banca
Spa. banqueta
berry (n) baya
Pue.R. cereza
berth (n) litera
Chi. camarote
biceps (n) bíceps
Mex. conejos
bifocals (n) lentes bifocales
Arg. anteojos bifocales
Cub., Pue.R. espejuelos bifocales
Spa. gafas bifocales
big toe (n phr) dedo gordo
Arg., Cub., Dom.R., Spa., Venz.
dedo gordo del pie
big-nosed (adj) narizón
Arg., Bol., Chi., Uru. narigón
Dom.R. narizú
bike, mountain (n phr) montañera
Arg. bicicleta todo terreno
Chi., Col., Venz. bicicleta de
montaña
Dom.R., Pue.R. mountain bike
ElS., Gua., Hon. bicicleta
montañesa
Mex. bicicleta de campotraviesa
Spa. bicicleta de montaña,
mountain bike
bike, road (n phr) bicicleta de camino
Arg., Cub., Uru. bicicleta
Col. bicicleta de ruta, bicicleta
para carretera
Dom.R. bicicleta de carrera
Mex. bicicleta turismo

Spa. bicicleta de carreras
bike, tandem (n phr) bicicleta para dos personas
Col. bicicleta de dos personas, bicicleta doble, tándem
Mex. bicicleta doble
Pue.R. doblecleta
Spa. tándem
bikini briefs (n phr) minitrusa
Arg. bombacha
Bol., Chi. bikini
Col. calzoncillos
Dom.R. tangas
Ecu. calzón bikini
Pan. calzoncillo corto
Pue.R. panticitos del bikini
Spa. braguita de bikini
Venz. interiores bikini
billboard (n) anuncio panorámico
Chi., Cub. cartelera
Col. cartelera, valla
Cos.R. rótulo
Dom.R. valla
Mex. anuncio
Pue.R. billboard
birthmark (n) marca de nacimiento
Cub., Ecu., Per., Venz. lunar
Dom.R., Spa. antojo
Mex. mancha de nacimiento
biscuit (n) bizcocho, galleta
Arg. galletita
Dom.R. bizcochito
Mex. bisquet
Pue.R. panecillo
black currant (n phr) casis
Col., Mex. grosella
Pan. pasita
blackbird (n) mirlo
Pan. talingo
blanket (n) cobija

Arg., Bol., Col., Cub., Uru. frazada
Ecu. colcha
Pue.R. frisa
Spa. manta
blender (n) licuadora
Cub., Dom.R., Spa., Venz. batidora
blimp (n) dirigible no rígido
Col., Spa. dirigible
Cub., Venz. zepelín
blinds (n) persianas
Col. cortinas
blinker (light) (n) intermitente, luz intermitente
Arg. guiño
Bol. guiñador
Pan. luz direccional
Venz. luz de cruce
blond (hair) (adj) rubio
Col. mono
Mex. güero
Pan. fulo
Venz. catire
blond (person) (n) rubio/a
Col. mono/a
Cos.R. macho (person with light hair)
Mex. güero/a
Pan. fulo/a
Venz. catire/a
bloom (v) florecer
Col. dar flor
Pue.R. retollar
blowtorch (n) soplete
Pan., Pue.R. antorcha
blue (eyes) (adj) azul
Col. ojiazul
Cos.R. macho (person with light-colored eyes)

---

blue jeans (n phr) jeans
    Arg., Cub., Uru. vaqueros
    Col., Venz. blue jeans
    Mex. pantalón de mezclilla
    Pue.R. mahones
    Spa. pantalones vaqueros,
    vaqueros
blueberry (n) arándano
    Mex. mora azul
    Per. mora
bluefish (n) pomátomo
    Mex. anjova, pez azul
board (v) embarcarse
    Chi., Col., Dom.R., Mex. abordar
    Spa., Venz. embarcar
boat (n) barco
    Cub., Venz. bote
boathouse (n) caseta de botes
    Col. cobertizo para las lanchas,
    garaje para botes
    Dom.R. casa-botes
    Gua. cobertizo de lanchas
bookkeeper (n) contador
    Cub. tenedor de libros
    Spa. contable
bookstore (n) librería
    Puc.R. tienda de libros
boring (adj) aburrido
    Col. harto, tedioso
boss (n) jefe
    Col. patrón
bothersome (adj) molesto
    Col. incómodo, inoportuno
    Venz. molestoso
bottle opener (n phr) destapador
    Chi., Cos.R. abridor
    Pan., Uru. abridor, saca corcho
    Pue.R. abridor de botellas
    Spa. abrebotellas
bow tie (n phr) corbata mariposa

    Arg. moñito
    Bol. corbata de gato
    Col. corbatín
    Cub., Spa. pajarita
    Dom.R. corbata de lacito
    Mex. corbata de moñito
    Pan. corbata de gatito
    Per. corbata michi
    Pue.R. lazo
    Uru., Venz. corbata de lazo
bowl (n) plato hondo
    Chi. bol
    Col. recipiente hondo, tazón,
    vasija
    Mex. tazón
    Pan. vasija
    Spa. cuenco
bowl, mixing (n phr) tazón para medir
    Arg. bol
    Col. vasija para mezclar
    ElS., Gua., Hon., Venz. tazón
    para mezclar
    Mex. tazón para batir
    Pan. platón, vasija
bowl, salad (n phr) ensaladera
    Col., Pan. plato para ensalada
bowl, soup (n phr) tazón
    Col., Venz. plato de sopa
    Cub., Dom.R., Ecu. plato sopero
    Pan. plato hondo, plato para sopa
    Pue.R. sopera
box spring (n phr) colchón de resortes
    Chi. catre
    Dom.R., Mex., Venz. box spring
    Pan. esprín
    Spa. somier
boxer (n) boxeador
    Chi. pugilista
boxer shorts (n phr) calzoncillos
    Cub. calzones

ABBREVIATIONS: Arg.=Argentina Bol.=Bolivia Chi.=Chile Col.=Colombia
Cos.R.=Costa Rica Cub.=Cuba Dom.R.=Dominican Republic Ecu.=Ecuador ElS.=El
Salvador Gua.=Guatemala Hon.=Honduras Mex.=Mexico Pan.=Panama Per.=Peru
Pri.=Primary Term Pue.R.=Puerto Rico Spa.=Spain Uru.=Uruguay Venz.=Venezuela

Dom.R. calzoncillos boxer
Pan. calzoncillo largo
boy (n) niño
   Arg., Pue.R., Uru. nene
   Col. chino
   Dom.R. muchachito
   Mex. chamaco
boyfriend (n) novio
   Chi. pololo
   Col. pretendiente
   Ecu., Per. enamorado
bra, brassiere (n) sostén
   Arg. corpiño
   Col. brassiere
   Cub. ajustador
   Dom.R., Pan. brasier
   Mex. brasiere
   Spa. sujetador
   Uru. soutien
bracelet (n) pulsera
   Cub. pulso
   Dom.R. guillo
braid (hair) (n) trenza
   Pan. moño
   Venz. crineja
brass section (n phr) bronces
   Col. cobres, instrumentos
   metálicos de viento
   Mex. metales
   Spa. instrumentos de metal
brat (n) mocoso
   Col. niño/a malcriado/a
   Cub., Pan. malcriado/a
   Dom.R. carajito/a, muchachito/a
   Pue.R. chiquillo/a
brave (adj) valiente
   Col. valeroso
   Dom.R. guapo
Brazil nut (n phr) nuez de Brasil
   Col. nuez del Brasil

bread, rye (n phr) pan negro
   Arg., Col., Cub., Dom.R., Ecu.,
   Spa., Venz. pan de centeno
   Chi. pan centeno
bread, sliced (n phr) pan de molde
   Arg. pan lactal
   Col. pan tajado
   Cos.R. pan cortado
   Dom.R. pan de sandwich
   Mex. pan de caja
   Pue.R. pan especial
   Venz. pan en rodajas
bread, white (n phr) pan blanco tajado
   Cub. pan de molde
   Pue.R. pan especial
   Arg., Col., Dom.R., Mex., Spa.,
   Venz. pan blanco
   Uru. pan blanco rebanado
break up (relationship) (v phr) romper
   Arg., Dom.R. cortar
   Chi., Mex. cortar, terminar
   Col. separarse
   Cub. pelearse
   Ecu., ElS., Gua., Hon., Venz.
   terminar
breast (n) seno
   Arg., Col., Cos.R., Uru. teta
   Chi. pechuga
   Dom.R., ElS., Gua., Hon., Spa.
   pecho
   Mex. chiche, chichi, busto
   Pan. pecho, teta
breaststroke (swimming) (n) estilo
braza
   Arg. brazada
   Chi., Col., Cub., Pue.R., Venz.
   estilo pecho
   Dom.R. brazado de pecho
   ElS., Gua., Hon. brazada de
   pecho

ABBREVIATIONS: Arg.=Argentina Bol.=Bolivia Chi.=Chile Col.=Colombia
Cos.R.=Costa Rica Cub.=Cuba Dom.R.=Dominican Republic Ecu.=Ecuador ElS.=El
Salvador Gua.=Guatemala Hon.=Honduras Mex.=Mexico Pan.=Panama Per.=Peru
Pri.=Primary Term Pue.R.=Puerto Rico Spa.=Spain Uru.=Uruguay Venz.=Venezuela

Mex. pecho
bridal shower (n phr) despedida de
soltera
Col. shower
bridge of nose (n phr) caballete
Chi., Dom.R. tabique
Mex., Venz. puente de la nariz
briefcase (n) portafolios
Bol. cartera, portafolio
Col., Cub., Per., Pue.R. maletín
briefs (n) calzoncillos
Col. trusa
Dom.R. pantaloncillos
Mex., Uru. calzones
Venz. interiores
brights (headlights) (n) luces fuertes
Arg., Chi., Dom.R., Mex., Pan.,
Venz. luces altas
Col. plenas
Cub., Pue.R., Spa. luces largas
Ecu. faros intensos
broad jump (n phr) salto de longitud
Chi., ElS., Gua., Hon. salto largo
Col. salto ancho
Pue.R. salto a lo largo
broadcast (n) emisión televisiva
Arg., Dom.R., Venz. programa
de televisión
Chi., Col., Cos.R., Gua., Hon.
transmisión
Cub. emisión
broadcast (v) emitir
Col., Cos.R., ElS., Gua., Hon.,
Venz. transmitir
brown (eyes) (adj) castaño
Arg., Col., Dom.R., Per., Spa.
marrón
Bol., Chi., Cos.R., Mex. café
brown (hair) (adj) moreno
Arg., Mex., Spa. castaño

Col. marrón, pelicastaño
Cub., Dom.R. trigueño
Uru. morocho
bruise (n) cardenal
Arg., Bol., Chi., Mex., Pan.
moretón
Col., Cub. morado
Cos.R. morete
Dom.R. hematoma, morado
ElS., Gua., Hon. magulladura
Spa. moratón
Venz. golpe, magulladura
brunch (n) brunch
Mex. almuerzo
Uru. desayuno
Venz. desayuno-almuerzo
brunette (person) (n) moreno/a
Arg., Uru. morocho/a
Col., Cub., Dom.R. trigueño/a
Spa. persona de pelo castaño
Brussels sprouts (n phr) coles de
Bruselas
Arg., Uru. repollitos de Bruselas
Chi. repollitos italianos
bucket (n) balde
Col., Mex., Spa. cubeta
Cub. cubo
bucksaw (n) sierra de ballesta
Spa. sierra de bastidor
Uru. serrucho
bud (n) brote
Col. botón, cogollo
Spa. capullo
buddy, pal (n) compañero/a
Chi., Cub. compadre
Col. amigazo/a
Dom.R. compinche, pana
ElS., Gua., Hon. cuate
Mex. amigocho, amigote, cuate
Pan., Pue.R. amigo/a

---

buffer storage (n phr) memoria
intermediaria
   Col. memoria intermedia,
   memoria temporal
   Mex. búfer
   Pue.R. buffer storage
   Venz. memoria de reserva,
   memoria intermedia, memoria
   temporal
buffet (n) aparador
   Col. mostrador
   Dom.R. despensa
   Gua. bufetera
   Mex. mesa de buffet
   Pue.R. chinero
bug (n) bicho, chinche
   Col., Per., Pue.R. insecto
   Dom.R. insecto, pajarito
bugle (n) clarín
   Col. corneta
   Spa. cornetín
building (n) edificio
   Col. construcción, edificación
bumblebee (n) abejorro
   Pue.R. avejita
bump (road) (n) bache
   Chi. lomo de toro
   Dom.R. hoyo
   Mex. tope
bumper (n) parachoques
   Arg. paragolpes
   Col. amortiguador
   Dom.R., Pan., Pue.R. bumper
   Mex. defensa
bumper car (n phr) carro loco
   Arg. autito chocador
   Dom.R. carrito chocón
   Mex., Per., Venz. carro chocón
   Spa. auto de choque
bun (hair) (n) moño

   Chi. tomate
   Mex. chongo
   Pan. cebolla
bun (n) panecillo
   Arg., Uru. pancito
   Bol., Spa. bollo
   Col. pancillo, pan pequeño
   Cos.R. bollito
   Mex. pan para hamburgeusas, pan
   para hot dogs
   Pan. pan para hamburguesas
bungalow (n) casa independiente
   Arg., Uru. bungalow
   Bol. cabañita
   Chi. cabaña, chalet
   Col. bungaló, cabaña, casita
   campestre, casita playera
   Dom.R. bungaloo
   ElS., Gua., Hon. casa campestre,
   casa de playa
   Mex. búngalo
   Pan. bungalu
   Spa. bungaló
   Venz. casa de campo
bunkbed (n) litera
   Chi. camarote
   Col., Dom.R., Pan. cama
   camarote
   Cub. cama litera
burial (n) entierro
   Chi., Mex. sepelio
   Col. exequias, sepelio
bus (n) autobús
   Arg. bus, ómnibus
   Col., Pan. bus
   Bol. colectivo
   Chi. micro
   Col. bus, buseta, colectivo
   Cos.R. bus, lata
   Cub., Dom.R., Pue.R. guagua

ABBREVIATIONS: Arg.=Argentina Bol.=Bolivia Chi.=Chile Col.=Colombia
Cos.R.=Costa Rica Cub.=Cuba Dom.R.=Dominican Republic Ecu.=Ecuador ElS.=El
Salvador Gua.=Guatemala Hon.=Honduras Mex.=Mexico Pan.=Panama Per.=Peru
Pri.=Primary Term Pue.R.=Puerto Rico Spa.=Spain Uru.=Uruguay Venz.=Venezuela

ElS., Gua. camioneta
Mex. camión
Per., Uru. ómnibus
bus driver (n phr) conductor de
autobús
   Arg. chofer de colectivo, chofer de
micro
   Chi. chofer
   Col. chofer de bus
   Cub. guagüero
   Dom.R., Pue.R. chofer de guagua
   Mex. camionero
   Pan. busero
bus stop (n phr) parada de autobús
   Arg., Per., Uru. parada del
ómnibus
   Bol. parada del colectivo
   Chi. parada del micro
   Col., Pan. parada de bus
   Cos.R. parada de lata, parada de
bus
   Cub., Dom.R., Pue.R. parada de
guagua
bush (n) arbusto
   Cub. mata
   Pue.R. arbolito, palito
business district (n phr) barrio
comercial
   Col., Cub., Mex., Pue.R. zona
comercial
   Dom.R. centro de negocios
   Spa. zona de negocios
businessman (n) hombre de negocios
   Arg., Chi. empresario
   Col. ejecutivo
   Pan. hombre profesional
businesswoman (n) mujer de negocios
   Arg., Chi., Cos.R. empresaria
   Col. ejecutiva
   Pan. mujer profesional

butcher block (n phr) bloque de
carnicero
   Arg. tabla de cocina
   Chi., Cub. tabla para cortar
   Col. tabla para cortar, tabla para
picar
   Pue.R. picador
butt (n) trasero
   Arg. cola, traste
   Chi. traste
   Col. cola, culo
   Cub. nalgas
   Mex. asentaderas
   Pan. nalga
   Per. poto
   Spa. culo
   Uru. cola
buttock (n) nalga
   Arg. cachete
   Chi. poto
   Mex. pompa, pompis
Bye! (int) ¡Adiós!
   Arg. ¡Chau!
   Chi. ¡Chao!
   Col. ¡Ciao!, ¡Hasta luego!
   Dom.R. ¡Bye!

When Bolivians talk to a friend,
they usually use the Quechuan
word *guayguay,* which means
"honey" or "dear."

ABBREVIATIONS: Arg.=Argentina Bol.=Bolivia Chi.=Chile Col.=Colombia
Cos.R.=Costa Rica Cub.=Cuba Dom.R.=Dominican Republic Ecu.=Ecuador ElS.=El
Salvador Gua.=Guatemala Hon.=Honduras Mex.=Mexico Pan.=Panama Per.=Peru
Pri.=Primary Term Pue.R.=Puerto Rico Spa.=Spain Uru.=Uruguay Venz.=Venezuela

C

cabbage, green (n phr) repollo verde
Cub., Ecu., Mex., Spa. col
Dom.R. lechuga repollada
cabbage, white (n phr) repollo
Cub., Spa. col
Mex. col blanca
cabin (n) cabaña, choza
Chi. refugio
cable television (n phr) televisión por cable
Arg., Cub. cable
Dom.R. telecable
Mex. cable, cablevisión
cactus (n) cacto
Arg., Chi., Dom.R., Mex., Pan., Pue.R., Spa. cactus
cake (n) pastel
Arg., Chi., Ecu., Uru., Venz. torta
Bol., Cos.R. queque
Col. ponqué, torta
Cub. cake
Dom.R., Pue.R. bizcocho
Pan. cake, dulce
Per. queque, torta
Spa. tarta
calf (n) ternera
Arg. ternero
Col., Spa. becerro, ternero
can opener (n phr) abrelatas
Chi. abridor de latas
Cos.R. abridor
canine (tooth) (n) canino
Cos.R. premolar
Cub., Mex., Spa. colmillo
canned food (n phr) alimentos enlatados

Chi. latas de conservas
Col., Cub., Dom.R., Pan. comida enlatada
cantaloupe (n) melón chino
Chi. melón calameño
Col. cantaloupe, melón
Cub. cantalupa
Pan., Per., Venz. melón
cap (n) gorra
Col., Dom.R. cachucha
cape (n) capa, capote
Mex. chal, quisquemel
car (n) carro
Arg., Chi., Col. auto, coche
Mex. auto, automóvil, coche
Spa. automóvil, coche
Uru. coche
car body (n phr) carrocería
Pan. chasis
car jack (crime) (v phr) sequestrar en auto
Bol. raptar
Col. asaltar
Cub. robarse un carro
Mex. asaltar con violencia
Pue.R. car jack
Spa. robar un vehículo con alguien dentro
Uru. atracar un coche
Venz. robar un carro
car, private (n phr) carro privado
Arg. auto particular
Chi., Ecu. carro particular
Spa., Uru. coche particular
cardigan (n) cardigán
Arg. chaleco, saco de lana
Chi. sweater
Col. suéter abierto
Ecu., Venz. suéter
Mex. chamarra tejida, suéter

Spa. chaqueta de punto
carousel (with horses) (n) caballitos
Arg., Uru. calesita
Chi., Col., Ecu., ElS., Gua.,
Hon., Pan., Venz. carrusel
carpool (v) compartir coches
Arg. hacer pool
Col. compartir viajes en carro
Gua. compartir carros
Mex. turnarse alternando coches
Venz. ir juntos en un carro
cartoon (n) dibujo animado
Col., Spa. dibujos animados
Cub., Dom.R., Pue.R.
muñequitos
Mex. caricatura
Pan. caricaturas
carving fork (n phr) trinche
Arg. tenedor
Col., ElS., Gua., Hon., Spa.
tenedor de trinchar
Pan., Pue.R. tenedor para servir
cashew (n) nuez de la India
Arg., Uru. castaña de cajú
Chi. castaña
Cub. anacardo
Dom.R. semilla de cajuil
Pan. pepita de marañón
cast (show) (n) equipo artístico
Chi., Pan.. Pue.R. elenco
Col., Mex., Spa., Venz. reparto
casual clothes (n phr) ropa informal
Dom.R. ropa casual
catfish (n) bagre
Spa. barbo
cave (n) cueva
Col. caverna
celesta (n) celesta
Col. celeste
cemetery (n) cementerio

Chi., Col. campo santo
Mex. panteón
certified public accountant (CPA) (n
phr) contador público certificado
Chi. contador
Cos.R. contador público
autorizado
Dom.R. contable, contador, CPA
Pan. contador público autorizado,
CPA
Spa. contable
chainsaw (n) serrucho eléctrico
Arg., Cos.R., Spa. motosierra
Chi., Uru. sierra eléctrica
Col., Mex., Pue.R. sierra de
cadena
chair, director's (n phr) silla de
director, silla plegable
Mex. silla ejecutiva, sillón
ejecutivo
chair, folding (n phr) silla plegable
Dom.R. silla plegadiza
chair, lounging (n phr) catre, chaise
Chi. asiento, poltrona
Col. silla de extensión
Mex. sillón reclinable
Pue.R. silla reclinable
Spa. hamaca
chair, rocking (n phr) mecedora
Arg. silla hamaca
Col. mecedor
Cub., Pue.R. sillón
chair, step (n phr) banco-escalera
Venz. silla con escalón
challenger (boxing) (n) contrincante
Col. contendor, retador
Dom.R., Mex. retador
Uru. aspirante
Venz. retador de boxeo
change (train) (v) transbordar

ABBREVIATIONS: Arg.=Argentina Bol.=Bolivia Chi.=Chile Col.=Colombia
Cos.R.=Costa Rica Cub.=Cuba Dom.R.=Dominican Republic Ecu.=Ecuador ElS.=El
Salvador Gua.=Guatemala Hon.=Honduras Mex.=Mexico Pan.=Panama Per.=Peru
Pri.=Primary Term Pue.R.=Puerto Rico Spa.=Spain Uru.=Uruguay Venz.=Venezuela

Arg. hacer una conexión
Col., Cub. cambiar de tren
Venz. hacer un transbordo de
trenes
channel (n) canal
Spa. cadena
chassis (n) chasis
Dom.R., Pue.R. chassis
Ecu., Pan., Per. bastidor
cheap (adj) barato
Col. asequible, ganga
Pan. runcho
cheater (n) tramposo
Col. embustero, estafador, pícaro
check in (baggage) (v phr) registrar el
equipaje
Chi. despachar
Dom.R., Venz. chequear el
equipaje
cheek (n) mejilla
Chi., Col., Dom.R., Mex., Pan.,
Per., Venz. cachete
Spa. carrillo
chef (n) chef
Col. cocinero, jefe de cocina
Per. jefe de cocina
Spa. cocinero
chest (n) pecho
Chi., Col. tórax
chestnut (n) castaña
Dom.R. pan de fruta
chicken (n) pollo
Pan. gallina
chief executive officer (CEO) (n phr)
jefe ejecutivo principal
Arg. presidente
Chi. gerente ejecutivo
Col. gerente general
Cos.R. director general, gerente
general

Dom.R. director ejecutivo
Gua. personero ejecutivo de más
alto rango
Mex. director general
Venz. oficial ejecutivo jefe
child (n) niño/a
Arg. chico/a
chin (n) barbilla
Arg. mentón, pera
Chi. pera
Col. mentón
Mex. barba
Per. quijada
china (n) porcelana
Chi. loza
Col., Dom.R., Mex. vajilla
Pan. loza, vajilla fina
chord (n) acorde
Col. cuerda
christening (n) bautizo
Arg., Col. bautismo
cicada (n) cigarra
Chi., Pue.R., Venz. chicharra
cigar (n) cigarro, puro
Cub. tabaco
cigarette (n) cigarrillo
Chi. pucho
Mex. cigarro
city (n) ciudad
Col. metrópoli, urbe
city block (n phr) manzana
Dom.R., Ecu., Pan. cuadra
Pue.R. bloque
city hall (n phr) ayuntamiento
Bol., Pue.R. alcaldía
Chi., Col., ElS., Gua., Hon.
municipalidad
Ecu. alcaldía, municipalidad
Uru. intendencia
clamp (n) abrazadera

Col. grapa
Cos.R. prensa
Mex. pinzas
cleft (chin) (n) hendidura
Chi. labio leporino
Cos.R. camanance
Dom.R. hoyito
Mex. barba partida
Per. barbida partida
Venz. barbilla hendida
click (computer) (v) hacer clic
Cub. pulsar
Pue.R. apretar
cliff (n) acantilado
Cub., Pan. precipicio
Cos.R. barranco
Mex. barranca
Pue.R. risco
climbing plant (n phr) trepadora
Bol., Col., Cub., Mex., Pue.R.
enredadera
cloak (n) capa
Col. manto
clogs (n) chanclos
Arg. ojotas
Chi. zancos
Col., Cub., Spa., Uru. zuecos
Dom.R., Mex., Pue.R. suecos
closet (clothes) (n) clóset
Arg. placard
Bol., Chi., Cos.R., Ecu., Uru.
ropero
Pan. estante
Spa. armario
closet (general) (n) armario
Chi. guardarropa
Col., Cos.R., Cub., Mex., Pan.,
Per. clóset
cloudy (adj) nublado
Chi. tapado

Col. cerrado, encapotado
Cos.R., Cub., Gua. cubierto,
nuboso
cloverleaf junction (n phr) trébol
Col. confluencia, empalme,
entronque en forma de trébol
Mex. paso a desnivel
coat (n) saco
Arg. tapado
Chi., Pue.R. chaqueta
Col., Cub., Mex., Pan., Spa.,
Venz. abrigo
coat, fur (n phr) saco de piel
Arg. tapado de piel
Chi., Col., Dom.R., Mex., Pan.,
Pue.R., Spa., Venz. abrigo de piel
Cub. abrigo de pieles
coat, mink (n phr) saco de visón
Arg. tapado de visón
Col., Mex., Pan., Pue.R. abrigo de
mink
Cub., Dom.R., Spa., Venz. abrigo
de visón
cocaine (n) cocaína
Col. coca
cocaine spoon (n phr) cuchara de
cocaína
Col. cuchara para la cocaína
Mex. grapas de cocaína
Spa. cuchara para cocaína
cockatoo (n) cacatúa
Chi. cata
coffee bar (n phr) café
Col., Pue.R., Spa. cafetería
Cos.R. café bar
coffee maker (n phr) cafetera
Dom.R. greca
coin purse (n phr) monedero
Dom.R. portamonedas
colander (n) colador

ABBREVIATIONS: Arg.=Argentina Bol.=Bolivia Chi.=Chile Col.=Colombia
Cos.R.=Costa Rica Cub.=Cuba Dom.R.=Dominican Republic Ecu.=Ecuador EIS.=El
Salvador Gua.=Guatemala Hon.=Honduras Mex.=Mexico Pan.=Panama Per.=Peru
Pri.=Primary Term Pue.R.=Puerto Rico Spa.=Spain Uru.=Uruguay Venz.=Venezuela

Bol., Col. coladera
Cos.R., Dom.R., Mex., Per.,
Spa., Uru. escurridor de verduras
colt (n) potro
Chi. potrillo
comb (n) peine
Chi. peineta
Col., Ecu., Pan., Pue.R. peinilla
commercial (n) anuncio
Arg. aviso, propaganda
Chi., Ecu., Per. propaganda
Col. anuncio comercial,
comercial, propaganda
Dom.R., Mex. comercial
Pan., Venz. comercial, propaganda
compact disk (n phr) disco compacto
Arg., Col., Pan. CD
Spa. CD, compact disk
compact disk player (n phr) tocadiscos
Arg. equipo de música para CD
Col. aparato de CD
Cos.R. CD-player
Cub. reproductor de compact-disc
Dom.R. CD player, tocador de
discos compactos
ElS., Gua., Venz. reproductor de
discos compactos
Mex. tocadiscos para discos
compactos
Spa. reproductor de CD
comptroller (n) controlador
Cos.R. auditor
Dom.R. contralor
Venz. interventor
computer (n) computadora
Col. computador
Spa. ordenador
condominium (n) condominios
Cub., ElS., Gua., Pue.R., Spa.
condominio

conduct (music) (v) dirigir
Col. conducir
conga drum (n phr) conga
Cub. tumbadora
Venz. tambor de conga
consultant (n) consejero
Arg., Col., Mex., Pan., Spa.
asesor
Chi., Cos.R., Cub., Dom.R.,
Ecu., Per. consultor
Venz. asesor, consultor
contestant (n) competidor
Chi. concursante
Cub., Pue.R. participante
contrabassoon (n) contrabajón
Mex. contrafagot
convertible (n) convertible
Spa. descapotable
cookie (n) galleta
Arg. masita
Cos.R., Pue.R., Uru. galletita
Cub. galletica
ElS., Gua., Hon. galleta dulce
Per. galleta de dulce
Spa. pasta
cookie cutters (n phr) cortadores de
galletas
Arg. moldes
Chi., Dom.R., Venz. moldes de
galletas
copier (n) copiadora
Spa. fotocopiadora
corkscrew (n) sacacorchos
Chi. destapador
corn (n) maíz
Bol., Chi., Ecu., Per., Uru. choclo
(choclo in Arg. is sweet corn)
Cub. mazorca (on the cob)
Mex. elote (on the cob)
cornet (n) cornetín

Mex., Spa. corneta
cottage (n) casa de campo
  Arg. casa, casa-quinta, quinta
  Chi. cabaña, chalet
  Col. casita de campo
counselor (n) consejero
  Ecu., Mex., Spa. asesor
counter (n) mostrador
  Arg. mesada
  Pue.R. counter
courthouse (n) tribunal de justicia
  Col. edificio de los tribunales
  Cub., Mex., Pue.R. corte
  Dom.R. palacio de justicia
  Spa. juzgado, palacio de justicia
crab (n) cangrejo
  Chi. jaiba, pancora
cracker (n) galleta
  Arg. galletita
  Dom.R. galletica
  Venz. galleta de soda
cradle, crib (n) cuna
  Dom.R. catre
cranberry (n) arándano agrio
  Mex. mora roja
  Pue.R. cranberry
  Venz. cereza agria
crash (vehicle) (v) chocar
  Col. estrellar
crawl (swimming) (n) crawl
  Chi. estilo libre
  Gua., Spa. estilo crol
  Pue.R., Uru. brazada
crayfish (n) cangrejo de río
  Chi. camarón de agua dulce
  Col., Dom.R. jaiba
  Pue.R. juey
cream puff (n phr) repolla
  Bol., ElS., Gua., Hon., Spa.
  bollo de crema

Chi. repollito
Pan. ecler
Uru. bomba de crema
Venz. pastel de crema
creamer (n) cremera
  Arg. lechera
  Spa. jarrita para leche
crease (pants) (n) raya
  Col. arruga, pliego
  Cub., ElS., Gua., Hon. pliegue
  Dom.R., Pue.R. filo
  Pan. doblez
croissant (n) croissant
  Arg., Col. medialuna
  Chi. media luna
  Dom.R. cruasant, pan camarón
  Mex. cuernito
  Per. cachito
crosswalk (n) paso de peatones
  Col. cruce peatonal
  Cub. acera
  Dom.R. cruce de peatones
cuckoo (n) cuco
  Col., Venz. cuclillo
  Mex. cucú
cucumber (n) pepino
  Pue.R. pepinillo
cuff (pants) (n) valenciana
  Arg. botamanga
  Bol. botapié
  Col., Spa. doblez
  Cub. dobladillo
  Dom.R. doblado
  Venz. ruedo doble
cufflinks (n) gemelos
  Chi. colleras
  Col., Ecu. mancornas
  Cub. yugos
  ElS., Gua., Hon., Mex.
  mancuernillas

Pan. mancuernas
Pue.R., Venz. yuntas
cup, coffee (n phr) taza para café
  Arg. pocillo, taza de café
curly (hair) (adj) rizado
  Arg., Pan. enrulado
  Bol., Chi., Venz. ondulado
  Col. crespo, ondulado
  Dom.R. duro, malo
  Mex. chino
  Per. crespo
cute (adj) mono
  Arg. divino
  Bol. amoroso
  Chi. simpático
  Col. primoroso
  Cub. guapo, lindo
  Dom.R., Ecu., Pan. gracioso
  Mex. chulo
  ElS., Gua., Hon., Per., Venz.
  chulo, lindo
  Pue.R. bonito, chulito
cutting board (n phr) tabla para cortar
  Col. tabla de cortar
  Pue.R. picador

"The idea of having a multicultural Spanish dictionary not only gives foreign language speakers a spectrum of the diversity of Spanish but also allows us, Hispanic speakers throughout the world, to understand each other better and to envision the divergence of our language sometimes as an asset and as a way of enrichment of our forms of expression."
—Nefertiti Casado-Hagan

D

Danish (n) pastelillo de fruta y nueces
  Mex. pan dulce
  Pan. danesa
  Per. pastel
  Venz. pastel danés
data (n) datos
  Col. información
date (v) tener una cita
  Arg. estar de novio
  Col. tener compromiso
  Dom.R., Gua., Mex., Venz. salir
  con
daycare center (n phr) guardería
infantil
  Arg., Dom.R. guardería
  Col. jardín de infantes
  Pue.R. nursery
deal (drugs) (v phr) vender
  Col., ElS., Gua. traficar con
  Mex., Venz. traficar
  Pue.R. distribuir
dear, darling, honey (n) querido/a
  Arg., Chi., ElS., Gua., Hon. mi
  amor
  Col. mi amor, amorcito, tesoro
  Cub. mi amor, mi cielo, mi vida
  Pan. cariño
  Pue.R. mi amor, mi vida
debug (computer) (v) depurar
  Dom.R. desinfectar
  Pue.R., Venz. limpiar
decanter (n) licorera
  Arg. jarra
  Col., Spa. garrafa
decelerate (v) disminuir la velocidad
  Chi., Dom.R., Pue.R., Spa.

reducir la velocidad
  Col., Cub. desacelerar
deer (n) venado
  Arg., Bol., Cos.R., ElS., Gua.,
  Hon., Spa., Uru. ciervo
delay (n) retraso
  Arg. demora
  Chi. atraso
  Col. atraso, demora, retardo
delete (v) borrar, eliminar
  Arg. deletear
delicious (adj) delicioso
  Arg., Pue.R. rico
  Per. exquisito
delightful (adj) divino
  Chi. agradable
  Col. agradable, deleitable,
  encantador, exquisito
  ElS., Gua., Hon. muy agradable
  Venz. rico
demitasse (n) tacita de café
  Arg. pocillo, taza de café
  Col. tacita
  Pue.R. pocillito de café
department store (n phr) grandes
almacenes
  Cub. tienda
  Col. almacén grande
  Cos.R. tienda de departamentos
  Dom.R., ElS., Gua., Hon.,
  Pue.R., Venz. tienda por
  departamentos
  Mex. tienda departamental
  Pan. almacén
departure (n) salida
  Chi. embarque
detour (n) desvío
  Mex. desviación
difficult (adj) difícil
  Col. dificultoso, peliagudo,

trabajoso
dimple (n) hoyuelo
   Bol. hoyo
   Chi., Dom.R., Mex. hoyito
   Cos.R., ElS., Gua., Hon.
camanance
dining car (train) (n phr) coche
comedor
   Col. vagón-restaurante
   Spa. coche restaurante
   Venz. carro comedor
dinner (n) cena
   Arg., Col., Per., Pue.R. comida
dipstick (n) indicador del nivel de
aceite
   Col. varilla para medir el aceite
   Pue.R. varilla de aceite
   Venz. indicador de medir el aceite
dishes (n) platos
   Pan. trastos, vajilla
dishwasher (n) lavaplatos
   Arg. lavavajilla
   Col., Cub., Pue.R. lavadora de
platos
   Spa. lavavajillas
   Uru. lava vajilla
display cabinet (n phr) vitrina
   Arg. aparador
   Pue.R. chinero
ditch (n) zanja
   Col., Spa. cuneta
   Cos.R. sanja
   Uru. pozo
diver (n) buceador, buzo
   Chi. hombre rana
   Cub. clauadista
divorce (v) divorciarse
   Col. apartarse, desunirse,
separarse
divorced (adj) divorciado

   Col. separado
doctor (n) médico
   Arg., Col., Chi. doctor
doctor's office (n phr) consultorio
médico
   Pue.R. oficina del médico, oficina
del doctor
dog tag (n phr) placa de identificación
   Mex. etiqueta
doghouse (n) perrera
   Arg. cucha
   Chi., Venz. casa de perro
door-to-door salesperson (n phr)
vendedor a domicilio
   Col. vendedor puerta a puerta
   Cos.R. representante de ventas
double chin (n phr) papada
   Chi. doble pera
   Dom.R. doble barbilla
double feature (movies) (n phr) doble
función
   Bol. película doble
   Col. doble
   Dom.R. doble presentación
   Mex. programa doble
   Spa. sesión de dos películas
seguidas
   Uru. función doble
   Venz. cine continuado
doughnut (n) dónut
   Chi. rosca
   Col. dona, rosca
   ElS., Gua., Hon., Mex., Pan.,
Pue.R. dona
dove (n) paloma
   Col. palomo, tórtola
   Pue.R. pichón
dowel (n) clavija
   Gua. tarugo
   Mex. espiga, pasador

downtown (n) centro de la ciudad
  Pue.R. centro del pueblo, pueblo
dragonfly (n) libélula
  Chi. matapiojos
  Cub. caballito del diablo
  Pan. caballito
draining spoon (n phr) cuchara para
escurrir
  Col. cuchara de escurrir
  Spa. espumadera
drawer (n) gaveta
  Arg., Chi., Col., Ecu., Mex., Per.,
  Spa., Uru. cajón
drawer knob (n phr) perilla
  Col. botón, pomo
  Dom. R. manubrio
  Pan. agarrador
  Venz. manilla
dress (oneself) (v) vestirse
  Col. ponerse la ropa
dress (woman's) (n) vestido
  Arg., Col., Pan. traje
  Bol. falda
  Cos.R., Uru. pollera
  Pue.R. traje de mujer
dress up (v phr) vestirse de etiqueta
  Arg. arreglarse
  Chi., Col. vestirse elegante
  Dom.R. arreglarse, vestirse formal
  Pue.R. engalanarse
dresser (n) ropero
  Arg., Chi., Col., Cub., Per.
  cómoda
  Venz. gavetero
  Pue.R., Spa. tocador
drill bit (n phr) broca
  Pue.R., Venz. barrena
drill, hand (n phr) taladro de mano
  Arg., Ecu., Per., Spa., Uru.
  taladradora de mano

  Chi. taladro
  Col., Mex. taladro manual
drive (car) (v) manejar
  Chi., Col., Pan., Spa. conducir
  Pue.R. guiar
drive (computer) (n) unidad de disco
  Dom. R., Pue.R. drive
drive-in (n) motocine
  Col., Pue.R. drive-in
  Dom.R. auto-cinema
  Mex. autocinema
  Pan., Per., Venz. autocine
driver's license (n phr) licencia de
conducir
  Arg. carnet de conductor,
  permiso de conductor
  Chi. carnet de chofer
  Col. pase para conducir
  Cub., Venz. licencia de manejar
  Spa. carnet de conducir
driver's seat (n phr) asiento del
conductor
  Chi. asiento del chofer, asiento del
  piloto
  Cub. asiento del chofer
drizzle (n) llovizna
  Col. lluvia tenue
  Per. garúa
drug abuse (n phr) toxicomanía
  Col., Cub., Dom.R., Pue.R.
  abuso de drogas
drug addict (n phr) drogadicto
  Col. narcómano
drug addiction (n phr) drogadicción
  Col. narcomanía
  Pue.R. adicción a las drogas
drug deal (n phr) transacción de drogas
  Col., Dom.R., Gua., Spa., Uru.
  tráfico de drogas
  Ecu., Venz. negocio de drogas

Pue.R. negociación
drug dealer (n phr) traficante de drogas
Bol., Cos.R., Cub., Venz.
narcotraficante
drug habit (n phr) drogadicción
Col. narcomanía
Cub. vicio de drogas
drug store (n phr) farmacia
Col. botica, droguería
Ecu., Per. botica
drug test (n phr) prueba anti-doping
Col., Uru., Venz. prueba anti-
drogas
Cub., Mex., Pue.R. prueba de
drogas
Pan. prueba para drogas
drug user (n phr) consumidor de
drogas
Pue.R. usuario de drogas
drum (n) tambor
Dom.R. batería
drum, tap (v) tamborilear
Col., Spa. tocar el tambor
drummer (n) tamborilero
Col. el que toca el tambor, tambor
Dom.R. baterista
drunk (adj) borracho
Col. bebido
drive drunk (v phr) manejar borracho
Arg., Pue.R. conducir en estado
de embriaguez
Chi. manejar en estado de
ebriedad
Col. manejar embriagado
Cos.R. manejar tomado
Dom.R. manejar en estado de
embriaguez
Spa. conducir borracho, conducir
ebrio
drunkard (n) borracho

Col. beodo, borrachín
Dom.R. borrachón
dryer (n) secadora
Arg. secarropas
Pue.R. secadora de ropa
duo (n) dúo
Col. dueto
duplex (n) dúplex
Chi. casa pareada
Dom.R., Pue.R. casa dúplex

> Italian immigrants left their
> mark on Argentine Spanish.
> *Chau,* for example, comes
> from the Italian word *ciao.*

E

earrings (n) aretes
Arg. aros
Pue.R. pantallas
Spa. pendientes
Venz. zarcillos
earrings, clip (n phr) aretes de presión
Arg. aros de presión
Pue.R. pantallas de clips
Spa. pendientes de clip
Venz. zarcillos de presión
earrings, drop (n phr) pendientes
Arg. aros colgantes
Spa. pendientes largos
earrings, pierced (n phr) aretes de espiga
Arg. aros de agujero
Dom.R. aretes de hoyito
Pue.R. pantallas de gancho
Spa. pendientes de tornillo
Venz. zarcillos
earrings, screw (n phr) aretes de tornillo
Arg. aros de tornillo
Spa. pendientes de tornillo
Venz. zarcillos de tornillo
earthquake (n) terremoto
Chi., Mex. temblor
Col. remezón, sacudida, sismo, temblor de tierra
Dom.R., Pue.R. temblor de tierra
easel (n) caballete
Chi., Col., Spa. atril
editor (n) redactor
Col., Pue.R., Spa., Venz. editor
egg beater (n phr) batidor manual
Chi., Pue.R. batidora

Ecu. batidor de mano
elevator (n) ascensor
Cub., Mex., Pan., Pue.R. elevador
e-mail (n) correo electrónico
Arg., Dom.R., Mex., Pue.R., Spa. e-mail
emergency lights (n phr) luces de emergencia
Arg. balizas
Ecu. faros de emergencia
Pue.R. luces intermitentes
encrypt (computer) (v) ocultar
Col., Mex., Spa. encriptar
Uru. cifrar
Venz. cifrar, codificar
endive (n) escarola
Arg., Col., Spa. endibia
Col. endivia
English horn (n phr) corno inglés
Col. cuerno inglés
entrance fee (n phr) entrada
Col. precio de la entrada
Pue.R., Venz. precio de entrada
escalator (n) escalera mecánica
Col. escalera automática
Dom.R., Mex. escalera eléctrica
evil (adj) malvado
Arg. maldito, malo
Chi., Dom.R. malo
Col. maligno, malo
Venz. maligno
exciting (adj) emocionante
Col. conmovedor,impresionante
Pue.R. excitante
exhaust pipe (n phr) tubo de escape
Arg. caño de escape
Col. exosto
Mex. escape
expressway (n) autopista
Mex. vía rápida

Spa. carretera
eyeglasses (n) anteojos
   Col. gafas, lentes
   Cub., Pue.R. espejuelos
   Dom.R., Ecu., Pan., Per., Venz.
   ientes
   Spa. gafas

The name of a popular plantain dish in Cuba, *fufú de plátano* (known as *mofongo* in Puerto Rico) came from English slave ships. Centuries ago, Cubans heard the Englishmen shout, "Food! Food!" as their slaves fed them plantains. To the Cuban ear, this became *fufú*, a plantain dish still popular today. Billboards in Miami advertise Cuban restaurants serving the best *fufú* under the catchword *fufumania!*

F

factory (n) fábrica
Col. empresa, industria
Dom.R., Pue.R. factoría
fairground (n) parque de atracciones
Col. terreno para ferias, terreno
para circos
Dom.R., Ecu. parque de
diversiones
Mex. feria
Pue.R. feria, parque de diversiones
family member (n phr) familiar
Arg., Chi., Ecu., Mex., Pue.R.,
Venz. pariente
Col. miembro de la familia
fan belt (n phr) correa del ventilador
Mex. banda del ventilador
farmer (n) agricultor
Chi. ganadero
Col. campesino
Per. granjero
fender (n) ala
Arg. paragolpes
Col. guardabarro, guardafango
Cub., Ecu., ElS., Gua., Venz.
guardafango
Mex. defensa
Pue.R. fender
Spa. guardabarro
ferris wheel (n phr) noria
Chi., rueda gigante
Col. rueda de Chicago, rueda
giratoria gigante
Cub., Dom.R., Pan. estrella
Ecu. rueda muscovita
Mex. rueda de la fortuna
Venz. rueda

ferry (n) transbordador
Col., Cos.R., Dom.R., Spa.,
Venz. ferry
Cub. lancha
fiancé (male) (n) novio
Col., Cos.R., Dom.R., Pan.
prometido
Mex. comprometido
fiancée (female) (n) novia
Col., Cos.R., Dom.R., Pan.
prometida
Mex. comprometida
file cabinet (n phr) archivo
Chi. archivador
Mex. archivero
film (n) película
Arg., Cos.R., Ecu., Uru., Pan.
filme
Chi., Col., Cub. cinta
Venz. film
fire (v) despedir
Arg. echar
Col. destituir, echar
Cub., Dom.R botar
fire station (n phr) estación de
bomberos
Bol., Cos.R., Ecu., Spa., Uru.
parque de bomberos
Mex. departamento de bomberos
firefly (n) luciérnaga
Cub. cocuyo
Pue.R. cucubano
fireplace (n) chimenea
Arg. estufa, hogar
first class (adj phr) primera clase
Arg. primera
flat tire (n phr) llanta reventada
Arg., Dom.R. goma pinchada
Bol. llanta pinchada
Chi. pneumático pinchado

ABBREVIATIONS: Arg.=Argentina Bol.=Bolivia Chi.=Chile Col.=Colombia
Cos.R.=Costa Rica Cub.=Cuba Dom.R.=Dominican Republic Ecu.=Ecuador ElS.=El
Salvador Gua.=Guatemala Hon.=Honduras Mex.=Mexico Pan.=Panama Per.=Peru
Pri.=Primary Term Pue.R.=Puerto Rico Spa.=Spain Uru.=Uruguay Venz.=Venezuela

Col. llanta desinflada, llanta
pinchada
Cos.R., Per. llanta desinflada
Cub. goma ponchada
Ecu. tubo bajo
Gua. llanta pache, llanta pinchada
Mex. llanta pinchada, llanta
ponchada
Pan. flat
Pue.R. goma vacía
Spa. neumático pinchado, rueda
pinchada
Uru. llanta desinflada, neumático
desinflado
Venz. caucho pinchado
flight attendant (n phr) auxiliar de
vuelo, azafata
Col. cabinera
Cub., Mex., Pan., Venz.
aeromozo/a
float (parade) (n) carroza
Chi. carro alegórico
flock (n) rebaño
Arg. bandada
Chi. piño
Col. manada
florist's shop (n phr) florista
Col., Dom.R., Pan., Pue.R., Venz.
floristería
Cub. florería
flounder (n) lenguado, platija
Gua. róbalo
flower bed (n phr) macizo
Arg. cantero
Bol. macetero
Gua. arriate de flores
Mex. cama de flores
fly (pants) (n) bragueta
Chi. marrueco
Cub. portañuela

Dom.R. ziper
Pue.R. zipper
foal (n) potro
Col., Venz. potrillo
fog (n) niebla
Arg., Cub., Dom.R., Mex., Per.
neblina
Chi. camanchaca
Col. bruma, neblina
folder (n) carpeta de archivo
Bol. archivador
Dom.R., Mex., Pan., Pue.R.
folder
Spa. archivadora, carpeta
foliage (n) follaje
Col. espesura, frondosidad
formal wear (n phr) ropa formal
Dom.R. ropa de vestir
Mex. ropa de etiqueta
four-four, common time (n phr)
compás mayor
Spa. compás de cuatro por cuatro
four-wheel drive (n phr) propulsión
total
Arg., Chi., Col., Gua., Mex.
tracción en las cuatro ruedas
Cub., Venz. tracción de cuatro
ruedas
Dom.R. cuatro tracciónes
Spa. tracción a las cuatro ruedas
fox (n) zorro
Pan. zorra
frame (movie) (n phr) imagen
Col. cuadro
free admission (n phr) entrada libre
Chi., Cub., Dom.R., ElS., Gua.,
Pan., Pue.R. entrada gratis
Spa. entrada gratuita
freezer (n) congelador
Arg., Pue.R. freezer

Bol. refrigerador
French fries (n phr) papas fritas
Dom.R. papitas fritas
Spa. patatas fritas
French horn (n phr) corno francés
Col. cuerno francés
Spa. trompa de pistones
friendly (adj) amistoso
Col., Mex., Pue.R. amigable
Cub. simpático
fringe benefit (n phr) incentivo
Col. beneficio adicional, beneficio
suplementario
Cos.R. beneficio laborable
ElS., Gua. prestación
complementaria
fruit stand (n phr) puesto de frutas
Pue.R. frutería
fruit tree (n phr) árbol frutal
Arg. frutal
Pue.R. árbol de frutas
full-time (work) (adj) de jornada
completa
Arg. de horario completo
Col., Mex. de tiempo completo
Cub., Dom.R., Venz. a tiempo
completo
funeral home (n phr) funeraria
Spa. tanatorio
funicular (n) funicular
Mex., Venz. teleférico
funny (adj) divertido, gracioso
Chi. simpático
Col., Dom.R., Ecu., Pan. chistoso

Uruguay's *bandoneón* is an accordion-like instrument used to play tango music.

G

game show (television) (n phr) programa concurso
  Arg. programa de entretenimientos
  Col. programa de concurso
  Cos.R. concurso televisivo
  Dom.R., Gua., Mex., Venz. programa de concursos
garage (repairs) (n) garaje
  Arg. taller mecánico
  Col. taller
garage (storage) (n) garaje
  Dom.R. marquesina
garbage collector (n phr) basurero
  Col., Venz. recogedor de basura
garment (n) vestido
  Arg. prenda
  Cub. prenda de vestir, vestidura
  ElS., Gua., Spa. prenda de vestir
  Mex. ropa, traje
gas (vehicle) (n) gasolina
  Arg. nafta
gas pedal (n phr) acelerador
  Pue.R. pedal de la gasolina
  Venz. pedal de gasolina
gas tank (n phr) tanque de gasolina
  Arg. tanque de nafta
  Spa. depósito de gasolina
gearbox (n) caja de cambios
  ElS., Gua., Mex. caja de velocidades
  Pue.R. transmisión
gears (n) velocidades
  Arg., Chi., Cub., Dom.R., Pan., Pue.R., Uru., Venz. cambios
  Cos.R. marchas

get high (drugs) (v phr) colocarse
  Bol., Per. volar
  Chi. volarse
  Col. entrar en onda, sollarse, soltarse, volar
  Cub. cojer nota
  Dom.R. darse un viaje, ponerse high
  Mex. tocarse, traer un alucine
  Pue.R. elevarse, tripear
  Venz. meterse un viaje
get off (bus) (v phr) bajarse
  Bol., Cos.R., Dom.R., Per., Uru. apearse
get on (bus) (v phr) subirse
  Col. montarse
girl (n) niña
  Arg., Uru. chica, nena
  Dom.R. muchachita
  Mex. chamaca
girlfriend (n) novia
  Chi. polola
  Ecu., Per. enamorada
give birth (v phr) dar a luz
  Arg. tener un/a beba/bebe/bebé/hijo/hija
  Col. alumbrar, parir
  Cos.R., Dom.R., Pan. parir
glasses, opera (n phr) gemelos de teatro
  Col. binoculares, binóculos
  Cub. anteojos de teatro
  Venz. lentes de ópera
glasses, safety (n phr) anteojos de camino
  Chi. anteojos de seguridad
  Mex. gafas de protección
  Pue.R. anteojos de protección
  Spa. gafas de seguridad
  Venz. lentes protectores
gloomy (person) (adj) lúgubre

Col. sombrío
Cub. melancólico
Dom.R. de mal humor
Mex. triste
Venz. deprimido
goalie (n) portero
Arg., Chi., Per. arquero
Col. guarda-vallas
Cub. guardameta
Pan. goleador
Pue.R. porteador
Uru. golero
goatee (n) barbas de chivo
Col. chivera
Cub. chivo
Dom.R. chiva, chivita
Ecu. chivita
Spa. perilla
Venz. chiva
goggles, ski (n phr) anteojos para esquiar
Arg. antiparras
Mex. gogles para esquiar
Spa. gafas de esquí
goggles, swimming (n phr) anteojos para nadar
Arg. antiparras
Mex. gogles
Pue.R. goggles
Spa. gafas de buceo
golf ball (n phr) pelota de golf
Col., Mex., Pue.R. bola de golf
golf club (n phr) palo de golf
Col. taco de golf
Pan. club de golf
golf course (n phr) campo de golf
Arg. cancha de golf
Good evening! (int phr) ¡Buenas tardes!
Col., Ecu. ¡Buenas noches!

Good morning! (int phr) ¡Buenos días!
Arg. ¡Buen día!
Good night! (int phr) ¡Buenas noches!
Ecu. ¡Hasta mañana!
Goodbye! (int) ¡Adiós!
Arg. ¡Chau!
Chi. ¡Chao!
Col. ¡Hasta luego!, ¡Hasta pronto!
Dom.R. ¡Bye!
gooseberry (n) grosella silvestre
Pue.R. grosella
grapefruit (n) toronja
Arg., Chi., Spa., Uru. pomelo
grass (n) hierba
Chi. césped, pasto
Col. pasto, yerba
Mex., Per. pasto
Pue.R. yerba
grater (n) rallador
Col. rallo
Dom.R. guallo
Pue.R. guayo
gray (hair) (adj) canoso
Col. cano
Spa. blanco
green (eyes) (adj) verde
Col. ojiverde
Cos.R. gato
griddle (n) asador eléctrico
Col., Pan. sartén eléctrica
Spa. plancha
grocer (n) tendero
Arg., Uru. almacenero
Col. comerciante, vendedor
Cub. bodeguero
Dom.R. dependiente de colmado/supermercado/tienda
Ecu., Mex. abarrotero
grocery (n) tienda de comestibles

Arg., Uru. almacén
Col. mercado
Cos.R. compras
Cub., Per. bodega
Dom.R. bodega, supercolmado,
víveres
ElS. pulpería
Gua. tienda
Mex. super, tienda de abarrotes
Pan. abarrotería, tienda
Pue.R. colmado
Spa. supermercado
Venz. abastos, supermercado
ground floor (n phr) planta baja
Col. piso de abajo, primer piso
Dom.R. primer piso
grow up (v phr) crecer
Col. madurar
grumpy (adj) malhumorado
Chi. andar de malas pulgas
Col. gruñón, protestón,
refunfuñón, rezongón
Pue.R. de mal humor
Venz. cascarrabias
guardian (n) tutor
Col., Pan., Venz. guardián
guy (n) muchacho, tipo
Arg. pibe
Chi. cabro
Cos.R. mae, fulano/a
Cub., Pue.R. chico
Mex., Pan. fulano/a
guys (dual gender plural) (n)
muchachos, tipos
Arg., Ecu. chicos
Chi. cabros, chiquillos

Mexicans use a variety of English words with the original pronunciation, such as "ride," as in *pedir ride* ("to ask for a ride") or *te doy un ride* ("I'll give you a ride").

H

habit (n) vicio
  Col. hábito
hacksaw (n) sierra de metal
  Col. sierra para cortar metal
  Cub. serrucho
  Mex., Spa. sierra para metal
  Pue.R. segueta
  Venz. serrucho, sierra para metales
hair (n) cabello, pelo
  Arg. vello
  Col. cabellera, melena
hair dryer (n phr) secadora manual
  Arg. secador
  Chi., Spa., Venz. secador de pelo
  Cub. secadora de pelo
  Dom.R., Pue.R. blower
  Mex. pistola de pelo, secadora de pelo
hair gel (n phr) gel para el pelo
  Dom.R., ElS., Gua. gelatina para el pelo
  Ecu. gel fijador
  Mex. jalea
  Spa. gomina para el pelo
hair mousse (n phr) mousse para el pelo
  Dom.R. mus para el pelo
  ElS., Gua., Spa. espuma para el pelo
  Mex. mouse para el pelo
hair rollers (n phr) ruleros
  Chi. ondulines
  Col., Spa. rulos
  Cub., Pue.R. rolos
  ElS., Gua., Mex. tubos
  Pan., Venz. rollos

hairdresser (n) peluquero/a
  Col. barbero
  Mex., Pan. estilista
hairdresser's shop (n phr) peluquería
  Dom.R., Mex., Pan. salón de belleza
  Pue.R. beauty parlor, salón de belleza
hairspray (n) laca para el pelo
  Cub. espray de pelo
  Dom.R., Mex., Pan. spray para el pelo
  Pue.R. spray de pelo
hairy (adj) velloso
  Arg., Chi., Pue.R., Spa., Venz. peludo
  Bol., Dom.R., Ecu., Pan., Uru. velludo
  Col. mechudo, peludo
half-glasses (n) media luna
  Mex. lentes para leer
  Venz. medios-lentes
hammock (n) hamaca
  Venz. chinchorro
handbag (n) cartera
  Col., Cos.R., Gua., Mex., Pan. bolsa de mano
  Dom.R. bolso
  Spa., Venz. bolso de mano
handball (n) handbol
  ElS., Gua. balonmano
  Uru. pelota de mano
handlebar grips (bicycle) (n phr) puños
  Col. manillas
  Gua., Venz. agarraderas del manubrio
  Per. mangos
handlebars (bicycle) (n) guía
  Arg., Bol., Chi., Col., Mex., Pue.R., Venz. manubrio

Cub., Dom.R., Pan. timón
Ecu. manubrios
Gua. manubrio, timón
Spa., Uru. manillar
handsome (adj) guapo
Arg. buen mozo
Bol. churro
Chi., Dom.R. buenmozo
Col. bien parecido, buenmozo, churro, majo
Venz. bien parecido
hard drive (n phr) disco duro
Pue.R. hard drive
hard drugs (n phr) drogas duras
Col. drogas fuertes
hard liquor (n phr) licor espiritoso
Bol., Dom.R., Venz. licor fuerte
Col. licor de alto contenido alcohólico
ElS., Pan. licor
Mex. bebidas fuertes
Spa. bebida alcohólica fuerte
Uru. bebida alcohólica
hare (n) liebre
Pue.R. conejo
hat, top (n phr) sombrero de copa
Arg. galera
hatchet (n) hacha
Col. hachuela
hawk (n) halcón
Bol. alcón
Chi. peuco
hazelnut (n) avellana
Dom.R. coquito
headboard (n) cabecera
Ecu. espaldar
Pue.R. espaldal
headlights (n) faros
Arg., Cub. focos, luces
Chi., Pan., Pue.R. luces

Col. faroles delanteros
Dom.R., Mex., Venz. luces delanteras
head-on collision (n phr) choque de frente
Col. colisión frente a frente
Per. choque frente a frente
Spa., Uru. choque frontal
hedge (n) seto
Col. matorral
Mex. cercado de arbustos
heel (shoe) (n) taco
Col., Cub., Gua., Hon., Mex., Pan., Spa., Venz. tacón
heel, high (shoe) (n phr) taco alto
Col., Cub., ElS., Gua., Hon., Mex., Pan., Spa., Venz. tacón alto
Hello? (answering telephone) (int) ¿Dígame?
Arg., Bol. ¿Hola?
Cub. ¿Oigo?
Col., Cos.R., Dom.R., Ecu., ElS., Gua., Hon., Per., Venz. ¿Aló?
Mex. ¿Bueno?
Pan., Pue.R. ¿Haló?
Uru. ¿Aló?, ¿Hola?
herbalist's shop (n) botánica
Col. tienda botánica
Mex. tienda naturista
Spa. tienda de botánica
Uru. herbolario
hibiscus (n) hibisco
Pan. papo
high jump (n phr) salto de altura
Chi., Col., ElS., Gua., Hon. salto alto
Pue.R. salto a lo alto
hill (n) colina

Chi. cerro, loma
Cub., Pan. loma
Pue.R. cuesta
hit (song) (n) canción de moda
Col. éxito
Cos.R. éxito, hit
Cub., Dom.R. hit
hitchhike (v) hacer autostop
Arg., Chi. hacer dedo
Col. echar dedo
Cos.R. pedir ride
Dom.R. pedir bola
ElS., Gua., Hon. pedir jalón a
dedo
Per. tirar dedo
Pue.R. pedir pon
Venz. pedir cola
hoe (n) azada
Bol. azador
Col., Pan. asadón
Dom.R., Gua. azadón
Mex. talacho
Venz. azadón, pico
hole in one (n phr) hoyo en uno
Pue.R. bola en uno
holiday (n) día feriado
Arg. feriado
Col., Spa. día festivo
Mex. día de fiesta, día de
vacaciones
hood (n) capucha
Chi. capuchón
Cub. caperuza
horizontal bar (n phr) barra fija
Col., Pan., Pue.R., Venz. barra
horizontal
horseback riding (n phr) equitación
Col. montar a caballo
Cub. ir a caballo
horsefly, gadfly (n) tábano

Col. moscardón
Pue.R. caballito de San Pedro
hospital (n) hospital
Col. clínica
host (show) (n) presentador
Col. animador
Dom.R., Mex., Venz. anfitrión/a
Per. maestro de ceremonias
hot air balloon (n phr) globo
aerostático
Chi., Col. globo
Venz. globo de aire caliente
house robe (n phr) túnica
Col. vestido casero
Cub., Dom.R., Spa., Venz. bata
de casa
Pan. bata de estar en casa
How's it going? (phr) ¿Cómo te (le) va?
Arg., Mex., Pue.R., Uru. ¿Qué
tal?
Bol. ¿Cómo estás?
Dom.R. ¿Cómo tú estás?
Ecu. ¿Qué ha habido?, ¿Qué tal?
hubcap (n) tapacubos
Chi. taparuedas
Col. copa de la rueda
Cub. tambora
Ecu., Spa. tapacubo
Mex. tapón
Pan. rin
Pue.R. tapabocina
Uru. embellecedor
Venz. taza del caucho
hum (n) zumbido
Col. murmullo, susurro
hummingbird (n) colibrí
Arg., Col., Pan. picaflor
Ecu. chupaflor
hurdles race (n phr) vallas
Chi. obstáculos

Col. competencia de obstáculos
Cub., Dom.R., ElS., Gua.,
Hon., Venz. carrera de obstáculos
hurricane (n) huracán
Dom.R. ciclón
hut (n) choza
Arg. albergue, cabaña, casilla
Dom.R. casita de paja
hydrofoil boat (n phr) hidroala
Chi. hidroavión
Col. aereodeslizador
Mex. hidrofoil
hymn (n) cántico
Bol., Col., Dom.R., Mex., Spa.,
Venz. himno
Pue.R. canción, himno

What is traditionally seen as local Costa Rican Spanish is derived primarily from the *campesinos* (country-dwellers). To them, a *casado* is not a married man, but an everyday dish composed of meat or a fried egg, lettuce, rice, black beans, and a fried banana.

ABBREVIATIONS: Arg.=Argentina   Bol.=Bolivia   Chi.=Chile   Col.=Colombia
Cos.R.=Costa Rica   Cub.=Cuba   Dom.R.=Dominican Republic   Ecu.=Ecuador   ElS.=El
Salvador   Gua.=Guatemala   Hon.=Honduras   Mex.=Mexico   Pan.=Panama   Per.=Peru
Pri.=Primary Term   Pue.R.=Puerto Rico   Spa.=Spain   Uru.=Uruguay   Venz.=Venezuela

I J K

ice bucket (n phr) balde de hielo
Dom.R., Ecu., Gua., Mex., Venz.
hielera
Pue.R. cubeta de hielo
ice cream parlor (n phr) heladería
Mex. nevería
ice cream truck (n phr) heladero
Col. camión del helado, carrito de
helados
Mex. carro de helados
Spa. camión del helado
ice skating (n phr) patinaje sobre hielo
Chi., Cub. patinaje en hielo
Col. patinaje en el hielo
iceberg (n) iceberg
Chi. témpano de hielo
icing syringe (n phr) jeringuilla de
decoración
Col. jeringuilla para decorar
Venz. decorador para pasteleros
icon (computer) (n) icono
Cub. símbolo gráfico
Pue.R. icon
impolite (adj) descortés, mal educado
Col. desatento, grosero, ramplón
Spa. maleducado
impressive (adj) impresionante
Col. emocionante
index card (n phr) ficha
Col., Pue.R. tarjeta
infant (n) niño/a
Arg., Uru. chico/a, nene/a
Col. criatura, infante, menor
Cub., Mex., Spa. bebé
Gua. criatura
infomercial (n) comercial informativa

Col. anuncio informativo,
programa comercial para
promocionar algo
Cos.R. boletín informativo
Spa. telepromoción
Uru. información de interés
inhale (drugs) (v) aspirar
Arg., Col., Mex., Pue.R. inhalar
Cub., Dom.R. oler
inmate (n) preso
Col. encarcelado, prisionero,
recluso
Pan. reo
inner tube (bicycle tire) (n phr) tubo
Chi., Spa. cámara
Cos.R. neumático
Venz. tripa del caucho
instructor (sports) (n) instructor de
deportes
Arg., Bol., Chi., Cub. entrenador
Col. instructor deportivo
Pue.R. maestro de educación
física
Venz. entrenador de deportes
interviewee (n) entrevistado/a
Arg., Cos.R., Cub., Ecu., ElS.,
Gua., Hon., Per., Pue.R.
encuestado/a
interviewer (n) entrevistador/a
Arg., Cos.R., Cub., Ecu., ElS.,
Gua., Hon., Per., Pue.R.
encuestador/a
intoxicated (adj) borracho, embriagado
Spa. bajo la influencia
iris (n) lirio
Venz. iris
jack (car) (n) gato
Bol., Chi., Per. gata
Gua. triquet
jacket (n) chaqueta

Arg. campera
Dom.R., Pan. saco
Mex. chamarra
Per. casca
Pue.R. blazer (women), gabán
(men)
jam session (n phr) sesión de músicos
de jazz o rock que tocan por placer
propio
Chi. ensayo
Col. sesión de música
improvisado
Cub. descarga
Pue.R. jameo
Spa. jam session
janitor (n) conserje
Chi. limpiador
Col. portero
Cub. barrendero
jaw (n) mandíbula
Col. quijada
jazz music (n phr) música jazz
Col. música de jazz
Dom.R., Spa. jazz
jersey (n) jersey
Bol. saco
Col. chompa
Mex. playera de punto
Venz. suéter
jet (n) jet
Chi. avión a chorro
jet-lag, to have (v phr) tener jet lag
Dom.R. estar desorientado por
desfase de horarios
Mex. sentirse mal por la altura,
sentirse mal por el vuelo
Spa. tener desfase horario
joint (n) articulación
Dom.R., Spa. coyuntura
jungle (n) selva

Chi., Col., Dom.R., Pue.R.,
Venz. jungla
kettle (n) marmita
Arg., Uru. pava
Bol. caldera
Chi., Col., Per., Spa. tetera
Cub. caldero
Ecu. cantina de agua
Mex. olla grande
key (music) (n) tono
Col. tonalidad
keyboard (computer) (n) teclado
Pue.R. keyboard
kid (n) chico/a
Cub. chiquito/a
Col., Venz. niño/a
Dom.R. muchacho/a
kiwi (n) kiwi
Uru. quivi
knife sharpener (n phr) afilador de
cuchillo
Dom.R. amolador
knife, butter (n phr) cuchillo para
mantequilla
Arg. cuchillo para manteca
knit shirt (n phr) polo
Dom.R., Pan. suéter
Mex. playera
Per. camiseta

Chencha means "girlfriend" in
Venezuelan slang.

L

label (n) etiqueta
Dom.R., Pue.R. label
label, adhesive (n phr) etiqueta
adhesiva
Dom.R., Pue.R. label adhesiva
ladybug (n) mariquita
Arg. vaquita de San Antonio
Chi. chinita
Mex. catarina
Venz. coquito
LAN (local area network) (n phr) LAN
Mex. red local LAN
Spa., Venz. red de área local
lane (n) carril
Cub. línea
Venz. canal
laundry (n) lavandería
Arg. lavadero
lawn (n) césped
Arg., Bol., Mex., Per. pasto
Col. hierba, manga, pasto, prado
Cub., Dom.R. yerba
Dom.R., ElS., Gua., Hon., Venz.
grama
Pue.R. grama, pasto
lawn mower (n phr) cortacéspedes
Arg. máquina de cortar pasto
Bol. cortadora
Chi. cortapasto
Col. máquina para cortar el
pasto
Cub. máquina de cortar yerba
ElS., Gua., Hon. cortagrama
Mex. podadora de pasto
Per. cortador de césped, cortador
del pasto

Pue.R. cortadora de grama
Spa. cortacésped
Venz. cortagrama, segadora
lawn rake (n phr) barredora
Arg., Chi., Col., Cub., Dom.R.,
Mex., Pan. rastrillo
lawyer (n) abogado
Col. jurista
lawyer's office (n phr) bufete de
abogados
Arg. estudio de abogados
Col., Pue.R. oficina de abogados
Ecu. estudio juridico
lazy (adj) perezoso
Arg., Cub. vago
Bol., Chi., Venz. flojo
Col., Uru. haragán
Dom.R. haragán, vago
Mex. flojo, holgazán
leek (n) porro
Arg., Col., Dom.R., Ecu., ElS.,
Gua., Hon., Spa., Uru. puerro
Mex., Per. poro
leotard (n) leotardo
Chi. malla
Venz. mallas de ejercicio
level (n) nivel
Chi. nivelador
Uru. plomada
liar (n) mentiroso
Chi. chamullento
Col. embustero
librarian (n) bibliotecario/a
Dom.R. bibliotecólogo
light (weight) (adj) ligero
Arg., Chi. liviano
lighter (n) encendedor
Cub. fosforera
lightning (n) rayo, relámpago
Col. centella

lime (n) lima
  Cub., Pan. limón
lip synch (v phr) doblar
  Dom.R. hacer mímica
lipstick (n) lápiz labial
  Arg., Bol., Chi. rouge
  Col., Cub., Dom.R. pintalabios
  Mex. bilé
  Pan. lipstick
  Pue.R. lipstic
  Spa., Uru. lápiz de labios
liquor (n) bebidas fuertes
  Col., Cub., ElS., Gua., Hon.,
  Mex., Pan., Venz. licor
  Spa. bebida alcohólica fuerte
liquor store (n phr) tienda de bebidas
alcohólicas
  Bol., Col., Mex. licorería
  Dom.R., Pue.R. liquor store
  Pan. bodega
live broadcast (n phr) transmisión en
directa
  Arg. programa en vivo,
  transmisión en directo
  Bol., Col., ElS., Gua., Uru.
  transmisión en directo
  Chi., Per. transmisión en vivo y
  en directo
  Cos.R., Cub., Dom.R., Ecu.,
  Pan., Spa., Venz. transmisión en
  vivo
  Mex. transmisión directa,
  transmisión en vivo
living room (n phr) cuarto de estar,
sala
  Arg. living
loading dock (n phr) plataforma de
carga
  Col. muelle de carga
loafers (n) zapatos de andar

Chi., Col., Cub., Ecu., Venz.
mocasines
  Dom.R. zapatos bajitos
  ElS., Gua., Spa. zapatos estilo
  mocasín
  Mex. zapatos de casa
lobby (n) foyer
  Arg. hall de entrada, lobby,
  recepción
  Chi. hall de entrada, recepción
  Col. pasillo, vestíbulo
  Cub., ElS., Gua., Spa. vestíbulo
  Dom.R., Mex., Pue.R. lobby
  Pan. loby
  Venz. sala de espera, vestíbulo
local train (n phr) tren local
  Mex. metro
  Spa. tren de cercanías
locket (n) relicario
  Cub. guardapelo
  Dom.R. medallón
loud (noise) (adj) ruidoso
  Chi. fuerte
love seat (n phr) confidente
  Arg. silloncito
  Col., ElS., Gua., Venz. sofá para
  dos personas
  Dom.R., Mex. love seat
  Pue.R., Spa. sofá
love song (n phr) canción de amor
  Col., Pue.R. canción romántica
love, lovey (n) amor
  Chi. tesoro
  Col. amorcito, cariño
  Cos.R. amorcito
LSD (n) LSD
  Cos.R., Cub. ácido
lubrication (n) engrase
  Chi. lubrificación
  Col., Dom.R., Gua., Pan.

lubricación
Mex. engrasado
lunch (n) almuerzo
Dom.R., Mex., Spa. comida
lyrics (n) letra de una canción
Dom.R. letras de una canción

In comparison to other Latin American countries, the influence of the Indian language on the Spanish spoken in Ecuador is minimal. Indian words are used to name streets, businesses, buildings, etc. but hardly at all in conversation.

ABBREVIATIONS: Arg.=Argentina Bol.=Bolivia Chi.=Chile Col.=Colombia Cos.R.=Costa Rica Cub.=Cuba Dom.R.=Dominican Republic Ecu.=Ecuador ElS.=El Salvador Gua.=Guatemala Hon.=Honduras Mex.=Mexico Pan.=Panama Per.=Peru Pri.=Primary Term Pue.R.=Puerto Rico Spa.=Spain Uru.=Uruguay Venz.=Venezuela

M

Ma'am, Madam (n) Señora
  Cos.R., Pan. Doña
macaw (n) guacamayo
  ElS., Gua., Mex. guacamaya
mail room (n phr) cuarto de correos,
sala de correos
  Spa. cuarto del correo
main course (n phr) plato principal
  Cub. plato fuerte
  Col. entrada
  Mex. platillo principal
makeup kit (n phr) estuche de
maquillaje
  Col. juego de maquillaje
  Pue.R. cartera de maquillaje
manager (sports) (n) manager
deportivo
  Col., Pan. administrador
  deportivo
  Mex. técnico
  Venz. administrador deportivo,
  gerente deportivo
mandarine orange (n phr) mandarina
  Pue.R. china mandarina
mandolin (n) mandolina
  Chi. mandolín
manicurist (n) manicuro/a
  Chi. manicure
  Dom.R., Ecu., Mex., Pan., Per.,
  Venz. manicurista
maple (tree) (n) arce
  Gua., Mex. maple
marijuana (n) marihuana
  Col. yerba
  Cos.R. monte, mota
marijuana cigarette (n phr) cigarrillo
de marihuana
  Arg. porro
  Chi. pito
  Col. varillo
  Cos.R. puro
  Cub., Pue.R. pitillo de marihuana
  Dom.R. joint, tabaco de
  marihuana
marker (n) marcador
  Cub., Mex. plumón
  Spa. rotulador
matchstick (n) cerilla, fósforo
  Mex. cerillo
mattress (n) colchón
  Pue.R. matres
mayor (n) alcalde/sa
  Chi. prefecto
  Dom.R. síndico
  Mex. presidente municipal
  Uru. intendente
measuring cups (n phr) tazas para
medir
  Dom.R. tazas medidoras
measuring spoons (n phr) cucharas
para medir
  Dom.R. cucharas medidoras
meat grinder (n phr) molino de carne
  Arg., Col., Dom.R. moledora de
  carne
  Cub. molidora
  Pan., Pue.R. moledor de carne
median (n) centro de la calle
  Col. isla de tráfico, separador
  Pue.R. carril del centro
  Spa. mediana
  Venz. isla
men's (bathroom) (n) hombres
  Chi., Col., Cub., Dom.R., Mex.,
  Venz. caballeros
microwave (oven) (n) micro

ABBREVIATIONS: Arg.=Argentina Bol.=Bolivia Chi.=Chile Col.=Colombia
Cos.R.=Costa Rica Cub.=Cuba Dom.R.=Dominican Republic Ecu.=Ecuador ElS.=El
Salvador Gua.=Guatemala Hon.=Honduras Mex.=Mexico Pan.=Panama Per.=Peru
Pri.=Primary Term Pue.R.=Puerto Rico Spa.=Spain Uru.=Uruguay Venz.=Venezuela

Arg., Col., Cub., Uru. microonda
Chi., Mex., Pue.R., Spa., Venz.
microondas
middle finger (n phr) dedo del corazón
Arg. medio
Col. dedo corazón
Cub., Dom.R., Venz. dedo del
medio
Mex., Uru. dedo medio
midwife (n) partera
Col., Dom.R., ElS., Gua., Hon.,
Spa. comadrona
miniskirt (n) minifalda
Col., Pue.R. falda corta
mist (n) neblina
Arg., Pue.R. niebla
Col. bruma, llovizna, niebla
Pan. bajareque
mistress (n) amante
Cub., Spa. querida
Mex. concubina
Pue.R. chilla
mixer (n) batidora
Cub. mezclador
modular office (n phr) oficina modular
Dom.R. módulo
molar (n) muela
Col. molar
monitor (computer) (n) monitor
Arg., Chi. pantalla
monkey (n) mono
Col. mico
Mex. chango
moose (n) anta
Chi. ante
Col., Mex. alce, ante
Arg., Spa., Venz. alce
motherboard (n) placa madre
Col., Spa. tarjeta madre
Mex. tarjeta principal

Pan. mother board
Venz. placa base
motorcycle, motorbike (n)
motocicleta, moto
Pue.R. motora
mouse (n) ratón
Chi. laucha
move (v) mudarse
Bol. trasladarse
Col. cambiarse de casa
movie theater (n phr) sala de cine
Col., Ecu. teatro de cine
movie, G-rated (n phr) película para
todo público
Mex. película para todo público
clasificación A
movie, horror (n phr) película de
miedo
Arg., Col., Cos.R., Dom.R.
película de terror
Mex., Uru. película de horror
Pue.R., Venz. película de horror,
película de terror
movie, PG-rated (n phr) película para
todo público
Mex. película para adolescentes y
adultos clasificación B
Pue.R. película público general
Spa. película apta para todos los
públicos
Venz. película censura B
movie, western (n phr) película de
vaqueros
Arg. película de cowboys
Spa. western
movie, x-rated (n phr) película para
adultos
Col. película clasificación X
Cub. película pornográfica
Mex. película sólo para adultos

clasificación C
Pue.R. película X
muffin (n) panecillo
Arg., Col. muffin
Bol. pancito
Gua. mollete
Mex. mufin, panqué, pastelito
Per. quequito
Spa. magdalena
muffin pan (n phr) molde para
panecillos
Arg. molde para muffin
Bol. molde para pancitos
Mex. molde para mufin, molde
para pastelitos
Per. molde para quequitos
Spa. molde para magdalenas
muffler (n) mofle
Arg., Col., Ecu., Spa., Uru.
silenciador
Dom.R. muffler
Mex. mufler
Venz. amortiguador
mug (n) jarro
Arg. jarrita, jarrito
Chi. jarra, tazón
Cub. vaso
ElS., Gua. pocillo
Pue.R., Spa., Venz. jarra
mug, beer (n phr) jarra para cerveza
Arg. porrón
Mex. jarro de cerveza
Pue.R., Spa., Venz. jarra de
cerveza
mug, coffee (n phr) jarra para café
Arg. jarrito, jarrita
Cub. taza de café
ElS., Gua. pocillo para café
Mex. jarro para café
Pue.R. tazón de café

Venz. jarrita para café
mushroom (n) hongo
Col., Mex. champiñón
Spa. champiñón, seta
musical (movie) (n) película musical
Dom.R., Pue.R. músical
mussel (n) mejillón
Chi. choro
mustang (n) mustango
Arg. potro

> If you need a plumber in Chile, you'd call for a *gáfiter*, or *gas-fitter*, as they were originally called.

ABBREVIATIONS: Arg.=Argentina Bol.=Bolivia Chi.=Chile Col.=Colombia
Cos.R.=Costa Rica Cub.=Cuba Dom.R.=Dominican Republic Ecu.=Ecuador ElS.=El
Salvador Gua.=Guatemala Hon.=Honduras Mex.=Mexico Pan.=Panama Per.=Peru
Pri.=Primary Term Pue.R.=Puerto Rico Spa.=Spain Uru.=Uruguay Venz.=Venezuela

N

nail polish (n phr) esmalte de uñas
  Chi. cutex
  Col., Spa. pintauñas
  Cub., Venz. pintura de uñas
  Dom.R. cuté
nanny (n) niñera
  Chi., Col., Mex., Venz. nana
nape (n) nuca
  Col. cogote
naughty (adj) travieso
  Arg. liero
  Chi. malvado
  Col. juguetón, retozón
  Cub. pillo
  Dom.R. bellaco
  Pue.R. necio
navel (n) ombligo
  Arg., Chi. pupo
neck (guitar) (n) mástil
  Chi. cuello
necklace, pendant (n phr) collar con
medallón
  Chi. medallón
  Dom.R. pendiente con medalla
  Mex. pendiente con cadena
  Spa. colgante con cadena
nectarine (n) ciruela de negra
  Chi. durazno pelado
  Col., Cub. nectarina
  Cos.R., Dom.R. ciruela
  ElS., Gua. nectarino
  Mex. nectarín
  Pan. ciruela negra
  Pue.R., Venz. nectarine
  Spa. briñón
  Uru. pelón

neighborhood (n) vecindad
  Arg., Ecu., Pan., Uru. barrio
  Bol., Gua., Pue.R., Venz.
  vecindario
  Col., Dom.R., Per., Spa. barrio,
  vecindario
neon sign (n phr) anuncio de neón
  Arg. cartel de néon
  Col. aviso con luz de neón
  Dom.R. letrero de néon
network (television) (n) cadena
  Dom.R. telecadena
news brief (n phr) breves
  Chi. breves informativos
  Col. informativo breve
  Cos.R. resúmen noticioso
  Dom.R. titulares
  Gua. resúmen de noticias
  Mex. noticiero breve
  Per., Venz. resúmen de noticias
newscast (n) telediario
  Arg., Chi., Col., Ecu., Pan.
  noticiero
  Cos.R. telenoticiero
  Cub. reporte
  Dom.R. noticiero, telenoticiero
  Mex. noticias, noticiero
  Spa. noticiario
newsstand (n) puesto de periódicos
  Arg. puesto de diarios
  Col. puesto de periódicos y de
  revistas
nice (adj) simpático
  Col. agradable, amable, amigable
  Cub., Spa. amable
  Dom.R. chulo
  Pue.R. chévere
  Venz. agradable
nightgown (n) camisón
  Chi., Col. camisa de dormir

Cub., Pue.R. bata de dormir
Ecu. camisa de noche
Dom.R. pijama
nipple (n) pezón
Col. tetilla
nostril (n) ventanilla
Chi. narina
Cub. ventana de la nariz
Dom.R. hoyo de la nariz
Mex. poro de la nariz
Pue.R. roto de la nariz
Venz. orificio nasal
notebook (n) cuaderno
Cub. carpeta
Dom.R. libreta, mascota
Pue.R. libreta
nursery (plants) (n) semillero
Arg., Col., Dom.R. vivero
Mex. invernadero

> *Cacahuete* (peanut) comes from the Nahuatl (Aztec) language.

ABBREVIATIONS: Arg.=Argentina Bol.=Bolivia Chi.=Chile Col.=Colombia
Cos.R.=Costa Rica Cub.=Cuba Dom.R.=Dominican Republic Ecu.=Ecuador EIS.=El
Salvador Gua.=Guatemala Hon.=Honduras Mex.=Mexico Pan.=Panama Per.=Peru
Pri.=Primary Term Pue.R.=Puerto Rico Spa.=Spain Uru.=Uruguay Venz.=Venezuela

O

office cubicle (n phr) recinto
Bol. oficina
Col., Dom.R., Gua., Mex., Pan.,
Pue.R., Venz. cubículo
office divider (n phr) partidor
Bol., Ecu. divisor
Col. divisor, separador
Dom.R. división
Mex. biombo separador
office hours (n phr) horas de oficina
Cub. horas de trabajo
office manager (n phr) jefe de oficina
Col. administrador, gerente
Cub., Mex., Pue.R., Venz. gerente
de oficina
office suite (n phr) oficina
Venz. suite de oficinas
office supplies (n phr) artículos de
oficina
Cub. materiales de oficina
Ecu. útiles de oficina
offside (n) fuera de juego
Arg. offside
Col., ElS., Gua., Hon. de
posición adelantada
Mex. lateral
Pue.R. fuera de posición
oil can (n phr) aceitera
Arg., Cub., Venz. lata de aceite
Col. tarro de aceite
okra (n) quimbombó
Dom.R. molondrón
Mex. okra
olive (n) aceituna
Cos.R. oliva
omelet (n) omelete

Bol., Col., Cub., Per., Pue.R.,
Spa., Venz. tortilla
Dom.R. tortilla española
one-way ticket (n phr) billete sencillo
Arg. boleto de ida, pasaje de ida
Bol. billete de ida, billete de una
sola vía
Chi., Mex., Pan., Venz. boleto de
ida
Col. tiquete de una sola vía
Cos.R., Dom.R. pasaje de ida
Ecu., Spa. billete de ida
Per. boleto en un solo sentido
onion, pickling (n phr) cebollino
Chi. cebollín
Col. cebollina
Mex. cebolla de cambray
Spa. cebolleta
onion, red (Bermuda) (n phr) cebolla
roja
Ecu. cebolla colorada
Mex. cebolla morada
onion, vidalia (n phr) vidalia
Bol. cebolla
Col. cebolla vidalia
orange (n) naranja
Dom.R., Pue.R. china
orchard (n) huerto
Pue.R. hortaliza
ostrich (n) avestruz
Col. ñandú
ottoman (n) otomana
Mex. taburete
Pan. banquillo
Pue.R. banquillo , ottomán
outfit (n) conjunto
Chi. traje
Col. vestimenta
outgoing (adj) extrovertido
Arg. dado

Cub. sociable
overalls (n) mono
    Arg., Dom.R., Pue.R. mameluco
    Chi., Col., Pan. overol
    Cub. guardapolvo
    Mex. overales, pantalones de peto
    Per. coverall
    Uru. entero
overcoat (n) abrigo
    Arg. sobretodo
overwhelming (adj) abrumador
    Chi., Col. agobiante
owl (n) búho
    Arg., Col., Cub., Dom.R. lechuza
    Chi. chuncho
oyster (n) ostra
    Mex. ostión

Costa Ricans may refer to their wife as their *terciopelo* (velvet) or *anabelle*, an endearing combination of *anaconda* and *cascabel* (rattlesnake).

ABBREVIATIONS: Arg.=Argentina Bol.=Bolivia Chi.=Chile Col.=Colombia Cos.R.=Costa Rica Cub.=Cuba Dom.R.=Dominican Republic Ecu.=Ecuador EIS.=El Salvador Gua.=Guatemala Hon.=Honduras Mex.=Mexico Pan.=Panama Per.=Peru Pri.=Primary Term Pue.R.=Puerto Rico Spa.=Spain Uru.=Uruguay Venz.=Venezuela

P

pad (paper) (n) cuaderno
Arg., Mex., Per. bloc
Bol., Cub., Pan., Pue.R., Venz.
libreta
Col. bloc, cuaderno de notas,
libreta
Spa. bloc de notas
pad, legal (n phr) cuaderno legal
Arg., Chi. bloc
Bol. libreta legal
Dom.R., Pan., Pue.R., Venz.
libreta tamaño legal
Mex. bloc tamaño oficio
Spa. bloc tamaño legal
pad, writing (n phr) cuaderno
Arg., Chi. bloc
Col., Cub., Dom.R., Pue.R.,
Venz. libreta
Mex. bloc tamaño carta
Spa. bloc de notas
pad, yellow (n phr) cuaderno amarillo
Arg., Chi. bloc
Bol., Col. Dom.R. libreta amarilla
Mex., Spa. bloc amarillo
Pue.R., Venz. libreta de papel
amarilla
pail (n) balde
Cub. cubo
Mex., Pue.R. cubeta
Venz. balde, tobo
painter's knife (n phr) navaja de pintor
Mex. espátula, raspa
pajamas (n) piyamas
Col. pijama, piyama
Dom.R., Pue.R. pijamas
Spa. pijama

pallet (n) paleta
Chi. palé
Mex. palet, tarima
Uru. plataforma
palm (tree) (n) palma
Arg., Col., Mex. palmera
pancake (n) panqueque
Cub., Dom.R., Pan., Pue.R.
pancake
Mex. hotcake
Venz. panqueca
panties (n) calzones
Arg., Uru. bombachas
Cub., Pan. blúmer, pantis
Dom.R., Pue.R. panties
Mex. pantaleta
Spa. bragas
Venz. pantaletas
pantry (n) despensa
Bol., Mex. alacena
Dom.R. pantry
ElS., Gua., Hon. comedor
auxiliar, pantry
Pue.R. gabinete
pantyhose (n) media pantalón
Arg. medias largas
Dom.R. media panty, pantyhose
Mex. pantimedia
Pan. pantihose
Per. media nylon
Pue.R. medias nylon
Spa. panty
Uru. pantimedias
Venz. medias panty
papaya (n) papaya
Cub. fruta bomba
Dom.R., Pue.R. lechosa
Venz. lechoso
paperclip (n) clip
Arg., Uru. ganchito

ABBREVIATIONS: Arg.=Argentina Bol.=Bolivia Chi.=Chile Col.=Colombia Cos.R.=Costa Rica Cub.=Cuba Dom.R.=Dominican Republic Ecu.=Ecuador ElS.=El Salvador Gua.=Guatemala Hon.=Honduras Mex.=Mexico Pan.=Panama Per.=Peru Pri.=Primary Term Pue.R.=Puerto Rico Spa.=Spain Uru.=Uruguay Venz.=Venezuela

Bol., Cos.R., Cub., ElS., Gua.,
Hon. sujetapapel
Col. grapa, sujetador
parakeet (n) perico
Spa. periquito
park (n) parque
Arg. plaza
park (v) estacionar
Bol., Col., Cos.R., Cub.,
Dom.R., ElS., Gua., Hon., Pan.
parquear
Spa. aparcar
parka (n) parka
Pue.R. capa
parking lot (n phr) estacionamiento
Arg. playa de estacionamiento
Bol., Cos.R., Cub., Dom.R.
ElS., Gua., Hon. parqueo
Col., Pan. parqueadero
Pue.R. parking
Spa. parking, aparcamiento
parrot (n) loro
Col. cotorra, papagayo
Dom.R. cotorra
parsnip (n) chiriva
Col. chirivia, chirivía
Gua. chiviría
Uru. pastinaca
part (hair) (n) raya
Chi., Pan. partidura
Dom.R., Mex., Venz. partido
part-time (work) (adj) por parte de la
jornada
Cub., Per., Spa. a tiempo parcial
Mex. de medio tiempo, parte de
tiempo
Pue.R. part-time
pass (traffic) (v) pasar
Chi. ultrapasar
Cos.R. adelantarse

Dom.R., Mex. rebasar
Spa. adelantar
pastry brush (n phr) pincel de
repostería
Col., Gua., ElS., Pan. brocha de
repostería
pastry cutting wheel (n phr)
cortapastas
Col. rodete para cortar masa
patient (n) paciente
Arg., Bol., Cub., Cos.R., Ecu.,
Gua., Uru. enfermo/a
Col. doliente
PC (n) PC
Arg., Gua., Mex., Venz.
computadora personal
Bol. computador personal
Spa. ordenador personal (OP)
peach (n) durazno
Cub., Dom.R., Para., Per., Pue.R.,
Spa. melocotón
peak (mountain) (n) pico
Chi. cima
peanut (n) maní
Mex. cacahuate
Spa. cacahuete
peas, green (n phr) arvejas
Cub. chícharos, petit pois
Mex. chícharos
Pan. petit pois
Per. arvejitas
Pue.R., Spa. guisantes
pecan (n) pacana
Bol., ElS., Gua., Hon. pecana
Mex. nuez
peeler (n) pelador
Mex. pelapapas
pen (n) pluma
Arg., Chi., Uru. lapicera
Per. lapicero

Spa. bolígrafo
pen, ball-point (n phr) bolígrafo,
pluma
  Bol. punta bola
  Chi. lapicera de pasta
  Col. esfero
  Per. lapicero
pen, fountain (n phr) pluma de fuente
  Arg. lapicera fuente
  Bol., Mex., Pue.R., Venz. pluma
  fuente
  Chi. lapicera a fuente
  Per. lapicero de tinta
  Spa. pluma, pluma estilográfica
  Uru. estilográfica
penknife (n) navaja
  Chi., Spa., Venz. cortaplumas
  Pue.R. cuchilla
pepper shaker (n phr) pimentera
  Arg., Col., Gua., Mex., Per.
  pimentero
  Pue.R. pimienta
  Venz. pimientero
pepper, hot (n phr) chile
  Bol., Chi., Venz., Per. ají
  Col., Cub., Pan., Pue.R. ají
  picante
  Cos.R. chile picante
  Ecu. pimiento picante
  Spa. guindilla
pepper, sweet (n phr) pimiento morrón
  Col. pimentón rojo, pimentón
  verde
  Cos.R. chile dulce
  Pan. ají dulce, pimentón
  Per., Venz. pimentón
  Spa. pimiento
perennial (plant) (n) perenne
  Pue.R. permanente
performer (n) artista

  Col. intérprete
  Mex. intérprete, músico
pest (person) (n) machaca
  Bol. cargoso
  Chi. insoportable
  Col. apestoso, lagarto, peste
  Cub. chivón, ladilla
  Dom.R. pesta, plaga
  Ecu. necio/a
  ElS., Gua. tipo/a pesado/a
  Mex., Venz. fastidioso
  Pan. peste
  Pue.R. sabandija
  Spa. pelma, pelmazo
pet shop (n phr) pajarería
  Col. almacén de mascotas
  Dom.R. pet shop, tienda de
  mascotas
  ElS., Gua. tienda de mascotes
  Mex. tienda de animales
  domésticos, veterinaria
  Pue.R. pet shop, tienda de
  animales
  Spa. tienda de animales
petticoat (n) combinación
  Chi. enagüa
  Cub. sayuela
  Dom.R. mediofondo, refajo
  Mex. enaguas
  Pan. peticote
  Pue.R. refajo
  Venz. enaguas, fondo
pharmacist (n) farmacéutico
  Col. boticario, farmaceuta
  Venz. farmaceuta
piccolo (n) pícolo
  Col., Mex., Spa. flautín
pickle (n) pepino encurtido
  Cub. pepino
  Dom.R., Mex., Pue.R. pepinillo

Spa. pepinillo en vinagre
Venz. encurtido
pickup truck (n phr) camioneta
Cos.R., ElS., Gua., Hon., Pan.,
Per. pickup
Mex., Venz. camioneta pickup
pie (n) pastel, tarta
Bol., Cub., Dom.R. pie
Chi., Cos.R. torta
Mex. pay
Venz. tartaleta
pie pan (n phr) molde para pastel
Arg. molde para tartas
Chi. molde para pie
Dom.R. molde de bizcocho
Mex. molde para pay
pig (n) puerco
Per. cerdo, chancho
Bol. chancho, cuchi
Arg., Chi., Ecu., Uru. chancho
Col. cerdo, marrano
Cos.R. chancho, cochino
Cub., Venz. cerdo, cochino
ElS., Gua., Hon. coche, marrano
Mex. cochino, marrano
Pan. marrano
Dom.R., Pue.R., Spa. cerdo
pigtail (n) trenza
Bol., Cos.R. cola
Chi. colita, moño
Col., Dom.R., Mex., Venz. colita
Per. cachito
Spa., Uru. coleta
pillowcase (n) funda
Gua. sobrefunda
pilot (n) piloto
Col. aviador
pimp (n) chulo
Chi. cafiche
ElS., Gua., Hon. alcahuete

pimple (n) grano
Chi., Cos.R., Dom.R., Spa.
espinilla
Col., Venz. barro, espinilla
Mex. barro
Per. barrito
pincers (n) tenazas
Col., Mex. pinzas
pine cone (n phr) piña
Per. piñón
pineapple (n) piña
Uru. ananá
pinkie finger (n phr) dedo meñique
Cub. dedo chiquito
pistachio (n) pistacho
Mex. pistache
pitcher (n) jarra
Chi. jarrón
Gua. pichel
plain (topography) (n) llanura
Col., Dom.R. llano
Mex. esplanada, planicie
Pue.R. planicie
plane (carpentry) (n) plano
Arg., Col., Dom.R., Mex., Spa.,
Uru. cepillo
plantar arch (foot) (n phr) arco plantar
Arg., Mex., Venz. arco del pie
Col. arco de la planta del pie
Dom.R. puente
platform (train) (n) andén
Col., Cub., Per. plataforma
platter (n) fuente de servir
Col., Cub., Pan. bandeja
Mex. platón
pliers (n) pinzas
Chi., Cos.R., Dom.R., Per.,
Pue.R., Venz. alicate
Col., Pan., Spa. alicates
Mex. alicatas

---

plumber (n) plomero
Chi. gáfiter [from "gas fitter"]
Ecu. gasfitero
Spa. fontanero
pocket, back (n phr) bolsillo trasero
Dom.R. bolsillo de atrás
pocket, breast (n phr) bolsillo superior
Dom.R. bolsillo de la camisa
pole vault (n phr) salto con garrocha
Pue.R. salto con pértiga
Spa. salto de pértiga
Venz. salto de garrocha
police detective (n) agente
Chi., Cub., Mex., Pan., Venz.
detective
Col. agente de policía, detective
policíaco
Dom.R. detective policial
ElS., Gua., Hon. detective de la
policía
Spa. investigador
police officer (n phr) policía
Chi. carabinero
Col., Spa. agente de policía
Dom.R. agente policial
Venz. oficial de policía
police station (n phr) comisaría
Col., Cub., Gua., Pan., Pue.R.
estación de policía
Dom.R. destacamento policial
polite (adj) cortés, educado
Col. atento, culto
Mex. caballeroso
pollution (n) contaminación
Col. polución
pomegranate (n) granada
Cos.R. granadilla
pond (n) charca
Arg., Uru. charco
Chi. charco, laguna

Col., ElS., Gua., Hon., Mex.
estanque
Dom.R. laguna
Venz. estanque, laguna
pony (n) jaca
Col., Dom.R., Mex., Pan. pony
Cub., Ecu. caballito
Pue.R., Venz. caballito, pony
Arg., Spa. poni
Uru. poney
ponytail (hair) (n) cola de caballo
Arg. cola, colita
Pue.R. rabo de caballo
Spa. coleta
porch (n) pórtico
Cub. porche
Dom.R. galería
Gua. terraza cubierta
Pan. porch
porpoise (n) marsopa
Chi., Ecu. delfín
porter (n) maletero
Bol. maletera
Col., Cub. portero
Spa. mozo
Venz. cargador de maletas
post office (n phr) oficina de correos
Arg., Cub. correo
Col. oficina postal
post office box (n phr) apartado postal
Bol. casilla
Chi. casilla postal
Col. buzón postal
Spa. apartado de correos
pot (n) olla
Arg. cacerola
Spa. puchero
potato (n) papa
Cub., Spa. patata
potato masher (n phr) majador de

papas
　　Chi. moledor de papas
　　Mex. prensapapas
　　Per. machucador de papas
　　Uru. triturador de papas
pothole (n) pozo
　　Arg., Cub., Gua., Mex., Spa.
　　bache
　　Chi., Dom.R. hoyo
　　Col., Cos.R., Ecu., Pan. hueco
prairie (n) pradera
　　Dom.R. valle
prawn (n) gamba
　　Arg., camarón, langostino
　　Chi. camarón gigante
　　Col., Cub., Mex., Pan., Spa.
　　langostino
　　Ecu., Uru. camarón
praying mantis (n phr) manta religiosa
　　Pan. maría palito
　　Pue.R. mantilla
　　Spa. mantis religiosa
pregnant (adj) embarazada
　　Col. encinta, esperando, preñada
　　Pan., Per. encinta
　　Venz. en estado
preserves (n) conserva (de alimentos)
　　Chi., Col. conservas
　　Dom.R. preservas
　　Per., Spa. mermelada
pretty (adj) guapa
　　Arg., Cub., Pue.R. linda
　　Chi. bonita, preciosa
　　Col. bella, bonita, linda
　　Dom.R., Ecu., ElS., Gua., Pan.,
　　Uru. bonita
print shop (n phr) imprenta
　　Col. taller tipográfico, talleres
　　gráficos
printer (computer) (n) impresora

Pue.R. printer
prisoner (n) preso
　　Chi. reo
　　Col. encarcelado, prisionero,
　　recluso
　　Pan. prisionero
program (n) programa
　　Cub., Dom.R. show
props (n) accesorios
　　Col. ayudas de escenario, soporte
　　Mex. adornos
pruning shears (n phr) podadera
　　Arg., Dom.R., Spa. tijeras de
　　podar
　　Bol., Ecu., Pue.R. podadora
　　Col. tijeras para podar
　　Mex. podadoras
　　Venz. tijera podadora
pubic hair (n phr) vello pubiano
　　Col., Cos.R., ElS., Gua., Mex.,
　　Venz. vello púbico
　　Dom.R. vello
　　Uru. vello del pubis
puff pastry (n phr) hojaldre
　　Chi. masa de mil hojas
　　Venz. milhoja
pullover (n) pulóver
　　Arg. sweater
　　Bol. saco
　　Mex. suéter cerrado
　　Per. chompa
　　Spa. jersey
　　Venz. suéter
pumpkin (n) calabaza
　　Bol., Chi., Pan. zapallo
　　Venz. ahuyama

Q R

quick (adj) rápido
Chi. veloz
Col. presto, raudo, veloz
quiet (adj) silencioso
Chi., Col., Venz. callado
Dom.R., Pan. tranquilo
quit using drugs (v phr) dejar las
drogas
Col. cortar con el vicio, zafar
rabbi (n) rabino
Spa. rabí
racecar (n) coche de carrera
Arg., Chi. auto de carrera
Cub., ElS., Gua., Hon., Pan.,
Pue.R. carro de carrera
Col., Per., Venz. carro de carreras
Dom.R. auto de carrera, carro de
carrera
Spa. coche de carreras
radiator grill (n phr) rejilla del radiador
Arg., Col. parrilla del radiador
rain forest (n phr) selva tropical
Col. bosque tropical
raincoat (n) impermeable
Arg. piloto
Col., Spa. gabardina
Cub. capa de agua
Pan. capote
Pue.R. capa
range (mountain) (n) sierra
Chi. cordillera
Col. cadena
razor (n) rasuradora
Arg., Chi. gillette
Col. máquina de afeitar
Cub., Spa. cuchilla de afeitar

Dom.R., Pue.R. afeitadora
Mex. rastrillo
Pan. navaja
Venz. hojilla de afeitar
realtor (n) corredor de bienes raíces
Arg. inmobiliario
reamer (n) escariador
Mex. escariadora
Pue.R. arado
Spa. fresadora
Uru. escardador
rear window (n phr) ventana trasera
Arg. luneta
Col. ventanilla trasera
Pue.R. cristal trasero
rear-view mirror (n phr) espejo
retrovisor
Uru. espejo trasero
record album (n phr) álbum
Col. disco
recreational vehicle (n phr) vehículo de
recreo
Bol. vagoneta
Chi. casa rodante
Mex. camper
Pue.R. RV
Spa. caravana
Venz. vehículo recreacional
referee (n) árbitro
Arg. referee
Bol., Col., Ecu., Per. juez
Mex. refere
Pan. referí
reflector (bicycle) (n) reflector
Arg. faro, luz
refrigerator (n) refrigerador
Arg. heladera
Col., Dom.R., Pue.R., Venz.
nevera
Cos.R. refrí

Ecu., nevera, refrigeradora
Per. refrigeradora
Spa. frigorífoco, nevera
reindeer (n) reno
Dom.R. cervatillo
remote control (n phr) control remoto
Spa. mando a distancia
rent (housing) (v) alquilar
Chi., Col. arrendar
Mex., Pue.R. rentar
request stop (bus) (n phr) parada
facultativa
Col. solicitud para hacer
detener el bus
Mex. parada solicitada
Spa. parada discrecional
Venz. parada pedida
residencial area (n phr) zona
residencial
Arg. barrio residencial
Col. área residencial
Pue.R. área residencial, sector
residencial
resonant (adj) sonoro
Col. estruendoso, resonante
Mex. resonante
résumé (work history) (n) currículum
(vitae)
Col. hoja de vida
Mex. currículo
Pue.R. resumé
retirement home (n phr) hogar de
ancianos
Arg. asilo de ancianos
Col. ancianato
Mex. asilo
Pan. retiro para ancianos
reverse (n) marcha atrás
Col. reversa, reverso
Dom.R., Mex., Pan. reversa

Pue.R. riversa
Venz. retroceso
ride (bicycle) (v phr) montar en
bicicleta
Arg., Chi., Cos.R., Mex. andar en
bicicleta
Pue.R. correr bicicleta
right of way (n phr) prioridad
Arg., Cub., Pue.R. derecho de
paso
Chi., Mex. paso
Col. derecho a la vía
Dom.R., Ecu., Spa. preferencia
ElS., Gua., Pan. derecho de vía
Venz. prioridad de circulación
rim (bicycle wheel) (n) llanta
Chi., Col., Cos.R. aro
Mex. rin
Venz. rueda
ring (boxing) (n) ring de boxeo
Chi. cuadrilátero
Col., Pue.R., Uru. cuadrilátero de
boxeo
ring (n) anillo
Pan., Pue.R. sortija
ring, class (n phr) anillo de graduación
Pue.R. sortija de graduación
ring, diamond (n phr) anillo de
diamante
Pue.R. sortija de diamante
Spa. anillo de diamantes
ring, signet (n phr) sortija de sello
Col. anillo de sello
Spa. sello
ring, wedding (n phr) anillo de
matrimonio
Arg. alianza, anillo de casamiento
Per., Pue.R. aro de matrimonio
rise (bread) (v) leudarse
Bol., Chi., ElS., Gua., Hon.,

Mex., Spa. levantarse
Col. inflarse, levantarse
Cos.R., Dom.R., Ecu., Pan.,
Pue.R. crecer
road shoulder (n phr) lomo
Arg. banquina
Col. breda, orilla de la carretera
Cos.R. orilla de la carretera
ElS., Gua. borde de la carretera
Pue.R. paseo
Spa., Uru. arcén
Venz. hombrillo
road sign (n phr) letrero de carretera
Arg. cartel
Chi. señalización en la carretera
Col. aviso vial
Dom.R., Spa., Uru. señal de
tráfico
Per. señal del camino
Venz. señal de tránsito
road works (n phr) obras
Arg., Pue.R. construcción
Col. arreglos en la vía
Venz. mantenimiento de calles
roasting pan (n phr) sartén para asar
Col. bandeja para hornear
Spa. bandeja para el horno
Venz. olla para hornear
rock music (n phr) música rock
Col. música de rock
Dom.R., Spa. rock
roll (n) pancito
Col., Pan. panecillo
ElS., Gua., Spa. bollo
Pue.R. pan
rolling pin (n phr) rodillo
Arg. palo de amasar
Bol., Chi. fuslero
Per. amasador
rolodex (n) fichero giratorio

Pue.R. rolodex
root (hair) (n) raíz
Dom.R. crecimeinto
rotten (food) (adj) podrido
Mex. hechado a perder
round trip ticket (n phr) billete de ida
y vuelta
Arg. boleto de ida y vuelta, pasaje
de ida y vuelta
Chi., Pan., Per., Venz. boleto de
ida y vuelta
Col. tiquete de ida y vuelta
Cos.R., Dom.R. pasaje de ida y
vuelta
Mex. boleto de ida y vuelta,
boleto de viaje redondo
rubber band (n phr) cinta elástica
Arg., Dom.R., Pue.R. gomita
Bol., Chi. elástico
Col. caucho
Cub., Mex., Pan., Per., Venz. liga
ElS., Gua., Hon. hule
Spa., Uru. goma elástica
rubbers (shoes) (n) chanclos de goma
Arg. ojotas de goma
Chi., Uru. zapatos de goma
Col. zapatos de caucho
Cub., Pue.R. chancletas de goma
ElS., Gua., Hon. chanclas de hule
Mex. chanclas de plástico,
huaraches de plástico, sandalias de
plástico
Spa. chanclas
rush hour (n phr) hora pico
Arg. rush hour
Cub., Mex. hora de tráfico
Per. hora de entrada o salida a los
trabajos
Pue.R. hora del tapón
Spa. hora punta

rutabaga (n) nabo sueco
  Col. nabo de suecia, rutabaga

The Spanish spoken in Ecuador is less "anglicized" that that of the Caribbean countries, for example, probably because of their proximity to the United States and to several former British colonies.

S

sailboat (n) barco de vela
    Col. bote de vela
    Dom.R. velero
salary (n) sueldo
    Col. honorarios, paga, salario
    Mex., Pan. salario
salesperson (n) dependiente
    Chi. promotor/a, vendedor/a
    Col. empleado/a, vendedor/a
    Dom.R., Ecu., ElS., Gua., Hon.,
    Mex., Venz. vendedor/a
sandals (n) sandalias
    Cub., Pue.R. chancletas
sandbar (n) barra de arena
    Mex. banco de arena
satellite television (n phr) televisión por satélite
    Spa. televisión vía satélite
saucepan (n) cacerola
    Arg., Pue.R. olla
    Col. perol
    Spa. cazo
saw (n) sierra
    Arg., Cub., Per. serrucho
scab (n) costra
    Cub., Dom.R. postilla
scallion (n) cebolla verde
    Bol. cebollita verde
    Col. cebolla larga
    ElS., Gua., Hon., Venz. cebollín
    Pan. cebollina
    Mex. cebollino
scallop (n) venera
    Arg., Venz. vieira
    Chi. ostión
    ElS., Gua. concha, escalope

    Pan. conchuela
    Spa. concha
scanner, optical (n phr) explorador óptico
    Arg., Dom.R., Pue.R. scanner
    Chi., Cub., Mex., Pan., Spa. escáner
    Venz. copiador óptico
scared (adj) asustado
    Col. atemorizado
school (n) escuela
    Arg., Col., Gua. colegio
school day (n phr) día lectivo
    Col. día de colegio
    Dom.R., Per. día de clases
    Mex., Venz. día de escuela
    Pue.R. día de clase
scorpion (n) alacrán
    Arg., Chi., Col., Cos.R., Pan., Spa., Uru., Venz. escorpión
scraper (n) rascador
    Chi. raspadora
    Col. cuchilla raspadora
    Mex. raspa
    Pue.R. espátula
    Venz. raspador
screenplay (n) guión cinematográfico
    Bol. telón
    Dom.R., ElS., Gua., Hon. libreto
    Spa. argumento
screwdriver (n) destornillador
    Chi. llave
    Mex., Per. desarmador
scroll (computer) (v) desplazar
    Pan. mover
    Pue.R. scroll
scythe (n) guadaña
    Mex. zapapico
seamstress (n) costurera
    Arg., Chi., Col., Pan., Spa.

ABBREVIATIONS: Arg.=Argentina Bol.=Bolivia Chi.=Chile Col.=Colombia Cos.R.=Costa Rica Cub.=Cuba Dom.R.=Dominican Republic Ecu.=Ecuador ElS.=El Salvador Gua.=Guatemala Hon.=Honduras Mex.=Mexico Pan.=Panama Per.=Peru Pri.=Primary Term Pue.R.=Puerto Rico Spa.=Spain Uru.=Uruguay Venz.=Venezuela

modista
seashore (n) orilla del mar
  Chi., Col., Pue.R. costa
seat (bicycle) (n) asiento
  Bol., Col. silla
  Chi., Dom.R., Ecu., Pue.R.,
  Spa., Uru. sillín
second class (n phr) segunda clase
  Arg. segunda
  Dom.R. clase económica
sedan (n) sedán
  Spa. turismo
See you later! (int phr) ¡Hasta luego!
  Col. ¡Te veo luego!, ¡Te veo más
  tarde!, ¡Hasta pronto!
  Dom.R., ElS., Gua., Pan. ¡Nos
  vemos!
  Pue.R. ¡Hasta la vista!
seedling (n) planta de semillero
  Chi. brote
  Col. planta de vivero
  Cos.R. almácigo
  Mex. plantita
sell drugs (v phr) vender drogas
  Pue.R. tirar drogas
set (movie) (n) escenario
  Chi. estudios
  Col. decorado
  Spa. plató
shallot (n) chalote
  Mex. cebollino, cebollita
shampoo (n) champú
  Arg. shampoo
share needles (v phr) compartir agujas
  Col. compartir jeringas
  Mex. prestarse jeringas
  Venz. compartir inyectadoras
shed (n) cobertizo
  Chi. galpón
  Pue.R. casita de herramientas

sheep (n) oveja
  Mex. borrego
sheet, contour (n phr) sábana de cajón
  Arg. sábana de elástico
  Col. sábana de forro
  Spa. sábana bajera ajustable
  Venz. sábana de esquinera
shift gear (v phr) cambiar la velocidad
  Arg. hacer un cambio
  Chi. pasar la marcha, reducir la
  marcha
  Col. meter un cambio
  Pue.R. cambiar de cambios
  Spa. cambiar la marcha
shin (n) espinilla
  Chi. canilla
ship (n) buque
  Arg., Cos.R., Pan., Uru., Venz.
  barco
  Chi. barco, navío
  Col. barco, embarcación
shirt, dressy (n phr) camisa formal
  Arg., Dom.R., Mex., Pan., Uru.,
  Venz. camisa de vestir
shirt, long-sleeved (n phr) camisa de
manga larga
  Arg. remera de manga larga
shirt, short-sleeved (n phr) camisa de
manga corta
  Arg. remera de manga corta
shoe rack (n phr) zapatera
  Col. repisa para zapatos
shoelace (n) cordón
  Mex. agujeta
  Pue.R. gabete
shoes, hiking (n phr) botas
  Chi. bototos
  Col. zapatos de caminar
  Mex. botas de alpinismo
  Spa. botas de monte

shoes, patent leather (n phr) zapatos de charol
   Arg., Bol., Cos.R., Ecu., Per.,
   Pue.R. zapatos de cuero barnizado
   Dom.R. zapatos de cuero,
   zapatos de piel
   Venz. zapatos de cuero, zapatos de patente
shoes, tennis (n phr) zapatos de tenis
   Arg., Chi., Pan. zapatillas
   Col. zapatos tenis
   Dom.R., Mex. tenis
   Spa. zapatillas de deporte
   Venz. zapatos de goma
shoot (movie) (v) rodar
   Venz. filmar
shooting (movie) (n) rodaje
   Venz. filmación
shop sign (n phr) letrero comercial
   Arg. cartel
   Col. anuncio de almacén
shop window (n phr) vitrina
   Arg. vidriera
   Cos.R., Cub., Per., Spa. escaparate
   Mex. aparador
shoreline (n) costa
   Col. litoral, orilla
short (adj) pequeño
   Arg., Per., Spa. bajo
   Chi., Pan., Pue.R. corto
   Col., Dom.R. bajito
   Mex. bajo, chaparro, corto
short (person) (adj) pequeño
   Arg., Uru. bajito, petiso
   Col. bajito, bajo
   Dom.R. bajito
   Mex. de estatura baja, chaparro
   Venz. bajo
shorts (n) pantalones cortos
   Arg., Chi., Col., Dom.R., Mex.,

   Venz. shorts
   Cub. bermudas
   Pan. pantaloncitos cortos
   Pue.R. pantalón corto
shot glass (n phr) copa de trago
   Chi. medida para bebida
   Col. copa de aguardiente, copita
   Dom.R. vaso de trago corto
   Mex. caballo (big), caballito (small), vaso tequilero
   Pue.R. vasito
   Spa. chupito
shot put (n phr) lanzamiento de peso
   Pue.R. lanzamiento de pesa
shovel (n) pala
   Per. palana
show (movie) (v) proyectar
   Arg. dar, pasar
   Col. presentar
   Dom.R. pasar
   Venz. mostrar
shredder (n) trituradora
   Mex. picadora de papel
shrimp (n) camarón
   Chi. langostino
   Spa. gamba
shrub (n) arbusto
   Cub. mata
shutters (n) postigos
   Col., Ecu., Gua. persianas
   Mex. contraventanas
shy (adj) tímido
   Cub., Pan. penoso
sick leave (n phr) permiso de convalecencia
   Arg., Bol., ElS., Gua., Hon. permiso por enfermedad
   Col., Dom.R. licencia por enfermedad
   Cub. días de enfermedad

ABBREVIATIONS: Arg.=Argentina Bol.=Bolivia Chi.=Chile Col.=Colombia Cos.R.=Costa Rica Cub.=Cuba Dom.R.=Dominican Republic Ecu.=Ecuador ElS.=El Salvador Gua.=Guatemala Hon.=Honduras Mex.=Mexico Pan.=Panama Per.=Peru Pri.=Primary Term Pue.R.=Puerto Rico Spa.=Spain Uru.=Uruguay Venz.=Venezuela

Venz. permiso de convalescencia
sickle (n) hoz
  Mex. pico
  Pue.R. yunta
side entrance (n phr) puerta lateral
  Arg. puerta de servicio
  Col. entrada lateral
  Cub. puerta del costado
  Mex. puerta del lado
sidewalk (n) acera
  Arg., Chi., Cos.R., Ecu., Per.,
  Uru. vereda
  Col. andén
  Mex. banqueta
sieve (n) cedazo
  Arg., Spa. tamiz
  Chi., Cub., Venz. colador
  Col. coladera, tamiz
  Mex. coladera
silverware (n) cubiertos
  Col. platería
sing harmony (v phr) cantar en
armonía
  Pue.R. cantar afinados
sinus (n) seno
  Mex., Spa. seno nasal
  Venz. cavidad
sitar (n) sitar
  Venz. guitarra oriental
sitcom, situation comedy (n phr)
comedia de situación
  Chi., Col., Cub., Dom.R., Spa.
  comedia
skeleton (n) esqueleto
  Col. osamenta
  Mex. calaca
ski jump (n phr) trampolín
  Venz. salto en esquíes
skimmer (n) espumadera
  Col. desnatadora

  Mex. desnatador
skirt (n) falda
  Arg., Uru. pollera
  Cub. saya
skull (n) cráneo
  Col., Cos.R., Mex. calavera
sledgehammer (n) almádena
  Chi., Dom.R., Mex. mazo
  Pue.R. marrón
sleeping car (train) (n phr) coche cama
  Col. litera
sleepy (adj) soñoliento
  Dom.R. asueñado
  Mex. adormilado
slip (n) combinación
  Chi., Pue.R. enagüa
  Cub. sayuela
  Dom.R. mediofondo
  Pan. peticote
  Mex., Venz. fondo
slippers (n) pantuflas
  Arg. chinelas
  Col. babuchas
  Cos.R., Pan. chancletas
  Cub. zapalillas
  Spa. zapatillas de casa
small (adj) chiquito, pequeño
  Arg., Chi. chico
  Col. chico, corto, menudo
smelt (n) eperlano
  Chi. pejerrey
snack (n) merienda
  Col. bocadillo, refrigerio
  Dom.R. picadera
  Mex. botana
  Spa. snack
snail (n) caracol
  Dom.R. babosa
snake (n) culebra
  Arg., Bol., Mex., Uru. víbora

Chi., Cub. serpiente
snapper (n) pargo
Dom.R., Pue.R. chillo
Mex. guachinango, huachinango
snare (of drum) (n) cuerdas
Col. bordón, tirante
snare drum (n phr) tarola
Col. tambor militar pequeño
Cos.R. redoblante
sneakers (n) snikers
Arg., Chi., Pan., Per., Uru. zapatillas
Col., Cos.R., Cub., Dom.R., Pue.R. tenis
Ecu. zapatos de caucho
ElS., Gua., Hon. zapatos de lona con suela de hule
Mex. tenis de lona
Spa. zapatillas de lona
Venz. zapatos de goma
snifter (n) copa ancha de boca estrecha
Chi. copa de cognac
snoop (n) fisgón
Chi. intruso
Col., Cub. entremetido, metiche, metido
Dom.R. curioso, entrometido, metiche
Ecu., Mex. metiche
Gua. entrometido, shute
Pan. vidajeno/a
Pue.R. ligón
Venz. averiguador
soap opera (n phr) telenovela
Arg., Cub. novela
soccer (n) fútbol
Pue.R. balompié
sock (n) calcetín
Arg., Uru. media (tres cuartos), soquete

Col., Cub., Dom.R., Ecu., Pan., Pue.R., Venz. media
soft drugs (n phr) drogas blandas
Col. drogas más suaves
Mex. drogas suaves
software (n) software
Spa. programas
song (n) canción
Arg. tema
Col. canto
sound effects (n phr) efectos sonoros
Arg., Col., Mex., Pan., Pue.R., Spa., Venz. efectos de sonido
sound track (n phr) banda sonora
Arg. banda de sonido
Mex., Pue.R. música
Venz. pista de sonido
sour (adj) agrio
Col. ácido, acre
Pan. ácido
soybeans (n) frijoles de soja
Chi., Spa. soja
Col., Gua. semillas de soya
Cub., Venz. soya
Uru. porotos de soja
spade (n) pala
Chi. pica
Venz. pico
spare parts (n phr) repuestos
Cub., Spa. piezas de repuesto
Mex. refacciones
Pue.R. repuestas
spare tire (n phr) rueda de repuesto
Arg. goma de auxilio, rueda de auxilio
Bol., Ecu., Gua., Pan. llanta de repuesto
Cub., Dom.R. goma de repuesto
Mex. llanta de refacción
Pue.R. goma de repuesta

Venz. caucho de repuesto
spectacles (n) anteojos
  Col. gafas, lentes
  Cub., Venz. espejuelos
speed limit (n phr) límite de velocidad
  Mex., Pue.R. velocidad máxima
speedometer (n) velocímetro
  Chi. cuenta kilómetros
  Cub. cuentakilómetro
spider (n) araña
  Dom.R. cacata
spine (n) columna vertebral
  Col. espinazo
  Ecu. espina dorsal, espinaso
  Gua. espina dorsal
spoiled (child) (adj) mimado
  Arg., Cub., Pan., Pue.R.
  malcriado
  Chi. regalón
  Col. consentido,
  malacostumbrado, malcriado
  Cos.R. chineado
  Dom.R. ñoño
  Ecu. consentido
  Mex. chiqueado, consentido
  Per. engreído
spoke (bicycle wheel) (n) faro
  Arg., Cub., Gua., Mex. rayo
  Col. radio, rayo
  Spa., Venz. radio
sports car (n phr) carro deportivo
  Arg., Chi. auto deportivo
  Bol. coche sport
  Cub. carro de deporte
  Spa., Uru. coche deportivo
sprinkler (n) rociador
  Arg. regador
  Cub. regadera
  Mex. regilete
  Spa. aspersor

sprint (v) esprintar
  Chi. picar
  Col., Dom.R. correr a toda
  velocidad
  Cub. correr
squash (n) chilacayote
  Bol. zapallito
  Col., Cos.R., Cub., Ecu., Spa.
  calabaza
  Dom.R., Venz. auyama
  Pan. chayote
  Uru. zapallo
squid (n) calamar
  Chi. jibia
stadium (n) estadio
  Pue.R. parque
stair machine (n phr) escaladora
  Cos.R. máquina escalera
  Dom.R. máquina de hacer
  ejercicios
  Mex. escalera
stall (car) (v) calar
  Arg., Cub., Ecu., Mex., Pan. parar
  Chi. pararse
  Col. vararse
  Cos.R. quedar varado
  Pue.R. inundar
  Spa. calarse
  Venz. apagarse el carro
stallion (n) padrillo
  Arg., Col., Dom.R., Spa., Venz.
  semental
  Chi. garañón
  Gua. garañón, semental
staple (n) grapa
  Arg. ganchito
  Chi. corchete
  Cub. presilla
  Per. grampa
staple remover (n phr) uñas

Bol., Ecu., ElS., Gua., Hon.
sacagrapas
Chi. saca corchetes
Col. removedor de grapas
Dom. R. uñas saca grapas
Mex. uña quitagrapas
Spa. quitagrapas
Venz. saca-grapas
stapler (n) engrapadora
Arg. abrochadora
Chi. corchetera
Cub. presilladora
Per. engrampador
Puc.R., Spa. grapadora
start (car) (v) arrancar
Chi., Dom.R. encender, prender
Col. poner en marcha
Pue.R. prender
starter (n) arranque
Chi. salir
Cos.R., Mex. arrancador
Cub., Spa. motor de arranque
Pue.R. estarter
station wagon (n phr) camioneta
Cos.R., Ecu., Per., Spa.
combinable
Bol. vagoneta
Cub. pisicorre
Dom.R. station, van
Pue.R. guagüita
stationary bicycle (n phr) bicicleta
estacionaria
Mex. bicicleta fija
Pan. bicicleta estable
Spa. bicicleta estática
steering wheel (n phr) volante
Chi. manubrio
Col., Cub., Gua., Pan. timón
Dom.R., Pue.R. guía
stick shift (n phr) palanca de cambios

Arg. cambio
Cos.R. marcha
Mex. palanca de velocidades
Spa. cambio manual
stool (n) banco
Chi. piso
Dom.R. banqueta, banquito
stop (sign) (int) alto
Arg., Chi., Col., Pue.R. pare
Spa. stop
storage room (n phr) almacenaje
Arg., Col. depósito
Bol., Dom.R., Pue.R., Spa.
almacén
Chi. despensa
Cos.R., Ecu., Gua. bodega
Mex. almacén, bodega
store (computer data) (v) almacenar
Arg. grabar, guardar
Dom.R. archivar
Mex., Pan. guardar
Venz. guarder
storm (n) tormenta
Col. aguacero, borrasca,
tempestad, temporal
stove (n) estufa
Arg., Bol., Chi., Per., Spa., Uru.
cocina
straight (hair) (adj) lacio
Chi., Col., Spa., Venz. liso
Dom.R. bueno
strawberry (n) fresa
Arg. frutilla
stream (n) arroyo
Col. arroyuelo, riachuelo
Dom.R., Pue.R. riachuelo
street lamp (n phr) farol
Dom.R. palo de luz
Pan. poste de luz
Spa. farola

---

street, cobblestone (n phr) calle de
guijarro
   Arg., Bol., Col., Ecu., Venz. calle
   empedrada
   Chi. calle de adoquines, calle de
   paralelepípedos
   Gua. calle de adoquín
   Mex. calle adoquinada
   Pan. calle de ladrillo
   Per. calle de piedras
   Pue.R., Spa., Uru. calle de
   adoquines
street, dead-end (n phr) calle sin salida
   Col., Mex. calle cerrada
   Venz. calle ciega
street, one-way (n phr) calle de una
mano
   Chi. vía única
   Col., Mex., Per. calle de un solo
   sentido
   Cos.R., Dom.R., Pue.R., Venz.
   calle de una vía
   Ecu. calle de una sola dirección
   ElS., Gua., Hon. calle de una sola
   vía
   Pan. calle de una vía, one way
   Spa. calle de dirección única
string quartet (n phr) cuarteto de
cuerdas
   Spa. cuarteto de cuerda
strum (v) guitarrear
   Col. rasgar, rasguear
   Cos.R. rasgar
   Spa. rasguear
strumming (n) guitarreo
   Col. rasgueo, rasgueado
   Cos.R. rasgueo
   Spa. rasgueado
stud (n) tachuela
   Mex. espárrago, espiga, pasador,

   viga vertical
stump (n) tocón
   Dom.R. cabo
   Mex. parte del tronco
stunt (n) acrobática
   Col., Mex. truco
   Dom.R., Pue.R. doblaje
   Spa., Venz. acrobacia
stuntman (n) acróbata
   Arg. extra
   Col. aquel que realiza los trucos
   Dom.R., Mex., Pue.R. doble
   Spa. doble, especialista
   Venz. especialista en acrobacias
subtitles (n) subtítulos
   Cub., Pan., Uru. leyendas
suburb (n) barrio
   Col. barrio en las afueras,
   suburbio
   Cub., Dom.R., Gua. suburbio
   Mex. colonia, fraccionamiento
succulent (plant) (n) suculenta
   Mex. carnosa
suit (n) traje
   Bol., Per. terno
   Col., Pan. vestido
suit, double-breasted (n phr) traje
cruzado
   Gua. traje traslapado
suit, tailored (n phr) traje sastre
   Col. vestido hecho a la medida
   Pan. vestido sastre
   Venz. traje a la medida
suit, three-piece (n phr) terno
   Bol., Dom.R., Mex., Pue.R.,
   Venz. traje de tres piezas
   Pan. vestido de tres piezas
suitcase (n) maleta
   Arg. valija
sunroof (n) sunroof

Chi., Spa. techo solar
Col. techo corredizo
Mex. quemacocos
Venz. techo corredizo, techo
descapotable
sunscreen (n) loción solar
Arg. pantalla solar, protector
Chi., Cos.R. protector solar
Dom.R. bloqueador solar
Mex., Per. bronceador
Spa. crema de protección solar
Venz. protector de sol
surf the net (v phr) surfear la Internet
Arg. navegar la red
Bol., Ecu. navegar en el Internet
Chi., Gua. navegar por la Internet
Col. navegar la red, navegar por
Internet
Cub., Spa., Uru. navegar por la
red
Dom.R. surfear en el Internet
Mex. accesar a la red, buscar en la
red, usar la red
Venz. explorar el Internet
suspenders (n) ligas
Chi. suspensores
Cub., Gua., Pan., Spa., Venz.
tirantes
Dom.R. breteles
Mex. ligeros
swamp (n) marisma
Chi. ciénaga, pantano
Col., Dom.R., Ecu., Mex., Venz.
pantano
Uru. terreno pantanoso
sweater (n) suéter
Arg. pulover
Chi. chomba
Per. chompa
Spa. jersey

sweatshirt (n) camisa de trabajo
Arg. buzo
Chi., Col., Mex., Pue.R. sudadera
Dom.R. abrigo, sudadera
Gua. sudadero
Spa. jersey
sweet potato (n phr) batata
Bol., Ecu., Gua., Mex., Pan., Per.
camote
Chi. papa dulce
Cub., Uru. boniato
sweetheart (n) enamorado/a
Chi. pololo/a
Mex. corazón
Spa. cariño, querido
swimming pool (n phr) piscina
Arg. pileta
Mex. alberca
Swiss roll (n phr) rollo
Spa. brazo de gitano
Uru. rosca
Venz. bollo de pan
swordfish (n) pez espada
Chi. albacora

ABBREVIATIONS: Arg.=Argentina Bol.=Bolivia Chi.=Chile Col.=Colombia
Cos.R.=Costa Rica Cub.=Cuba Dom.R.=Dominican Republic Ecu.=Ecuador EIS.=El
Salvador Gua.=Guatemala Hon.=Honduras Mex.=Mexico Pan.=Panama Per.=Peru
Pri.=Primary Term Pue.R.=Puerto Rico Spa.=Spain Uru.=Uruguay Venz.=Venezuela

T

table leaf (n phr) tablero
Chi. tabla
Col. hoja, lámina
Mex. tablón de extensión
table, kitchen (n phr) mesa de cocina
Pan. mesita de cocina
table, night (n phr) mesilla de noche
Arg. mesa de luz, mesita de luz
Bol. mesita de noche, velador
Chi. velador
Col., ElS., Gua., Hon., Pue.R.,
Venz. mesa de noche
Cub., Dom.R., Pan. mesita de
noche
table, serving (n phr) mesita de servicio
Arg. mesita rodante
Col. mesa de servicio
Venz. mesa de servir
tack (n) tachuela
Spa. chincheta
tailcoat (n) frac
Venz. smoking
tailor (n) sastre
Col. costurero, modisto
Spa. costurero
talk show (n phr) programa de
entrevistas
Col. programa de charlas
talkative (adj) hablador, locuaz
Arg. charlatán
Col. charlatán, dicharachero,
garlador
Pan. conversador
tambourine (n) pandero
Chi., Col., Cub., Dom.R., Ecu.,
Pue.R., Spa. pandereta

tan (skin) (adj) bronceado
Arg., Chi., Cub., Dom.R.
quemado
Col. tostado
tan (v) broncearse
Arg., Chi., Cub., Dom.R.
quemarse
Col. dorarse al sol
tape (cassette) (n) cinta
Arg., Col., Venz. casete
Cub., Dom.R., Mex. cassette
tape (n) cinta adhesiva
Ecu. cinta pegante
Mex. durex
Pue.R. tape
Spa. celo
tape dispenser (n phr) carrete de cinta
Col. dispensador de cinta pegante
Dom.R. rollo de tape
Mex. dispensador de durex,
portarrollo
Spa. carrete de celo
Venz. dispensador de cinta
adhesiva
tape measure (n phr) metro
Arg., Col., Dom.R., Mex., Spa.
cinta métrica
Chi. huincha
Cub. centímetro
Pan. cinta de medir
taro (n) taro
Cub. malanga
Dom.R. yautía
tart (n) moldecito
Bol., Chi., Pue.R., Uru., Venz.
tarta
Col. torta
Dom.R. dulcito relleno
Gua. pastelito
Mex. tartaleta

Spa. pastel de frutas
tasty (adj) sabroso
    Arg., Col., Spa. rico
tattler (n) charlatán
    Chi., Gua. chismoso/a
    Cub. chismoso, chivato
    Dom.R., Pue.R. sinvergüenza
    Mex. hablador
    Spa. chivato
taxi (n) taxi
    Venz. libre
taxi driver (n phr) conductor de taxi
    Arg., Cub., Dom.R., Gua., Mex.,
    Per., Spa. taxista
    Chi., Col., Cos.R. chofer de taxi
    Venz. conductor de libre
taxi stand (n phr) parada de taxi
    Venz. parada de libres, parada de
    taxis
teenager (n) adolescente
    Dom.R. teenager
teeth (n) dientes
    Col. dentadura
telephone booth (n phr) cabina
telefónica
    Mex. teléfono público
television set (n phr) televisor
    Col., Mex., Spa. televisión
television viewer (n phr) televidente
    Col. teleaudiencia
temporary worker (n phr) temporero
    Bol. temporal
    Chi. jornalero
    Col., Cos.R., Gua., Venz.
    empleado/a temporal
    Mex. trabajador eventual
    Uru. temporario
tenor drum (n phr) teno
    Col. tambor de tenor
    Spa. tenor

tent (n) carpa
    Chi., Cos.R., Dom.R., Mex.,
    Spa., Venz. tienda de campaña
    Pan. tolda
termite (n) termita
    Cos.R., Cub., Dom.R., Pan.,
    Pue.R. comején
    Chi. polilla
    Ecu., ElS., Gua., Hon. comején
terrifying (adj) aterrador
    Bol. miedoso
    Col. aterrorizante, horripilante,
    temible, terrorífico
three-ring binder (n phr) carpeta de
argollas
    Arg. carpeta con ganchos
    Chi. archivador
    Col. folder de argollas
    Dom.R. carpeta de tres hoyos
    Pan. portafolio
    Spa. carpeta de tres anillos
through train (n phr) tren directo
    Venz. tren expreso
thumb (n) pulgar
    Arg. dedo gordo
ticket (n) billete
    Arg., Cub. boleto, pasaje
    Chi., Mex., Pan., Per., Pue.R.
    boleto
    Col. tiquete
    Cos.R. pasaje
    Dom.R. pasaje, ticket
    Venz. boleto, ticket
ticket collector (n phr) revisor
    Chi., Ecu. conductor
    Col. recolector de tiquetes
    Mex. persona que recoge los
    boletos
    Per. boletero
    Venz. chequeador de boletos,

chequeador de tickets
ticket, speeding (n phr) multa por
exceso de velocidad
  Mex. infracción por exceso de
  velocidad
  Pan. boleta por velocidad
ticket, traffic (n phr) multa
  Mex. infracción
  Pan. boleta
tights (n) leotardo
  Chi. medias gruesas
  Col. media pantalón
  Mex., Venz. mallas
  Pue.R. tights
  Spa. leotardos, medias
timetable (n) horario
  Col. itinerario
timpani (n) timbal
  Col., Cub. tímpanos
tip of nose (n phr) lóbulo
  Chi., Col., Mex., Spa., Venz.
  punta de la nariz
tire (bicycle) (n) neumático
  Arg., Dom.R., Pue.R. goma
  Bol., Col., Cos.R., Gua., Mex.,
  Pan., Per. llanta
  Cub. rueda
  Venz. caucho
tire (car) (n) llanta
  Arg., Cub. goma, rueda
  Chi., Col. pneumático
  Dom.R., Pue.R. goma
  Spa. rueda
  Venz. caucho
toast (n) tostada
  Mex., Pan. pan tostado
toaster (n) tostador
  Chi., Col., Cub., Dom.R., Ecu.,
  Pue.R., Spa., Venz. tostadora
toddler (n) pequeñito/a

Arg. beba, bebe, bebé
  Col. niño/a chiquito/a
  ElS., Gua., Hon. niño/a que
  empieza a andar
  Mex. niño/a de edad pre-escolar,
  niño/a que empieza a andar
  Spa. niño/a
  Venz. niñito/a
tomato (n) tomate
  Mex. jitomate
tom-tom (n) tam-tam
  Col. tantán
  Spa. tamtan
tone (n) sonoridad
  Col., Dom.R., Mex. tono
toner (n) tinta
  Dom. R. toner
  Mex. tonificador
toner cartridge (n phr) cartucho de
tinta
  Dom.R. cartucho del toner
  Mex. cartucho tonificador
tongs (n) tenazas
  Arg., Col., Spa. pinzas
tonsil (n) amígdala
  Mex. angina
toothpaste (n) dentífrico, pasta de
dientes
  Col. crema dental
  Per., Pue.R. pasta dental
townhouse (n) casa en hilera
  Bol., Uru. casa pegada
  Col. casa de ciudad, casa
  particular en la ciudad
  Dom.R., Pue.R. townhouse
  Gua. casa particular en complejos
  residenciales
  Mex. dúplex horizontal
  Spa. casa adosada
traffic (n) tráfico

Chi., Cos.R., Dom.R. tránsito
traffic island (n phr) isleta
   Arg., Col., Venz. isla
traffic jam (n phr) congestionamiento
   Arg., Per., Uru. embotellamiento
   Chi. atascamiento, congestión,
   taco
   Col. trancón
   Cos.R. atasco, presa
   Cub. tráfico, tranque
   Dom.R., Pue.R. tapón
   Pan. tranque
   Spa. atasco
trailer (n) remolque
   Chi., Cos.R., Cub., Dom.R., Pan.
   trailer
train (for job) (v) capacitar
   Col., Cub., Dom.R., Ecu., Pan.,
   Venz. entrenar
tread (tire) (n) ranuras
   Mex. dibujo de llanta
   Spa. cubierta
   Venz. huella del caucho
treadmill (n) rueda de andar
   Col. caminador
   Cos.R. banda sin fin
   Dom.R. máquina de caminar
   Mex., Uru. caminadora
   Pue.R. máquina de correr
treble (stereo) (n) de agudos
   Col. tonos agudos
   Spa. agudos
tree (n) árbol
   Dom.R. mata
tremendous (adj) imponente
   Arg., Chi., Cub., Mex., Venz.
   tremendo
   Col. asombroso, formidable
trench coat (n phr) trinchera
   Col., Spa. impermeable

Mex. gabardina
trifocals (n) trifocales
   Spa. gafas trifocales
   Venz. lentes trifocales
triple jump (n phr) salto triple
   Arg., Col. triple salto
trolley (n) tranvía
   Chi. trole
   Dom.R. carrito
   Mex. trolebús
trowel (n) desplantador
   Chi. paleta
   Mex. palustre
   Pue.R. palaustre
   Venz. aplanadora
trunk (car) (n) baúl
   Bol., Per. maletera
   Chi. porta equipaje
   Cub., Pan., Spa. maletero
   Mex. cajuela
   Venz. maleta
t-shirt (n) camiseta
   Arg. remera
   Chi. polera
   Dom.R. polo-shirt
tumbler (n) vaso para whiskey
   Arg. vaso
tuna (n) atún
   Cub., Pue.R. tuna
tune up (v phr) revisar
   Cub. reglar
   Dom.R. arreglar
   Gua., Mex. afinar
   Venz. entonar
turkey (n) pavo
   Cub. guanajo
   Mex. guajolote
turn on (television) (v phr) prender
   Bol., Chi., Cub., Ecu., Gua.,
   Spa., Uru. encender

ABBREVIATIONS: Arg.=Argentina Bol.=Bolivia Chi.=Chile Col.=Colombia
Cos.R.=Costa Rica Cub.=Cuba Dom.R.=Dominican Republic Ecu.=Ecuador EIS.=El
Salvador Gua.=Guatemala Hon.=Honduras Mex.=Mexico Pan.=Panama Per.=Peru
Pri.=Primary Term Pue.R.=Puerto Rico Spa.=Spain Uru.=Uruguay Venz.=Venezuela

turn right, left (v phr) doblar a la
derecha, izquierda
    Cos.R. virar a la derecha,
    izquierda
    Mex. dar vuelta a la derecha,
    izquierda
    Spa. torcer a la derecha, izquierda
turner (n) pala
    Pan. espátula
    Venz. paleta
turning light (n phr) luz direccional
    Arg. guiño
    Chi. luz del indicador
    Col. luz para doblar
    Cub., Spa. intermitente
    Dom.R. luz de doblar
    Gua. pidevías
    Mex. dirrecional
    Per. luz para voltear
    Uru. señal intermitente
    Venz. señal de cruce
turtleneck (n) cuello vuelto
    Arg. polera
    Chi. beatle
    Col. buzo
    Dom.R., Pan., Venz. cuello
    tortuga
    Mex., Pue.R. cuello de tortuga
    Per. cuello Jorge Chavez
    Spa. polo de cuello alto
    Uru. rompeviento
tuxedo (n) smoking
    Cub., Pue.R. tuxedo
    Pan. toxido
two-four time (n phr) compás menor,
compasillo
    Spa. compás de dos por cuatro

> The grass-covered plains of South America are known as the *pampa*. A windstorm moving across the *pampa* is called a *pampero*.

U V W

umpire (baseball) (n) umpire
   Cub., Ecu., Uru., Venz. árbitro
   Mex. ampayer
underpass (n) paso subterráneo
   Chi. paso nivel
   Col. pasadizo subterráneo
   Spa. paso inferior
underwear (n) ropa interior
   Cos.R., Bol., Uru. ropa blanca
   Cub. ropa de interior
undress (v) desvestirse
   Col., Venz. quitarse la ropa
upper floor (n phr) planta alta
   Col. piso superior
   Dom.R. piso de arriba
   Spa. planta superior
uptown (n) distrito residencial
   Dom.R. área residencial
use drugs (v phr) drogarse
   Col. consumir drogas, usar drogas
   ElS., Gua., Hon. consumir drogas
vacant (adj) libre
   Col. desocupado
   Dom.R. vacante
   Mex., Venz. vacío
vacuum cleaner (n phr) aspiradora
   Cub., Cos.R. aspirador
valve (trumpet) (n) pistón
   Mex. llave
van (n) camión
   Arg., Chi., Cub., Dom.R., Pue.R. van
   Col., Uru. furgón
   Cos.R., Mex. camioneta
   Ecu. buseta
   Pan. busito, van

   Per. microbus
   Spa. furgoneta
   Venz. camioneta, furgoneta
vegetable garden (n phr) huerto
   Arg. huerta, quinta
   Spa. huerta
vest (n) chaleco
   Arg. camiseta, musculosa
videocassette (n) videocasete
   Col. casete para vídeo
   Dom.R. casette
   Spa. cinta de vídeo
videocassette recorder (VCR) (n phr) videograbadora
   Arg., Mex. videocasetera
   Chi. VCR
   Col. grabadora de vídeo, VCR
   Spa. vídeo
videogame (n) videojuego
   Col., Cos.R., Dom.R., Mex., Venz. juego de vídeo
village (n) aldea
   Arg. pueblo
   Col. población
   Cub. pueblecito
   Dom.R. pueblito
violoncello (n) violoncelo
   Spa. violonchelo
vise (n) prensa
   Mex., Uru. torno
v-neck (n) cuello de pico
   Arg., Chi., Col., Gua., Mex., Venz. cuello en V
   Dom.R., Pan., Per., Pue.R. cuello V
   Uru. escote en V
vulture (n) buitre
   Chi. jote
   Cub. aura tiñosa
waffle (n) gofre

Col. barquillo, waffle
Gua. wafle
Mex. waffle
wagon (n) carreta
Bol., Ecu., Gua., Spa. vagón
waist (n) cintura
Col. cinto, talle
waiter (n) camarero
Arg., Bol., Cos.R., Dom.R., Uru.
mozo
Chi. garzón, mesero, mozo
Col., Cub., Dom.R., ElS., Gua.,
Hon., Mex., Pan., Pue.R. mesero
Venz. mesonero
wake (n) velorio
Col. velación
Cos.R. vela
Dom.R. funeral
Spa. velatorio
wallet (n) billetera, cartera
Dom.R. cartera de hombre
walrus (n) morsa
Dom.R. foca marina
WAN (wide area network) (n phr)
WAN
Col. red de área extendida
Cub., Mex., Spa. red de área
amplia
Uru. red de área ancha
Venz. red de área extensa
warden (prison) (n) director/a de la
cárcel
Col. carcelero, guarda
Venz. carcelero, guardián de la
cárcel
wart (n) verruga
Mex. mezquino
Per. callo
washer (n) arandela
Mex. rodana

wasp (n) avispa
Pan. abejorro
watch television (v phr) ver tele(visión)
Col. mirar televisión
Spa. ver la televisión
water fountain (n phr) fuente de agua
Arg., Chi., Mex., Venz. bebedero
Dom.R. neverita
water skiing (n phr) esquí acuático
Chi. ski acuático
Cos.R., Ecu., ElS., Gua., Hon.,
Per., Venz. esquí náutico
waterfall (n) cascada
Dom.R. caída de agua
Spa. catarata
watering can (n phr) regadera
Mex. regador de plantas
Venz. lata de regar
watermelon (n) sandía
Cub. melón de agua
wavy (hair) (adj) ondulado
Venz. crespo
wear (clothing) (v) llevar
Arg., Bol., Gua., Pan., Venz. usar
Chi. ponerse, vestir
Col. tener puesto
Cub. llevar puesto, tener puesto
Dom.R. llevar puesto, ponerse
Mex. ponerse
weather report (n phr) boletín
meteorológico
Arg. pronóstico del tiempo
Col. reporte del estado del tiempo
Venz. reporte del tiempo, reporte
meteorológico
weather reporter (n phr) meteorólogo
Venz. reportero del tiempo,
reportero meteorológico
website (n) sitio web
Arg. página principal

Dom.R., Pue.R. web-site
Gua. sitio de la red
Venz. lugar del Web, página del
Web
weed (n) mala hierba
Arg. maleza, yuyo
Chi., Ecu. maleza
Dom.R. maleza, pajón
Mex. hierba silvestre
Pue.R. yerba mala
weekday (n) día de entre semana
Arg., Col., Dom.R., Pue.R.,
Venz. día de semana
Cub., Gua., Spa. día entre semana
weight lifting (n phr) levantamiento de
pesas
Chi. alterofilismo
wetlands (n) pantano
Chi. marisma
Mex. terreno pantanoso
What's up? (int phr) ¿Qué pasa?
Chi. ¿Qué hay?
Col. ¿En qué andas/an?, ¿Qué
hay?
Dom.R. ¿Qué hay de nuevo?
Pan. ¿Quiubo?
wine shop (n phr) bodega
Col. taberna
Dom.R. tienda de vinos
Ecu. tienda de licores
Mex., Pue.R. vinatería
Uru. vinería
wipers (windshield) (n)
limpiaparabrisas
Col. limpiabrisas
Cub., Per. parabrisas
Dom.R. limpiavidrios
Pue.R. wipers
Venz. limpia-parabrisas
woodcock (n) chocha

Col. gallineta
ElS., Gua., Hon. gallina sorda,
gallineta
Venz. perdiz
word processing (n phr) procesamiento
de palabras
Arg., Mex. procesamiento de
textos
Cub., Ecu. procesamiento de
texto
Pue.R. word processing
work day (n phr) día hábil
Col. día laborable, día de trabajo
Cub., Per., Pue.R. día de trabajo
Dom.R., Spa. día laborable
wrong (adj) equivocado
Col. erróneo
Pue.R., Spa. incorrecto

> In Mexico, many of the rivers, volcanoes, hills, and streets bear Aztec names, such as Tehuantepec, Tololotlán, Popocatépetl and Ixtaccíhuatl.

X Y Z

xylophone (n) xilófono
    Cub. marimba
yellow jacket (n phr) avispa con pintas
amarillas
    Cub., Pan. abispa
zucchini (n) calabacín
    Chi. zapallito italiano
    Mex. calabacita

> Cuba's *marimba,* a type of
> xylophone, comes from a Bantu
> word.

ABBREVIATIONS: Arg.=Argentina Bol.=Bolivia Chi.=Chile Col.=Colombia
Cos.R.=Costa Rica Cub.=Cuba Dom.R.=Dominican Republic Ecu.=Ecuador EIS.=El
Salvador Gua.=Guatemala Hon.=Honduras Mex.=Mexico Pan.=Panama Per.=Peru
Pri.=Primary Term Pue.R.=Puerto Rico Spa.=Spain Uru.=Uruguay Venz.=Venezuela

PART II: SPANISH - ENGLISH

A

a tiempo completo Cub., Dom.R., Venz. (adj phr) full-time (work)
a tiempo parcial Cub., Per., Spa. (adj phr) part-time (work)
abarrotería Pan. (n) grocery
abarrotero Ecu., Mex. (n) grocer
abastos Venz. (n) grocery
abdomen Pri. (n) abdomen
abejorro Pan. (n) wasp
abejorro Pri. (n) bumblebee
abispa Cub., Pan. (n phr) yellow jacket
abogado Pri. (n) lawyer
abordar Chi., Col., Dom.R., Mex. (v) board
abrazadera Pri. (n) clamp
abreboca Pan. (n) appetizer
abrebotellas Spa. (n) bottle opener
abrelatas Pri. (n) can opener
abridor Chi., Cos.R., Pan., Uru (n) bottle opener
abridor Cos.R. (n) can opener
abridor de botellas Pue.R. (n phr) bottle opener
abridor de latas Chi. (n phr) can opener
abrigo Col., Cub., Mex., Pan., Spa., Venz. (n) coat
abrigo de mink Col., Mex., Pan., Pue.R. (n phr) coat, mink
abrigo de piel Chi., Col., Dom.R.,

Mex., Pan., Pue.R., Spa., Venz. (n phr) coat, fur
abrigo de pieles Cub. (n phr) coat, fur
abrigo de visón Cub., Dom.R., Spa., Venz. (n phr) coat, mink
abrigo Dom.R. (n) sweatshirt
abrigo Pri. (n) overcoat
abrochadora Arg. (n) stapler
abrumador Pri. (adj) overwhelming
aburrido Pri. (adj) boring
abuso de drogas Col., Cub., Dom.R., Pue.R. (n phr) drug abuse
acantilado Pri. (n) cliff
accesar a la red Mex. (v phr) surf the net
accesorios Pri. (n) props
aceitera Pri. (n) oil can
aceituna Pri. (n) olive
acelerador Pri. (n) gas pedal
acera Cub. (n) crosswalk
acera Pri. (n) sidewalk
ácido Col., Pan. (adj) sour
ácido Cos.R., Cub. (n) LSD
acorde Pri. (n) chord
acre Col. (adj) sour
acrobacia Spa., Venz. (n) stunt
acróbata Pri. (n) stuntman
acrobática Pri. (n) stunt
actor Pri. (n) actor
actriz Pri. (n) actress
adelantar Spa. (v) pasar (traffic)
adelantarse Cos.R. (v) pasar (traffic)
adicción a las drogas Pue.R. (n phr)

drug addiction
adicción Col., Cos.R., Dom.R., Mex.,
Pan., Pue.R. (n) addiction
adicto Pri. (adj) addicted
¡Adiós! Pri. (int) Bye!
¡Adiós! Pri. (int) Goodbye!
administrador Col. (n) office manager
administrador deportivo Col., Pan.,
Venz. (n phr) manager (sports)
adolescente Pri. (n) teenager
adormilado Mex. (adj) sleepy
adornos Mex. (n) props
adulto Pri. (n) adult
aereodeslizador Col. (n) hydrofoil boat
aerobic Spa. (n) aerobics
aeróbicos Dom.R., ElS., Gua., Hon.,
Pan., Pue.R., Uru. (n) aerobics
aerobics Col., Mex. (n) aerobics
aerobismo Pri. (n) aerobics
aerolínea Pri. (n) airline
aeromozo/a Cub., Mex., Pan., Venz.
(n) flight attendant
aeronave Col. (n) airplane
afeitadora Dom.R., Pue.R. (n) razor
aficionado Col., Mex., Venz. (n)
amateur
afilador de cuchillo Pri. (n phr) knife
sharpener
afinar Gua., Mex. (v) tune up
agarraderas del manubrio Gua., Venz.
(n phr) handlebar grips (bicycle)
agarrador Pan. (n) drawer knob
agente de policía Col. (n phr) police
detective
agente de policía Col., Spa. (n phr)
police officer
agente policial Dom.R. (n phr)
police officer
agente Pri. (n) police detective
agobiante Chi., Col. (adj)

overwhelming
agradable Col., Venz. (adj) nice
agricultor Pri. (n) farmer
agrio Pri. (adj) sour
aguacate Pri. (n) avocado
agudos Spa. (n) treble (stereo)
agujeta Mex. (n) shoelace
ahuyama Venz. (n) pumpkin
aire acondicionado Pri. (n phr) air
conditioning
airecondicionado Cos.R. (n) air
conditioning
ají Bol., Chi., Venz., Per. (n) pepper,
hot
ají dulce Pan. (n phr) pepper, sweet
ají picante Col., Cub., Pan., Pue.R.
(n phr) pepper, hot
ajustador Cub. (n) bra, brassiere
al revés Cub. (adv phr) backstroke
(swimming)
ala Pri. (n) fender
alacena Bol., Mex. (n) pantry
alacrán Pri. (n) scorpion
albacora Chi. (n) swordfish
albaricoque Pri. (n) apricot
alberca Mex. (n) swimming pool
albergue Arg. (n) hut
albornoz Spa. (n) bathrobe
álbum Pri. (n) record album
alcachofa Pri. (n) artichoke
alcahuete ElS., Gua., Hon. (n) pimp
alcalde/sa Pri. (n) mayor
alcaldía Bol., Ecu., Pue.R. (n) city hall
alcaucil Arg., Uru. (n) artichoke
alce Arg., Col., Mex., Spa., Venz. (n)
moose
alcón Bol. (n) hawk
aldea Pri. (n) village
alianza Arg. (n) ring, wedding
alicatas Mex. (n) pliers

ABBREVIATIONS: Arg.=Argentina Bol.=Bolivia Chi.=Chile Col.=Colombia
Cos.R.=Costa Rica Cub.=Cuba Dom.R.=Dominican Republic Ecu.=Ecuador ElS.=El
Salvador Gua.=Guatemala Hon.=Honduras Mex.=Mexico Pan.=Panama Per.=Peru
Pri.=Primary Term Pue.R.=Puerto Rico Spa.=Spain Uru.=Uruguay Venz.=Venezuela

alicate Chi., Cos.R., Dom.R., Per., Pue.R., Venz. (n) pliers
alicates Col., Pan., Spa. (n) pliers
alimentos enlatados Pri. (n phr) canned food
almacén Arg., Uru. (n) grocery
almacén Bol., Dom.R., Mex., Pue.R., Spa. (n) storage room
almacén de mascotas Col. (n phr) pet shop
almacén grande Col. (n phr) department store
almacén Pan. (n) department store
almacenaje Pri. (n) storage room
almacenar Pri. (v) store (computer data)
almacenero Arg., Uru. (n) grocer
almácigo Cos.R. (n) seedling
almádena Pri. (n) sledgehammer
almuerzo Mex. (n) brunch
almuerzo Pri. (n) lunch
¿Aló? Col., Cos.R., Dom.R., Ecu., ElS., Gua., Hon., Per., Uru., Venz. (int) Hello? (answering telephone)
alquilar Pri. (v) rent (housing)
alterofilismo Chi. (n) weight lifting
alto Pri. (int) stop (sign)
alubias negras Spa. (n phr) beans, black
alubias rojas Spa. (n phr) beans, kidney
alubias Spa. (n) beans
alumbrar Col. (v phr) give birth
amable Col., Cub., Spa. (adj) nice
amador Chi. (n) amateur
amante Pri. (n) mistress
amasador Per. (n) rolling pin
amateur Pri. (n) amateur
amigable Col. (adj) nice
amigable Col., Mex., Pue.R. (adj)

friendly
amigazo/a Col. (n) buddy, pal
amígdala Pri. (n) tonsil
amigo/a Pan., Pue.R. (n) buddy, pal
amigocho Mex. (n) buddy, pal
amigote Mex. (n) buddy, pal
amistoso Pri. (adj) friendly
amolador Dom.R. (n) knife sharpener
amor, mi Arg., Chi., Col., Cub., ElS., Gua., Hon., Pue.R. (n) dear, honey, sweetheart
amor, mi Pri. (n) love, lovey
amorcito Col. (n) dear, darling, honey
amorcito Col., Cos.R. (n) love, lovey
amoroso Bol. (adj) cute
amortiguador Col. (n) bumper
amortiguador Venz. (n) muffler
ampayer Mex. (n) umpire (baseball)
anacardo Cub. (n) cashew
ananá Uru. (n) pineapple
anchoa Pri. (n) anchovy
anchoveta Chi., Per. (n) anchovy
ancianato Col. (n) retirement home
andar de malas pulgas Chi. (adj phr) grumpy
andar en bicicleta Arg., Chi., Cos.R., Mex. (v phr) ride (bicycle)
andén Col. (n) sidewalk
andén Pri. (n) platform (train)
anfitrión/a Dom.R., Mex., Venz. (n) host (show)
angina Mex. (n) tonsil
anillo de casamiento Arg. (n phr) ring, wedding
anillo de diamante Pri. (n phr) ring, diamond
anillo de diamantes Spa. (n phr) ring, diamond
anillo de graduación Pri. (n phr) ring, class

anillo de matrimonio Pri. (n phr) ring,
wedding
anillo de sello Col. (n phr) ring, signet
anillo Pri. (n) ring
animador Col. (n) host (show)
anjova Mex. (n) bluefish
anta Pri. (n) moose
ante Chi., Col. (n) moose
anteojos bifocales Arg. (n phr) bifocals
anteojos de camino Pri. (n phr) glasses,
safety
anteojos de protección Pue.R. (n phr)
glasses, safety
anteojos de seguridad Chi. (n phr)
glasses, safety
anteojos de teatro Cub. (n phr) glasses,
opera
anteojos para esquiar Pri. (n phr)
goggles, ski
anteojos para nadar Pri. (n phr)
goggles, swimming
anteojos Pri. (n) eyeglasses
anteojos Pri. (n) spectacles
antiparras Arg. (n) goggles, ski
antiparras Arg. (n) goggles, swimming
antiperspirante ElS., Gua., Hon.,
Mex., Pue.R. (n) antiperspirant
antojo Dom.R., Spa. (n) birthmark
antorcha Pan., Pue.R. (n) blowtorch
anuncio comercial Col. (n phr)
commercial
anuncio de almacén Col. (n phr) shop
sign
anuncio de neón Pri. (n phr) neon sign
anuncio informativo Col. (n)
infomercial
anuncio Mex. (n) billboard
anuncio panorámico Pri. (n phr)
billboard
anuncio Pri. (n) commercial

apagarse el carro Venz. (v phr) stall
(car)
aparador Arg. (n) display cabinet
aparador Mex. (n) shop window
aparador Pri. (n) buffet
aparato de CD Col. (n phr) compact
disk player
aparcamiento Spa. (n) parking lot
aparcar Spa. (v) park
apartado de correos Spa. (n phr) post
office box
apartado postal Pri. (n phr) post office
box
apartamento Pri. (n) apartment
apartarse Col. (v) divorce
apearse Bol., Cos.R., Dom.R., Per.,
Uru. (v) get off (bus)
aperitivo Pri. (n) appetizer
apestoso Col. (n) pest (person)
aplanadora Venz. (n) trowel
aposento Dom.R. (n) bedroom
apretar Pue.R. (v) click (computer)
aquel que realiza los trucos Col. (n
phr) stuntman
arado Pue.R. (n) reamer
araña Pri. (n) spider
arándano agrio Pri. (n phr) cranberry
arándano Pri. (n) blueberry
arandela (n) washer
árbitro Cub., Ecu., Uru., Venz. (n)
umpire (baseball)
árbitro Pri. (n) referee
árbol de frutas Pue.R. (n phr) fruit
tree
árbol frutal Pri. (n phr) fruit tree
árbol Pri. (n) tree
arbolito Pue.R. (n) bush
arbusto Pri. (n) bush
arbusto Pri. (n) shrub
arce Pri. (n) maple (tree)

arcén Spa., Uru. (n) road shoulder
archivador Bol. (n) folder
archivador Chi. (n) file cabinet
archivador Chi. (n) three-ring binder
archivadora Spa. (n) folder
archivar Dom.R. (v) store (computer data)
archivero Mex. (n) file cabinet
archivo Pri. (n) file cabinet
arco de la planta del pie Col. (n phr) plantar arch (foot)
arco del pie Arg., Mex., Venz. (n phr) plantar arch (foot)
arco plantar Pri. (n phr) plantar arch (foot)
área residencial Col., Pue.R. (n phr) residencial area
área residencial Dom.R. (n phr) uptown
aretes de espiga Pri. (n phr) earrings, pierced
aretes de hoyito Dom.R. (n phr) earrings, pierced
aretes de presión Pri. (n phr) earrings, clip
aretes de tornillo Pri. (n phr) earrings, screw
aretes Pri. (n) earrings
argumento Spa. (n) screenplay
armario Pri. (n) closet (general)
armario Spa. (n) closet (clothes)
aro Chi., Col., Cos.R. (n) rim (bicycle wheel)
aro de matrimonio Per., Pue.R. (n phr) ring, wedding
aros Arg. (n) earrings
aros colgantes Arg. (n phr) earrings, drop
aros de agujero Arg. (n phr) earrings, pierced

aros de presión Arg. (n phr) earrings, clip
aros de tornillo Arg. (n phr) earrings, screw
arquero Arg., Chi., Per. (n) goalie
arrancador Cos.R., Mex. (n) starter
arrancar Pri. (v) start (car)
arranque Pri. (n) starter
arreglar Dom.R. (v) tune up
arreglarse Arg., Dom.R. (v) dress up
arreglos en la vía Col. (n phr) road works
arrendar Chi., Col. (v) rent (housing)
arriate de flores Gua. (n phr) flower bed
arroyo Pri. (n) stream
arroyuelo Col. (n) stream
arruga Col. (n) crease (pants)
articulación Pri. (n) joint
artículos de oficina Pri. (n phr) office supplies
artista Col. (n) actor
artista Col. (n) actress
artista Pri. (n) performer
arvejas Pri. (n) peas, green
arvejitas Per. (n) peas, green
asadón Col., Pan. (n) hoe
asador eléctrico Pri. (n phr) griddle
asaltar Col. (v) car jack (crime)
asaltar con violencia Mex. (v phr) car jack (crime)
ascensor Pri. (n) elevator
asentaderas Mex. (n) butt
asequible Col. (adj) cheap
asesor Arg., Col., Mex., Pan., Spa., Venz. (n) consultant
asesor Ecu., Mex., Spa. (n) counselor
asiento Chi. (n) chair, lounging
asiento del chofer Chi., Cub. (n phr) driver's seat

asiento del conductor Pri. (n phr) driver's seat
asiento del piloto Chi. (n phr) driver's seat
asiento Pri. (n) seat (bicycle)
asilo de ancianos Arg. (n phr) retirement home
asilo Mex. (n) retirement home
asombroso Col. (adj) tremendous
asombroso Pri. (adj) amazing
aspersor Spa. (n) sprinkler
aspirador Cub., Cos.R. (n) vacuum cleaner
aspiradora Pri. (n) vacuum cleaner
aspirante Uru. (n) challenger (boxing)
aspirar Pri. (v) inhale (drugs)
asueñado Dom.R. (adj) sleepy
asustado Pri. (adj) scared
atascamiento Chi. (n) traffic jam
atasco Cos.R., Spa. (n) traffic jam
atemorizado Col. (adj) scared
atento Col. (adj) polite
aterrador Pri. (adj) terrifying
aterrorizante Col. (adj) terrifying
atleta Pri. (n) athlete
atracar un coche Uru. (v phr) car jack (crime)
atraso Chi., Col. (n) delay
atril Chi., Col., Spa. (n) easel
atún Pri. (n) tuna
auditor Cos.R. (n) comptroller
aura tiñosa Cub. (n phr) vulture
autito chocador Arg. (n phr) bumper car
auto Arg., Chi., Col., Mex. (n) car
auto de carrera Arg., Chi., Dom.R. (n phr) racecar
auto de choque Spa. (n phr) bumper car
auto deportivo Arg., Chi. (n phr) sports car
auto particular Arg. (n phr) car, private
autobús Pri. (n) bus
autocine Pan., Per., Venz. (n) drive-in
auto-cinema Dom.R. (n) drive-in
autocinema Mex. (n) drive-in
automóvil Mex., Spa. (n) car
autopista Pri. (n) expressway
auxiliar de vuelo, azafata Pri. (n phr) flight attendant
auyama Dom.R., Venz. (n) squash
avejita Pue.R. (n) bumblebee
avejón Dom.R. (n) beetle
avellana Pri. (n) hazelnut
averiguador Venz. (n) snoop
avestruz Pri. (n) ostrich
aviador Col. (n) pilot
avión a chorro Chi. (n) jet
avión Pri. (n) airplane
aviso Arg. (n) commercial
aviso con luz de neón Col. (n phr) neon sign
aviso vial Col. (n phr) road sign
avispa (n) wasp
avispa con pintas amarillas (n phr) yellow jacket
axila Pri. (n) armpit
ayudas de escenario Col. (n phr) props
ayuntamiento Pri. (n) city hall
azada Pri. (n) hoe
azadón Dom.R., Gua., Venz. (n) hoe
azador Bol. (n) hoe
azul Pri. (adj) blue (eyes)

Peru's *olluco*, a tuber similar to the potato, gets its name from the Quechuan *ulluku*.

ABBREVIATIONS: Arg.=Argentina Bol.=Bolivia Chi.=Chile Col.=Colombia Cos.R.=Costa Rica Cub.=Cuba Dom.R.=Dominican Republic Ecu.=Ecuador EIS.=El Salvador Gua.=Guatemala Hon.=Honduras Mex.=Mexico Pan.=Panama Per.=Peru Pri.=Primary Term Pue.R.=Puerto Rico Spa.=Spain Uru.=Uruguay Venz.=Venezuela

B

babosa Dom.R. (n) snail
babuchas Col. (n) slippers
babysitter Arg. (n) babysitter
bache Arg., Cub., Gua., Mex., Spa. (n)
    pothole
bache Pri. (n) bump (road)
bagel Bol., Col., Pue.R. (n) bagel
bagre Pri. (n) catfish
baguette Pri. (n) baguette
bajareque Pan. (n) mist
bajarse Pri. (v) get off (bus)
bajito Col., Dom.R. (adj) short
bajito Col., Dom.R., Uru. (adj) short
    (person)
bajo Arg., Mex., Per., Spa. (adj) short
bajo Col. (n) bass (stereo)
bajo Col., Venz. (adj) short (person)
bajo la influencia Spa. (adj phr)
    intoxicated
bajo Pri. (n) bass (voice)
balaustrada Col. (n) balcony
balcón Pri. (n) balcony
balconcillo Col. (n) balcony
balde Pri. (n) bucket
balde Pri. (n) pail
balde de hielo Pri. (n phr) ice bucket
balizas Arg. (n) emergency lights
balompié Pue.R. (n) soccer
balón de fútbol Col. (n phr) ball
    (soccer)
balón Spa. (n) ball (soccer)
baloncesto Pri. (n) basketball
balonmano ElS., Gua., Hon. (n)
    handball
bañador Spa. (n) bathing suit
banana Arg., Uru. (n) banana

banano Col., Cos.R., Ecu. (n) banana
banca Arg. (n) bench
banco de arena Mex. (n phr) sandbar
banco Pri. (n) bench
banco Pri. (n) stool
banco-escalera Pri. (n) chair, step
banda de sonido Arg. (n phr) sound
    track
banda del ventilador Mex. (n phr) fan
    belt
banda sin fin Cos.R. (n phr) treadmill
banda sonora Pri. (n phr) sound track
bandada Arg. (n) flock
bandeja Col., Cub., Pan. (n) platter
bandeja para el horno Spa. (n phr)
    roasting pan
bandeja para hornear Col. (n phr)
    roasting pan
banjo Pri. (n) banjo
baño Pri. (n) bathroom
banqueta Dom.R. (n) stool
banqueta Mex. (n) sidewalk
banqueta Spa. (n) bench
banquillo Pan., Pue.R. (n) ottoman
banquina Arg. (n) road shoulder
banquito Dom.R. (n) stool
banyo Spa. (n) banjo
bar Pri. (n) bar
barato Pri. (adj) cheap
barba Mex. (n) chin
barba partida Mex. (n phr) cleft (chin)
barbas de chivo Pri. (n phr) goatee
barbero Col. (n) hairdresser
barbero Pri. (n) barber
barbida partida Per. (n phr) cleft (chin)
barbilla hendida Venz. (n phr) cleft
    (chin)
barbilla Pri. (n) chin
barbo Spa. (n) catfish
barco Arg., Chi., Col., Cos.R., Pan.,

Uru., Venz. (n) ship
barco de vela Pri. (n phr) sailboat
barco Pri. (n) boat
barman Pri. (n) bartender
barquillo Col. (n) waffle
barra (entre compases) Col. (n) bar
(music)
barra de arena Pri. (n phr) sandbar
barra de pan Spa. (n phr) baguette
barra fija Pri. (n phr) horizontal bar
barra horizontal Col., Pan., Pue.R.,
Venz. (n phr) horizontal bar
barraca Pue.R. (n) barracks
barracas Pan. (n) barracks
barranca Mex. (n) cliff
barranco Cos.R. (n) cliff
barredora Pri. (n) lawn rake
barrena Pue.R., Venz. (n) drill bit
barrendero Cub. (n) janitor
barriga Per. (n) abdomen
barriga Pri. (n) belly
barrio Arg., Col., Dom.R., Ecu., Pan.,
Per., Spa., Uru. (n) neighborhood
barrio comercial Pri. (n phr) business
district
barrio en las afueras Col. (n phr)
suburb
barrio Pri. (n) suburb
barrio residencial Arg. (n phr)
residencial area
barrito Per. (n) pimple
barro Col., Mex., Venz. (n) pimple
bartender Cub., Dom.R. (n) bartender
basketball Mex., Pan. (n) basketball
basketbol Arg., Per., Uru. (n)
basketball
bastidor Ecu., Pan., Per. (n) chassis
basurero Pri. (n) garbage collector
bata de baño Pri. (n phr) bathrobe
bata de casa Cub., Dom.R., Spa.,

Venz. (n phr) house robe
bata de dormir Cub., Pue.R. (n phr)
nightgown
bata de estar en casa Pan. (n phr)
house robe
batata Pri. (n) sweet potato
batería Dom.R. (n) drum
baterista Dom.R. (n) drummer
bathing suit Pri. (n phr) traje de baño
batidor de mano Ecu. (n phr) egg
beater
batidor manual Pri. (n phr) egg beater
batidora Chi., Pue.R. (n) egg beater
batidora Cub., Dom.R., Spa., Venz.
(n) blender
batidora Pri. (n) mixer
batón Bol. (n) bathrobe
baúl Pri. (n) trunk (car)
bautismo Arg., Col. (n) christening
bautizo Pri. (n) christening
baya Pri. (n) berry
beatle Chi. (n) turtleneck
beauty parlor Pue.R. (n phr)
hairdresser's shop
beba Arg. (n) toddler
beba Arg., Uru. (n) baby
bebe Arg. (n) toddler
bebé Arg. (n) toddler
bebe Arg., Uru. (n) baby
bebé Cub., Mex., Spa. (n) infant
bebé Pri. (n) baby
bebedero Arg., Chi., Mex., Venz. (n)
water fountain
bebida alcohólica fuerte Spa. (n phr)
hard liquor
bebida alcohólica fuerte Spa. (n phr)
liquor
bebida alcohólica Pri. (n phr)
alcoholic beverage
bebida alcohólica Uru. (n phr) hard

---

liquor
bebidas fuertes Mex. (n phr) hard
liquor
bebidas fuertes Pri. (n phr) liquor
bebido Col. (adj) drunk
becerro Col., Spa. (n) calf
bella Col. (adj) pretty
bellaco Dom.R. (adj) naughty
bello Chi., Col., Cos.R., Cub.,
Dom.R. (adj) beautiful
beneficio adicional Col. (n phr)
fringe benefit
beneficio laborable Cos.R. (n phr)
fringe benefit
beneficio suplementario Col. (n phr)
fringe benefit
beodo Col. (n) drunkard
berbiquí Mex. (n) awl
bermudas Cub. (n) shorts
betabel Mex. (n) beet
beterraga Bol., Chi., Per. (n) beet
bibliotecario/a Pri. (n) librarian
bibliotecólogo Dom.R. (n) librarian
bíceps Pri. (n) biceps
bicho, chinche Pri. (n) bug
bicicleta Arg., Cub., Uru. (n) bike,
road
bicicleta de camino Pri. (n phr) bike,
road
bicicleta de campotraviesa Mex. (n
phr) bike, mountain
bicicleta de carrera Dom.R. (n phr)
bike, road
bicicleta de carreras Spa. (n phr) bike,
road
bicicleta de dos personas Col. (n phr)
bike, tandem
bicicleta de montaña Chi., Col., Spa.,
Venz. (n phr) bike, mountain
bicicleta de ruta Col. (n phr) bike,

road
bicicleta doble Col., Mex. (n phr)
bike, tandem
bicicleta estable Pan. (n phr)
stationary bicycle
bicicleta estacionaria Pri. (n phr)
stationary bicycle
bicicleta estática Spa. (n phr)
stationary bicycle
bicicleta fija Mex. (n phr) stationary
bicycle
bicicleta montañesa ElS., Gua., Hon.
(n phr) bike, mountain
bicicleta para carretera Col. (n phr)
bike, road
bicicleta para dos personas Pri. (n phr)
bike, tandem
bicicleta todo terreno Arg. (n phr)
bike, mountain
bicicleta turismo Mex. (n phr) bike,
road
bien parecido Col., Venz. (adj phr)
handsome
bikini Bol., Chi. (n) bikini briefs
bilé Mex. (n) lipstick
billboard Pue.R. (n) billboard
billete de ida Bol., Ecu., Spa. (n phr)
one-way ticket
billete de ida y vuelta Pri. (n phr)
round trip ticket
billete de una sola vía Bol. (n phr)
one-way ticket
billete Pri. (n) ticket
billete sencillo Pri. (n phr) one-way
ticket
billetera, cartera (n) wallet
binoculares Col. (n) glasses, opera
binóculos Col. (n) glasses, opera
biombo separador Mex. (n phr) office
divider

bisquet Mex. (n) biscuit
bizcochito Dom.R. (n) biscuit
bizcocho Dom.R., Pue.R. (n) cake
bizcocho, galleta Pri. (n) biscuit
blanco Spa. (adj) gray (hair)
blazer Pue.R. (n) jacket (women's)
bloc amarillo Mex., Spa. (n phr) pad,
   yellow
bloc Arg., Chi. (n) pad, legal
bloc Arg., Chi. (n) pad, writing
bloc Arg., Chi. (n) pad, yellow
bloc Arg., Col., Mex., Per. (n) pad
   (paper)
bloc de notas Spa. (n phr) pad (paper)
bloc de notas Spa. (n phr) pad, writing
bloc tamaño carta Mex. (n phr) pad,
   writing
bloc tamaño legal Spa. (n phr) pad,
   legal
bloc tamaño oficio Mex. (n phr) pad,
   legal
bloque de carnicero Pri. (n phr)
   butcher block
bloque Pue.R. (n) city block
bloqueador solar Dom.R. (n phr)
   sunscreen
blower Dom.R., Pue.R. (n) hair dryer
blue jeans Col., Venz. (n phr) blue
   jeans
blúmer Cub., Pan. (n) panties
bocadillo Col. (n) snack
bocaditos Per. (n) appetizer
bocas Cos.R. (n) appetizer
bocina Arg., Chi., Dom.R., Uru. (n)
   bell (bicycle)
bodega (n) wine shop
bodega Cos.R., Ecu., Gua., Mex. (n)
   storage room
bodega Cub., Dom.R., Per. (n) grocery
bodega Pan. (n) liquor store

bodeguero Cub. (n) grocer
bol Arg. (n) bowl, mixing
bol Chi. (n) bowl
bola de balompié Pue.R. (n phr) ball
   (soccer)
bola de golf Col., Mex., Pue.R. (n phr)
   golf ball
bola en uno Pue.R. (n phr) hole in one
boleta Pan. (n) ticket, traffic
boleta por velocidad Pan. (n phr)
   ticket, speeding
boletero Per. (n) ticket collector
boletín informativo Cos.R. (n phr)
   infomercial
boletín meteorológico (n phr) weather
   report
boleto Arg., Chi., Cub., Mex., Pan.,
   Per., Pue.R., Venz. (n) ticket
boleto de ida Arg., Chi., Mex., Pan.,
   Venz. (n phr) one-way ticket
boleto de ida y vuelta Arg., Chi., Mex.,
   Pan., Per., Venz. (n phr) round
   trip ticket
boleto de viaje redondo Mex. (n phr)
   round trip ticket
boleto en un solo sentido Per. (n phr)
   one-way ticket
bolígrafo, pluma Pri. (n) pen, ball-
   point
bolígrafo Spa. (n) pen
bollito Cos.R. (n) bun
bollo Bol., Spa. (n) bun
bollo de crema Bol., ElS., Gua., Hon.,
   Spa. (n phr) cream puff
bollo de pan Venz. (n phr) Swiss roll
bollo ElS., Gua., Hon., Spa. (n) roll
bolsa de mano Col., Cos.R., Gua.,
   Mex., Pan. (n phr) handbag
bolsas Dom.R. (n) bags (under
   eyes)

ABBREVIATIONS: Arg.=Argentina Bol.=Bolivia Chi.=Chile Col.=Colombia
Cos.R.=Costa Rica Cub.=Cuba Dom.R.=Dominican Republic Ecu.=Ecuador ElS.=El
Salvador Gua.=Guatemala Hon.=Honduras Mex.=Mexico Pan.=Panama Per.=Peru
Pri.=Primary Term Pue.R.=Puerto Rico Spa.=Spain Uru.=Uruguay Venz.=Venezuela

bolsillo de atrás Dom.R. (n phr) pocket, back

bolsillo de la camisa Dom.R. (n phr) pocket, breast

bolsillo superior Pri. (n phr) pocket, breast

bolsillo trasero Pri. (n phr) pocket, back

bolso de mano Spa., Venz. (n phr) handbag

bolso Dom.R. (n) handbag

bomba de crema Uru. (n phr) cream puff

bombacha Arg. (n) bikini briefs

bombachas Arg., Uru. (n) panties

boniato Cub., Uru. (n) sweet potato

bonita Chi., Col., Dom.R., Ecu., ElS., Gua., Hon., Pan., Uru. (adj) pretty

bonito Pue.R. (adj) cute

bonito, hermoso Pri. (adj) beautiful

boquerón Cos.R., Dom.R., Per., Pue.R. (n) anchovy

borde de la carretera ElS., Gua., Hon. (n phr) road shoulder

bordón Col. (n) snare (of drum)

borrachín Col. (n) drunkard

borracho, embriagado (adj) intoxicated

borracho Pri. (adj) drunk

borracho Pri. (n) drunkard

borrachón Dom.R. (n) drunkard

borrar, eliminar Pri. (v) delete

borrego Mex. (n) sheep

bosque tropical Col. (n phr) rain forest

botamanga Arg. (n) cuff (pants)

botana Mex. (n) snack

botánica Pri. (n) herbalist's shop

botapié Bol. (n) cuff (pants)

botar Cub., Dom.R (v) fire

botas de alpinismo Mex. (n phr) shoes, hiking

botas de monte Spa. (n phr) shoes, hiking

botas Pri. (n) shoes, hiking

bote de vela Col. (n phr) sailboat

bote Cub., Venz. (n) boat

botica Col., Ecu., Per. (n) drug store

boticario Col. (n) pharmacist

botón Col. (n) bud

botón Col. (n) drawer knob

bototos Chi. (n) shoes, hiking

box spring Dom.R., Mex., Venz. (n phr) box spring

boxeador Pri. (n) boxer

bragas Spa. (n) panties

bragueta Pri. (n) fly (pants)

braguita de bikini Spa. (n phr) bikini briefs

brasier Dom.R., Pan. (n) bra, brassiere

brasiere Mex. (n) bra, brassiere

brassiere Col. (n) bra, brassiere

bravo Col., Cub., Venz. (adj) angry

brazada Arg. (n) breaststroke (swimming)

brazada de pecho ElS., Gua., Hon. (n phr) breaststroke (swimming)

brazada Pue.R., Uru. (n) crawl (swimming)

brazado de pecho Dom.R. (n phr) breaststroke (swimming)

brazo de gitano Spa. (n phr) Swiss roll

breda Col. (n) road shoulder

breteles Dom.R. (n) suspenders

breves informativos Chi. (n phr) news brief

breves Pri. (n) news brief

brifión Spa. (n) nectarine

broca Pri. (n) drill bit

brocha de repostería Col., Gua., ElS.,

ABBREVIATIONS: Arg.=Argentina Bol.=Bolivia Chi.=Chile Col.=Colombia Cos.R.=Costa Rica Cub.=Cuba Dom.R.=Dominican Republic Ecu.=Ecuador ElS.=El Salvador Gua.=Guatemala Hon.=Honduras Mex.=Mexico Pan.=Panama Per.=Peru Pri.=Primary Term Pue.R.=Puerto Rico Spa.=Spain Uru.=Uruguay Venz.=Venezuela

Hon., Pan. (n phr) pastry brush
broche para el pelo Pri. (n phr)
barrette
bronceado Pri. (adj) tan (skin)
bronceador Mex., Per. (n) sunscreen
broncearse Pri. (v) tan
bronces Pri. (n) bronze section
brote Chi. (n) seedling
brote Pri. (n) bud
brotes de soja Arg., Uru. (n phr) bean
sprouts
bruma Col. (n) fog
bruma Col. (n) mist
brunch Pri. (n) brunch
buceador, buzo Pri. (n) diver
¡Buen día! Arg. (int phr) Good
morning!
¡Buenas noches! Col., Ecu. (int phr)
Good evening!
¡Buenas noches! Pri. (int phr) Good
night!
¡Buenas tardes! Pri. (int phr) Good
evening!
buen mozo Arg. (adj phr) handsome
buenmozo Chi., Col., Dom.R. (adj)
handsome
bueno Dom.R. (adj) straight (hair)
¿Bueno? Mex. (int) Hello? (answering
telephone)
¡Buenos días! Pri. (int phr) Good
morning!
búfer Mex. (n) buffer storage
bufete de abogados Pri. (n phr)
lawyer's office
bufetera Gua. (n) buffet
buffer storage Pue.R. (n phr) buffer
storage
búho Pri. (n) owl
buitre (n) vulture
bumper Dom.R., Pan., Pue.R. (n)

bumper
bungaló Col., Spa. (n) bungalow
búngalo Mex. (n) bungalow
bungaloo Dom.R. (n) bungalow
bungalow Arg., Uru. (n) bungalow
bungalu Pan. (n) bungalow
buque Pri. (n) ship
bus Arg., Col., Cos.R., Pan. (n) bus
buscar en la red Mex. (v phr) surf the
net
busero Pan. (n) bus driver
buseta Col. (n) bus
buseta Ecu. (n) camión
buseta Ecu. (n) van
busito Pan. (n) camión
busito Pan. (n) van
busto Mex. (n) breast
butaca Cub., Dom.R., Pue.R. (n)
armchair
buzo Arg. (n) sweatshirt
buzo Col. (n) turtleneck
buzón postal Col. (n phr) post office
box
¡Bye! Dom.R. (int) Bye!
¡Bye! Dom.R. (int) Goodbye!

While Guatemala's official language is Spanish, the country has twenty-one non-official Mayan tongues. The Mayan influence is evident in the name of Guatemala's currency, the *quetzal*, and in the names of its major cities: Q u e t z a l t e n a n g o , Chiquimula, Escuintla, and Mazatenango.

C

caballeroso Mex. (adj) polite
caballete Pri. (n phr) bridge of nose
caballete Pri. (n) easel
caballito Cub., Ecu., Pue.R., Venz. (n)
pony
caballito de San Pedro Pue.R. (n phr)
horsefly, gadfly
caballito del diablo Cub. (n phr)
dragonfly
caballito Mex. (n) shot glass (small)
caballito Pan. (n) dragonfly
caballitos Pri. (n) carousel (with
horses)
caballo Mex. (n) shot glass (big)
cabaña Arg. (n) hut
cabaña Chi. (n) cottage
cabaña Chi., Col. (n) bungalow
cabaña, choza Pri. (n) cabin
cabañita Bol. (n) bungalow
cabellera Col. (n) hair
cabello, pelo Pri. (n) hair
cabina telefónica Pri. (n phr) telephone
booth
cabinera Col. (n) flight attendant
cable Arg., Cub., Mex. (n) cable
television
cablevisión Mex. (n) cable television
cabo Dom.R. (n) stump
cabro Chi. (n) guy
cabros Chi. (n) guys (dual gender
plural)
cacahuate Mex. (n) peanut
cacahuete Spa. (n) peanut
cacata Dom.R. (n) spider
cacatúa Pri. (n) cockatoo
cacerola Arg. (n) pot

cacerola Pri. (n) saucepan
cachete Arg. (n) buttock
cachete Chi., Col., Dom.R., Mex.,
Pan., Per., Venz. (n) cheek
cachito Per. (n) croissant
cachito Per. (n) pigtail
cachucha Col., Dom.R. (n) cap
cacto Pri. (n) cactus
cactus Arg., Chi., Dom.R., Mex., Pan.,
Pue.R., Spa. (n) cactus
cadena Col. (n) range (mountain)
cadena Pri. (n) network (television)
cadena Spa. (n) channel
café bar Cos.R. (n phr) coffee bar
café Bol., Chi., Cos.R., Mex. (adj)
brown (eyes)
café Pri. (n) coffee bar
cafetera Pri. (n) coffee maker
cafetería Col., Pue.R., Spa. (n) coffee
bar
cafiche Chi. (n) pimp
caída de agua Dom.R. (n phr) waterfall
caja de cambios Pri. (n phr) gearbox
caja de velocidades ElS., Gua., Hon.,
Mex. (n phr) gearbox
cajón Arg., Chi., Col., Ecu., Mex.,
Per., Spa., Uru. (n) drawer
cajuela Mex. (n) trunk (car)
cake Cub., Pan. (n) cake
calabacín (n) zucchini
calabacita Mex. (n) zucchini
calabaza Col., Cos.R., Cub., Ecu., Spa.
(n) squash
calabaza Pri. (n) pumpkin
calaca Mex. (n) skeleton
calamar Pri. (n) squid
calar Pri. (v) stall (car)
calarse Spa. (v) stall (car)
calavera Col., Cos.R., Mex. (n) skull
calcetín Pri. (n) sock

caldera Bol. (n) kettle
caldero Cub. (n) kettle
calesita Arg., Uru. (n) carousel (with horses)
callado Chi., Col., Venz. (adj) quiet
calle adoquinada Mex. (n phr) street, cobblestone
calle cerrada Col., Mex. (n phr) street, dead-end
calle ciega Venz. (n phr) street, dead-end
calle de adoquín Gua. (n phr) street, cobblestone
calle de adoquines Chi., Pue.R., Spa., Uru. (n phr) street, cobblestone
calle de dirección única Spa. (n phr) street, one-way
calle de guijarro Pri. (n phr) street, cobblestone
calle de ladrillo Pan. (n phr) street, cobblestone
calle de paralelepípedos Chi. (n phr) street, cobblestone
calle de piedras Per. (n phr) street, cobblestone
calle de un solo sentido Col., Mex., Per. (n phr) street, one-way
calle de una mano Pri. (n phr) street, one-way
calle de una sola dirección Ecu. (n phr) street, one-way
calle de una sola vía ElS., Gua., Hon. (n phr) street, one-way
calle de una vía Cos.R., Dom.R., Pan., Pue.R., Venz. (n phr) street, one-way
calle empedrada Arg., Bol., Col., Ecu., Venz. (n phr) street, cobblestone
calle sin salida Pri. (n phr) street, dead-end
callejón Pri. (n) alley
callejuela Col. (n) alley
callo Per. (n) wart
calzón bikini Ecu. (n phr) bikini briefs
calzoncillo corto Pan. (n phr) bikini briefs
calzoncillo largo Pan. (n phr) boxer shorts
calzoncillos boxer Dom.R. (n phr) boxer shorts
calzoncillos Col. (n) bikini briefs
calzoncillos Pri. (n) boxer shorts
calzoncillos Pri. (n) briefs
calzones Cub. (n) boxer shorts
calzones Mex., Uru. (n) briefs
calzones Pri. (n) panties
cama camarote Col., Dom.R., Pan. (n phr) bunkbed
cama camera Arg. (n phr) bed, king-sized
cama camera Arg. (n phr) bed, queen-sized
cama de flores Mex. (n phr) flower bed
cama de matrimonio Spa. (n phr) bed, double
cama de soltero Chi. (n phr) bed, single
cama doble Pri. (n phr) bed, double
cama doble Pri. (n phr) bed, queen-sized
cama grande Pri. (n phr) bed, king-sized
cama imperial Gua. (n phr) bed, single
cama individual Mex., Venz. (n phr) bed, single
cama king Pan., Venz. (n phr) bed, king-sized
cama king size Col., Dom.R. (n phr) bed, king-sized

cama king-size Mex. (n phr) bed, king-sized

cama litera Cub. (n phr) bunkbed

cama matrimonial Gua., Mex. (n phr) bed, double

cama matrimonial Pan. (n phr) bed, queen-sized

cama Pri. (n) bed, single

cama queen size Dom.R. (n phr) bed, queen-sized

cama queen Venz. (n phr) bed, queen-sized

cama queen-size Mex. (n phr) bed, queen-sized

cama sencilla Col., Ecu., Pue.R. (n phr) bed, single

cama tres cuartos Pan. (n phr) bed, single

camanance Cos.R. (n) cleft (chin)

camanance Cos.R., ElS., Gua., Hon. (n) dimple

camanchaca Chi. (n) fog

cámara Chi., Spa. (n) inner tube (bicycle tire)

camarero (n) waiter

camarón Arg., Ecu., Uru. (n) prawn

camarón de agua dulce Chi. (n phr) crayfish

camarón gigante Chi. (n phr) prawn

camarón Pri. (n) shrimp

camarote Chi. (n) berth

camarote Chi. (n) bunkbed

cambiar de cambios Pue.R. (v phr) shift gear

cambiar de tren Col., Cub. (v phr) change (train)

cambiar la marcha Spa. (v phr) shift gear

cambiar la velocidad Pri. (v phr) shift gear

cambiarse de casa Col. (v phr) move

cambio Arg. (n) stick shift

cambio automático Spa. (n phr) automatic transmission

cambio manual Spa. (n phr) stick shift

cambios Arg., Chi., Cub., Dom.R., Pan., Pue.R., Uru., Venz. (n) velocidades

cambur Venz. (n) banana

caminador Col. (n) treadmill

caminadora Mex., Uru. (n) treadmill

camión del helado Col., Spa. (n phr) ice cream truck

camión Mex. (n) bus

camión Pri. (n) van

camionero Mex. (n) bus driver

camioneta Cos.R., Mex., Venz. (n) camión

camioneta Cos.R., Mex., Venz. (n) van

camioneta ElS., Gua., Hon. (n) bus

camioneta pickup Mex., Venz. (n phr) pickup truck

camioneta Pri. (n) pickup truck

camioneta Pri. (n) station wagon

camisa de dormir Chi., Col. (n phr) nightgown

camisa de manga corta Pri. (n phr) shirt, short-sleeved

camisa de manga larga Pri. (n phr) shirt, long-sleeved

camisa de noche Ecu. (n phr) nightgown

camisa de trabajo Pri. (n phr) sweatshirt

camisa de vestir Arg., Dom.R., Mex., Pan., Uru., Venz. (n phr) shirt, dressy

camisa formal Pri. (n phr) shirt, dressy

camiseta Arg. (n) vest

camiseta Per. (n) knit shirt

ABBREVIATIONS: Arg.=Argentina Bol.=Bolivia Chi.=Chile Col.=Colombia Cos.R.=Costa Rica Cub.=Cuba Dom.R.=Dominican Republic Ecu.=Ecuador ElS.=El Salvador Gua.=Guatemala Hon.=Honduras Mex.=Mexico Pan.=Panama Per.=Peru Pri.=Primary Term Pue.R.=Puerto Rico Spa.=Spain Uru.=Uruguay Venz.=Venezuela

camiseta Pri. (n) t-shirt
camisón Pri. (n) nightgown
camote Bol., Ecu., Gua., Mex., Pan.,
Per. (n) sweet potato
campanilla Bol. (n) bell (bicycle)
camper Mex. (n) recreational vehicle
campera Arg. (n) jacket
campesino Col. (n) farmer
campo de golf Pri. (n phr) golf course
campo santo Chi., Col. (n phr)
cemetery
canal Pri. (n) channel
canal Venz. (n) lane
canasta Arg., Mex., Pan., Per., Uru. (n)
basket (basketball)
canasto Dom.R., Pue.R. (n) basket
(basketball)
cancha de golf Arg. (n phr) golf course
canción de amor Pri. (n phr) love song
canción de moda Pri. (n phr) hit
(song)
canción Pri. (n) song
canción Pue.R. (n) hymn
canción romántica Col., Pue.R. (n
phr) love song
cangrejo de río Pri. (n phr) crayfish
cangrejo Pri. (n) crab
canilla Chi. (n) shin
canino Pri. (n) canine (tooth)
cano Col. (adj) gray (hair)
caño de escape Arg. (n phr) exhaust
pipe
canoso Pri. (adj) gray (hair)
cantaloupe Col. (n) cantaloupe
cantalupa Cub. (n) cantaloupe
cantar afinados Pue.R. (v phr) sing
harmony
cantar en armonía Pri. (v phr) sing
harmony
cantero Arg. (n) flower bed

cántico Pri. (n) hymn
cantina de agua Ecu. (n phr) kettle
cantina Mex., Pan. (n) bar
cantinero Col., Ecu., ElS., Gua., Hon.,
Mex., Pan., Pue.R. (n) bartender
canto Col. (n) song
capa de agua Cub. (n phr) raincoat
capa Pri. (n) cloak
capa Pue.R. (n) parka
capa Pue.R. (n) raincoat
capa, capote Pri. (n) cape
capacitar Pri. (v) train (for job)
caperuza Cub. (n) hood
capote Pan. (n) raincoat
capucha Pri. (n) hood
capuchón Chi. (n) hood
capul Col. (n) bangs (hair)
capullo Spa. (n) bud
car jack Pue.R. (v phr) car jack (crime)
carabinero Chi. (n) police officer
caracol Pri. (n) snail
carajito/a Dom.R. (n) brat
caraotas negras Venz. (n phr) beans,
black
caraotas Venz. (n) beans
caravana Spa. (n) recreational vehicle
carcelero Col., Venz. (n) warden
(prison)
cardenal Pri. (n) bruise
cardigán Pri. (n) cardigan
cargador de maletas Venz. (n phr)
porter
cargoso Bol. (n) pest (person)
caricatura Mex. (n) cartoon
caricaturas Pan. (n) cartoon
cariño Col. (n) love, lovey
cariño Pan. (n) dear, darling, honey
cariño Spa. (n) sweetheart
carnet de conducir Spa. (n phr) driver's
license

carnet de chofer Chi. (n phr) driver's license

carnet de conductor Arg. (n phr) driver's license

carnosa Mex. (n) succulent (plant)

carpa Pri. (n) tent

carpeta con ganchos Arg. (n phr) three-ring binder

carpeta Cub. (n) notebook

carpeta de archivo Pri. (n phr) folder

carpeta de argollas Pri. (n phr) three-ring binder

carpeta de tres anillos Spa. (n phr) three-ring binder

carpeta de tres hoyos Dom.R. (n phr) three-ring binder

carpeta Spa. (n) folder

carrera de obstáculos Cub., Dom.R., ElS., Gua., Hon., Venz. (n phr) hurdles race

carreta (n) wagon

carrete de celo Spa. (n phr) tape dispenser

carrete de cinta Pri. (n phr) tape dispenser

carretera Spa. (n) expressway

carril del centro Pue.R. (n phr) median

carril Pri. (n) lane

carrillo Spa. (n) cheek

carrito chocón Dom.R. (n phr) bumper car

carrito de helados Col. (n phr) ice cream truck

carrito Dom.R. (n) trolley

carro alegórico Chi. (n) float (parade)

carro chocón Mex., Per., Venz. (n phr) bumper car

carro comedor Venz. (n phr) dining car (train)

carro de carrera Cub., Dom.R., ElS., Gua., Hon., Pan., Pue.R. (n phr) racecar

carro de carreras Col., Per., Venz. (n phr) racecar

carro de deporte Cub. (n phr) sports car

carro de helados Mex. (n phr) ice cream truck

carro deportivo Pri. (n phr) sports car

carro loco Pri. (n phr) bumper car

carro particular Chi., Ecu. (n phr) car, private

carro Pri. (n) car

carro privado Pri. (n phr) car, private

carrocería Pri. (n) car body

carroza Pri. (n) float (parade)

carrusel Chi., Col., Ecu., ElS., Gua., Hon., Pan., Venz. (n) carousel (with horses)

cartel Arg. (n) road sign

cartel Arg. (n) shop sign

cartel de neón Arg. (n phr) neon sign

cartelera Chi., Col., Cub. (n) billboard

cartera Bol. (n) briefcase

cartera de hombre Dom.R. (n phr) wallet

cartera de maquillaje Pue.R. (n phr) makeup kit

cartera Pri. (n) handbag

cartucho de tinta Pri. (n phr) toner cartridge

cartucho del toner Dom.R. (n phr) toner cartridge

cartucho tonificador Mex. (n phr) toner cartridge

casa adosada Spa. (n phr) townhouse

casa Arg. (n) cottage

casa campestre ElS., Gua., Hon. (n phr) bungalow

casa de campo Pri. (n) cottage

casa de campo Venz. (n phr) bungalow

casa de ciudad Col. (n phr) townhouse

casa de perro Chi., Venz. (n phr) doghouse

casa de playa ElS., Gua., Hon. (n phr) bungalow

casa dúplex Dom.R., Pue.R. (n phr) duplex

casa en hilera Pri. (n phr) townhouse

casa independiente Pri. (n phr) bungalow

casa pareada Chi. (n phr) duplex

casa particular en complejos residenciales Gua. (n phr) townhouse

casa particular en la ciudad Chi. (n phr) townhouse

casa pegada Bol., Uru. (n phr) townhouse

casa rodante Chi. (n phr) recreational vehicle

casa-botes Dom.R. (n) boathouse

casa-quinta Arg. (n) cottage

casca Per. (n) jacket

cascada (n) waterfall

cascarrabias Venz. (adj) grumpy

caseta de botes Pri. (n phr) boathouse

casete Arg., Col., Venz. (n) tape (cassette)

casete para vídeo Col. (n) videocassette

casette Cub., Dom.R. (n) videocassette

casilla Arg. (n) hut

casilla Bol. (n) post office box

casilla postal Chi. (n phr) post office box

casis Pri. (n) black currant

casita campestre Col. (n phr) bungalow

casita de campo Col. (n) cottage

casita de herramientas Pue.R. (n phr) shed

casita de paja Dom.R. (n) hut

casita playera Col. (n phr) bungalow

cassette Dom.R., Mex. (n) tape (cassette)

castaña Chi. (n) cashew

castaña de cajú Arg., Uru. (n phr) cashew

castaña Pri. (n) chestnut

castaño Arg., Mex., Spa. (adj) brown (hair)

castaño Pri. (adj) brown (eyes)

cata Chi. (n) cockatoo

catarata Spa. (n) waterfall

catarina Mex. (n) ladybug

catire Venz. (adj) blond (hair)

catire/a Venz. (n) blond (person)

catre Chi. (n) box spring

catre Dom.R. (n) cradle, crib

catre, chaise Pri. (n) chair, lounging

caucho Col. (n) rubber band

caucho de repuesto Venz. (n phr) spare tire

caucho pinchado Venz. (n phr) flat tire

caucho Venz. (n) tire (bicycle)

caucho Venz. (n) tire (car)

caverna Col. (n) cave

cavidad Venz. (n) sinus

cazo Spa. (n) saucepan

CD Arg., Col., Pan., Spa. (n) compact disk

CD player Dom.R. (n phr) compact disk player

CD-player Cos.R. (n) compact disk player

cebolla Bol. (n) onion, vidalia

cebolla colorada Ecu. (n phr) onion, red (Bermuda)

cebolla de cambray Mex. (n phr) onion, pickling

cebolla larga Col. (n phr) scallion

---

cebolla morada Mex. (n phr) onion, red (Bermuda)
cebolla Pan. (n) bun (hair)
cebolla roja Pri. (n phr) onion, red (Bermuda)
cebolla verde Pri. (n phr) scallion
cebolla vidalia Col. (n phr) onion, vidalia
cebolleta Spa. (n) onion, pickling
cebollín Chi. (n) onion, pickling
cebollín ElS., Gua., Hon., Venz. (n) scallion
cebollina Col. (n) onion, pickling
cebollina Pan. (n) scallion
cebollino Mex. (n) scallion
cebollino Mex. (n) shallot
cebollino Pri. (n) onion, pickling
cebollita Mex. (n) shallot
cebollita verde Bol. (n phr) scallion
cedazo Pri. (n) sieve
celesta Pri. (n) celesta
celeste Col. (n) celesta
celo Spa. (n) tape
cementerio Pri. (n) cemetery
cena Pri. (n) dinner
centella Col. (n) lightning
centímetro Cub. (n) tape measure
centro de la calle Pri. (n phr) median
centro de la ciudad Pri. (n phr) downtown
centro de negocios Dom.R. (n phr) business district
centro del pueblo Pue.R. (n phr) downtown
cepillo Arg., Col., Dom.R., Mex., Spa., Uru. (n) plane (carpentry)
cercado de arbustos Mex. (n phr) hedge
cerdo Col., Cub., Dom.R., Per., Pue.R., Spa., Venz. (n) pig

cereza agria Venz. (n phr) cranberry
cereza Pue.R. (n) berry
cerilla, fósforo Pri. (n) matchstick
cerillo Mex. (n) matchstick
cerquillo Cub., Ecu., Per. (n) bangs (hair)
cerrado Col. (adj) cloudy
cerro Chi. (n) hill
cervatillo Dom.R. (n) reindeer
césped Chi. (n) hierba
césped Pri. (n) lawn
cesta Pri. (n) basket (basketball)
cesto Bol. (n) basket (basketball)
chabacano Mex. (n) apricot
chal, quisquemel Mex. (n) cape
chaleco Arg. (n) cardigan
chaleco Pri. (n) vest
chalet Chi. (n) bungalow
chalet Chi. (n) cottage
chalote Pri. (n) shallot
chamaca Mex. (n) girl
chamaco Mex. (n) boy
chamarra Mex. (n) jacket
chamarra tejida Mex. (n phr) cardigan
champiñón Col., Mex., Spa. (n) mushroom
champú Pri. (n) shampoo
chamullento Chi. (n) liar
chancho Arg., Bol., Chi., Cos.R., Ecu., Per., Uru. (n) pig
chanclas de hule ElS., Gua., Hon. (n phr) rubbers (shoes)
chanclas de plástico Mex. (n phr) rubbers (shoes)
chanclas Spa. (n) rubbers (shoes)
chancletas Cos.R., Pan. (n) slippers
chancletas Cub., Pue.R. (n) sandals
chancletas de goma Cub., Pue.R. (n phr) rubbers (shoes)
chanclos de goma Pri. (n phr)

rubbers (shoes)
chanclos Pri. (n) clogs
chango Mex. (n) monkey
chaparro Mex. (adj) short
chaparro Mex. (adj) short (person)
chaqueta Chi., Pue.R. (n) coat
chaqueta de punto Spa. (n phr)
     cardigan
chaqueta Pri. (n) jacket
charca Pri. (n) pond
charco Arg., Chi., Uru. (n) pond
charlatán Arg., Col. (adj) talkative
charlatán Pri. (n) tattler
chasis Pan. (n) car body
chasis Pri. (n) chassis
chasquillas Chi. (n) bags (under eyes)
chassis Dom.R., Pue.R. (n) chassis
¡Chao! Chi. (int) Bye!
¡Chao! Chi. (int) Goodbye!
¡Chau! Arg. (int) Bye!
¡Chau! Arg. (int) Goodbye!
chauchas Arg., Uru. (n) beans, broad
chauchas Arg., Uru. (n) beans, green
chayote Pan. (n) squash
chef Pri. (n) chef
chequeador de boletos Venz. (n phr)
     ticket collector
chequeador de tickets Venz. (n phr)
     ticket collector
chequear el equipaje Dom.R., Venz.
     (v phr) check in (baggage)
chévere Pue.R. (adj) nice
chica Arg., Uru. (n) girl
chícharos Cub., Mex. (n) peas, green
chicharra Chi., Pue.R., Venz. (n)
     cicada
chiche Mex. (n) breast
chichi Mex. (n) breast
chico Arg., Chi., Col. (adj) small
chico Cub., Pue.R. (n) guy

chico/a Arg. (n) child
chico/a Pri. (n) kid
chico/a Arg. (n) child
chicos Arg., Ecu. (n) guys (dual gender
     plural)
chilacayote Pri. (n) squash
chile dulce Cos.R. (n phr) pepper,
     sweet
chile picante Cos.R. (n phr) pepper,
     hot
chile Pri. (n) pepper, hot
chilla Pue.R. (n) mistress
chillo Dom.R., Pue.R. (n) snapper
chimenea Pri. (n) fireplace
china Dom.R., Pue.R. (n) orange
china mandarina Pue.R. (n phr)
     mandarine orange
chincheta Spa. (n) tack
chinchorro Venz. (n) hammock
chineado Cos.R. (adj) spoiled (child)
chinelas Arg. (n) slippers
chinero Pue.R. (n) buffet
chinero Pue.R. (n) display cabinet
chinita Chi. (n) ladybug
chino Col. (n) boy
chino Mex. (adj) curly (hair)
chiqueado Mex. (adj) spoiled (child)
chiquillo/a Pue.R. (n) brat
chiquillos Chi. (n) guys (dual gender
     plural)
chiquito, pequeño Pri. (adj) small
chiquito/a Cub. (n) kid
chiriva Pri. (n) parsnip
chirivia Col. (n) parsnip
chirivía Col. (n) parsnip
chismoso/a Chi., Cub., Gua. (n) tattler
chistoso Col., Dom.R., Ecu., Pan.
     (adj) funny
chiva Dom.R., Venz. (n) goatee
chivato Cub., Spa. (n) tattler

chivera Col. (n) goatee
chiviría Gua. (n) parsnip
chivita Dom.R., Ecu. (n) goatee
chivo Cub. (n) goatee
chivón Cub. (n) pest (person)
chocar Pri. (v) crash (traffic)
chocha (n) woodcock
choclo Arg. (n) sweet corn
choclo Bol., Chi., Ecu., Per., Uru. (n)
   corn
chofer Chi. (n) bus driver
chofer de bus Col. (n phr) bus driver
chofer de colectivo Arg. (n phr) bus
   driver
chofer de guagua Dom.R., Pue.R. (n
   phr) bus driver
chofer de micro Arg. (n phr) bus driver
chofer de taxi Chi., Col., Cos.R. (n
   phr) taxi driver
chomba Chi. (n) sweater
chompa Col. (n) jersey
chompa Per. (n) pullover
chompa Per. (n) sweater
chongo Mex. (n) bun (hair)
choque de frente Pri. (n phr) head-on
   collision
choque frente a frente Per. (n phr)
   head-on collision
choque frontal Spa., Uru. (n phr)
   head-on collision
choro Chi. (n) mussel
choza Pri. (n) hut
chulito Pue.R. (adj) cute
chulo Dom.R. (adj) nice
chulo ElS., Gua., Hon., Mex., Per.,
   Venz. (adj) cute
chulo Pri. (n) pimp
chuncho Chi. (n) owl
chupaflor Ecu. (n) hummingbird
chupito Spa. (n) shot glass

churro Bol., Col. (adj) handsome
¡Ciao! Col. (int) Bye!
ciclón Dom.R. (n) hurricane
cielo, mi Cub. (n) dear, darling, honey
ciénaga Chi. (n) swamp
ciervo Arg., Bol., Cos.R., ElS., Gua.,
   Hon., Spa., Uru. (n) deer
cifrar Uru., Venz. (v) encrypt
   (computer)
cigarra Pri. (n) cicada
cigarrillo de marihuana Pri. (n phr)
   marijuana cigarette
cigarrillo Pri. (n) cigarette
cigarro Mex. (n) cigarette
cigarro, puro Pri. (n) cigar
cima Chi. (n) peak (mountain)
cine continuado Venz. (n phr) double
   feature (movies)
cinta adhesiva Pri. (n phr) tape
cinta Chi., Col., Cub. (n) film
cinta de medir Pan. (n phr) tape
   measure
cinta de vídeo Spa. (n) videocassette
cinta elástica Pri. (n phr) rubber
   band
cinta métrica Arg., Col., Dom.R.,
   Mex., Spa. (n phr) tape measure
cinta pegante Ecu. (n phr) tape
cinta Pri. (n) tape (cassette)
cinto Col. (n) waist
cintura (n) waist
cinturón Pri. (n) belt
ciruela Cos.R., Dom.R. (n) nectarine
ciruela de negra Pri. (n phr) nectarine
ciruela negra Pan. (n phr) nectarine
ciudad Pri. (n) city
clarín Pri. (n) bugle
clase económica Dom.R. (n phr)
   second class
clauadista Cub. (n) diver

clavija Pri. (n) dowel
clínica Col. (n) hospital
clip Pri. (n) paperclip
clóset Col., Cos.R., Cub., Mex., Pan.,
    Per. (n) closet (general)
clóset Pri. (n) closet (clothes)
club de golf Pan. (n phr) golf club
cobertizo de lanchas Gua. (n phr)
    boathouse
cobertizo para las lanchas Col. (n phr)
    boathouse
cobertizo Pri. (n) shed
cobija Pri. (n) blanket
cobres Col. (n) bronze section
coca Col. (n) cocaine
cocaína Pri. (n) cocaine
coche Arg., Chi., Col., Mex., Spa.,
    Uru. (n) car
coche cama Pri. (n phr) sleeping car
    (train)
coche comedor Pri. (n phr) dining car
    (train)
coche de carrera Pri. (n phr) racecar
coche de carreras Spa. (n phr) racecar
coche deportivo Spa., Uru. (n phr)
    sports car
coche ElS., Gua., Hon. (n) pig
coche particular Spa., Uru. (n phr)
    car, private
coche restaurante Spa. (n phr) dining
    car (train)
coche sport Bol. (n phr) sports car
cochino Cos.R., Cub., Mex., Venz.
    (n) pig
cocina Arg., Bol., Chi., Per., Spa., Uru.
    (n) stove
cocinar en el horno Spa. (v phr) bake
cocinero Col., Spa. (n) chef
cocuyo Cub. (n) firefly
codificar Venz. (v) encrypt (computer)

cogollo Col. (n) bud
cogote Col. (n) nape
cojer nota Cub. (v phr) get high
    (drugs)
col blanca Mex. (n phr) cabbage, white
col Cub., Ecu., Mex., Spa. (n) cabbage,
    green
col Cub., Spa. (n) cabbage, white
cola Arg. (n) ponytail (hair)
cola Arg., Col., Uru. (n) butt
cola Bol., Cos.R. (n) pigtail
cola de caballo Pri. (n phr) ponytail
    (hair)
coladera Bol., Col. (n) colander
coladera Col., Mex. (n) sieve
colador Chi., Cub., Venz. (n) sieve
colador Pri. (n) colander
colcha Ecu. (n) blanket
colchón de resortes Pri. (n phr) box
    spring
colchón Pri. (n) mattress
colectivo Bol., Col. (n) bus
colegio Arg., Col., Gua. (n) school
coles de Bruselas Pri. (n phr) Brussels
    sprouts
coleta Spa. (n) ponytail (hair)
coleta Spa., Uru. (n) pigtail
colgante con cadena Spa. (n phr)
    necklace, pendant
colibrí Pri. (n) hummingbird
colina Pri. (n) hill
colisión frente a frente Col. (n phr)
    head-on collision
colita Arg. (n) ponytail (hair)
colita Chi., Col., Dom.R., Mex., Venz.
    (n) pigtail
collar con medallón Pri. (n phr)
    necklace, pendant
colleras Chi. (n) cufflinks
colmado Pue.R. (n) grocery

colmillo Cub., Mex., Spa. (n) canine
(tooth)
colocarse Pri. (v) get high (drugs)
colonia Mex. (n) suburb
columna vertebral Pri. (n phr) spine
comadrona Col., Dom.R., ElS., Gua.,
Hon., Spa. (n) midwife
combinable Cos.R., Ecu., Per., Spa. (n)
station wagon
combinación Pri. (n) petticoat
combinación Pri. (n) slip
comedia Chi., Col., Cub., Dom.R.,
Spa. (n) sitcom, situation comedy
comedia de situación Pri. (n phr)
sitcom, situation comedy
comedor auxiliar ElS., Gua.. Hon. (n)
pantry
comején Ecu., ElS., Gua (n) termite
comejón Cos.R., Cub., Dom.R., Pan.,
Pue.R. (n) termite
comercial Col., Dom.R., Mex., Pan.,
Venz. (n) commercial
comercial informativa Pri. (n phr)
infomercial
comerciante Col. (n) grocer
comida Arg., Col., Per., Pue.R. (n)
dinner
comida Dom.R., Mex., Spa. (n) lunch
comida enlatada Col., Cub., Dom.R.,
Pan. (n phr) canned food
comisaría Pri. (n) police station
cómoda Arg., Chi., Col., Cub., Per. (n)
dresser
¿Cómo estás? Bol. (phr) How's it
going?
¿Cómo te (le) va? Pri. (phr) How's it
going?
¿Cómo tú estás? Dom.R. (phr)
How's it going?
compact disk Spa. (n phr) compact

disk
compadre Chi., Cub. (n) buddy, pal
compañero/a Pri. (n) buddy, pal
compañía de aviación Col. (n phr)
airline
compartir agujas Pri. (v phr) share
needles
compartir carros Gua. (v phr) carpool
compartir coches Pri. (v phr) carpool
compartir inyectadoras Venz. (v phr)
share needles
compartir jeringas Col. (v phr) share
needles
compartir viajes en carro Col. (v phr)
carpool
compás de cuatro por cuatro Spa. (n
phr) four-four, common time
compás de dos por cuatro Spa. (n phr)
two-four time
compás mayor Pri. (n phr) four-four,
common time
compás menor, compasillo Pri. (n phr)
two-four time
compás Pri. (n) bar (music)
competencia de obstáculos Col. (n
phr) hurdles race
competidor Pri. (n) contestant
compinche Dom.R. (n) buddy, pal
compras Cos.R. (n) grocery
comprometida Mex. (n) fiancée
(female)
comprometido Mex. (n) fiancé (male)
computador Col. (n) computer
computador personal Bol. (n phr) PC
computadora personal Arg., Gua.,
Mex., Venz. (n phr) PC
computadora Pri. (n) computer
concha ElS., Gua., Hon., Spa. (n)
scallop
conchuela Pan. (n) scallop

concubina Mex. (n) mistress
concursante Chi. (n) contestant
concurso televisivo Cos.R. (n phr) game show (television)
condominio Cub., ElS., Gua., Hon., Pue.R., Spa. (n) condominium
condominios Pri. (n) condominium
conducir borracho Spa. (v phr) drive drunk
conducir Chi., Col., Pan., Spa. (v) drive (car)
conducir Col. (v) conduct (music)
conducir ebrio Spa. (v phr) drive drunk
conducir en estado de embriaguez Arg., Pue.R. (v phr) drive drunk
conductor Chi., Ecu. (n) ticket collector
conductor de autobús Pri. (n phr) bus driver
conductor de libre Venz. (n phr) taxi driver
conductor de taxi Pri. (n phr) taxi driver
conejo Pue.R. (n) hare
conejos Mex. (n) biceps
confidente Pri. (n) love seat
confluencia Col. (n) cloverleaf junction
conga Pri. (n) conga drum
congelador Pri. (n) freezer
congestión Chi. (n) traffic jam
congestionamiento Pri. (n) traffic jam
conjunto Pri. (n) outfit
conmovedor Col. (adj) emocionante
consejero Pri. (n) consultant
consejero Pri. (n) counselor
consentido Col., Ecu., Mex. (adj) spoiled (child)
conserje Pri. (n) janitor
conserva (de alimentos) Pri. (n) preserves
conservas Chi., Col. (n) preserves
construcción Arg., Pue.R. (n) road works
construcción Col. (n) building
consultor Chi., Cos.R., Cub., Dom.R., Ecu., Per., Venz. (n) consultant
consultorio médico Pri. (n phr) doctor's office
consumidor de drogas Pri. (n phr) drug user
consumir drogas Col., ElS., Gua., Hon. (v phr) use drugs
contable Dom.R., Spa. (n) certified public accountant (CPA)
contable Spa. (n) bookkeeper
contador Chi., Dom.R. (n) certified public accountant (CPA)
contador Pri. (n) bookkeeper
contador público autorizado Cos.R., Pan. (n phr) certified public accountant (CPA)
contador público certificado Pri. (n phr) certified public accountant (CPA)
contaminación Pri. (n) pollution
contendor Col. (n) challenger (boxing)
contrabajo Col. (n) bass (voice)
contrabajón Pri. (n) contrabassoon
contrafagot Mex. (n) contrabassoon
contralor Dom.R. (n) comptroller
contraventanas Mex. (n) shutters
contrincante Pri. (n) challenger (boxing)
control remoto Pri. (n phr) remote control
controlador Pri. (n) comptroller
conversador Pan. (adj) talkative
convertible Pri. (n) convertible
copa ancha de boca estrecha Pri. (n

phr) snifter
copa de aguardiente Col. (n phr) shot glass
copa de cognac Chi. (n phr) snifter
copa de la rueda Col. (n phr) hubcap
copa de trago Pri. (n phr) shot glass
copiador óptico Venz. (n phr) scanner, optical
copiadora Pri. (n) copier
copita Col. (n) shot glass
coquito Dom.R. (n) hazelnut
coquito Venz. (n) ladybug
corazón Mex. (n) sweetheart
corbata de gatito Pan. (n phr) bow tie
corbata de gato Bol. (n phr) bow tie
corbata de lacito Dom.R. (n phr) bow tie
corbata de lazo Uru., Venz. (n phr) bow tie
corbata de moñito Mex. (n phr) bow tie
corbata mariposa Pri. (n phr) bow tie
corbata michi Per. (n phr) bow tie
corbatín Col. (n) bow tie
corchete Chi. (n) staple
corchetera Chi. (n) stapler
cordillera Chi. (n) range (mountain)
cordón Pri. (n) shoelace
corneta Col. (n) bugle
corneta Mex., Spa. (n) cornet
cornetín Pri. (n) cornet
cornetín Spa. (n) bugle
corno francés Pri. (n phr) French horn
corno inglés Pri. (n phr) English horn
corpiño Arg. (n) bra, brassiere
correa Col., Dom.R., Pan., Pue.R. (n) belt
correa del ventilador Pri. (n phr) fan belt
corredor de bienes raíces Pri. (n phr)

realtor
correo Arg., Cub. (n) post office
correo electrónico Pri. (n phr) e-mail
correr a toda velocidad Col., Dom.R. (v phr) sprint
correr bicicleta Pue.R. (v phr) ride (bicycle)
correr Cub. (v) sprint
cortacésped Spa. (n) lawn mower
cortacéspedes Pri. (n) lawn mower
cortador de césped Per. (n phr) lawn mower
cortador del pasto Per. (n phr) lawn mower
cortadora Bol. (n) lawn mower
cortadora de grama Pue.R. (n phr) lawn mower
cortadores de galletas Pri. (n phr) cookie cutters
cortagrama ElS., Gua., Hon., Venz. (n) lawn mower
cortapastas Pri. (n) pastry cutting wheel
cortapasto Chi. (n) lawn mower
cortaplumas Chi., Spa., Venz. (n) penknife
cortar Arg., Chi., Dom.R., Mex. (v) break up (relationship)
cortar con el vicio Col. (v phr) quit using drugs
corte Cub., Mex., Pue.R. (n) courthouse
cortés, educado Pri. (adj) polite
cortinas Col. (n) blinds
corto Chi., Mex., Pan., Pue.R. (adj) short
corto Col. (adj) small
costa Chi., Col., Pue.R. (n) seashore
costa Pri. (n) shoreline
costra Pri. (n) scab

ABBREVIATIONS: Arg.=Argentina Bol.=Bolivia Chi.=Chile Col.=Colombia Cos.R.=Costa Rica Cub.=Cuba Dom.R.=Dominican Republic Ecu.=Ecuador ElS.=El Salvador Gua.=Guatemala Hon.=Honduras Mex.=Mexico Pan.=Panama Per.=Peru Pri.=Primary Term Pue.R.=Puerto Rico Spa.=Spain Uru.=Uruguay Venz.=Venezuela

costurera Pri. (n) seamstress
costurero Col., Spa. (n) tailor
cotorra Col., Dom.R. (n) parrot
counter Pue.R. (n) counter
coverall Per. (n) overalls
coyuntura Dom.R., Spa. (n) joint
CPA Dom.R., Pan. (n) certified public
accountant (CPA)
cranberry Pue.R. (n) cranberry
cráneo Pri. (n) skull
crawl Pri. (n) crawl (swimming)
crecer Cos.R., Dom.R., Ecu., Pan.,
Pue.R. (v) rise (bread)
crecer Pri. (v) grow up
crecimeinto Dom.R. (n) root (hair)
crema de protección solar Spa. (n phr)
sunscreen
crema dental Col. (n phr) toothpaste
cremera Pri. (n) creamer
crespo Col., Per. (adj) curly (hair)
crespo Venz. (adj) wavy (hair)
criatura Col. (n) infant
criatura Gua. (n) infant
crineja Venz. (n) braid (hair)
cristal trasero Pue.R. (n phr) rear
window
croissant Pri. (n) croissant
cruasant Dom.R. (n) croissant
cruce de peatones Dom.R. (n phr)
crosswalk
cruce peatonal Col. (n phr) crosswalk
cuaderno amarillo Pri. (n phr) pad,
yellow
cuaderno de notas Col. (n phr) pad
(paper)
cuaderno legal Pri. (n phr) pad, legal
cuaderno Pri. (n) notebook
cuaderno Pri. (n) pad (paper)
cuaderno Pri. (n) pad, writing
cuadra Dom.R., Ecu., Pan. (n) city

block
cuadrilátero Chi. (n) ring (boxing)
cuadrilátero de boxeo Col., Pue.R.,
Uru. (n phr) ring (boxing)
cuadro Col. (n) frame (movie)
cuartel Pri. (n) barracks
cuarteto de cuerda Spa. (n phr) string
quartet
cuarteto de cuerdas Pri. (n phr) string
quartet
cuarto Arg., Col., Cub., Dom.R.,
Mex., Pue.R. (n) bedroom
cuarto de baño Bol., Chi., Cos.R.,
Ecu., Spa., Uru., Venz. (n phr)
bathroom
cuarto de correos, sala de correos Pri.
(n phr) mail room
cuarto de estar, sala Pri. (n phr) living
room
cuarto del correo Spa. (n phr) mail
room
cuate ElS., Gua., Hon., Mex. (n)
buddy, pal
cuatro tracciónes Dom.R. (n phr)
four-wheel drive
cubeta Col., Mex., Spa. (n) bucket
cubeta de hielo Pue.R. (n phr) ice
bucket
cubeta Mex., Pue.R. (n) pail
cubículo Col., Dom.R., Gua., Mex.,
Pan., Pue.R., Venz. (n) office
cubicle
cubierta Spa. (n) tread (tire)
cubierto Cos.R., Cub., Gua. (adj)
cloudy
cubiertos Pri. (n) silverware
cubo Pri. (n) bucket
cubo Cub. (n) pail
cucaracha Chi. (n) beetle
cucha Arg. (n) doghouse

cuchara de cocaína Pri. (n phr) cocaine
spoon
cuchara de escurrir Col. (n phr)
draining spoon
cuchara para cocaína Spa. (n phr)
cocaine spoon
cuchara para escurrir Pri. (n phr)
draining spoon
cuchara para la cocaína Col. (n phr)
cocaine spoon
cucharas medidoras Dom.R. (n phr)
measuring spoons
cucharas para medir Pri. (n phr)
measuring spoons
cuchi Bol. (n) pig
cuchilla de afeitar Cub., Spa. (n phr)
razor
cuchilla Pue.R. (n) penknife
cuchilla raspadora Col. (n phr) scraper
cuchillo para manteca Arg. (n phr)
knife, butter
cuchillo para mantequilla Pri. (n phr)
knife, butter
cuclillo Col., Venz. (n) cuckoo
cuco Pri. (n) cuckoo
cucú Mex. (n) cuckoo
cucubano Pue.R. (n) firefly
cuello Chi. (n) neck (guitar)
cuello de pico Pri. (n phr) v-neck
cuello de tortuga Mex., Pue.R. (n phr)
turtleneck
cuello en V Arg., Chi., Col., Gua.,
Mex., Venz. (n phr) v-neck
cuello Jorge Chavez Per. (n phr)
turtleneck
cuello tortuga Dom.R., Pan., Venz.
(n phr) turtleneck
cuello V Dom.R., Pan., Per., Pue.R. (n
phr) v-neck
cuello vuelto Pri. (n phr) turtleneck

cuenco Spa. (n) bowl
cuenta kilómetros Chi. (n phr)
speedometer
cuentakilómetro Cub. (n) speedometer
cuerda Col. (n) chord
cuerdas Pri. (n) snare (of drum)
cuernito Mex. (n) croissant
cuerno francés Col. (n phr) French
horn
cuerno inglés Col. (n phr) English
horn
cuesta Pue.R. (n) hill
cueva Pri. (n) cave
cuidador de niños Venz. (n phr)
babysitter
cuidadora de niños Per. (n phr)
babysitter
cuidar a un bebé/niño/niña Mex. (v
phr) babysit
cuidar a un/a beba/bebe/chico/chica/
nene/nena Arg., Uru. (v phr)
babysit
cuidar niños Chi., Col., Ecu., Per.,
Pue.R., Venz. (v phr) babysit
culebra Pri. (n) snake
culo Col., Spa. (n) butt
culto Col. (adj) polite
cuna Pri. (n) cradle, crib
cuneta Col., Spa. (n) ditch
curioso Dom.R. (n) snoop
currículo Mex. (n) résumé (work
history)
currículum (vitae) Pri. (n) résumé
(work history)
cuté Dom.R. (n) nail polish
cutex Chi. (n) nail polish

D

dado Arg. (adj) outgoing
damasco Arg., Chi., Uru. (n) apricot
danesa Pan. (n) Danish
dar a luz Pri. (v phr) give birth
dar Arg. (v) show (movie)
dar flor Col. (v phr) bloom
dar vuelta a la derecha, izquierda Mex.
(v phr) turn right, left
darse un viaje Dom.R. (v phr) get high
(drugs)
datos Pri. (n) data
de agudos Pri. (n phr) treble (stereo)
de estatura baja Mex. (adj) short
(person)
de horario completo Arg. (adj phr)
full-time (work)
de jornada completa Pri. (adj phr)
full-time (work)
de mal humor Dom.R. (ad phrj)
gloomy (person)
de mal humor Pue.R. (adj phr)
grumpy
de medio tiempo Mex. (adj phr)
part-time (work)
de posición adelantada Col., ElS.,
Gua., Hon. (n phr) offside
de tiempo completo Col., Mex. (adj
phr) full-time (work)
decorado Col. (n) set (movie)
decorador para pasteleros Venz. (n
phr) icing syringe
dedo chiquito Cub. (n phr) pinkie
finger
dedo corazón Col. (n phr) middle
finger
dedo del corazón Pri. (n phr) middle
finger
dedo del medio Cub., Dom.R., Venz.
(n phr) middle finger
dedo gordo Arg. (n phr) thumb
dedo gordo del pie Arg., Cub.,
Dom.R., Spa., Venz. (n phr) big
toe
dedo gordo Pri. (n phr) big toe
dedo medio Mex., Uru. (n phr) middle
finger
dedo meñique Pri. (n phr) pinkie
finger
defensa Mex. (n) bumper
defensa Mex. (n) fender
defensa Pri. (n) back (soccer)
defensor Spa. (n) back (soccer)
dejar las drogas Pri. (v phr) quit using
drugs
deleitable Col. (adj) divino
deletear Arg. (v) delete
delfín Chi., Ecu. (n) porpoise
delicioso Pri. (adj) delicious
delightful Pri. (adj) divino
demora Arg., Col. (n) delay
dentadura Col. (n) teeth
dentífrico, pasta de dientes Pri. (n phr)
toothpaste
departamento Arg., Bol., Chi., Mex.
(n) apartment
departamento de bomberos Mex. (n
phr) fire station
dependencia Pri. (n) addiction
dependiente de colmado Dom.R. (n
phr) grocer
dependiente de supermercado Dom.R.
(n phr) grocer
dependiente de tienda Dom.R. (n phr)
grocer
dependiente Pri. (n) salesperson
deportista Pan. (n) athlete

---

depósito Arg., Col. (n) storage room
depósito de gasolina Spa. (n phr) gas tank
deprimido Venz. (adj) gloomy (person)
depurar Pri. (v) debug (computer)
derecho a la vía Col. (n phr) right of way
derecho de paso Arg., Cub., Pue.R. (n phr) right of way
derecho de vía ElS., Gua., Hon., Pan. (n phr) right of way
desacelerar Col., Cub. (v) decelerate
desarmador Mex., Per. (n) screw driver
desatento Col. (adj) impolite
desayuno Uru. (n) brunch
desayuno-almuerzo Venz. (n) brunch
descapotable Spa. (n) convertible
descarga Cub. (n) jam session
desembarque Chi. (n) arrival
desinfectar Dom.R. (v) debug (computer)
desnatador Mex. (n) skimmer
desnatadora Col. (n) skimmer
desocupado Col. (adj) vacant
desodorante Pri. (n) antiperspirant
despachar Chi. (v) check in (baggage)
despedida de soltera Pri. (n phr) bridal shower
despedir Pri. (v) fire
despensa Chi. (n) storage room
despensa Dom.R. (n) buffet
despensa Pri. (n) pantry
desplantador Pri. (n) trowel
desplazar Pri. (v) scroll (computer)
destacamento policial Dom.R. (n phr) police station
destapador Chi. (n) corkscrew
destapador Pri. (n) bottle opener
destituir Col. (v) fire
destornillador Pri. (n) screwdriver

desunirse Col. (v) divorce
desvestirse Pri. (v) undress
desviación Mex. (n) detour
desvío Pri. (n) detour
detective Chi., Cub., Mex., Pan., Venz. (n) police detective
detective de la policía ElS., Gua., Hon. (n phr) police detective
detective policíaco Col. (n phr) police detective
detective policial Dom.R. (n phr) police detective
día de clase Pue.R. (n phr) school day
día de clases Dom.R., Per. (n phr) school day
día de colegio Col. (n phr) school day
día de entre semana (n phr) weekday
día de escuela Mex., Venz. (n phr) school day
día de fiesta Mex. (n phr) holiday
día de semana Arg., Col., Dom.R., Pue.R., Venz. (n phr) weekday
día de trabajo Col., Cub., Per., Pue.R. (n phr) work day
día de vacaciones Mex. (n phr) holiday
día entre semana Cub., Gua., Spa. (n phr) weekday
día feriado Pri. (n phr) holiday
día festivo Col., Spa. (n phr) holiday
día hábil (n phr) work day
día laborable Col., Dom.R., Spa. (n phr) work day
día lectivo Pri. (n phr) school day
días de enfermedad Cub. (n phr) sick leave
dibujo animado Pri. (n phr) cartoon
dibujo de llanta Mex. (n phr) tread (tire)
dibujos animados Col., Spa. (n phr) cartoon

---

dicharachero Col. (adj) talkative
dientes Pri. (n) teeth
difícil Pri. (adj) difficult
dificultoso Col. (adj) difficult
¿Dígame? Pri. (int) Hello? (answering telephone)
director ejecutivo Dom.R. (n phr) chief executive officer (CEO)
director general Cos.R., Mex. (n phr) chief executive officer (CEO)
director/a de la cárcel (n phr) warden (prison)
dirigible Col., Spa. (n) blimp
dirigible no rígido Pri. (n phr) blimp
dirigir Pri. (v) conduct (music)
dirreccional Mex. (n) turning light
disco Col. (n) record album
disco compacto Pri. (n phr) compact disk
disco duro Pri. (n phr) hard drive
disminuir la velocidad Pri. (v phr) decelerate
dispensador de cinta adhesiva Venz. (n phr) tape dispenser
dispensador de cinta pegante Col. (n phr) tape dispenser
dispensador de durex Mex. (n phr) tape dispenser
distribuir Pue.R. (v) deal (drugs)
distrito residencial Pri. (n phr) uptown
divertido, gracioso Pri. (adj) funny
divino Arg. (adj) cute
división Dom.R. (n) office divider
divisor Bol., Col., Ecu. (n) office divider
divorciado Pri. (adj) divorced
divorciarse Pri. (v) divorce
dobladillo Cub. (n) cuff (pants)
doblado Dom.R. (n) cuff (pants)
doblaje Dom.R., Pue.R. (n) stunt

doblar a la derecha, izquierda Pri. (v phr) turn right, left
doblar Pri. (v) lip synch
doble barbilla Dom.R. (n phr) double chin
doble Col. (n) double feature (movies)
doble Dom.R., Mex., Pue.R., Spa. (n) stuntman
doble función Pri. (n phr) double feature (movies)
doble pera Chi. (n phr) double chin
doble presentación Dom.R. (n phr) double feature (movies)
doblecleta Pue.R. (n) bike, tandem
doblez Col., Spa. (n) cuff (pants)
doblez Pan. (n) crease (pants)
doctor Arg., Col., Chi. (n) doctor
doliente Col. (n) patient
dona Col., ElS., Gua., Hon., Mex., Pan., Pue.R. (n) doughnut
Doña Cos.R., Pan. (n) Ma'am, Madam
dónut Pri. (n) doughnut
dorarse al sol Col. (v phr) tan
dormitorio Pri. (n) bedroom
dorso Mex. (n) backstroke (swimming)
drive Dom. R., Pue.R. (n) drive (computer)
drive-in Col., Pue.R. (n) drive-in
drogadicción Pri. (n) drug addiction
drogadicción Pri. (n) drug habit
drogadicto Pri. (n) drug addict
drogarse Pri. (v) use drugs
drogas blandas Pri. (n phr) soft drugs
drogas duras Pri. (n phr) hard drugs
drogas fuertes Col. (n phr) hard drugs
drogas más suaves Col. (n phr) soft drugs
drogas suaves Mex. (n phr) soft drugs
droguería Col. (n) drug store

ABBREVIATIONS: Arg.=Argentina Bol.=Bolivia Chi.=Chile Col.=Colombia Cos.R.=Costa Rica Cub.=Cuba Dom.R.=Dominican Republic Ecu.=Ecuador ElS.=El Salvador Gua.=Guatemala Hon.=Honduras Mex.=Mexico Pan.=Panama Per.=Peru Pri.=Primary Term Pue.R.=Puerto Rico Spa.=Spain Uru.=Uruguay Venz.=Venezuela

dueto Col. (n) duo
dulce Pan. (n) cake
dulcito relleno Dom.R. (n phr) tart
dúo Pri. (n) duo
dúplex horizontal Mex. (n phr)
   townhouse
dúplex Pri. (n) duplex
durazno pelado Chi. (n phr) nectarine
durazno Pri. (n) peach
durex Mex. (n) tape
duro Dom.R. (adj) curly (hair)

> The word *cancha*, meaning "field" in some Spanish-speaking countries, comes from the identical Quechuan term meaning "an enclosure for cattle."

E

echar Arg., Col. (v) fire
echar dedo Col. (v phr) hitchhike
ecler Pan. (n) cream puff
edificación Col. (n) building
edificio Chi., Col. (n) apartment
  building
edificio de apartamentos Pri. (n phr)
  apartment building
edificio de departamentos Arg., Bol.,
  Mex. (n phr) apartment building
edificio de los tribunales Col. (n phr)
  courthouse
edificio de pisos Spa. (n phr)
  apartment building
edificio Pri. (n) building
editor Col., Pue.R., Spa., Venz. (n)
  editor
efectos de sonido Arg., Col., Mex.,
  Pan., Pue.R., Spa., Venz. (n phr)
  sound effects
efectos sonoros Pri. (n phr) sound
  effects
ejecutiva Col. (n) businesswoman
ejecutivo Col. (n) businessman
ejotes ElS., Gua., Hon., Mex. (n)
  beans, green
el que toca el tambor Col. (n phr)
  drummer
elástico Bol., Chi. (n) rubber band
elenco Chi., Pan.. Pue.R. (n) cast
  (show)
elevador Cub., Mex., Pan., Pue.R. (n)
  elevator
elevarse Pue.R. (v) get high (drugs)
elote Mex. (n) corn (on the cob)
e-mail Arg., Dom.R., Mex., Pue.R.,

Spa. (n) e-mail
embarazada Pri. (adj) pregnant
embarcación Col. (n) ship
embarcar Spa., Venz. (v) board
embarcarse Pri. (v) board
embarque Chi. (n) departure
embellecedor Uru. (n) hubcap
emborrachar Pri. (v) become
  intoxicated
embotellamiento Arg., Per., Uru. (n)
  traffic jam
embriagarse Chi. (v) become
  intoxicated
embustero Col. (n) cheater
embustero Col. (n) liar
emisión Cub. (n) broadcast
emisión televisiva Pri. (n phr)
  broadcast
emitir Pri. (v) broadcast
emocionante Col. (adj) exciting
empalme Col. (n) cloverleaf junction
empleado/a Col. (n) salesperson
empleado/a temporal Col., Cos.R.,
  Gua., Venz. (n phr) temporary
  worker
empresa Col. (n) factory
empresaria Arg., Chi., Cos.R. (n)
  businesswoman
empresario Arg., Chi. (n) businessman
en estado Venz. (adj phr) pregnant
enagüa Chi. (n) petticoat
enagüa Chi., Pue.R. (n) slip
enaguas Mex., Venz. (n) petticoat
enamorada Ecu., Per. (n) girlfriend
enamorado Ecu., Per. (n) boyfriend
enamorado/a Pri. (n) sweetheart
encantador Col. (adj) divino
encapotado Col. (adj) cloudy
encarcelado Col. (n) inmate
encarcelado Col. (n) prisoner

encendedor Pri. (n) lighter
encender Bol., Chi., Cub., Ecu., Gua.,
Spa., Uru. (v) turn on (television)
encender Chi., Dom.R. (v) start (car)
encinta Col., Pan., Per. (adj) pregnant
encriptar Col., Mex., Spa. (v) encrypt
(computer)
encuestado/a Arg., Cos.R., Cub., Ecu.,
ElS., Gua., Hon., Per., Pue.R. (n)
interviewee
encuestador/a Arg., Cos.R., Cub.,
Ecu., ElS., Gua., Hon., Per.,
Pue.R. (n) interviewer
encurtido Venz. (n) pickle
endibia Arg., Col., Spa. (n) endive
endivia Col. (n) endive
enfermo/a Arg., Bol., Cub., Cos.R.,
Ecu., Gua., Uru. (n) patient
enfogono Pue.R. (adj) angry
enfurecido Ecu. (adj) angry
engalanarse Pue.R. (v) dress up
engrampador Per. (n) stapler
engrapadora Pri. (n) stapler
engrasado Mex. (n) lubrication
engrase Pri. (n) lubrication
engreído Per. (adj) spoiled (child)
enojado Pri. (adj) angry
¿En qué andas/an? Col. (int phr)
What's up?
enredadera Bol., Col., Cub., Mex.,
Pue.R. (n) climbing plant
enrulado Arg., Pan. (adj) curly (hair)
ensaladera Pri. (n) bowl, salad
ensayo Chi. (n) jam session
entero Uru. (n) overalls
entierro Pri. (n) burial
entonar Venz. (v) tune up
entrada Arg., Dom.R., Ecu., Uru. (n)
appetizer
entrada Col. (n) main course

entrada gratis Chi., Cub., Dom.R.,
ElS., Gua., Hon., Pan., Pue.R.
(n phr) free admission
entrada gratuita Spa. (n phr) free
admission
entrada lateral Col. (n phr) side
entrance
entrada libre Pri. (n phr) free
admission
entrada Pri. (n) entrance fee
entrar en onda Col. (v phr) get high
(drugs)
entremés Venz. (n) appetizer
entremetido Col., Cub., Dom.R., Gua.
(n) snoop
entrenador Arg., Bol., Chi., Cub. (n)
instructor (sports)
entrenador de deportes Venz. (n phr)
instructor (sports)
entrenar Col., Cub., Dom.R., Ecu.,
Pan., Venz. (v) train (for job)
entrevistado/a Pri. (n) interviewee
entrevistador/a Pri. (n) interviewer
entronque en forma de trébol Col. (n
phr) cloverleaf junction
eperlano Pri. (n) smelt
equipaje Pri. (n) baggage
equipo artístico Pri. (n phr) cast
(show)
equipo de música para CD Arg. (n
phr) compact disk player
equitación Pri. (n) horseback riding
equivocado (adj) wrong
erróneo Col. (adj) wrong
escaladora Pri. (n) stair machine
escalera automática Col. (n phr)
escalator
escalera eléctrica Dom.R., Mex. (n
phr) escalator
escalera mecánica Pri. (n phr)

ABBREVIATIONS: Arg.=Argentina Bol.=Bolivia Chi.=Chile Col.=Colombia
Cos.R.=Costa Rica Cub.=Cuba Dom.R.=Dominican Republic Ecu.=Ecuador ElS.=El
Salvador Gua.=Guatemala Hon.=Honduras Mex.=Mexico Pan.=Panama Per.=Peru
Pri.=Primary Term Pue.R.=Puerto Rico Spa.=Spain Uru.=Uruguay Venz.=Venezuela

escalator
escalera Mex. (n) stair machine
escalope ElS., Gua., Hon. ElS., Gua.,
Hon. (n) scallop
escáner Chi., Cub., Mex., Pan., Spa.
(n) scanner, optical
escaparate Cos.R., Cub., Per., Spa. (n)
shop window
escape Mex. (n) exhaust pipe
escarabajo Pri. (n) beetle
escardador Uru. (n) reamer
escariador Pri. (n) reamer
escariadora Mex. (n) reamer
escarola Pri. (n) endive
escenario Pri. (n) set (movie)
escorpión Arg., Chi., Col., Cos.R.,
Pan., Spa., Uru., Venz. (n)
scorpion
escote en V Uru. (n phr) v-neck
escuela Pri. (n) school
escurridor de verduras Cos.R.,
Dom.R., Mex., Per., Spa., Uru.
(n phr) colander
esfero Col. (n) pen, ball-point
esmalte de uñas Pri. (n phr) nail polish
espaldal Pue.R. (n) cabecera
espaldar Ecu. (n) cabecera
espantoso Arg., Chi., Col. (adj) awful
espárrago Mex. (n) stud
espátula Mex. (n) painter's knife
espátula Pan. (n) turner
espátula Pue.R. (n) scraper
especialista en acrobacias Venz. (n
phr) stuntman
especialista Spa. (n) stuntman
espejo retrovisor Pri. (n phr) rear-view
mirror
espejo trasero Uru. (n phr) rear-view
mirror
espejuelos bifocales Cub., Pue.R. (n

phr) bifocals
espejuelos Cub., Pue.R. (n) eye glasses
espejuelos Cub., Venz. (n) spectacles
esperando Col. (adj) pregnant
espesura Col. (n) foliage
espiga Mex. (n) dowel
espiga Mex. (n) stud
espina dorsal Ecu., Gua. (n phr) spine
espinaso Ecu. (n) spine
espinazo Col. (n) spine
espinilla Chi., Col., Cos.R., Dom.R.,
Spa., Venz. (n) pimple
espinilla Pri. (n) shin
esplanada Mex. (n) plain (topography)
espray de pelo Cub. (n phr)
hairspray
esprín Pan. (n) box spring
esprintar Pri. (v) sprint
espuma para el pelo ElS., Gua., Hon.,
Spa. (n phr) hair mousse
espumadera Pri. (n) skimmer
espumadera Spa. (n) draining spoon
esqueleto Pri. (n) skeleton
esquí acuático (n phr) water skiing
esquí náutico Cos.R., Ecu., ElS., Gua.,
Hon., Per., Venz. (n phr) water
skiing
estación de bomberos Pri. (n phr) fire
station
estación de policía Col., Cub., Gua.,
Pan., Pue.R. (n phr) police station
estacionamiento Pri. (n) parking lot
estacionar Pri. (v) park
estadio Pri. (n) stadium
estafador Col. (n) cheater
estanque Col., ElS., Gua., Hon., Mex.,
Venz. (n) pond
estante Pan. (n) closet (clothes)
**estar bajo la influencia del alcohol o
de las drogas** Spa. (v phr) become

intoxicated

estar de novio Arg. (v phr) date

estar desorientado por desfase de horarios Dom.R. (v phr) jet-lag, to have

estarter Pue.R. (n) starter

estilista Mex., Pan. (n) hairdresser

estilo braza Pri. (n phr) breaststroke (swimming)

estilo crol Gua., Spa. (n phr) crawl (swimming)

estilo espalda Pri. (n phr) backstroke (swimming)

estilo libre Chi. (n phr) crawl (swimming)

estilo pecho Chi., Col., Cub., Pue.R., Venz. (n phr) breaststroke (swimming)

estilográfica Uru. (n) pen, fountain

estrella Cub., Dom.R., Pan. (n) ferris wheel

estrellar Col. (v) crash (traffic)

estruendoso Col. (adj) resonant

estuche de maquillaje Pri. (n phr) makeup kit

estudio de abogados Arg. (n phr) lawyer's office

estudio juridico Ecu. (n phr) lawyer's office

estudios Chi. (n) set (movie)

estufa Arg. (n) fireplace

estufa Pri. (n) stove

estupendo Col. (adj) amazing

etiqueta adhesiva Pri. (n phr) label, adhesive

etiqueta Mex. (n) dog tag

etiqueta Pri. (n) label

excitante Pue.R. (adj) emocionante

exciting Pri. (adj) emocionante

exequias Col. (n) burial

éxito Col., Cos.R. (n) hit (song)

exosto Col. (n) exhaust pipe

explorador óptico Pri. (n phr) scanner, optical

explorar el Internet Venz. (v phr) surf the net

exquisito Col. (adj) divino

exquisito Per. (adj) delicious

extra Arg. (n) stuntman

extrovertido Pri. (adj) outgoing

Shorts is used in Mexico with the same meaning and pronunciation as in English. *Pants* retains its original pronuciation in Mexican Spanish but refers only to sweatpants.

F

fábrica Pri. (n) factory
factoría Dom.R., Pue.R. (n) factory
faja Cos.R. (n) belt
falda Bol. (n) dress (woman's)
falda corta Col., Pue.R. (n) miniskirt
falda Pri. (n) skirt
familiar Pri. (n) family member
farmaceuta Col., Venz. (n) pharmacist
farmacéutico Pri. (n) pharmacist
farmacia Pri. (n) drug store
faro Arg. (n) reflector (bicycle)
faro Pri. (n) spoke (bicycle wheel)
farol Pri. (n) street lamp
farola Spa. (n) street lamp
faroles delanteros Col. (n phr)
    headlights
faros de emergencia Ecu. (n phr)
    emergency lights
faros intensos Ecu. (n phr) brights
    (headlights)
faros Pri. (n) headlights
fastidioso Mex., Venz. (n) pest (person)
fender Pue.R. (n) fender
fenomenal Col. (adj) amazing
feria Mex., Pue.R. (n) fairground
feriado Arg. (n) holiday
ferry Col., Cos.R., Dom.R., Spa.,
    Venz. (n) ferry
fichero giratorio Pri. (n phr) rolodex
film Venz. (n) film
filmación Venz. (n) shooting (movie)
filmar Venz. (v) shoot (movie)
filme Arg., Cos.R., Ecu., Uru., Pan.
    (n) film
filo Dom.R., Pue.R. (n) crease (pants)
fisgón Pri. (n) snoop

flat Pan. (n) flat tire
flautín Col., Mex., Spa. (n) piccolo
fleco Mex. (n) bangs (hair)
flequillo Pri. (n) bangs (hair)
flojo Bol., Chi., Mex., Venz. (adj) lazy
florecer Pri. (v) bloom
florería Cub. (n) florist's shop
florista Pri. (n) florist's shop
floristería Col., Dom.R., Pan., Pue.R.,
    Venz. (n) florist's shop
foca marina Dom.R. (n phr) walrus
focos Arg., Cub. (n) headlights
folder de argollas Col. (n phr) three-
    ring binder
folder Dom.R., Mex., Pan., Pue.R. (n)
    folder
follaje Pri. (n) foliage
fondo Mex., Venz. (n) slip
fondo Venz. (n) petticoat
fontanero Spa. (n) plumber
formidable Col. (adj) tremendous
fosforera Cub. (n) lighter
fotocopiadora Spa. (n) copier
foyer Pri. (n) lobby
frac Pri. (n) tailcoat
fraccionamiento Mex. (n) suburb
frazada Arg., Bol., Col., Cub., Uru. (n)
    blanket
freezer Arg., Pue.R. (n) freezer
frejoles Ecu. (n) beans
fresa Pri. (n) strawberry
fresadora Spa. (n) reamer
frigorífoco Spa. (n) refrigerator
frijol nacido Pan. (n phr) bean sprouts
frijoles Col., Cub., Gua., Hon., Mex.,
    Pan. (n) beans
frijoles colorados Cub. (n phr) beans,
    kidney
frijoles de media luna Pri. (n phr)
    beans, lima

ABBREVIATIONS: Arg.=Argentina Bol.=Bolivia Chi.=Chile Col.=Colombia
Cos.R.=Costa Rica Cub.=Cuba Dom.R.=Dominican Republic Ecu.=Ecuador ElS.=El
Salvador Gua.=Guatemala Hon.=Honduras Mex.=Mexico Pan.=Panama Per.=Peru
Pri.=Primary Term Pue.R.=Puerto Rico Spa.=Spain Uru.=Uruguay Venz.=Venezuela

frijoles de soja Pri. (n phr) soybeans
frijoles negros Col., Cub., ElS., Gua.,
Hon., Mex., Pan. (n phr) beans,
black
frijoles Pri. (n) beans, black
frisa Pue.R. (n) blanket
frondosidad Col. (n) foliage
fruta bomba Cub. (n phr) papaya
frutal Arg. (n) fruit tree
frutería Pue.R. (n) fruit stand
frutilla Arg. (n) strawberry
fuente de agua (n phr) water fountain
fuente de servir Pri. (n phr) platter
fuera de juego Pri. (n phr) offside
fuera de posición Pue.R. (n phr)
offside
fuerte Chi. (adj) loud (noise)
fulano/a Cos.R., Mex., Pan. (n) guy
fulo Pan. (adj) blond (hair)
fulo/a Pan. (n) blond (person)
función doble Uru. (n phr) double
feature (movies)
funda Pri. (n) pillowcase
funeral Dom.R. (n) wake
funeraria Pri. (n) funeral home
funicular Pri. (n) funicular
furgón Col., Uru. (n) van
furgoneta Spa., Venz. (n) van
furioso Dom.R. (adj) angry
fuslero Bol., Chi. (n) rolling pin
fútbol Pri. (n) soccer

In many Spanish-speaking countries, the maple tree is known as *el árbol de arce.* In Mexico, people are more familiar with *el árbol de maple,* pronouncing *maple* as it would be read in Spanish.

G

gabán Pue.R. (n) jacket (men's)
gabardina Col., Spa. (n) raincoat
gabardina Mex. (n) trench coat
gabete Pue.R. (n) shoelace
gabinete Pue.R. (n) pantry
gafas bifocales Spa. (n phr) bifocals
gafas Col. (n) spectacles
gafas Col., Spa. (n) eyeglasses
gafas de buceo Spa. (n phr) goggles,
  swimming
gafas de esquí Spa. (n phr) goggles, ski
gafas de protección Mex. (n phr)
  glasses, safety
gafas de seguridad Spa. (n phr) glasses,
  safety
gafas trifocales Spa. (n phr) trifocals
gáfiter [from "gas fitter"] Chi. (n)
  plumber
galán Col. (n) actor
galera Arg. (n) hat, top
galería Dom.R. (n) porch
galleta Pri. (n) cookie
galleta Pri. (n) cracker
galleta de dulce Per. (n phr) cookie
galleta de soda Venz. (n phr) cracker
galleta dulce ElS., Gua., Hon. (n phr)
  cookie
galletica Dom.R. (n) cracker
galletica Cub. (n) cookie
galletita Arg. (n) biscuit
galletita Arg. (n) cracker
galletita Arg., Cos.R., Pue.R., Uru. (n)
  cookie
gallina Pan. (n) chicken
gallina sorda ElS., Gua., Hon. (n phr)
  woodcock

gallineta Col., ElS., Gua., Hon. (n)
  woodcock
gallusa Pan. (n) bangs (hair)
galpón Chi. (n) shed
gamba Pri. (n) prawn
gamba Spa. (n) shrimp
ganadero Chi. (n) farmer
ganchito Arg. (n) staple
ganchito Arg., Uru. (n) paperclip
ganchito de pelo Venz. (n phr) barrette
gancho para el pelo Dom.R., Pan.,
  Per., Spa. (n phr) barrette
ganga Col. (adj) cheap
garaje para botes Col. (n phr)
  boathouse
garaje Pri. (n) garage (repairs)
garaje Pri. (n) garage (storage)
garañón Chi., Gua. (n) stallion
garlador Col. (adj) talkative
garrafa Col., Spa. (n) decanter
garúa Per. (n) drizzle
garzón Chi. (n) waiter
gasfitero Ecu. (n) plumber
gasolina Pri. (n) gasolina (vehicle)
gata Bol., Chi., Per. (n) jack (car)
gato Cos.R. (adj) green (eyes)
gato Pri. (n) jack (car)
gaveta Pri. (n) drawer
gavetero Venz. (n) dresser
gears Pri. (n) velocidades
gel fijador Ecu. (n phr) hair gel
gel para el pelo Pri. (n phr) hair gel
gelatina para el pelo Dom.R., ElS.,
  Gua., Hon. (n phr) hair gel
gemelos de teatro Pri. (n phr) glasses,
  opera
gemelos Pri. (n) cufflinks
gerente Col. (n) office manager
gerente de oficina Cub., Mex.,
  Pue.R., Venz. (n phr) office

ABBREVIATIONS: Arg.=Argentina Bol.=Bolivia Chi.=Chile Col.=Colombia
Cos.R.=Costa Rica Cub.=Cuba Dom.R.=Dominican Republic Ecu.=Ecuador ElS.=El
Salvador Gua.=Guatemala Hon.=Honduras Mex.=Mexico Pan.=Panama Per.=Peru
Pri.=Primary Term Pue.R.=Puerto Rico Spa.=Spain Uru.=Uruguay Venz.=Venezuela

manager
gerente deportivo Venz. (n phr)
manager (sports)
gerente ejecutivo Chi. (n phr) chief
executive officer (CEO)
gerente general Col., Cos.R. (n phr)
chief executive officer (CEO)
germinados de soja Pri. (n phr) bean
sprouts
gillette Arg., Chi. (n) razor
globo aerostático Pri. (n phr) hot air
balloon
globo Chi., Col. (n) hot air balloon
globo de aire caliente Venz. (n phr)
hot air balloon
gofre (n) waffle
goggles Pue.R. (n) goggles, swimming
gogles Mex. (n) goggles, swimming
gogles para esquiar Mex. (n phr)
goggles, ski
goleador Pan. (n) goalie
golero Uru. (n) goalie
golpe Venz. (n) bruise
goma Arg., Cub., Dom.R., Pue.R. (n)
tire (car)
goma Arg., Dom.R., Pue.R. (n) tire
(bicycle)
goma de auxilio Arg. (n phr) spare tire
goma de repuesta Pue.R. (n phr) spare
tire
goma de repuesto Cub., Dom.R. (n
phr) spare tire
goma elástica Spa., Uru. (n phr) rubber
band
goma pinchada Arg., Dom.R. (n phr)
flat tire
goma ponchada Cub. (n phr) flat tire
goma vacía Pue.R. (n phr) flat tire
gomina para el pelo Spa. (n phr) hair
gel

gomita Arg., Dom.R., Pue.R. (n)
rubber band
gorra Pri. (n) cap
grabadora de vídeo Col. (n phr)
videocassette recorder (VCR)
grabar Arg. (v) store (computer data)
gracioso Dom.R., Ecu., Pan. (adj) cute
grama Dom.R., ElS., Gua., Hon.,
Pue.R., Venz. (n) lawn
grampa Per. (n) staple
granada Pri. (n) pomegranate
granadilla Cos.R. (n) pomegranate
grandes almacenes Pri. (n phr)
department store
granjero Per. (n) farmer
grano Pri. (n) pimple
grapa Col. (n) clamp
grapa Col. (n) paperclip
grapa Pri. (n) staple
grapadora Pue.R., Spa. (n) stapler
grapas de cocaína Mex. (n phr) cocaine
spoon
grass Pri. (n) hierba
graves Pri. (n) bass (stereo)
greca Dom.R. (n) coffee maker
grosella Col., Mex. (n) black currant
grosella Pue.R. (n) gooseberry
grosella silvestre Pri. (n phr)
gooseberry
grosero Col. (adj) impolite
grufión Col. (adj) grumpy
guacamaya ElS., Gua., Hon., Mex. (n)
macaw
guacamayo Pri. (n) macaw
guachinango Mex. (n) snapper
guadaña Pri. (n) scythe
guagua Chi. (n) baby
guagua Cub., Dom.R., Pue.R. (n) bus
guagüero Cub. (n) bus driver
guagüita Pue.R. (n) station wagon

guajolote Mex. (n) turkey
guallo Dom.R. (n) grater
guanajo Cub. (n) turkey
guandules Dom.R. (n) beans, broad
guapa Pri. (adj) pretty
guapo Cub. (adj) cute
guapo Pri. (adj) handsome
guapo Dom.R. (adj) brave
guarda Col. (n) warden (prison)
guardabarro Col., Spa. (n) fender
guardafango Col., Cub., Ecu., ElS.,
    Gua., Hon., Venz. (n) fender
guardameta Cub. (n) goalie
guardapelo Cub. (n) locket
guardapolvo Cub. (n) overalls
guardar Arg., Mex., Pan. (v) store
    (computer data)
guardarropa Chi. (n) closet (general)
guarda-vallas Col. (n) goalie
guarder Venz. (v) store (computer data)
guardería Arg., Dom.R. (n) daycare
    center
guardería infantil Pri. (n phr)
    daycare center
guardián Col., Pan., Venz. (n) guardian
guardián de la cárcel Venz. (n phr)
    warden (prison)
guata Chi. (n) abdomen
guata Chi. (n) belly
guayo Pue.R. (n) grater
güero Mex. (adj) blond (hair)
güero/a Mex. (n) blond (person)
guía Dom.R., Pue.R. (n) steering wheel
guía Pri. (n) handlebars (bicycle)
guiar Pue.R. (v) drive (car)
guillo Dom.R. (n) bracelet
guiñador Bol. (n) blinker (light)
guindilla Spa. (n) pepper, hot
guineo Col., Dom.R., Ecu., Pan.,
    Pue.R. (n) banana

guiño Arg. (n) blinker (light)
guiño Arg. (n) turning light
guión cinematográfico Pri. (n phr)
    screenplay
guisantes Pue.R., Spa. (n) peas, green
guitarra oriental Venz. (n phr) sitar
guitarrear Pri. (v) strum
guitarreo Pri. (n) strumming

"Irrational as life itself,
Spanish is not cast in stone.
It is a constant process of
dynamic expressions of
people from town and
country."
—Carolina Valencia

ABBREVIATIONS: Arg.=Argentina Bol.=Bolivia Chi.=Chile Col.=Colombia
Cos.R.=Costa Rica Cub.=Cuba Dom.R.=Dominican Republic Ecu.=Ecuador ElS.=El
Salvador Gua.=Guatemala Hon.=Honduras Mex.=Mexico Pan.=Panama Per.=Peru
Pri.=Primary Term Pue.R.=Puerto Rico Spa.=Spain Uru.=Uruguay Venz.=Venezuela

H

habas limas Cub. (n phr) beans, lima
habas Pri. (n) beans, broad
habas Spa. (n) beans, lima
habichuelas de soya Pue.R. (n phr)
  bean sprouts
habichuelas Dom.R., Pue. R. (n) beans
habichuelas negras Pue.R. (n phr)
  beans, black
habichuelas Pri. (n) beans, green
habichuelas Pri. (n) beans, kidney
habichuelas rojas Dom.R. (n phr)
  beans, kidney
habichuelas verdes Pue.R. (n phr)
  beans, green
habitación Pan. (n) bedroom
hábito Col. (n) addiction
hábito Col. (n) habit (drugs)
hablador Mex. (n) tattler
hablador, locuaz Pri. (adj) talkative
hacer autostop Pri. (v phr) hitchhike
hacer clic Pri. (v phr) click (computer)
hacer de niñero/a Pri. (v phr) babysit
hacer dedo Arg., Chi. (v phr) hitchhike
hacer mímica Dom.R. (v phr) lip
  synch
hacer pool Arg. (v phr) carpool
hacer un cambio Arg. (v phr) shift gear
hacer un transbordo de trenes Venz.
  (v phr) change (train)
hacer una conexión Arg. (v phr)
  change (train)
hacha Pri. (n) hatchet
hachuela Col. (n) hatchet
hairy Pri. (adj) velloso
halcón Pri. (n) hawk
hall de entrada Arg., Chi. (n phr)
  lobby
¿Haló? Pan., Pue.R. (int) Hello?
  (answering telephone)
hamaca Pri. (n) hammock
hamaca Spa. (n) chair, lounging
handbol Pri. (n) handball
haragán Col., Dom.R., Uru. (adj) lazy
hard drive Pue.R. (n phr) hard drive
harto Col. (adj) boring
¡Hasta la vista! Pue.R. (int phr) See
  you later!
¡Hasta luego! Col. (int phr) Bye!
¡Hasta luego! Col. (int phr) Goodbye!
¡Hasta luego! Pri. (int phr) See you
  later!
¡Hasta mañana! Ecu. (int phr) Good
  night!
¡Hasta pronto! Col. (int phr)
  Goodbye!
¡Hasta pronto! Col. (int phr) See you
  later!
headboard Pri. (n) cabecera
hebilla Arg., Bol., Col., Cub., Pue.R.
  (n) barrette
hechado a perder Mex. (adj phr)
  rotten (food)
heladera Arg. (n) refrigerator
heladería Pri. (n) ice cream parlor
heladero Pri. (n) ice cream truck
hematoma Dom.R. (n) bruise
hendidura Pri. (n) cleft (chin)
herbolario Uru. (n) herbalist's shop
hibisco Pri. (n) hibiscus
hidroala Pri. (n) hydrofoil boat
hidroavión Chi. (n) hydrofoil boat
hidrofoil Mex. (n) hydrofoil boat
hielera Dom.R., Ecu., Gua., Mex.,
  Venz. (n) ice bucket
hierba Col. (n) lawn
hierba silvestre Mex. (n phr) weed

himno Bol., Col., Dom.R., Mex., Pue.R., Spa., Venz. (n) hymn
hit Cos.R., Cub., Dom.R. (n) hit (song)
hogar Arg. (n) fireplace
hogar de ancianos Pri. (n phr) retirement home
hoja Col. (n) table leaf
hoja de vida Col. (n phr) résumé (work history)
hojaldre Pri. (n) puff pastry
hojilla de afeitar Venz. (n phr) razor
¿Hola? Arg., Bol., Uru. (int) Hello? (answering telephone)
holgazán Mex. (adj) lazy
hombre de negocios Pri. (n phr) businessman
hombre profesional Pan. (n phr) businessman
hombre rana Chi. (n) diver
hombrillo Venz. (n) road shoulder
hongo Pri. (n) mushroom
honorarios Col. (n) salary
hora de entrada o salida a los trabajos Per. (n phr) rush hour
hora de tráfico Cub., Mex. (n phr) rush hour
hora del tapón Pue.R. (n phr) rush hour
hora pico Pri. (n phr) rush hour
hora punta Spa. (n phr) rush hour
horario Pri. (n) timetable
horas de oficina Pri. (n phr) office hours
horas de trabajo Cub. (n phr) office hours
hornada Pri. (n) batch
horneada Chi. (n) batch
hornear Pri. (v) bake
horrible Pri. (adj) awful

horripilante Col. (adj) terrifying
hortaliza Pue.R. (n) orchard
hospital Pri. (n) hospital
hotcake Mex. (n) pancake
hoyito Chi., Dom.R., Mex. (n) dimple
hoyito Dom.R. (n) cleft (chin)
hoyo Bol. (n) dimple
hoyo Chi., Dom.R. (n) pothole
hoyo de la nariz Dom.R. (n phr) nostril
hoyo Dom.R. (n) bump (road)
hoyo en uno Pri. (n phr) hole in one
hoyuelo Pri. (n) dimple
hoz Pri. (n) sickle
huachinango Mex. (n) snapper
huaraches de plástico Mex. (n phr) rubbers (shoes)
hueco Col., Cos.R., Ecu., Pan. (n) pothole
huella del caucho Venz. (n phr) tread (tire)
huerta Arg., Spa. (n) vegetable garden
huerto Pri. (n) orchard
huerto Pri. (n) vegetable garden
huincha Chi. (n) tape measure
hule ElS., Gua., Hon. (n) rubber band
huracán Pri. (n) hurricane

I J K

iceberg Pri. (n) iceberg
icon Pue.R. (n) icon (computer)
icono Pri. (n) icon (computer)
imagen Pri. (n) frame (movie)
impermeable Col., Spa. (n) trench coat
impermeable Pri. (n) raincoat
impolite Pri. (adj) descortés, mal educado
imponente Pri. (adj) tremendous
imprenta Pri. (n) print shop
impresionante Col. (adj) emocionante
impresora Pri. (n) printer (computer)
impressive Pri. (adj) impresionante
incentivo Pri. (n) fringe benefit
incómodo Col. (adj) bothersome
incorrecto Pue.R., Spa. (adj) wrong
increíble Arg., Chi., Dom.R. (adj) amazing
index card Pri. (n phr) ficha
indicador de medir el aceite Venz. (n phr) dipstick
indicador del nivel de aceite Pri. (n phr) dipstick
industria Col. (n) factory
infante Col. (n) infant
inflarse Col. (v) rise (bread)
información Col. (n) data
información de interés Uru. (n phr) infomercial
informativo breve Col. (n phr) news brief
infracción Mex. (n) ticket, traffic
infracción por exceso de velocidad Mex. (n phr) ticket, speeding
inhalar Arg., Col., Mex., Pue.R. (v) inhale (drugs)

inmobiliario Arg. (n) realtor
inoportuno Col. (adj) bothersome
insecto Col., Dom.R., Per., Pue.R. (n) bug
insoportable Chi. (n) pest (person)
instructor de deportes Pri. (n phr) instructor (sports)
instructor deportivo Col. (n phr) instructor (sports)
instrumentos de metal Spa. (n phr) bronze section
instrumentos metálicos de viento Col. (n phr) bronze section
intendencia Uru. (n) city hall
intendente Uru. (n) mayor
interiores bikini Venz. (n) bikini briefs
interiores Venz. (n) briefs
intermitente Cub., Spa. (n) turning light
intermitente, luz intermitente Pri. (n) blinker (light)
intérprete Col., Mex. (n) performer
interventor Venz. (n) comptroller
intruso Chi. (n) snoop
inundar Pue.R. (v) stall (car)
invernadero Mex. (n) nursery (plants)
investigador Spa. (n) police detective
ir a caballo Cub. (v phr) ride horseback
ir juntos en un carro Venz. (v phr) carpool
iris Venz. (n) iris
isla Arg., Col., Venz. (n) traffic island
isla de tráfico Col. (n phr) median
isla Venz. (n) median
isleta Pri. (n) traffic island
itinerario Col. (n) timetable
jaca Pri. (n) pony
jaiba Chi. (n) crab
jaiba Col., Dom.R. (n) crayfish
jalea Mex. (n) hair gel

---

jam session Spa. (n phr) jam session
jameo Pue.R. (n) jam session
jardín de infantes Col. (n phr) daycare
center
jarra Arg. (n) decanter
jarra Chi., Pue.R., Spa., Venz. (n) mug
jarra de cerveza Pue.R., Spa., Venz.
(n phr) mug, beer
jarra para café Pri. (n phr) mug, coffee
jarra para cerveza Pri. (n phr) mug,
beer
jarra Pri. (n) pitcher
jarrita Arg. (n) mug
jarrita Arg. (n) mug, coffee
jarrita para café Venz. (n phr) mug,
coffee
jarrita para leche Spa. (n phr) creamer
jarrito Arg. (n) mug
jarrito Arg. (n) mug, coffee
jarro de cerveza Mex. (n phr) mug,
beer
jarro para café Mex. (n phr) mug,
coffee
jarro Pri. (n) mug
jarrón Chi. (n) pitcher
jazz Dom.R., Spa. (n) jazz music
jeans Pri. (n) blue jeans
jefe de cocina Col., Per. (n) chef
jefe de oficina Pri. (n phr) office
manager
jefe ejecutivo principal Pri. (n phr)
chief executive officer (CEO)
jefe Pri. (n) boss
jeringuilla de decoración Pri. (n phr)
icing syringe
jeringuilla para decorar Col. (n phr)
icing syringe
jersey Pri. (n) jersey
jersey Spa. (n) pullover
jersey Spa. (n) sweater

jersey Spa. (n) sweatshirt
jet Pri. (n) jet
jibia Chi. (n) squid
jitomate Mex. (n) tomato
joint Dom.R. (n) marijuana cigarette
jornalero Chi. (n) temporary worker
jote Chi. (n) vulture
judías verdes Spa. (n phr) beans, green
juego de maquillaje Col. (n phr)
makeup kit
juego de vídeo Col., Cos.R., Dom.R.,
Mex., Venz. (n) videogame
juey Pue.R. (n) crayfish
juez Bol., Col., Ecu., Per. (n) referee
juguetón Col. (adj) naughty
jungla Chi., Col., Dom.R., Pue.R.,
Venz. (n) selva
jungle Pri. (n) selva
jurista Col. (n) lawyer
juzgado Spa. (n) courthouse
keyboard Pue.R. (n) keyboard
(computer)
kiwi Pri. (n) kiwi

Cuba's *casabe*, a bread made
from the cassava plant, comes
from the French *cassave* and
the Haitian *kasabi*. It is a
popular snack served with
olive oil and garlic.

L

label adhesiva Dom.R., Pue.R. (n phr) label, adhesive
label Dom.R., Pue.R. (n) label
labio leporino Chi. (n phr) cleft (chin)
laca para el pelo Pri. (n phr) hairspray
lacio Pri. (adj) straight (hair)
ladilla Cub. (n) pest (person)
lagarto Col. (n) pest (person)
laguna Chi., Dom.R., Venz. (n) pond
lámina Col. (n) table leaf
lámina de aluminio Cos.R., ElS., Gua., Hon., Pan., Per. (n phr) aluminum foil
LAN Pri. (n) LAN (local area network)
lancha Cub. (n) ferry
langostino Arg., Col., Cub., Mex., Pan., Spa. (n) prawn
langostino Chi. (n) shrimp
lanzamiento de pesa Pue.R. (n phr) shot put
lanzamiento de peso Pri. (n phr) shot put
lapicera a fuente Chi. (n phr) pen, fountain
lapicera Arg., Chi., Uru. (n) pen
lapicera de pasta Chi. (n phr) pen, ball-point
lapicera fuente Arg. (n phr) pen, fountain
lapicero de tinta Per. (n phr) pen, fountain
lapicero Per. (n) pen
lapicero Per. (n) pen, ball-point
lápiz de labios Spa., Uru. (n phr) lipstick

lápiz labial Pri. (n phr) lipstick
lata Cos.R. (n) bus
lata de aceite Arg., Cub., Venz. (n phr) oil can
lata de regar Venz. (n phr) watering can
latas de conservas Chi. (n phr) canned food
lateral Mex. (n) offside
laucha Chi. (n) mouse
laundry Pue.R. (n) dry cleaner's
lava vajilla Uru. (n phr) dishwasher
lavadero Arg. (n) laundry
lavadora de platos Col., Cub., Pue.R. (n phr) dishwasher
lavandería Pri. (n) laundry
lavaplatos Pri. (n) dishwasher
lavaplatos Spa. (n) dishwasher
lavavajilla Arg. (n) dishwasher
lavavajillas Spa. (n) dishwasher
lazo Pue.R. (n) bow tie
lechera Arg. (n) creamer
lechosa Dom.R., Pue.R. (n) papaya
lechoso Venz. (n) papaya
lechuga repollada Dom.R. (n phr) cabbage, green
lechuza Arg., Col., Cub., Dom.R. (n) owl
lenguado, platija Pri. (n) flounder
lentes bifocales Pri. (n phr) bifocals
lentes Col. (n) spectacles
lentes Col., Dom.R., Ecu., Pan., Per., Venz. (n) eyeglasses
lentes de ópera Venz. (n phr) glasses, opera
lentes para leer Mex. (n phr) half-glasses
lentes protectores Venz. (n phr) glasses, safety
lentes trifocales Venz. (n phr)

trifocals
leotardo Pri. (n) leotard
leotardo Pri. (n) tights
leotardos Spa. (n) tights
letra de una canción Pri. (n phr) lyrics
letras de una canción Dom.R. (n phr) lyrics
letrero comercial Pri. (n phr) shop sign

letrero de carretera Pri. (n phr) road sign
letrero de néon Dom.R. (n phr) neon sign
leudarse Pri. (v) rise (bread)
levantamiento de pesas (n phr) weight lifting
levantarse Bol., Chi., Col., ElS., Gua., Hon., Mex., Spa. (v) rise (bread)
leyendas Cub., Pan., Uru. (n) subtitles
lezna Pri. (n) awl
libélula Pri. (n) dragonfly
libre Pri. (adj) vacant
libre Venz. (n) taxi
librería Pri. (n) bookstore
libreta amarilla Bol., Col. Dom.R. (n phr) pad, yellow
libreta Bol., Col., Cub., Pan., Pue.R., Venz. (n) pad (paper)
libreta Col., Cub., Dom.R., Pue.R., Venz. (n) pad, writing
libreta de papel amarilla Pue.R., Venz. (n phr) pad, yellow
libreta Dom.R., Pue.R. (n) notebook
libreta legal Bol. (n phr) pad, legal
libreta tamaño legal Dom.R., Pan., Pue.R., Venz. (n phr) pad, legal
libreto Dom.R., ElS., Gua., Hon. (n) screenplay
licencia de conducir Pri. (n phr) driver's license

licencia por enfermedad Col., Dom.R. (n phr) sick leave
licencia de manejar Cub., Venz. (n phr) driver's license
licor Col., Cub., Gua., Mex., Pan., Venz. (n) liquor
licor de alto contenido alcohólico Col. (n phr) hard liquor
licor ElS., Pan. (n) hard liquor
licor espiritoso Pri. (n phr) hard liquor
licor fuerte Bol., Dom.R., Venz. (n phr) hard liquor
licorera Pri. (n) decanter
licorería Bol., Col., Mex. (n) liquor store
licuadora Pri. (n) blender
liebre Pri. (n) hare
liero Arg. (adj) naughty
liga Cub., Mex., Pan., Per., Venz. (n) rubber band
ligas Pri. (n) suspenders
ligero Pri. (adj) light (weight)
ligeros Mex. (n) suspenders
ligón Pue.R. (n) snoop
lima Pri. (n) lime
límite de velocidad Pri. (n phr) speed limit
limón Cub., Pan. (n) lime
limpiabrisas Col. (n) wipers (windshield)
limpiador Chi. (n) janitor
limpiaparabrisas (n) wipers (windshield)
limpia-parabrisas Venz. (n) wipers (windshield)
limpiar Pue.R., Venz. (v) debug (computer)
limpiavidrios Dom.R. (n) wipers (windshield)
linda Arg., Col., Cub., Pue.R. (adj)

pretty
lindo Arg., Col., Ecu., Pue.R., Venz. (adj) beautiful
lindo Cub., ElS., Gua., Hon., Per., Venz. (adj) cute
línea aérea Col., Dom.R. (n phr) airline
línea Cub. (n) lane
lipstic Pue.R. (n) lipstick
lipstick Pan. (n) lipstick
liquor store Dom.R., Pue.R. (n phr) liquor store
lirio Pri. (n) iris
liso Chi., Col., Spa., Venz. (adj) straight (hair)
litera Col. (n) sleeping car (train)
litera Pri. (n) berth
litera Pri. (n) bunkbed
litoral Col. (n) shoreline
liviano Arg., Chi. (adj) light (weight)
living Arg. (n) living room
llano Col., Dom.R. (n) plain (topography)
llanta Bol., Col., Cos.R., Gua., Mex., Pan., Per. (n) tire (bicycle)
llanta de refacción Mex. (n phr) spare tire
llanta de repuesto Bol., Ecu., Gua., Pan. (n phr) spare tire
llanta desinflada Col., Cos.R., Per., Uru. (n phr) flat tire
llanta pache Gua. (n phr) flat tire
llanta pinchada Bol., Col., Gua., Mex. (n phr) flat tire
llanta ponchada Mex. (n phr) flat tire
llanta Pri. (n) rim (bicycle wheel)
llanta Pri. (n) tire (car)
llanta reventada Pri. (n phr) flat tire
llanura Pri. (n) plain (topography)
llave Chi. (n) screwdriver

llave Mex. (n) valve (trumpet)
llegada Pri. (n) arrival
llevar (v) wear (clothing)
llevar puesto Cub., Dom.R. (v phr) wear (clothing)
llovizna Col. (n) mist
llovizna Pri. (n) drizzle
lluvia tenue Col. (n phr) drizzle
lobby Arg., Dom.R., Mex., Pue.R. (n) lobby
lóbulo Pri. (n) tip of nose
loby Pan. (n) lobby
loción solar Pri. (n phr) sunscreen
loma Chi., Cub., Pan. (n) hill
lomo de toro Chi. (n phr) bump (road)
lomo Pri. (n) road shoulder
loro Pri. (n) parrot
lote Cos.R. (n) batch
love seat Dom.R., Mex. (n phr) love seat
loza Chi., Pan. (n) china
LSD Pri. (n) LSD
lubricación Col., Dom.R., Gua., Pan. (n) lubrication
lubrificación Chi. (n) lubrication
luces altas Arg., Chi., Dom.R., Mex., Pan., Venz. (n phr) brights (headlights)
luces Arg., Chi., Cub., Pan., Pue.R. (n) headlights
luces de emergencia Pri. (n phr) emergency lights
luces delanteras Dom.R., Mex., Venz. (n phr) headlights
luces fuertes Pri. (n phr) brights (headlights)
luces intermitentes Pue.R. (n phr) emergency lights
luces largas Cub., Pue.R., Spa. (n phr) brights (headlights)

ABBREVIATIONS: Arg.=Argentina Bol.=Bolivia Chi.=Chile Col.=Colombia Cos.R.=Costa Rica Cub.=Cuba Dom.R.=Dominican Republic Ecu.=Ecuador ElS.=El Salvador Gua.=Guatemala Hon.=Honduras Mex.=Mexico Pan.=Panama Per.=Peru Pri.=Primary Term Pue.R.=Puerto Rico Spa.=Spain Uru.=Uruguay Venz.=Venezuela

luciérnaga Pri. (n) firefly
lugar del Web Venz. (n phr) website
lúgubre Pri. (adj) gloomy (person)
lunar Cub., Ecu., Per., Venz. (n)
  birthmark
luneta Arg. (n) rear window
luz Arg. (n) reflector (bicycle)
luz de cruce Venz. (n) blinker (light)
luz de doblar Dom.R. (n phr) turning
  light
luz del indicador Chi. (n phr) turning
  light
luz direccional (n phr) turning light
luz direccional Pan. (n) blinker (light)
luz para doblar Col. (n phr) turning
  light
luz para voltear Per. (n phr) turning
  light

The original inhabitants of modern-day Ecuador were the Quitu and the Cara Indians. In the fifteenth century they were conquered by the Incas, who came from what is now Peru. All inhabitants of the Incan empire spoke Quechua.

M

macetero Bol. (n) flower bed
machaca Pri. (n) pest (person)
macho Cos.R. (adj) blue (light-colored eyes)
macho Cos.R. (n) blond (person with light hair)
machucador de papas Per. (n phr) potato masher
macizo Pri. (n) flower bed
madurar Col. (v) grow up
mae Cos.R. (n) guy
maestro de ceremonias Per. (n phr) host (show)
maestro de educación física Pue.R. (n phr) instructor (sports)
magdalena Spa. (n) muffin
magulladura ElS., Gua., Hon., Venz. (n) bruise
mahones Pue.R. (n) blue jeans
maíz Pri. (n) corn
majador de papas Pri. (n phr) potato masher
majo Col. (adj) handsome
mala hierba (n phr) weed
malacostumbrado Col. (adj) spoiled (child)
malanga Cub. (n) taro
malcriado Arg., Col., Cub., Pan., Pue.R. (adj) spoiled (child)
malcriado Cub., Pan. (n) brat
maldito Arg. (adj) evil
maleducado Spa. (adj) spoiled (child)
maleta Pri. (n) suitcase
maleta Venz. (n) trunk (car)
maletas Cos.R. (n) baggage
maletera Bol. (n) porter

maletera Bol., Per. (n) trunk (car)
maletero Cub., Pan., Spa. (n) trunk (car)
maletero Pri. (n) porter
maletín Col., Cub., Per., Pue.R. (n) briefcase
maletín Pri. (n) attaché case
maleza Arg., Chi., Dom.R., Ecu. (n) weed
malhumorado Pri. (adj) grumpy
maligno Col., Venz. (adj) evil
malla Chi. (n) leotard
mallas de ejercicio Venz. (n phr) leotard
mallas Mex., Venz. (n) tights
malo Arg., Chi., Col., Dom.R. (adj) evil
malo Dom.R. (adj) curly (hair)
malvado Chi. (adj) naughty
malvado Pri. (adj) evil
mameluco Arg., Dom.R., Pue.R. (n) overalls
manada Col. (n) flock
manager deportivo Pri. (n phr) manager (sports)
mancha de nacimiento Mex. (n phr) birthmark
mancornas Col., Ecu. (n) cufflinks
mancuernas Pan. (n) cufflinks
mancuernillas ElS., Gua., Hon., Mex. (n) cufflinks
mandarina Pri. (n) mandarine orange
mandíbula Pri. (n) jaw
mando a distancia Spa. (n phr) remote control
mandolín Chi. (n) mandolin
mandolina Pri. (n) mandolin
manejar borracho Pri. (v phr) drive drunk
manejar embriagado Col. (v phr)

drive drunk
manejar en estado de ebriedad Chi.
(v phr) drive drunk
manejar en estado de embriaguez
Dom.R. (v phr) drive drunk
manejar Pri. (v) drive (car)
manejar tomado Cos.R. (v phr) drive
drunk
manga Col. (n) lawn
mangos Per. (n) handlebar grips
(bicycle)
maní Pri. (n) peanut
manicure Chi. (n) manicurist
manicurista Dom.R., Ecu., Mex.,
Pan., Per., Venz. (n) manicurist
manicuro/a Pri. (n) manicurist
manilla Venz. (n) drawer knob
manillar Spa., Uru. (n) handlebars
(bicycle)
manillas Col. (n) handlebar grips
(bicycle)
manta religiosa Pri. (n phr) praying
mantis
manta Spa. (n) blanket
mantenimiento de calles Venz. (n phr)
road works
mantilla Pue.R. (n) praying mantis
mantis religiosa Spa. (n phr) praying
mantis
manto Col. (n) cloak
manubrio Arg., Bol., Chi., Col., Gua.,
Mex., Pue.R., Venz. (n)
handlebars (bicycle)
manubrio Chi. (n) steering wheel
manubrio Dom. R. (n) drawer knob
manubrios Ecu. (n) handlebars
(bicycle)
manzana de Adán Pri. (n phr) Adam's
apple
manzana Pri. (n) city block

maple Gua., Mex. (n) maple (tree)
máquina de afeitar Col. (n phr) razor
máquina de caminar Dom.R. (n phr)
treadmill
máquina de correr Pue.R. (n phr)
treadmill
máquina de cortar yerba Cub. (n phr)
lawn mower
máquina de cortar pasto Arg. (n phr)
lawn mower
máquina de hacer ejercicios Dom.R.
(n phr) stair machine
máquina escalera Cos.R. (n phr) stair
machine
máquina para cortar el pasto Col. (n
phr) lawn mower
marca de nacimiento Pri. (n phr)
birthmark
marcador Pri. (n) marker
marcha atrás Pri. (n phr) reverse
marcha Cos.R. (n) stick shift
marchas Cos.R. (n) velocidades
maría palito Pan. (n phr) praying
mantis
marihuana Pri. (n) marijuana
marimba Cub. (n) xylophone
mariquita Pri. (n) ladybug
marisma Chi. (n) wetlands
marisma Pri. (n) swamp
marmita Pri. (n) kettle
marquesina Dom.R. (n) garage
(storage)
marrano Col., ElS., Gua., Hon.,
Mex., Pan. (n) pig
marrón Arg., Col., Dom.R., Per.,
Spa. (adj) brown (eyes)
marrón Col. (adj) brown (hair)
marrón Pue.R. (n) sledgehammer
marrueco Chi. (n) fly (pants)
marsopa Pri. (n) porpoise

masa de mil hojas Chi. (n phr) puff
  pastry
mascota Dom.R. (n) notebook
masita Arg. (n) cookie
mástil Pri. (n) neck (guitar)
mata Cub. (n) bush
mata Cub. (n) shrub
mata Dom.R. (n) tree
matapiojos Chi. (n) dragonfly
materiales de oficina Cub. (n phr)
  office supplies
matorral Col. (n) hedge
matres Pue.R. (n) mattress
maya Arg. (n) bathing suit
mazo Chi., Dom.R., Mex. (n)
  sledgehammer
mecedor Col. (n) chair, rocking
mecedora Pri. (n) chair, rocking
mechudo Col. (adj) velloso
medallón Chi. (n) necklace, pendant
medallón Dom.R. (n) locket
media (tres cuartos)Arg., Uru. (n) sock
media Col., Cub., Dom.R., Ecu., Pan.,
  Pue.R., Venz. (n) sock
media luna Chi. (n phr) croissant
media luna Pri. (n phr) half-glasses
media nylon Per. (n phr) pantyhose
media pantalón Col. (n phr) tights
media pantalón Pri. (n phr) pantyhose
media panty Dom.R. (n phr)
  pantyhose
medialuna Arg., Col. (n) croissant
mediana Spa. (n) median
medias gruesas Chi. (n phr) tights
medias largas Arg. (n phr) pantyhose
medias nylon Pue.R. (n phr)
  pantyhose
medias panty Venz. (n phr) pantyhose
medias Spa. (n) tights
médico Pri. (n) doctor

medida para bebida Chi. (n phr) shot
  glass
medio Arg. (n) middle finger
mediofondo Dom.R. (n) petticoat
mediofondo Dom.R. (n) slip
medios-lentes Venz. (n) half-glasses
mejilla Pri. (n) cheek
mejillón Pri. (n) mussel
melena Col. (n) hair
melocotón Cub., Dom.R., Para., Per.,
  Pue.R., Spa. (n) peach
melón calameño Chi. (n phr)
  cantaloupe
melón chino Pri. (n phr) cantaloupe
melón Col., Pan., Per., Venz. (n)
  cantaloupe
melón de agua Cub. (n phr)
  watermelon
memoria de reserva Venz. (n phr)
  buffer storage
memoria intermedia Col., Venz. (n
  phr) buffer storage
memoria intermediaria Pri. (n phr)
  buffer storage
memoria temporal Col., Venz. (n phr)
  buffer storage
menor Col. (n) infant
mentiroso Pri. (n) liar
mentón Arg., Col. (n) chin
menudo Col. (adj) small
mercado Col. (n) grocery
merienda Pri. (n) snack
mermelada Per., Spa. (n) preserves
mesa de buffet Mex. (n phr) buffet
mesa de cocina Pri. (n phr) table,
  kitchen
mesa de luz Arg. (n phr) table, night
mesa de noche Col., ElS., Gua., Hon.,
  Pue.R., Venz. (n phr) table, night
mesa de servicio Col. (n phr) table,

serving
mesa de servir Venz. (n phr) table,
serving
mesada Arg. (n) counter
mesero Chi., Col., Cub., Dom.R.,
ElS., Gua., Hon., Mex., Pan.,
Pue.R. (n) waiter
mesilla de noche Pri. (n phr) table,
night
mesita de cocina Pan. (n phr) table,
kitchen
mesita de luz Arg. (n phr) table, night
mesita de noche Bol., Cub., Dom.R.,
Pan.(n phr) table, night
mesita de servicio Pri. (n phr) table,
serving
mesita rodante Arg. (n phr) table,
serving
mesonero Venz. (n) waiter
metales Mex. (n) bronze section
meteorólogo (n phr) weather reporter
meter un cambio Col. (v phr) shift
gear
meterse un viaje Venz. (v phr) get high
(drugs)
metiche Col., Cub., Dom.R., Ecu.,
Mex. (n) snoop
metido Col., Cub. (n) snoop
metro Mex. (n) local train
metro Pri. (n) tape measure
metrópoli Col. (n) city
mezclador Cub. (n) mixer
mezquino Mex. (n) wart
mico Col. (n) monkey
micro Chi. (n) bus
micro Pri. (n) microwave (oven)
microbus Per. (n) van
microonda Arg., Col., Cub., Uru. (n)
microwave (oven)
microondas Chi., Mex., Pue.R., Spa.,

Venz. (n) microwave (oven)
miedoso Bol. (adj) terrifying
miembro de la familia Col. (n phr)
family member
milhoja Venz. (n) puff pastry
mimado Pri. (adj) spoiled (child)
minifalda Pri. (n) miniskirt
minitrusa Pri. (n) bikini briefs
mirar televisión Col. (v phr) watch
television
mirlo Pri. (n) blackbird
mocasines Chi., Col., Cub., Ecu.,
Venz. (n) loafers
mocoso Pri. (n) brat
modista Arg., Chi., Col., Pan., Spa.
(n) seamstress
modisto Col. (n) tailor
módulo Dom.R. (n) modular office
mofle Pri. (n) muffler
molar Col. (n) molar
molde de bizcocho Dom.R. (n phr)
pie pan
molde para magdalenas Spa. (n phr)
muffin pan
molde para muffin Arg. (n phr) muffin
pan
molde para mufin Mex. (n phr) muffin
pan
molde para pancitos Bol. (n phr)
muffin pan
molde para panecillos Pri. (n phr)
muffin pan
molde para pastel Pri. (n phr) pie pan
molde para pastelitos Bol. (n phr)
muffin pan
molde para pay Mex. (n phr) pie pan
molde para pie Chi. (n phr) pie pan
molde para quequitos Per. (n phr)
muffin pan
molde para tartas Arg. (n phr) pie pan

moldecito Pri. (n) tart
moldes Arg. (n) cookie cutters
moldes de galletas Chi., Dom.R.,
  Venz. (n phr) cookie cutters
moledor de carne Pan., Pue.R. (n phr)
  meat grinder
moledor de papas Chi. (n phr) potato
  masher
moledora de carne Arg., Col., Dom.R.
  (n phr) meat grinder
molesto Pri. (adj) bothersome
molesto Pue.R. (adj) angry
molestoso Venz. (adj) bothersome
molidora Cub. (n) meat grinder
molino de carne Pri. (n phr) meat
  grinder
mollete Gua. (n) muffin
molondrón Dom.R. (n) okra
monedero Pri. (n) coin purse
moñito Arg. (n) bow tie
monitor Pri. (n) monitor (computer)
mono Col. (adj) blond (hair)
mono Pri. (adj) cute
mono Pri. (n) monkey
mono Pri. (n) overalls
moño Chi. (n) pigtail
moño Pan. (n) braid (hair)
moño Pri. (n) bun (hair)
mono/a Col. (n) blond (person)
montañera Pri. (n) bike, mountain
montar a caballo Col. (v phr) ride
  horseback
montar en bicicleta Pri. (v phr) ride
  (bicycle)
montarse Col. (v) get on (bus)
monte Cos.R. (n) marijuana
mora azul Mex. (n phr) blueberry
mora Per. (n) blueberry
mora roja Mex. (n phr) cranberry
morado Col., Cub. (n) bruise

morado Dom.R. (n) bruise
moratón Spa. (n) bruise
moreno Pri. (adj) brown (hair)
moreno/a Pri. (n) brunette (person)
morete Cos.R. (n) bruise
moretón Arg., Bol., Chi., Mex., Pan.
  (n) bruise
morocho Uru. (adj) brown (hair)
morocho/a Arg., Uru. (n) brunette
  (person)
morsa (n) walrus
moscardón Col. (n) horsefly, gadfly
mostrador Col. (n) buffet
mostrador Pri. (n) counter
mostrar Venz. (v) show (movie)
mota Cos.R. (n) marijuana
mother board Pan. (n phr)
  motherboard
motocicleta, moto Pri. (n) motorcycle,
  motorbike
motocine Pri. (n) drive-in
motor de arranque Cub., Spa. (n phr)
  starter
motora Pue.R. (n) motorcycle,
  motorbike
motosierra Arg., Cos.R., Spa. (n)
  chainsaw
mountain bike Dom.R., Pue.R., Spa.
  (n phr) bike, mountain
mouse para el pelo Mex. (n phr) hair
  mousse
mousse para el pelo Pri. (n phr) hair
  mousse
mover Pan. (v) scroll (computer)
mozo Arg., Bol., Chi., Cos.R.,
  Dom.R., Uru. (n) waiter
mozo Spa. (n) porter
muchachita Dom.R. (n) girl
muchachito Dom.R. (n) boy
muchachito/a Dom.R. (n) brat

muchacho, tipo Pri. (n) guy
muchacho/a Dom.R. (n) kid
muchachos, tipos Pri. (n) guys (dual
    gender plural)
mudarse Pri. (v) move
muela Pri. (n) molar
muelle de carga Col. (n phr) loading
    dock
muffin Arg., Col. (n) muffin
muffler Dom.R. (n) muffler
mufin Mex. (n) muffin
mufler Mex. (n) muffler
mujer de negocios Pri. (n phr)
    businesswoman
mujer profesional Pan. (n phr)
    businesswoman
multa por exceso de velocidad Pri. (n
    phr) ticket, speeding
multa Pri. (n) ticket, traffic
muñequitos Cub., Dom.R., Pue.R.
    (n) cartoon
municipalidad Chi., Col., Ecu., ElS.,
    Gua., Hon. (n) city hall
murmullo Col. (n) hum
mus para el pelo Dom.R. (n phr)
    hair mousse
musculosa Arg. (n) vest
música de jazz Col. (n phr) jazz music
música de rock Col. (n phr) rock
    music
música jazz Pri. (n phr) jazz music
música Mex., Pue.R. (n) sound track
música rock Pri. (n phr) rock music
músical Dom.R., Pue.R. (n) musical
    (movie)
músico Mex. (n) performer
mustango Pri. (n) mustang
muy agradable ElS., Gua., Hon. (adj
    phr) divino

> Uruguayans are familiar with *pato* (literally meaning "duck"), a game played on horseback using a six-handled ball.

N

nabo de suecia Col.
nabo sueco Pri. (n phr) rutabaga
nafta Arg. (n) gasolina (vehicle)
nalga Pan. (n) butt
nalga Pri. (n) buttock
nalgas Cub. (n) butt
nana Chi., Col., Mex., Venz. (n)
    nanny
nana Mex. (n) babysitter
ñandú Col. (n) ostrich
naranja Pri. (n) orange
narcomanía Col. (n) drug addiction
narcomanía Col. (n) drug habit
narcómano Col. (adj) addicted
narcómano Col. (n) drug addict
narcotraficante Bol., Cos.R., Cub.,
    Venz. (n) drug dealer
narigón Arg., Bol., Chi., Uru. (adj)
    big-nosed
narina Chi. (n) nostril
narizón Pri. (adj) big-nosed
narizú Dom.R. (adj) big-nosed
navaja de pintor Pri. (n phr) painter's
    knife
navaja Pan. (n) razor
navaja Pri. (n) penknife
navegar en el Internet Bol., Ecu. (v
    phr) surf the net
navegar la red Arg., Col. (v phr) surf
    the net
navegar por Internet Col. (v phr)
    surf the net
navegar por la Internet Chi., Gua. (v
    phr) surf the net
navegar por la red Cub., Spa., Uru. (v
    phr) surf the net

navío Chi. (n) ship
neblina Arg., Col., Cub., Dom.R.,
    Mex., Per. (n) fog
neblina Pri. (n) mist
necio Pue.R. (adj) naughty
necio/a Ecu. (n) pest (person)
nectarín Mex. (n) nectarine
nectarina Col., Cub. (n) nectarine
nectarine Pue.R., Venz. (n) nectarine
nectarino ElS., Gua., Hon. (n)
    nectarine
negociación Pue.R. (n) drug deal
negocio de drogas Ecu., Venz. (n phr)
    drug deal
nena Arg., Uru. (n) girl
nene Arg., Pue.R., Uru. (n) boy
nene/a Uru. (n) child
neumático Cos.R. (n) inner tube
    (bicycle tire)
neumático desinflado Uru. (n phr)
    flat tire
neumático pinchado Spa. (n phr) flat
    tire
neumático Pri. (n) tire (bicycle)
nevera Col., Dom.R., Ecu., Pue.R.,
    Spa., Venz. (n) refrigerator
nevería Mex. (n) ice cream parlor
neverita Dom.R. (n) water fountain
niebla Arg., Col., Pue.R. (n) mist
niebla Pri. (n) fog
niña Pri. (n) girl
niñera Pri. (n) nanny
niñero/a Pri. (n) babysitter
niñito/a Venz. (n) toddler
niño Pri. (n) boy
niño/a chiquito/a Col. (n phr) toddler
niño/a Col., Venz. (n) kid
niño/a de edad pre-escolar Mex. (n
    phr) toddler
niño/a malcriado/a Col. (n phr) brat

niño/a Pri. (n) child
niño/a Pri. (n) infant
niño/a que empieza a andar ElS.,
     Gua., Hon., Mex. (n phr) toddler
niño/a Spa. (n) toddler
nivel Pri. (n) level
nivelador Chi. (n) level
no profesional Cub. (n phr) amateur
nodriza Chi. (n) babysitter
ñoñio Dom.R. (adj) spoiled (child)
noria Pri. (n) ferris wheel
¡Nos vemos! Dom.R., ElS., Gua.,
     Hon., Pan. (int phr) See you later!
noticiario Spa. (n) newscast
noticias Mex. (n) newscast
noticiero Arg., Chi., Col., Dom.R.,
     Ecu., Mex., Pan. (n) newscast
noticiero breve Mex. (n phr) news brief
novato Per. (n) amateur
novela Arg., Cub. (n) soap opera
novia Pri. (n) fiancée (female)
novia Pri. (n) girlfriend
novio Pri. (n) boyfriend
novio Pri. (n) fiancé (male)
nublado Pri. (adj) cloudy
nuboso Cos.R., Cub., Gua. (adj)
     cloudy
nuca Pri. (n) nape
nuez Cub. (n) Adam's apple
nuez de Adán Arg. (n phr) Adam's
     apple
nuez de Brasil Pri. (n phr) Brazil nut
nuez de la garganta Spa. (n phr)
     Adam's apple
nuez de la India Pri. (n phr) cashew
nuez del Brasil Col. (n phr) Brazil nut
nuez Mex. (n) pecan
nursery Pue.R. (n) daycare center

> Spanish explorers in Puerto Rico adopted many words from *los indios tainos*, the first inhabitants of the island, including Coamo, Bayamón, Caguas, Humacao (geographical names), *anón*, and *guamá* (fruits).

O

obras Pri. (n) road works
obstáculos Chi. (n) hurdles race
ocultar Pri. (v) encrypt (computer)
offside Arg. (n) offside
oficial de policía Venz. (n phr) police
  officer
oficial ejecutivo jefe Venz. (n phr)
  chief executive officer (CEO)
oficina Bol. (n) office cubicle
oficina de abogados Col., Pue.R. (n
  phr) lawyer's office
oficina de correos Pri. (n phr) post
  office
oficina del doctor Pue.R. (n phr)
  doctor's office
oficina del médico Pue.R. (n phr)
  doctor's office
oficina modular Pri. (n phr) modular
  office
oficina postal Col. (n phr) post office
oficina Pri. (n) office suite
¿Oigo? Cub. (int) Hello? (answering
  telephone)
ojeras Pri. (n) bags (under eyes)
ojiazul Col. (adj) blue (eyes)
ojiverde Col. (adj) green (eyes)
ojotas Arg. (n) clogs
ojotas de goma Arg. (n phr) rubbers
  (shoes)
okra Mex. (n) okra
oler Cub., Dom.R. (v) inhale (drugs)
oliva Cos.R. (n) olive
olla Arg., Pue.R. (n) saucepan
olla grande Mex. (n phr) kettle
olla para hornear Venz. (n phr)
  roasting pan

olla Pri. (n) pot
ombligo Pri. (n) belly button
ombligo Pri. (n) navel
omelete Pri. (n) omelet
ómnibus Arg., Per., Uru. (n) bus
ondulado (adj) wavy (hair)
ondulado Bol., Chi., Col., Venz. (adj)
  curly (hair)
ondulines Chi. (n) hair rollers
one way Pan. (n phr) street, one-way
ordenador personal (OP) Spa. (n phr)
  PC
ordenador Spa. (n) computer
orificio nasal Venz. (n phr) nostril
orilla Col. (n) shoreline
orilla de la carretera Col., Cos.R. (n
  phr) road shoulder
orilla del mar Pri. (n phr) seashore
osamenta Col. (n) skeleton
ostión Chi. (n) scallop
ostión Mex. (n) oyster
ostra Pri. (n) oyster
otomana Pri. (n) ottoman
ottomán Pue.R. (n) ottoman
oveja Pri. (n) sheep
overales Mex. (n) overalls
overol Chi., Col., Pan. (n) overalls

African slaves were brought to
Argentina in colonial times. It
is believed that the word
mucama (maid) is of African
origin.

P

pacana Pri. (n) pecan
paciente Pri. (n) patient
padrillo Pri. (n) stallion
paga Col. (n) salary
página del Web Venz. (n phr) website
página principal Arg. (n phr) website
pajarería Pri. (n) pet shop
pajarita Cub., Spa. (n) bow tie
pajarito Dom.R. (n) bug
pajón Dom.R. (n) weed
pala Pri. (n) shovel
pala Pri. (n) spade
pala Pri. (n) turner
palacio de justicia Dom.R., Spa. (n phr) courthouse
palana Per. (n) shovel
palanca de cambios Pri. (n phr) stick shift
palanca de velocidades Mex. (n phr) stick shift
palaustre Pue.R. (n) trowel
palé Chi. (n) pallet
palet Mex. (n) pallet
paleta Chi. (n) trowel
paleta Pri. (n) pallet
paleta Venz. (n) turner
palito Pue.R. (n) bush
palma Pri. (n) palm (tree)
palmera Arg., Col., Mex. (n) palm (tree)
palo de amasar Arg. (n phr) rolling pin
palo de golf Pri. (n phr) golf club
palo de luz Dom.R. (n phr) street lamp
paloma Pri. (n) dove
palomo Col. (n) dove
palta Arg., Bol., Chi., Per., Uru.

(n) avocado
palustre Mex. (n) trowel
pan blanco Arg., Col., Dom.R., Mex., Spa., Venz. (n phr) bread, white
pan blanco rebanado Uru. (n phr) bread, white
pan blanco tajado Pri. (n phr) bread, white
pan camarón Dom.R. (n phr) croissant
pan centeno Chi. (n phr) bread, rye
pan cortado Cos.R. (n phr) bread, sliced
pan de caja Mex. (n phr) bread, sliced
pan de centeno Arg., Col., Cub., Dom.R., Ecu., Spa., Venz. (n phr) bread, rye
pan de fruta Dom.R. (n phr) chestnut
pan de molde Cub. (n phr) bread, white
pan de molde Pri. (n phr) bread, sliced
pan de sandwich Dom.R. (n phr) bread, sliced
pan dulce Mex. (n phr) Danish
pan en rodajas Venz. (n phr) bread, sliced
pan especial Pue.R. (n phr) bread, sliced
pan especial Pue.R. (n phr) bread, white
pan flauta Pan. (n phr) baguette
pan francés Bol., Chi., Col., Dom.R., Pan., Venz. (n phr) baguette
pan lactal Arg. (n phr) bread, sliced
pan negro Pri. (n phr) bread, rye
pan para hamburgeusas Mex., Pan. (n phr) bun
pan para hot dogs Mex. (n phr) bun
pan pequeño Col. (n phr) bun

pan Pue.R. (n) roll
pan tajado Col. (n phr) bread, sliced
pan tostado Mex., Pan. (n phr) toast
pana Dom.R. (n) buddy, pal
panadería Pri. (n) bakery
pancake Cub., Dom.R., Pan., Pue.R.
   (n) pancake
pancillo Col. (n) bun
pancito Arg., Uru. (n) bun
pancito Bol. (n) muffin
pancito Pri. (n) roll
pancora Chi. (n) crab
pandereta Chi., Col., Cub., Dom.R.,
   Ecu., Pue.R., Spa. (n) tambourine
pandero Pri. (n) tambourine
panecillo Col., Pan. (n) roll
panecillo Pri. (n) bun
panecillo Pri. (n) muffin
panecillo Pue.R. (n) biscuit
panqué Mex. (n) muffin
panqueca Venz. (n) pancake
panqueque Pri. (n) pancake
pantaleta Mex. (n) panties
pantaletas Venz. (n) panties
pantalla Arg., Chi. (n) monitor
   (computer)
pantalla solar Arg. (n phr) sunscreen
pantallas de clips Pue.R. (n phr)
   earrings, clip
pantallas de gancho Pue.R. (n phr)
   earrings, pierced
pantallas Pue.R. (n) earrings
pantalón corto Pue.R. (n phr) shorts
pantalón de mezclilla Mex. (n phr)
   blue jeans
pantaloncillos Dom.R. (n) briefs
pantaloncitos cortos Pan. (n phr)
   shorts
pantalones cortos Pri. (n phr) shorts
pantalones de peto Mex. (n phr)

overalls
pantalones vaqueros Spa. (n phr) blue
   jeans
pantano (n) wetlands
pantano Chi., Col., Dom.R., Ecu.,
   Mex., Venz. (n) swamp
panteón Mex. (n) cemetery
panticitos del bikini Pue.R. (n phr)
   bikini briefs
panties Dom.R., Pue.R. (n) panties
pantihose Pan. (n) pantyhose
pantimedia Mex. (n) pantyhose
pantimedias Uru. (n) pantyhose
pantis Cub., Pan. (n) panties
pantry Dom.R., ElS., Gua.. Hon. (n)
   pantry
pantuflas Pri. (n) slippers
panty Spa. (n) pantyhose
pantyhose Dom.R. (n) pantyhose
panza Arg., Col., Cos.R., Dom.R.,
   Mex., Uru. (n) belly
papa dulce Chi. (n phr) sweet potato
papa Pri. (n) potato
papada Pri. (n phr) double chin
papagayo Col. (n) parrot
papas fritas Pri. (n phr) French fries
papaya Pri. (n) papaya
papel aluminio Chi., Pan. (n phr)
   aluminum foil
papel de aluminio Pri. (n phr)
   aluminum foil
papitas fritas Dom.R. (n phr) French
   fries
papo Pan. (n) hibiscus
parabrisas Cub., Per. (n) wipers
   (windshield)
parachoques Pri. (n) bumper
parada de autobús Pri. (n phr) bus
   stop
parada de bus Col., Cos.R., Pan. (n

ABBREVIATIONS: Arg.=Argentina Bol.=Bolivia Chi.=Chile Col.=Colombia
Cos.R.=Costa Rica Cub.=Cuba Dom.R.=Dominican Republic Ecu.=Ecuador ElS.=El
Salvador Gua.=Guatemala Hon.=Honduras Mex.=Mexico Pan.=Panama Per.=Peru
Pri.=Primary Term Pue.R.=Puerto Rico Spa.=Spain Uru.=Uruguay Venz.=Venezuela

phr) bus stop

parada de guagua Cub., Dom.R., Pue.R. (n phr) bus stop

parada de lata Cos.R. (n phr) bus stop

parada de libres Venz. (n phr) taxi stand

parada de taxi Pri. (n phr) taxi stand

parada de taxis Venz. (n phr) taxi stand

parada del colectivo Bol. (n phr) bus stop

parada del micro Chi. (n phr) bus stop

parada del ómnibus Arg., Per., Uru. (n phr) bus stop

parada discrecional Spa. (n phr) request stop (bus)

parada facultativa Pri. (n phr) request stop (bus)

parada pedida Venz. (n phr) request stop (bus)

parada solicitada Mex. (n phr) request stop (bus)

paragolpes Arg. (n) bumper

paragolpes Arg. (n) fender

parar Arg., Cub., Ecu., Mex., Pan. (v) stall (car)

pararse Chi. (v) stall (car)

pare Arg., Chi., Col., Pue.R. stop (sign)

pargo Pri. (n) snapper

pariente Arg., Chi., Ecu., Mex., Pue.R., Venz. (n) family member

parir Col., Cos.R., Dom.R., Pan. (v phr) give birth

parka Pri. (n) parka

parking Pue.R., Spa. (n) parking lot

parque de atracciones Pri. (n phr) fairground

parque de bomberos Bol., Cos.R., Ecu., Spa., Uru. (n phr) fire

station

parque de diversiones Dom.R., Ecu., Pue.R. (n phr) fairground

parque Pri. (n) park

parque Pue.R. (n) stadium

parqueadero Col., Pan. (n) parking lot

parquear Bol., Col., Cos.R., Cub., Dom.R., ElS., Gua., Hon., Pan. (v) park

parqueo Bol., Cos.R., Cub., Dom.R. ElS., Gua., Hon. (n) parking lot

parrilla del radiador Arg., Col. (n phr) radiator grill

parte de tiempo Mex. (adj phr) part-time (work)

parte del tronco Mex. (n phr) stump

partera Pri. (n) midwife

participante Cub., Pue.R. (n) contestant

partido Dom.R., Mex., Venz. (n) part (hair)

partidor Pri. (n) office divider

partidura Chi., Pan. (n) part (hair)

part-time Pue.R. (adj) part-time (work)

pasadizo Col. (n) alley

pasadizo subterráneo Col. (n phr) underpass

pasador Mex. (n) dowel

pasador Mex. (n) stud

pasaje Arg., Cos.R., Cub., Dom.R. (n) ticket

pasaje de ida Arg., Cos.R., Dom.R. (n phr) one-way ticket

pasaje de ida y vuelta Arg., Cos.R., Dom.R. (n phr) round trip ticket

pasaje Per. (n) alley

pasar Arg., Dom.R. (v) show (movie)

pasar la marcha Chi. (v phr) shift gear

pasar Pri. (v) pasar(traffic)

pase para conducir Col. (n phr)

driver's license
paseo Pue.R. (n) road shoulder
pasillo Col. (n) lobby
pasita Pan. (n) black currant
paso a desnivel Mex. (n) cloverleaf
junction
paso Chi., Mex. (n) right of way
paso de peatones Pri. (n phr) crosswalk
paso inferior Spa. (n phr) underpass
paso nivel Chi. (n phr) underpass
paso subterráneo Pri. (n phr)
underpass
pasta dental Per., Pue.R. (n phr)
toothpaste
pasta Spa. (n) cookie
pastel danés Venz. (n phr) Danish
pastel de crema Venz. (n phr) cream
puff
pastel de frutas Spa. (n phr) tart
pastel Dom.R., Pan., Per., Pue.R. (n)
pie
pastel Per. (n) Danish
pastel Pri. (n) cake
pastel, tarta Pri. (n) pie
pastelería Chi., Col. (n) bakery
pastelillo de fruta y nueces Pri. (n phr)
Danish
pastelito Gua. (n) tart
pastelito Mex. (n) muffin
pastinaca Uru. (n) parsnip
pasto Arg., Bol., Col., Mex., Per.,
Pue.R. (n) lawn
pasto Chi., Col., Mex., Per. (n) grass
patata Cub., Spa. (n) potato
patatas fritas Spa. (n phr) French fries
patinaje en el hielo Col. (n phr) ice
skating
patinaje en hielo Chi., Cub. (n phr)
ice skating
patinaje sobre hielo Pri. (n phr) ice

skating
patrón Col. (n) boss
pava Arg., Uru. (n) kettle
pava Cos.R. (n) bangs (hair)
pavo Pri. (n) turkey
pay Mex. (n) pie
PC Pri. (n) PC
pecana Bol., ElS., Gua., Hon. (n)
pecan
pecho Dom.R., ElS., Gua., Hon., Pan.,
Spa. (n) breast
pecho Mex. (n) breaststroke
(swimming)
pecho Pri. (n) chest
pechuga Chi. (n) breast
pedal de gasolina Venz. (n phr) gas
pedal
pedal de la gasolina Pue.R. (n phr) gas
pedal
pedir bola Dom.R. (v phr) hitchhike
pedir cola Venz. (v phr) hitchhike
pedir jalón a dedo ElS., Gua., Hon.
(v phr) hitchhike
pedir pon Pue.R. (v phr) hitchhike
pedir ride Cos.R. (v phr) hitchhike
peine Pri. (n) comb
peineta Chi. (n) comb
peinilla Col., Ecu., Pan., Pue.R. (n)
comb
pejerrey Chi. (n) smelt
pelador Pri. (n) peeler
pelapapas Mex. (n) peeler
pelearse Cub. (v) break up
(relationship)
peliagudo Col. (adj) difficult
pelicastaño Col. (adj) brown (hair)
película apta para todos los públicos
Spa. (n phr) movie, PG-rated
película censura B Venz. (n phr)
movie, PG-rated

película censurada Col., Dom.R. (n phr) banned film

película clasificación X Col. (n phr) movie, x-rated

película de cowboys Arg. (n phr) movie, western

película de horror Mex., Pue.R., Uru., Venz. (n phr) movie, horror

película de miedo Pri. (n phr) movie, horror

película de terror Arg., Col., Cos.R., Dom.R., Pue.R., Venz. (n phr) movie, horror

película de vaqueros Pri. (n phr) movie, western

película doble Bol. (n phr) double feature (movies)

película musical Pri. (n phr) musical (movie)

película para adolescentes y adultos clasificación B Mex. (n phr) movie, PG-rated

película para adultos Pri. (n phr) movie, x-rated

película para todo público clasificación A Mex. (n phr) movie, G-rated

película para todo público Pri. (n phr) movie, G-rated

película para todo público Pri. (n phr) movie, PG-rated

película pornográfica Cub. (n phr) movie, x-rated

película Pri. (n) film

película prohibida Pri. (n phr) banned film

película público general Pue.R. (n phr) movie, PG-rated

película sólo para adultos clasificación C Mex. (n phr) movie, x-rated

película X Pue.R. (n phr) movie, x-rated

pelma Spa. (n) pest (person)

pelmazo Spa. (n) pest (person)

pelón Uru. (n) nectarine

pelota de fútbol Pri. (n phr) ball (soccer)

pelota de golf Pri. (n phr) golf ball

pelota de mano Uru. (n phr) handball

peludo Arg., Chi., Col., Pue.R., Spa., Venz. (adj) velloso

peluquería Pri. (n) hairdresser's shop

peluquero Arg., Ecu., Mex., Per. (n) barber

peluquero/a Pri. (n) hairdresser

pendiente con cadena Mex. (n phr) necklace, pendant

pendiente con medalla Dom.R. (n phr) necklace, pendant

pendientes de clip Spa. (n phr) earrings, clip

pendientes de tornillo Spa. (n phr) earrings, pierced

pendientes de tornillo Spa. (n phr) earrings, screw

pendientes largos Spa. (n phr) earrings, drop

pendientes Pri. (n phr) earrings, drop

pendientes Spa. (n) earrings

penoso Cub., Pan. (adj) shy

pepinillo Dom.R., Mex., Pue.R. (n) pickle

pepinillo en vinagre Spa. (n phr) pickle

pepinillo Pue.R. (n) cucumber

pepino Cub. (n) pickle

pepino encurtido Pri. (n phr) pickle

pepino Pri. (n) cucumber

pepita de marañón Pan. (n phr) cashew

pequeñito/a Pri. (n) toddler

ABBREVIATIONS: Arg.=Argentina Bol.=Bolivia Chi.=Chile Col.=Colombia Cos.R.=Costa Rica Cub.=Cuba Dom.R.=Dominican Republic Ecu.=Ecuador ElS.=El Salvador Gua.=Guatemala Hon.=Honduras Mex.=Mexico Pan.=Panama Per.=Peru Pri.=Primary Term Pue.R.=Puerto Rico Spa.=Spain Uru.=Uruguay Venz.=Venezuela

pequeño Pri. (adj) short
pequeño Pri. (adj) short (person)
pera Arg., Chi. (n) chin
perdiz Venz. (n) woodcock
perenne Pri. (n) perennial (plant)
perezoso Pri. (adj) lazy
perico Pri. (n) parakeet
perilla Pri. (n) drawer knob
perilla Spa. (n) goatee
periquito Spa. (n) parakeet
permanente Pue.R. (n) perennial
   (plant)
permiso de conductor Arg. (n phr)
   driver's license
permiso de convalecencia Pri. (n phr)
   sick leave
permiso de convalescencia Venz. (n
   phr) sick leave
permiso por enfermedad Arg., Bol.,
   ElS., Gua., Hon. (n phr) sick
   leave
perol Col. (n) saucepan
perrera Pri. (n) doghouse
persianas Col., Ecu., Gua. (n) shutters
persianas Pri. (n) blinds
persona de pelo castaño Spa. (n phr)
   brunette (person)
persona mayor Col. (n phr) adult
persona que recoge los boletos Mex.
   (n phr) ticket collector
personero ejecutivo de más alto rango
   Gua. (n phr) chief executive
   officer (CEO)
pesta Dom.R. (n) pest (person)
peste Col., Pan. (n) pest (person)
pet shop Dom.R., Pue.R. (n phr) pet
   shop
peticote Pan. (n) petticoat
peticote Pan. (n) slip
petiso Arg., Uru. (adj) short (person)

petit pois Cub., Pan. (n phr) peas,
   green
peuco Chi. (n) hawk
pez azul Mex. (n phr) bluefish
pez espada Pri. (n phr) swordfish
pezón Pri. (n) nipple
pibe Arg. (n) guy
pica Chi. (n) spade
picadera Dom.R. (n) snack
picador Pue.R. (n phr) cutting board
picador Pue.R. (n) butcher block
picadora de papel Mex. (n phr)
   shredder
picaflor Arg., Col., Pan. (n)
   hummingbird
picar Chi. (v) sprint
pícaro Col. (n) cheater
pichel Gua. (n) pitcher
pichón Pue.R. (n) dove
pickup Cos.R., ElS., Gua., Hon., Pan.,
   Per. (n) pickup truck
pico Mex. (n) sickle
pico Pri. (n) peak (mountain)
pico Venz. (n) hoe
pico Venz. (n) spade
pícolo Pri. (n) piccolo
pidevías Gua. (n) turning light
pie Bol., Dom.R. (n) pie
piezas de repuesto Cub., Spa. (n phr)
   spare parts
pijama Col., Spa. (n) pajamas
pijama Dom.R. (n) nightgown
pijamas Dom.R., Pue.R. (n) pajamas
pileta Arg. (n) swimming pool
pillo Cub. (adj) naughty
piloto Arg. (n) raincoat
piloto Pri. (n) pilot
pimentera Pri. (n) pepper shaker
pimentero Arg., Col., Gua., Mex., Per.
   (n) pepper shaker

ABBREVIATIONS: Arg.=Argentina Bol.=Bolivia Chi.=Chile Col.=Colombia
Cos.R.=Costa Rica Cub.=Cuba Dom.R.=Dominican Republic Ecu.=Ecuador ElS.=El
Salvador Gua.=Guatemala Hon.=Honduras Mex.=Mexico Pan.=Panama Per.=Peru
Pri.=Primary Term Pue.R.=Puerto Rico Spa.=Spain Uru.=Uruguay Venz.=Venezuela

pimentón Pan., Per., Venz. (n) pepper, sweet

pimentón rojo Col. (n phr) pepper, sweet

pimentón verde Col. (n phr) pepper, sweet

pimienta Pue.R. (n) pepper shaker

pimientero Venz. (n) pepper shaker

pimiento morrón Pri. (n phr) pepper, sweet

pimiento picante Ecu. (n phr) pepper, hot

pimiento Spa. (n) pepper, sweet

piña Pri. (n) pine cone

piña Pri. (n) pineapple

pincel de repostería Pri. (n phr) pastry brush

piño Chi. (n) flock

piñón Per. (n) pine cone

pintalabios Col., Cub., Dom.R. (n) lipstick

pintauñas Col., Spa. (n) nail polish

pintura de uñas Cub., Venz. (n phr) nail polish

pinzas Arg., Col., Spa. (n) tongs

pinzas Col., Mex. (n) pincers

pinzas Mex. (n) clamp

pinzas Pri. (n) pliers

pipa Col. (n) belly

piscina Pri. (n) swimming pool

pisicorre Cub. (n) station wagon

piso Chi. (n) stool

piso de abajo Col. (n phr) ground floor

piso de arriba Dom.R. (n phr) planta alta

piso Spa. (n) apartment

piso superior Col. (n phr) planta alta

pista de sonido Venz. (n phr) sound track

pistache Mex. (n) pistachio

pistacho Pri. (n) pistachio

pistola de pelo Mex. (n phr) hair dryer

pistón Pri. (n) valve (trumpet)

pitillo de marihuana Cub., Pue.R. (n phr) marijuana cigarette

pito Chi. (n) marijuana cigarette

piyama Col. (n) pajamas

piyamas Pri. (n) pajamas

placa base Venz. (n phr) motherboard

placa de identificación Pri. (n phr) dog tag

placa madre Pri. (n phr) motherboard

placard Arg. (n) closet (clothes)

plaga Dom.R. (n) pest (person)

plancha Spa. (n) griddle

planicie Mex., Pue.R. (n) plain (topography)

plano Pri. (n) plane (carpentry)

planta baja Pri. (n phr) ground floor

planta de semillero Pri. (n phr) seedling

planta de vivero Col. (n phr) seedling

planta superior Spa. (n phr) planta alta

plantita Mex. (n) seedling

plataforma Col., Cub., Per. (n) platform (train)

plataforma de carga Pri. (n phr) loading dock

plataforma Uru. (n) pallet

plátano Pri. (n) banana

platería Col. (n) silverware

platillo principal Mex. (n phr) main course

plato de sopa Col., Venz. (n phr) bowl, soup

plato fuerte Cub. (n phr) main course

plato hondo Pan. (n phr) bowl, soup

plato hondo Pri. (n) bowl

plato para ensalada Col., Pan. (n phr)

bowl, salad
plato para sopa Pan. (n phr) bowl, soup
plato principal Pri. (n phr) main course
plato sopero Cub., Dom.R., Ecu. (n phr) bowl, soup
plató Spa. (n) set (movie)
platón Mex. (n) platter
platón Pan. (n) bowl, mixing
platos Pri. (n) dishes
playa de estacionamiento Arg. (n phr) parking lot
playera de punto Mex. (n phr) jersey
playera Mex. (n) knit shirt
plaza Arg. (n) park
plenas Col. (n) brights (headlights)
pliego Col. (n) crease (pants)
pliegue Cub., ElS., Gua., Hon. (n) crease (pants)
plomada Uru. (n) level
plomero Pri. (n) plumber
pluma de fuente Pri. (n phr) pen, fountain
pluma estilográfica Spa. (n phr) pen, fountain
pluma fuente Bol., Mex., Pue.R., Venz. (n phr) pen, fountain
pluma Pri. (n) pen
pluma Spa. (n) pen, fountain
plumón Cub., Mex. (n) marker
pneumático Chi., Col. (n) tire (car)
pneumático pinchado Chi. (n phr) flat tire
población Col. (n) village
pocillito de café Pue.R. (n phr) demitasse
pocillo Arg. (n phr) cup, coffee
pocillo Arg. (n) demitasse
taza de café Arg. (n phr) demitasse

pocillo ElS., Gua., Hon. (n) mug
pocillo para café ElS., Gua., Hon. (n phr) mug, coffee
podadera Pri. (n) pruning shears
podadora Bol., Ecu., Pue.R. (n) pruning shears
podadora de pasto Mex. (n phr) lawn mower
podadoras Mex. (n) pruning shears
podrido Pri. (adj) rotten (food)
polera Arg. (n) turtleneck
polera Chi. (n) t-shirt
policía Pri. (n) police officer
polilla Chi. (n) termite
político Pri. (n) politician
pollera Arg., Uru. (n) skirt
pollera Cos.R., Uru. (n) dress (woman's)
pollina Dom.R., Venz. (n) bangs (hair)
pollo Pri. (n) chicken
polo de cuello alto Spa. (n phr) turtleneck
polo Pri. (n) knit shirt
polola Chi. (n) girlfriend
pololo Chi. (n) boyfriend
pololo/a Chi. (n) sweetheart
polo-shirt Dom.R. (n) t-shirt
poltrona Chi. (n) chair, lounging
polución Col. (n) pollution
pomátomo Pri. (n) bluefish
pomelo Arg., Chi., Spa., Uru. (n) grapefruit
pomo Col. (n) drawer knob
pompa Mex. (n) buttock
pompis Mex. (n) buttock
poner en marcha Col. (v phr) start (car)
ponerse Chi., Dom.R., Mex. (v) wear (clothing)
ponerse high Dom.R. (v phr) get

ABBREVIATIONS: Arg.=Argentina Bol.=Bolivia Chi.=Chile Col.=Colombia Cos.R.=Costa Rica Cub.=Cuba Dom.R.=Dominican Republic Ecu.=Ecuador ElS.=El Salvador Gua.=Guatemala Hon.=Honduras Mex.=Mexico Pan.=Panama Per.=Peru Pri.=Primary Term Pue.R.=Puerto Rico Spa.=Spain Uru.=Uruguay Venz.=Venezuela

high (drugs)
ponerse la ropa Col. (v phr) dress (oneself)
poney Uru. (n) pony
poni Arg., Spa. (n) pony
ponqué Col. (n) cake
pony Col., Dom.R., Mex., Pan., Pue.R., Venz. (n) pony
por parte de la jornada Pri. (adj phr) part-time (work)
porcelana Pri. (n) china
porch Pan. (n) porch
porche Cub. (n) porch
poro de la nariz Mex. (n phr) nostril
poro Mex., Per. (n) leek
porotos de soja Uru. (n phr) soybeans
porotos negros Arg., Uru. (n phr) beans, black
porotos Pri. (n) beans
porro Arg. (n) marijuana cigarette
porro Pri. (n) leek
porrón Arg. (n) mug, beer
porta equipaje Chi. (n phr) trunk (car)
portafolio Bol. (n) briefcase
portafolio Mex. (n) attaché case
portafolio Pan. (n) three-ring binder
portafolios Arg. (n) attaché case
portafolios Pri. (n) briefcase
portamonedas Dom.R. (n) coin purse
portañuela Cub. (n) fly (pants)
portarrollo Mex. (n) tape dispenser
porteador Pue.R. (n) goalie
portero Col. (n) janitor
portero Col., Cub. (n) porter
portero Pri. (n) goalie
pórtico Pri. (n) porch
poste de luz Pan. (n phr) street lamp
postigos Pri. (n) shutters
postilla Cub., Dom.R. (n) scab
poto Chi. (n) buttock

poto Per. (n) butt
potrillo Chi. (n) colt
potrillo Col., Venz. (n) foal
potro Arg. (n) mustang
potro Pri. (n) colt
potro Pri. (n) foal
pozo Pri. (n) pothole
pozo Uru. (n) ditch
pradera Pri. (n) prairie
prado Col. (n) lawn
precio de entrada Pue.R., Venz. (n phr) entrance fee
precio de la entrada Col. (n phr) entrance fee
precio del billete de avión Spa. (n phr) airfare
precio del boleto Venz. (n phr) airfare
precio del pasaje Pri. (n phr) airfare
preciosa Chi. (adj) pretty
precioso Arg., Col. (adj) beautiful
precipicio Cub., Pan. (n) cliff
prefecto Chi. (n) mayor
preferencia Dom.R., Ecu., Spa. (n) right of way
premolar Cos.R. (n) canine (tooth)
preñada Col. (adj) pregnant
prenda Arg. (n) garment
prenda de vestir Cub., ElS., Gua., Hon., Spa. (n phr) garment
prender Chi., Dom.R., Pue.R. (v) start (car)
prender Pri. (v) turn on (television)
prensa Cos.R. (n) clamp
prensa Pri. (n) vise
prensapapas Mex. (n) potato masher
presa Cos.R. (n) traffic jam
presentador Pri. (n) host (show)
presentar Col. (v) show (movie)
preservas Dom.R. (n) preserves
presidente Arg. (n) chief executive

---

officer (CEO)
presidente municipal Mex. (n phr) mayor
presilla Cub. (n) staple
presilladora Cub. (n) stapler
preso Pri. (n) inmate
preso Pri. (n) prisoner
prestación complementaria ElS., Gua., Hon. (n phr) fringe benefit
prestarse jeringas Mex. (v phr) share needles
presto Col. (adj) quick
pretendiente Col. (n) boyfriend
primer piso Col., Dom.R. (n phr) ground floor
primer plato Ecu. (n phr) appetizer
primera Arg. (adj) first class
primera clase Pri. (adj phr) first class
primoroso Col. (adj) cute
printer Pue.R. (n) printer (computer)
prioridad de circulación Venz. (n phr) right of way
prioridad Pri. (n) right of way
prisionero Col. (n) inmate
prisionero Col., Pan. (n) prisoner
procesamiento de palabras (n phr) word processing
procesamiento de texto Cub., Ecu. (n phr) word processing
procesamiento de textos Arg., Mex. (n phr) word processing
programa comercial para promocionar algo Col. (n) infomercial
programa concurso Pri. (n phr) game show (television)
programa de charlas Col. (n phr) talk show
programa de concurso Col. (n phr) game show (television)
programa de concursos Dom.R., Gua.,

Mex., Venz. (n phr) game show (television)
programa de entretenimientos Arg. (n phr) game show (television)
programa de entrevistas Pri. (n phr) talk show
programa de televisión Arg., Dom.R., Venz. (n phr) broadcast
programa doble Mex. (n phr) double feature (movies)
programa en vivo Arg. (n phr) live broadcast
programa Pri. (n) program
programas Spa. (n) software
prometida Col., Cos.R., Dom.R., Pan. (n) fiancée (female)
prometido Col., Cos.R., Dom.R., Pan. (n) fiancé (male)
promotor/a Chi. (n) salesperson
pronóstico del tiempo Arg. (n phr) weather report
propaganda Arg., Chi., Col., Ecu., Pan., Per., Venz. (n) commercial
propiedad horizontal Uru. (n phr) apartment building
propulsión total Pri. (n phr) four-wheel drive
protector Arg. (n) sunscreen
protector de sol Venz. (n phr) sunscreen
protector solar Chi., Cos.R. (n phr) sunscreen
protestón Col. (adj) grumpy
proyectar Pri. (v) show (movie)
prueba anti-doping Pri. (n phr) drug test
prueba anti-drogas Col., Uru., Venz. (n phr) drug test
prueba de drogas Cub., Mex., Pue.R. (n phr) drug test

ABBREVIATIONS: Arg.=Argentina Bol.=Bolivia Chi.=Chile Col.=Colombia Cos.R.=Costa Rica Cub.=Cuba Dom.R.=Dominican Republic Ecu.=Ecuador ElS.=El Salvador Gua.=Guatemala Hon.=Honduras Mex.=Mexico Pan.=Panama Per.=Peru Pri.=Primary Term Pue.R.=Puerto Rico Spa.=Spain Uru.=Uruguay Venz.=Venezuela

prueba para drogas Pan. (n phr) drug
test
puchero Spa. (n) pot
pucho Chi. (n) cigarette
pueblecito Cub. (n) village
pueblito Dom.R. (n) village
pueblo Arg. (n) village
pueblo Pue.R. (n) downtown
puente de la nariz Mex., Venz. (n phr)
bridge of nose
puente Dom.R. (n) plantar arch (foot)
puerco Pri. (n) pig
puerro Arg., Col., Dom.R., Ecu., ElS.,
Gua., Hon., Spa., Uru. (n) leek
puerta de servicio Arg. (n phr) side
entrance
puerta del costado Cub. (n phr) side
entrance
puerta del lado Mex. (n phr) side
entrance
puerta lateral Pri. (n phr) side entrance
puesto de diarios Arg. (n phr)
newsstand
puesto de frutas Pri. (n phr) fruit stand
puesto de periódicos Pri. (n phr)
newsstand
puesto de periódicos y de revistas Col.
(n phr) newsstand
pugilista Chi. (n) boxer
pulgar Pri. (n) thumb
pulover Arg. (n) sweater
pulóver Pri. (n) pullover
pulpería ElS. (n) grocery
pulsar Cub. (v) click (computer)
pulsera Pri. (n) bracelet
pulso Cub. (n) bracelet
puños Pri. (n) handlebar grips (bicycle)
punta bola Bol. (n phr) pen, ball-
point
punta de la nariz Chi., Col., Mex.,

Spa., Venz. (n phr) tip of nose
punzón Bol., Col., Spa., Venz. (n) awl
pupo Arg., Chi. (n) navel
pupo Chi. (n) belly button
puro Cos.R. (n) marijuana cigarette

Uruguayans relax in the
confitería, a tearoom which
serves tea, sandwiches, and
cakes.

Q R

quedar varado Cos.R. (v phr) stall (car)
¿Qué ha habido? Ecu. (phr) How's it
    going?
¿Qué hay de nuevo? Dom.R. (int phr)
    What's up?
¿Qué hay? Chi., Col. (int phr) What's
    up?
quemacocos Mex. (n) sunroof
quemado Arg., Chi., Cub., Dom.R.
    (adj) tan (skin)
quemarse Arg., Chi., Cub., Dom.R.
    (v) tan
¿Qué pasa? (int phr) What's up?
queque Bol., Cos.R., Per. (n) cake
quequito Per. (n) muffin
querida Cub., Spa. (n) mistress
querido Spa. (n) sweetheart
querido/a Pri. (n) dear, darling, honey
¿Qué tal? Arg., Ecu., Mex., Pue.R.,
    Uru. (phr) How's it going?
quijada Col. (n) jaw
quijada Per. (n) chin
quimbombó Pri. (n) okra
quinta Arg. (n) cottage
quinta Arg. (n) vegetable garden
quitagrapas Spa. (n) staple remover
quitarse la ropa Col., Venz. (v phr)
    undress
¿Quiubo? Pan. (int phr) What's up?
quivi Uru. (n) kiwi
rabí Spa. (n) rabbi
rabino Pri. (n) rabbi
rabo de caballo Pue.R. (n phr) ponytail
    (hair)
radio Col., Spa., Venz. (n) spoke
    (bicycle wheel)

raíz Pri. (n) root (hair)
rallador Pri. (n) grater
rallo Col. (n) grater
ramplón Col. (adj) impolite
ranuras Pri. (n) tread (tire)
rápido Pri. (adj) quick
raptar Bol. (v) car jack (crime)
rascador Pri. (n) scraper
rasgar Col., Cos.R. (v) strum
rasgueado Col., Spa. (n) strumming
rasguear Col., Spa. (v) strum
rasgueo Col., Cos.R. (n) strumming
raspa Mex. (n) painter's knife
raspa Mex. (n) scraper
raspador Venz. (n) scraper
raspadora Chi. (n) scraper
rastrillo Arg., Chi., Col., Cub.,
    Dom.R., Mex., Pan. (n) lawn
    rake
rastrillo Mex. (n) razor
rasuradora Pri. (n) razor
ratón Pri. (n) mouse
raudo Col. (adj) quick
raya Pri. (n) crease (pants)
raya Pri. (n) part (hair)
rayo Arg., Col., Cub., Gua., Mex. (n)
    spoke (bicycle wheel)
rayo, relámpago Pri. (n) lightning
rebaño Pri. (n) flock
rebasar Dom.R., Mex. (v) pasar
    (traffic)
recámara Mex. (n) bedroom
recepción Arg., Chi. (n) lobby
recinto Pri. (n) office cubicle
recipiente hondo Col. (n) bowl
recluso Col. (n) inmate
recluso Col. (n) prisoner
recogedor de basura Col., Venz. (n
    phr) garbage collector
recolector de tiquetes Col. (n phr)

ticket collector

red de área amplia Cub., Mex., Spa. (n phr) WAN (wide area network)

red de área ancha Uru. (n phr) WAN (wide area network)

red de área extendida Col. (n phr) WAN (wide area network)

red de área extensa Venz. (n phr) WAN (wide area network)

red de área local Spa., Venz. (n phr) LAN (local area network)

red local LAN Mex. (n phr) LAN (local area network)

redactor Pri. (n) editor

redoblante Cos.R. (n) snare drum

reducir la marcha Chi. (v phr) shift gear

reducir la velocidad Chi., Dom.R., Pue.R., Spa. (v phr) decelerate

refacciones Mex. (n) spare parts

refajo Dom.R., Pue.R. (n) petticoat

refere Mex. (n) referee

referee Arg. (n) referee

referí Pan. (n) referee

reflector Pri. (n) reflector (bicycle)

refrí Cos.R. (n) refrigerator

refrigerador Bol. (n) freezer

refrigerador Pri. (n) refrigerator

refrigeradora Ecu., Per. (n) refrigerator

refrigerio Col. (n) snack

refugio Chi. (n) cabin

refunfuñón Col. (adj) grumpy

regadera (n) watering can

regadera Cub. (n) sprinkler

regador Arg. (n) sprinkler

regador de plantas Mex. (n phr) watering can

regalón Chi. (adj) spoiled (child)

regilete Mex. (n) sprinkler

región abdominal Col. (n phr)

abdomen

registrar el equipaje Pri. (v phr) check in (baggage)

reglar Cub. (v) tune up

rejilla del radiador Pri. (n phr) radiator grill

relicario Pri. (n) locket

remera Arg. (n) t-shirt

remera de manga corta Arg. (n phr) shirt, short-sleeved

remera de manga larga Arg. (n phr) shirt, long-sleeved

remezón Col. (n) earthquake

remolacha Pri. (n) beet

remolque Pri. (n) trailer

removedor de grapas Col. (n phr) staple remover

reno Pri. (n) reindeer

rentar Mex., Pue.R. (v) rent (housing)

reo Chi. (n) prisoner

reo Pan. (n) inmate

reparto Col., Mex., Spa., Venz. (n) cast (show)

repisa para zapatos Col. (n phr) shoe rack

repolla Pri. (n) cream puff

repollito Chi. (n) cream puff

repollitos de Bruselas Arg., Uru. (n phr) Brussels sprouts

repollitos italianos Chi. (n phr) Brussels sprouts

repollo Pri. (n) cabbage, white

repollo verde Pri. (n phr) cabbage, green

reporte Cub. (n) newscast

reporte del estado del tiempo Col. (n phr) weather report

reporte del tiempo Venz. (n phr) weather report

reporte meteorológico Venz. (n phr)

---

weather report
reportero del tiempo Venz. (n phr)
weather reporter
reportero meteorológico Venz. (n phr)
weather reporter
repostería Pue.R. (n) bakery
representante de ventas Cos.R. (n phr)
door-to-door salesperson
reproductor de CD Spa. (n phr)
compact disk player
reproductor de compact-disc Cub. (n
phr) compact disk player
reproductor de discos compactos ElS.,
Gua., Hon., Venz. (n phr)
compact disk player
repuestas Pue.R. (n) spare parts
repuestos Pri. (n) spare parts
resonante Col., Mex. (adj) resonant
resumé Pue.R. (n) résumé (work
history)
resúmen de noticias Gua. (n phr) news
brief
resúmen de noticias Per., Venz. (n phr)
news brief
resúmen noticioso Cos.R. (n phr) news
brief
retador Col., Dom.R., Mex. (n)
challenger (boxing)
retador de boxeo Venz. (n phr)
challenger (boxing)
retardo Col. (n) delay
retiro para ancianos Pan. (n phr)
retirement home
retollar Pue.R. (v) bloom
retoños de soya ElS., Gua., Hon. (n
phr) bean sprouts
retozón Col. (adj) naughty
retraso Pri. (n) delay
retroceso Venz. (n) reverse
reversa Col., Dom.R., Mex., Pan. (n)

reverse
reverso Col. (n) reverse
revisar Pri. (v) tune up
revisor Pri. (n) ticket collector
rezongón Col. (adj) grumpy
riachuelo Col., Dom.R., Pue.R. (n)
stream
rico Arg., Col., Spa. (adj) tasty
rico Arg., Pue.R. (adj) delicious
rico Venz. (adj) divino
rin Mex. (n) rim (bicycle wheel)
rin Pan. (n) hubcap
ring de boxeo Pri. (n phr) ring
(boxing)
risco Pue.R. (n) cliff
riversa Pue.R. (n) reverse
rizado Pri. (adj) curly (hair)
róbalo Gua. (n) flounder
robar un carro Venz. (v phr) car jack
(crime)
robar un vehículo con alguien dentro
Spa. (v phr) car jack (crime)
robarse un carro Cub. (v phr) car jack
(crime)
rociador Pri. (n) sprinkler
rock Dom.R., Spa. (n) rock music
rodaje Pri. (n) shooting (movie)
rodana Mex. (n) washer
rodar Pri. (v) shoot (movie)
rodete para cortar masa Col. (n phr)
pastry cutting wheel
rodillo Pri. (n) rolling pin
rollo de tape Dom.R. (n phr) tape
dispenser
rollo Pri. (n) Swiss roll
rollos Pan., Venz. (n) hair rollers
rolodex Pue.R. (n) rolodex
rolos Cub., Pue.R. (n) hair rollers
romper Pri. (v) break up (relationship)
rompeviento Uru. (n) turtleneck

ropa blanca Cos.R., Bol., Uru. (n phr) underwear

ropa casual Dom.R. (n phr) casual clothes

ropa de etiqueta Mex. (n phr) formal wear

ropa de interior Cub. (n phr) underwear

ropa de vestir Dom.R. (n phr) formal wear

ropa formal Pri. (n phr) formal wear

ropa informal Pri. (n phr) casual clothes

ropa interior Pri. (n phr) underwear

ropa Mex. (n) garment

ropero Bol., Chi., Cos.R., Ecu., Uru. (n) closet (clothes)

ropero Pri. (n) dresser

rosca Chi., Col. (n) doughnut

rosca de pan Pri. (n phr) bagel

rosca Uru. (n) Swiss roll

roto de la nariz Pue.R. (n phr) nostril

rotulador Spa. (n) marker

rótulo Cos.R. (n) billboard

rouge Arg., Bol., Chi. (n) lipstick

rubio Pri. (adj) blond (hair)

rubio/a Pri. (n) blond (person)

rueda Arg., Cub., Spa. (n) tire (car)

rueda Cub. (n) tire (bicycle)

rueda de andar Pri. (n phr) treadmill

rueda de auxilio Arg. (n phr) spare tire

rueda de Chicago Col. (n phr) ferris wheel

rueda de la fortuna Mex. (n phr) ferris wheel

rueda de repuesto Pri. (n phr) spare tire

rueda gigante Chi. (n phr) ferris wheel

rueda giratoria gigante Col. (n phr) ferris wheel

rueda muscovita Ecu. (n phr) ferris wheel

rueda pinchada Spa. (n phr) flat tire

rueda Venz. (n) ferris wheel

rueda Venz. (n) rim (bicycle wheel)

ruedo doble Venz. (n phr) cuff (pants)

ruidoso Pri. (adj) loud (noise)

ruleros Pri. (n) hair rollers

rulos Col., Spa. (n) hair rollers

runcho Pan. (adj) cheap

rush hour Arg. (n phr) rush hour

rutabaga Col. (n) rutabaga

RV Pue.R. (n) recreational vehicle

In Venezuela, *chamo* is a general, widely used greeting for people of all ages. Initially, it referred only to children.

ABBREVIATIONS: Arg.=Argentina Bol.=Bolivia Chi.=Chile Col.=Colombia Cos.R.=Costa Rica Cub.=Cuba Dom.R.=Dominican Republic Ecu.=Ecuador ElS.=El Salvador Gua.=Guatemala Hon.=Honduras Mex.=Mexico Pan.=Panama Per.=Peru Pri.=Primary Term Pue.R.=Puerto Rico Spa.=Spain Uru.=Uruguay Venz.=Venezuela

S

sábana bajera ajustable Spa. (n phr) sheet, contour

sábana de cajón Pri. (n phr) sheet, contour

sábana de elástico Arg. (n phr) sheet, contour

sábana de esquinera Venz. (n phr) sheet, contour

sábana de forro Col. (n phr) sheet, contour

sabandija Pue.R. (n) pest (person)

sabroso Pri. (adj) tasty

saca corchetes Chi. (n phr) staple remover

saca corcho Pan., Uru. (n phr) bottle opener

sacacorchos Pri. (n) corkscrew

sacagrapas Bol., Ecu., ElS., Gua., Hon. (n) staple remover

saca-grapas Venz. (n) staple remover

saco Bol. (n) jersey

saco Bol. (n) pullover

saco de lana Arg. (n phr) cardigan

saco de piel Pri. (n phr) coat, fur

saco de visón Pri. (n phr) coat, mink

saco Dom.R., Pan. (n) jacket

saco Pri. (n) coat

sacudida Col. (n) earthquake

sala de espera Venz. (n phr) lobby

salario Col., Mex., Pan. (n) salary

salida Pri. (n) departure

salir Chi. (n) starter

salir con Dom.R., Gua., Mex., Venz. (v phr) date

salón de belleza Dom.R., Mex., Pan., Pue.R. (n phr) hairdresser's shop

salto a lo alto Pue.R. (n phr) high jump

salto a lo largo Pue.R. (n phr) broad jump

salto alto Chi., Col., ElS., Gua., Hon. (n phr) high jump

salto ancho Col. (n phr) broad jump

salto con garrocha Pri. (n phr) pole vault

salto con pértiga Pue.R. (n phr) pole vault

salto de altura Pri. (n phr) high jump

salto de garrocha Venz. (n phr) pole vault

salto de longitud Pri. (n phr) broad jump

salto de pértiga Spa. (n phr) pole vault

salto en esquíes Venz. (n phr) ski jump

salto largo Chi., ElS., Gua., Hon. (n phr) broad jump

salto triple Pri. (n phr) triple jump

sandalias de plástico Mex. (n phr) rubbers (shoes)

sandalias Pri. (n) sandals

sandía (n) watermelon

sanja Cos.R. (n) ditch

sartén eléctrica Col., Pan. (n phr) griddle

sartén para asar Pri. (n phr) roasting pan

sastre Pri. (n) tailor

saya Cub. (n) skirt

sayuela Cub. (n) petticoat

sayuela Cub. (n) slip

scanner Arg., Dom.R., Pue.R. (n) scanner, optical

scroll Pue.R. (v) scroll (computer)

secador Arg. (n) hair dryer

secador de pelo Chi., Spa., Venz. (n phr) hair dryer

secadora de pelo Cub., Mex. (n phr) hair dryer
secadora de ropa Pue.R. (n phr) dryer
secadora manual Pri. (n phr) hair dryer
secadora Pri. (n) dryer
secarropas Arg. (n) dryer
sector residencial Pue.R. (n phr) residencial area
sedán Pri. (n) sedan
segadora Venz. (n) lawn mower
segueta Pue.R. (n) hacksaw
segunda Arg. (n) second class
segunda clase Pri. (n phr) second class
sello Spa. (n) ring, signet
selva tropical Pri. (n phr) rain forest
semental Arg., Col., Dom.R., Gua., Spa., Venz. (n) stallion
semilla de cajuil Dom.R. (n phr) cashew
semillas de soya Col., Gua. (n phr) soybeans
semillero Pri. (n) nursery (plants)
señal de cruce Venz. (n phr) turning light
señal de tráfico Dom.R., Spa., Uru. (n phr) road sign
señal de tránsito Venz. (n phr) road sign
señal del camino Per. (n phr) road sign
señal intermitente Uru. (n phr) turning light
señalización en la carretera Chi. (n phr) road sign
seno nasal Mex., Spa. (n phr) sinus
seno Pri. (n) breast
seno Pri. (n) sinus
señora Dom.R. (n) wife
Señora Pri. (n) Ma'am, Madam
sentirse mal por el vuelo Mex. (v phr) jet-lag, to have

sentirse mal por la altura Mex. (v phr) jet-lag, to have
separado Col. (adj) divorced
separador Col. (n) median
separador Col. (n) office divider
separarse Col. (v) break up (relation ship)
separarse Col. (v) divorce
sepelio Chi., Col., Mex. (n) burial
sequestrar en auto Pri. (v phr) car jack (crime)
serpiente Chi., Cub. (n) snake
serrucho Arg., Cub., Per. (n) saw
serrucho Cub., Venz. (n) hacksaw
serrucho eléctrico Pri. (n phr) chainsaw
serrucho Uru. (n) bucksaw
sesión de dos películas seguidas Spa. (n phr) double feature (movies)
sesión de música improvisado Col. (n phr) jam session
sesión de músicos de jazz o rock que tocan por placerpropio Pri. (n phr) jam session
seta Spa. (n) mushroom
seto Pri. (n) hedge
shampoo Arg. (n) shampoo
shorts Arg., Chi., Col., Dom.R., Mex., Venz. (n phr) shorts
show Cub., Dom.R. (n) program
shower Col. Pri. (n) bridal shower
shute Gua. (n) snoop
sierra de ballesta Pri. (n phr) bucksaw
sierra de bastidor Spa. (n phr) bucksaw
sierra de cadena Col., Mex., Pue.R. (n phr) chainsaw
sierra de metal Pri. (n phr) hacksaw
sierra eléctrica Chi., Uru. (n phr) chainsaw
sierra para cortar metal Col. (n phr)

hacksaw
sierra para metal Mex., Spa. (n phr)
hacksaw
sierra para metales Venz. (n phr)
hacksaw
sierra Pri. (n) range (mountain)
sierra Pri. (n) saw
silenciador Arg., Col., Ecu., Spa., Uru.
(n) muffler
silencioso Pri. (adj) quiet
silla Bol., Col. (n) seat (bicycle)
silla con coderas Mex. (n phr)
armchair
silla con escalón Venz. (n phr) chair,
step
silla de brazos Pri. (n phr) armchair
silla de director, silla plegable Pri. (n
phr) chair, director's
silla de extensión Col. (n phr) chair,
lounging
silla ejecutiva Mex. (n phr) chair,
director's
silla hamaca Arg. (n phr) chair, rocking
silla plegable Pri. (n phr) chair, folding
silla plegadiza Dom.R. (n phr) chair,
folding
silla reclinable Pue.R. (n phr) chair,
lounging
sillín Chi., Dom.R., Ecu., Pue.R.,
Spa., Uru. (n) seat (bicycle)
sillón Arg., Chi., Dom.R., Spa., Uru.
(n) armchair
sillón Cub., Pue.R. (n) chair, rocking
sillón ejecutivo Mex. (n phr) chair,
director's
sillón reclinable Mex. (n phr) chair,
lounging
silloncito Arg. (n) love seat
símbolo gráfico Cub. (n phr) icon
(computer)

simpático Chi. (adj) cute
simpático Chi. (adj) funny
simpático Cub. (adj) friendly
simpático Pri. (adj) nice
síndico Dom.R. (n) mayor
sinvergüenza Dom.R., Pue.R. (n)
tattler
sismo Col. (n) earthquake
sitar Pri. (n) sitar
sitio de la red Gua. (n phr) website
sitio web (n phr) website
ski acuático Chi. (n phr) water skiing
smoking Pri. (n) tuxedo
smoking Venz. (n) railcoat
snack Spa. (n) snack
snikers Pri. (n) sneakers
sobaco Pan. (n) armpit
sobrefunda Gua. (n) pillowcase
sobretodo Arg. (n) overcoat
sociable Cub. (adj) outgoing
sofá para dos personas Col., ElS.,
Gua., Hon., Venz. (n phr) love
seat
sofá Pue.R., Spa. (n) love seat
software Pri. (n) software
soja Chi., Spa. (n) soybeans
solicitud para hacer detener el bus
Col. (n phr) request stop (bus)
sollarse Col. (v) get high (drugs)
soltarse Col. (v) get high (drugs)
sombrero de copa Pri. (n phr) hat, top
sombrío Col. (adj) gloomy (person)
somier Spa. (n) box spring
soñoliento Pri. (adj) sleepy
sonoridad Pri. (n) tone
sonoro Pri. (adj) resonant
sopera Pue.R. (n phr) bowl, soup
soplete Pri. (n) blowtorch
soporte Col. (n) props
soquete Arg., Uru. (n) sock

sortija de diamante Pue.R. (n phr) ring, diamond
sortija de graduación Pue.R. (n phr) ring, class
sortija de sello Pri. (n phr) ring, signet
sortija Pan., Pue.R. (n) ring
sostén Pri. (n) bra, brassiere
soutien Uru. (n) bra, brassiere
soya Cub., Venz. (n) soybeans
spray de pelo Pue.R. (n phr) hairspray
spray para el pelo Dom.R., Mex., Pan. (n phr) hairspray
station Dom.R. (n) station wagon
stop Spa. stop (sign)
subirse Pri. (v) get on (bus)
subtítulos Pri. (n) subtitles
suburbio Col., Cub., Dom.R., Gua. (n) suburb
suculenta Pri. (n) succulent (plant)
sudadera Chi., Col., Dom.R., Mex., Pue.R. (n) sweatshirt
sudadero Gua. (n) sweatshirt
suecos Dom.R., Mex., Pue.R. (n) clogs
sueldo Pri. (n) salary
suéter abierto Col. (n phr) cardigan
suéter cerrado Mex. (n phr) pullover
suéter Dom.R., Pan. (n) knit shirt
suéter Ecu., Mex., Venz. (n) cardigan
suéter Pri. (n) sweater
suéter Venz. (n) jersey
suéter Venz. (n) pullover
suite de oficinas Venz. (n phr) office suite
sujetador Col. (n) paperclip
sujetador Spa. (n) bra, brassiere
sujetapapel Bol., Cos.R., Cub., ElS., Gua., Hon. (n) paperclip
sunroof Pri. (n) sunroof
super Mex. (n) grocery

supercolmado Dom.R. (n) grocery
supermercado Spa., Venz.
surfear en el Internet Dom.R. (v phr) surf the net
surfear la Internet Pri. (v phr) surf the net
suspensores Chi. (n) suspenders
susurro Col. (n) hum
sweater Arg. (n) pullover
sweater Chi. (n) cardigan

In Uruguay, the familiar Spanish *tú* (informal "you") becomes *vos,* and *eres* ("you are") becomes *sos.*

T

tabaco Cub. (n) cigar
tabaco de marihuana Dom.R. (n phr)
  marijuana cigarette
tábano Pri. (n) horsefly, gadfly
taberna Col. (n) bar
taberna Col. (n) wine shop
tabique Chi., Dom.R. (n) bridge of
  nose
tabla Chi. (n) table leaf
tabla de cocina Arg. (n phr) butcher
  block
tabla de cortar Col. (n phr) cutting
  board
tabla para cortar Chi., Col., Cub. (n
  phr) butcher block
tabla para cortar Pri. (n phr) cutting
  board
tabla para picar Col. (n phr) butcher
  block
tablero Pri. (n) table leaf
tablón de extensión Mex. (n phr) table
  leaf
taburete Mex. (n) ottoman
tachuela Pri. (n) stud
tachuela Pri. (n) tack
tacita Col. (n) demitasse
tacita de café Pri. (n phr) demitasse
taco alto Pri. (n phr) heel, high (shoe)
taco Chi. (n) traffic jam
taco de golf Col. (n phr) golf club
taco Pri. (n) heel (shoe)
tacón alto Col., Cub., ElS., Gua.,
  Hon., Mex., Pan., Spa., Venz. (n
  phr) heel, high (shoe)
tacón Col., Cub., ElS., Gua., Hon.,
  Mex., Pan., Spa., Venz. (n) heel

(shoe)
talacho Mex. (n) hoe
taladradora de mano Arg., Ecu., Per.,
  Spa., Uru. (n phr) drill, hand
taladro Chi. (n) drill, hand
taladro de mano Pri. (n phr) drill,
  hand
taladro manual Col., Mex. (n phr)
  drill, hand
talingo Pan. (n) blackbird
talle Col. (n) waist
taller Col. (n) garaje (repairs)
taller mecánico Arg. (n phr) garaje
  (repairs)
taller tipográfico Col. (n phr) print
  shop
talleres gráficos Col. (n phr) print shop
tambor Col. (n) drummer
tambor de conga Venz. (n phr) conga
  drum
tambor de tenor Col. (n phr) tenor
  drum
tambor militar pequeño Col. (n phr)
  snare drum
tambor Pri. (n) drum
tambora Cub. (n) hubcap
tamborilear Pri. (v) drum, tap
tamborilero Pri. (n) drummer
tamiz Arg., Col., Spa. (n) sieve
tam-tam Pri. (n) tom-tom
tamtan Spa. (n) tom-tom
tanatorio Spa. (n) funeral home
tanda Col. (n) batch
tándem Col., Spa. (n) bike, tandem
tangas Dom.R. (n) bikini briefs
tanque de gasolina Pri. (n phr) gas
  tank
tanque de nafta Arg. (n phr) gas tank
tantán Col. (n) tom-tom
tapa Spa. (n) appetizer

tapabocina Pue.R. (n) hubcap
tapacubo Ecu., Spa. (n) hubcap
tapacubos Pri. (n) hubcap
tapado Arg. (n) coat
tapado Chi. (adj) cloudy
tapado de piel Arg. (n phr) coat, fur
tapado de visón Arg. (n phr) coat, mink
taparuedas Chi. (n) hubcap
tape Pue.R. (n) tape
tapón Dom.R., Pue.R. (n) traffic jam
tapón Mex. (n) hubcap
tarifa aérea Col. (n phr) airfare
tarifa Arg., Ecu. (n) airfare
tarifa de vuelo Mex. (n phr) airfare
tarima Mex. (n) pallet
tarjeta Col., Pue.R. (n) index card
tarjeta madre Col., Spa. (n phr) motherboard
tarjeta principal Mex. (n phr) motherboard
taro Pri. (n) taro
tarola Pri. (n) snare drum
tarro de aceite Col. (n phr) oil can
tarta Bol., Chi., Pue.R., Uru., Venz. (n) tart
tarta Spa. (n) cake
tartaleta Mex. (n) tart
tartaleta Venz. (n) pie
tarugo Gua. (n) dowel
taxi Pri. (n) taxi
taxista Arg., Cub., Dom.R., Gua., Mex., Per., Spa. (n) taxi driver
taza de café Arg., Cub. (n phr) mug, coffee
taza del caucho Venz. (n phr) hubcap
taza para café Pri. (n phr) cup, coffee
tazas medidoras Dom.R. (n phr) measuring cups
tazas para medir Pri. (n phr) measuring cups
tazón Chi. (n) mug
tazón Col., Mex. (n) bowl
tazón de café Pue.R. (n phr) mug, coffee
tazón para batir Mex. (n phr) bowl, mixing
tazón para medir Pri. (n phr) bowl, mixing
tazón para mezclar ElS., Gua., Hon., Venz. (n phr) bowl, mixing
tazón Pri. (n) bowl, soup
techo corredizo Col., Venz. (n phr) sunroof
techo descapotable Venz. (n phr) sunroof
techo solar Chi., Spa. (n phr) sunroof
teclado Pri. (n) keyboard (computer)
técnico Mex. (n) manager (sports)
tedioso Col. (adj.) boring
teenager Dom.R. (n) teenager
teleaudiencia Col. (n) television viewer
telecable Dom.R. (n) cable television
telecadena Dom.R. (n) network (television)
telediario Pri. (n) newscast
teleférico Mex., Venz. (n) funicular
teléfono público Mex. (n phr) telephone booth
telenoticiero Cos.R., Dom.R. (n) newscast
telenovela Pri. (n) soap opera
telepromoción Spa. (n) infomercial
televidente Pri. (n) television viewer
televisión Col., Mex., Spa. (n) television set
televisión por cable Pri. (n phr) cable television
televisión por satélite Pri. (n phr) satellite television

televisión vía satélite Spa. (n phr) satellite television

televisor Pri. (n) television set

telón Bol. (n) screenplay

tema Arg. (n) song

temblor Chi., Mex. (n) earthquake

temblor de tierra Col., Dom.R., Pue.R. (n) earthquake

temible Col. (adj) terrifying

témpano de hielo Chi. (n phr) iceberg

temporal Bol. (n) temporary worker

temporario Uru. (n) temporary worker

temporero Pri. (n) temporary worker

tenazas Pri. (n) pincers

tenazas Pri. (n) tongs

tendero Pri. (n) grocer

tenedor Arg. (n) carving fork

tenedor de libros Cub. (n phr) bookkeeper

tenedor de trinchar Col., ElS., Gua., Hon., Spa. (n phr) carving fork

tenedor para servir Pan., Pue.R. (n phr) carving fork

tener compromiso Col. (v phr) date

tener desfase horario Spa. (v phr) jet-lag, to have

tener jet lag Pri. (v phr) jet-lag, to have

tener puesto Col., Cub. (v phr) wear (clothing)

tener un/a beba/bebe/bebé/hijo/hija Arg. (v phr) give birth

tener una cita Pri. (v phr) date

tenis Col., Cos.R., Cub., Dom.R., Pue.R. (n) sneakers

tenis de lona Mex. (n phr) sneakers

tenis Dom.R., Mex. (n) shoes, tennis

teno Pri. (n) tenor drum

tenor Spa. (n) tenor drum

terminar Chi., Ecu., ElS., Gua.,

Hon., Mex., Venz. (v) break up (relationship)

termita Pri. (n) termite

ternera Pri. (n) calf

ternero/a Arg., Col. (n) calf

terno Bol., Per. (n) suit

terno Pri. (n) suit, three-piece

terraza cubierta Gua. (n phr) porch

terraza Chi. (n) balcony

terremoto Pri. (n) earthquake

terreno pantanoso Mex. (n phr) wetlands

terreno pantanoso Uru. (n phr) swamp

terreno para circos Col. (n phr) fairground

terreno para ferias Col. (n phr) fairground

terrible Dom.R. (adj) awful

terrorífico Col. (adj) terrifying

tesoro Chi. (n) love, lovey

tesoro Col. (n) dear, darling, honey

teta Arg., Col., Cos.R., Pan., Uru. (n) breast

tetera Chi., Col., Per., Spa. (n) kettle

tetilla Col. (n) nipple

¡Te veo luego! Col. (int phr) See you later!

¡Te veo más tarde! Col. (int phr) See you later!

ticket Dom.R., Venz. (n) ticket

tienda botánica Col. (n phr) herbalist's shop

tienda Cub. (n) department store

tienda de abarrotes Mex. (n phr) grocery

tienda de animales domésticos Mex. (n phr) pet shop

tienda de animales Pue. R., Spa. (n phr) pet shop

tienda de bebidas alcohólicas Pri. (n

phr) liquor store

tienda de botánica Spa. (n phr) herbalist's shop

tienda de campaña Chi., Cos.R., Dom.R., Mex., Spa., Venz. (n phr) tent

tienda de comestibles Pri. (n phr) grocery

tienda de departamentos Cos.R. (n phr) department store

tienda de libros Pue.R. (n phr) bookstore

tienda de licores Ecu. (n phr) wine shop

tienda de mascotas Dom.R. (n phr) pet shop

tienda de mascotes ElS., Gua., Hon. (n phr) pet shop

tienda de vinos Dom.R. (n phr) wine shop

tienda departamental Mex. (n phr) department store

tienda Gua., Pan. (n) grocery

tienda naturista Mex. (n phr) herbalist's shop

tienda por departamentos Dom.R., ElS., Gua., Hon., Pue.R., Venz. (n phr) department store

tights Pue.R. (n) tights

tijera podadora Venz. (n phr) pruning shears

tijeras de podar Arg., Dom.R., Spa. (n phr) pruning shears

tijeras para podar Col. (n phr) pruning shears

timbal Pri. (n) timpani

timbre Pri. (n) bell (bicycle)

tímido Pri. (adj) shy

timón Col., Cub., Gua., Pan. (n) steering wheel

timón Cub., Dom.R., Pan. (n) handlebars (bicycle)

timón Gua. (n) handlebars (bicycle)

tímpanos Col., Cub. (n) timpani

tinta Pri. (n) toner

tipo/a pesado/a ElS., Gua., Hon. (n phr) pest (person)

tiquete Col. (n) ticket

tiquete de ida y vuelta Col. (n phr) round trip ticket

tiquete de una sola vía Col. (n phr) one-way ticket

tirante Col. (n) snare (of drum)

tirantes Cub., Gua., Pan., Spa., Venz. (n) suspenders

tirar dedo Per. (v phr) hitchhike

tirar drogas Pue.R. (v phr) sell drugs

titulares Dom.R. (n) news brief

tobo Venz. (n) pail

tocadiscos para discos compactos Mex. (n phr) compact disk player

tocadiscos Pri. (n) compact disk player

tocador de discos compactos Dom.R. (n phr) compact disk player

tocador Pue.R., Spa. (n) dresser

tocar el tambor Col., Spa. (v phr) drum, tap

tocarse Mex. (v) get high (drugs)

tocón Pri. (n) stump

tolda Pan. (n) tent

tomate Chi. (n) bun (hair)

tomate Pri. (n) tomato

tonalidad Col. (n) key (music)

toner Dom. R. (n) toner

tonificador Mex. (n) toner

tono Col., Dom.R., Mex. (n) tone

tono Pri. (n) key (music)

tonos agudos Col. (n phr) treble (stereo)

tope Mex. (n) bump (road)
tórax Chi., Col. (n) chest
torcer a la derecha, izquierda Spa. (v phr) turn right, left
torno Mex., Uru. (n) vise
toronja Pri. (n) grapefruit
torre de apartamentos Dom.R. (n phr) apartment building
torta Arg., Chi., Col., Ecu., Per., Uru., Venz. (n) cake
torta Chi., Cos.R. (n) pie
torta Col. (n) tart
tortilla Bol., Col., Cub., Per., Pue.R., Spa., Venz. (n) omelet
tortilla española Dom.R. (n phr) omelet
tórtola Col. (n) dove
tostada Pri. (n) toast
tostado Col. (adj) tan (skin)
tostador Pri. (n) toaster
tostadora Chi., Col., Cub., Dom.R., Ecu., Pue.R., Spa., Venz. (n) toaster
townhouse Dom.R., Pue.R. (n) townhouse
toxicomanía Pri. (n) drug abuse
toxido Pan. (n) tuxedo
traba Chi. (n) barrette
trabajador eventual Mex. (n phr) temporary worker
trabajoso Col. (adj) difficult
tracción a las cuatro ruedas Spa. (n phr) four-wheel drive
tracción de cuatro ruedas Cub., Venz. (n phr) four-wheel drive
tracción en las cuatro ruedas Arg., Chi., Col., Gua., Mex. (n phr) four-wheel drive
traer un alucine Mex. (v phr) get high (drugs)

traficante de drogas Pri. (n phr) drug dealer
traficar con Col., ElS., Gua., Hon. (v phr) deal (drugs)
traficar Mex., Venz. (v) deal (drugs)
tráfico Cub. (n) traffic jam
tráfico de drogas Col., Dom.R., Gua., Spa., Uru. (n phr) drug deal
tráfico Pri. (n) traffic
trago Chi. (n) alcoholic beverage
trailer Chi., Cos.R., Cub., Dom.R., Pan. (n) trailer
traje a la medida Venz. (n phr) suit, tailored
traje Arg., Col., Pan. (n) dress (woman's)
traje Chi. (n) outfit
traje cruzado Pri. (n phr) suit, double-breasted
traje de mujer Pue.R. (n phr) dress (woman's)
traje de tres piezas Bol., Dom.R., Mex., Pue.R., Venz. (n phr) suit, three-piece
traje Mex. (n) garment
traje Pri. (n) suit
traje sastre Pri. (n phr) suit, tailored
traje traslapado Gua. (n phr) suit, double-breasted
trampolín Pri. (n) ski jump
tramposo Pri. (n) cheater
trancón Col. (n) traffic jam
tranque Cub., Pan. (n) traffic jam
tranquilo Dom.R., Pan. (adj) quiet
transacción de drogas Pri. (n phr) drug deal
transbordador Pri. (n) ferry
transbordar Pri. (v) change (train)
tránsito Chi., Cos.R., Dom.R. (n) traffic

ABBREVIATIONS: Arg.=Argentina Bol.=Bolivia Chi.=Chile Col.=Colombia Cos.R.=Costa Rica Cub.=Cuba Dom.R.=Dominican Republic Ecu.=Ecuador ElS.=El Salvador Gua.=Guatemala Hon.=Honduras Mex.=Mexico Pan.=Panama Per.=Peru Pri.=Primary Term Pue.R.=Puerto Rico Spa.=Spain Uru.=Uruguay Venz.=Venezuela

transmisión automática Pri. (n phr) automatic transmission

transmisión Chi., Col., Cos.R., ElS., Gua., Hon. (n) broadcast

transmisión directa Mex. (n phr) live broadcast

transmisión en directa Pri. (n phr) live broadcast

transmisión en directo Arg. (n phr) live broadcast

transmisión en directo Bol., Col., ElS., Gua., Hon., Uru. (n phr) live broadcast

transmisión en vivo Cos.R., Cub., Dom.R., Ecu., Mex., Pan., Spa., Venz. (n phr) live broadcast

transmisión en vivo y en directo Chi., Per. (n phr) live broadcast

transmisión Pue.R. (n) gearbox

transmitir Col., Cos.R., ElS., Gua., Hon., Venz. (v) broadcast

tranvía Pri. (n) trolley

trasero Pri. (n) butt

trasladarse Bol. (v) move

traste Arg., Chi. (n) butt

trastos Pan. (n) dishes

travieso Pri. (adj) naughty

trébol Pri. (n) cloverleaf junction

tremendo Arg., Chi., Cub., Mex., Venz. (adj) tremendous

tren de cercanías Spa. (n phr) local train

tren directo Pri. (n phr) through train

tren expreso Venz. (n phr) through train

tren local Pri. (n phr) local train

trenza Pri. (n) braid (hair)

trenza Pri. (n) pigtail

trepadora Pri. (n) climbing plant

tribunal de justicia Pri. (n phr) courthouse

trifocales Pri. (n) trifocals

trigueño Cub., Dom.R. (adj) brown (hair)

trigueño/a Col., Cub., Dom.R. (n) brunette (person)

trinche Pri. (n) carving fork

trinchera Pri. (n) trench coat

tripa del caucho Venz. (n phr) inner tube (bicycle tire)

tripear Pue.R. (v) get high (drugs)

triple salto Arg., Col. (n phr) triple jump

triquet Gua. (n) jack (car)

triste Mex. (adj) gloomy (person)

triturador de papas Uru. (n phr) potato masher

trituradora Pri. (n) shredder

trole Chi. (n) trolley

trolebús Mex. (n) trolley

trompa de pistones Spa. (n phr) French horn

truco Col., Mex. (n) stunt

trusa Col. (n) briefs

trusa Cub. (n) bathing suit

tubo bajo Ecu. (n phr) flat tire

tubo de escape Pri. (n phr) exhaust pipe

tubo Pri. (n) inner tube (bicycle tire)

tubos ElS., Gua., Hon., Mex. (n) hair rollers

tumbadora Cub. (n) conga drum

tuna Cub., Pue.R. (n) tuna

túnica Pri. (n) house robe

turismo Spa. (n) sedan

turnarse alternando coches Mex. (v phr) carpool

tutor Pri. (n) guardian

tuxedo Cub., Pue.R. (n) tuxedo

ABBREVIATIONS: Arg.=Argentina Bol.=Bolivia Chi.=Chile Col.=Colombia Cos.R.=Costa Rica Cub.=Cuba Dom.R.=Dominican Republic Ecu.=Ecuador ElS.=El Salvador Gua.=Guatemala Hon.=Honduras Mex.=Mexico Pan.=Panama Per.=Peru Pri.=Primary Term Pue.R.=Puerto Rico Spa.=Spain Uru.=Uruguay Venz.=Venezuela

U V W

ultrapasar Chi. (v) pasar (traffic)
umpire Pri. (n) umpire (baseball)
uña quitagrapas Mex. (n phr) staple
  remover
uñas Pri. (n) staple remover
uñas saca grapas Dom. R. (n phr)
  staple remover
unidad de disco Pri. (n phr) drive
  (computer)
upper floor Pri. (n phr) planta alta
urbe Col. (n) city
usar Arg., Bol., Gua., Pan., Venz. (v)
  wear (clothing)
usar drogas Col. (v phr) use drugs
usar la red Mex. (v phr) surf the net
usuario de drogas Pue.R. (n phr) drug
  user
útiles de oficina Ecu. (n phr) office
  supplies
vacante Dom.R. (adj) vacant
vacío Mex., Venz. (adj) vacant
vago Arg., Cub., Dom.R. (adj) lazy
vagón Bol., Ecu., Gua., Spa. (n)
  wagon
vagoneta Bol. (n) recreational vehicle
vagoneta Bol. (n) station wagon
vagón-restaurante Col. (n) dining car
  (train)
vainitas Dom.R., Ecu., Per., Venz. (n)
  beans, green
vajilla Col., Dom.R., Mex. (n) china
vajilla fina Pan. (n phr) china
vajilla Pan. (n) dishes
valenciana Pri. (n) cuff (pants)
valeroso Col. (adj) brave
valiente Pri. (adj) brave

valija Arg. (n) suitcase
valla Col., Dom.R. (n) billboard
vallas Pri. (n) hurdles race
valle Dom.R. (n) prairie
van Arg., Chi., Cub., Dom.R., Pan.,
  Pue.R. (n) van
vaqueros Arg., Cub., Spa., Uru. (n)
  blue jeans
vaquita de San Antonio Arg. (n phr)
  ladybug
vararse Col. (v) stall (car)
varilla de aceite Pue.R. (n phr) dipstick
varilla para medir el aceite Col. (n phr)
  dipstick
varillo Col. (n) marijuana cigarette
vasija Col., Pan. (n) bowl
vasija Pan. (n) bowl, mixing
vasija para mezclar Col. (n phr) bowl,
  mixing
vasito Pue.R. (n) shot glass
vaso Arg. (n) tumbler
vaso Cub. (n) mug
vaso de trago corto Dom.R. (n phr)
  shot glass
vaso para whiskey Pri. (n) tumbler
vaso tequilero Mex. (n phr) shot glass
VCR Chi., Col. (n) videocassette
  recorder (VCR)
vecindad Pri. (n) neighborhood
vecindario Bol., Col., Dom.R., Gua.,
  Per., Pue.R., Spa., Venz. (n)
  neighborhood
vehículo de recreo Pri. (n phr)
  recreational vehicle
vehículo recreacional Venz. (n phr)
  recreational vehicle
vela Cos.R. (n) wake
velación Col. (n) wake
velador Bol., Chi. (n) table, night
velatorio Spa. (n) wake

---

velero Dom.R. (n) sailboat
vello Arg. (n) hair
vello del pubis Uru. (n phr) pubic hair
vello Dom.R. (n) pubic hair
vello pubiano Pri. (n phr) pubic hair
vello púbico Col., Cos.R., ElS., Gua.,
Mex., Venz. (n phr) pubic hair
velludo Bol., Dom.R., Ecu., Pan., Uru.
(adj) velloso
velocidad máxima Mex., Pue.R. (n
phr) speed limit
velocímetro Pri. (n) speedometer
velorio (n) wake
veloz Chi., Col. (adj) quick
venado Pri. (n) deer
vendedor a domicilio Pri. (n phr)
door-to-door salesperson
vendedor Col. (n) grocer
vendedor puerta a puerta Col. (n
phr) door-to-door salesperson
vendedor/a Chi., Col., Dom.R., Ecu.,
ElS., Gua., Hon., Mex., Venz.
(n) salesperson
vender drogas Pri. (v phr) sell drugs
vender Pri. (v phr) deal (drugs)
venera Pri. (n) scallop
ventana de la nariz Cub. (n phr) nostril
ventana trasera Pri. (n phr) rear
window
ventanilla Pri. (n) nostril
ventanilla trasera Col. (n phr) rear
window
ver la televisión Spa. (v phr) watch
television
ver tele(visión) (v phr) watch television
verde Pri. (adj) green (eyes)
vereda Arg., Chi., Cos.R., Ecu., Per.,
Uru. (n) sidewalk
verruga (n) wart
vestíbulo Col., Cub., ElS., Gua., Hon.,

Spa., Venz. (n) lobby
vestido casero Col. (n phr) house robe
vestido Col., Pan. (n) suit
vestido de baño Col., Ecu., Pan. (n
phr) bathing suit
vestido de tres piezas Pan. (n phr)
suit, three-piece
vestido hecho a la medida Col. (n phr)
suit, tailored
vestido Pri. (n) dress (woman's)
vestido Pri. (n) garment
vestido sastre Pan. (n phr) suit, tailored
vestidura Cub. (n) garment
vestimenta Col. (n) outfit
vestir Chi. (v) wear (clothing)
vestirse de etiqueta Pri. (v phr) dress
up
vestirse elegante Chi., Col. (v phr)
dress up
vestirse formal Dom.R. (v phr) dress
up
vestirse Pri. (v) dress (oneself)
veterinaria Mex. (n) pet shop
vía rápida Mex. (n phr) expressway
vía única Chi. (n phr) street, one-way
víbora Arg., Bol., Mex., Uru. (n) snake
vicio de drogas Cub. (n phr) drug
habit
vicio Pri. (n) habit (drugs)
vida, mi Cub., Pue.R. (n) dear, darling,
honey
vidajeno/a Pan. (n) snoop
vidalia Pri. (n) onion, vidalia
vídeo Spa. (n) videocassette recorder
(VCR)
videocasete Pri. (n) videocassette
videocasetera Arg., Mex. (n)
videocassette recorder (VCR)
videograbadora Pri. (n) videocassette
recorder (VCR)

ABBREVIATIONS: Arg.=Argentina Bol.=Bolivia Chi.=Chile Col.=Colombia
Cos.R.=Costa Rica Cub.=Cuba Dom.R.=Dominican Republic Ecu.=Ecuador ElS.=El
Salvador Gua.=Guatemala Hon.=Honduras Mex.=Mexico Pan.=Panama Per.=Peru
Pri.=Primary Term Pue.R.=Puerto Rico Spa.=Spain Uru.=Uruguay Venz.=Venezuela

videojuego Pri. (n) videogame
vidriera Arg. (n) shop window
vieira Arg., Venz. (n) scallop
vientre Col., Dom.R. (n) abdomen
viga vertical Mex. (n) stud
villorrio Col. (n) village
vinatería Mex., Pue.R. (n) wine shop
vinería Uru. (n) wine shop
violoncelo Pri. (n) violoncello
violonchelo Spa. (n) violoncello
virar a la derecha, izquierda Cos.R.
    (v phr) turn right, left
vitrina Pri. (n) display cabinet
vitrina Pri. (n) shop window
víveres Dom.R. (n) grocery
vivero Arg., Col., Dom.R. (n) nursery
    (plants)
volante Pri. (n) steering wheel
volar Bol., Col., Per. (v) get high
    (drugs)
volarse Chi. (v) get high (drugs)
waffle Col., Mex. (n) waffle
wafle Gua. (n) waffle
WAN (n) WAN (wide area network)
web-site Dom.R., Pue.R. (n) website
western Spa. (n) movie, western
wipers Pue.R. (n) wipers (windshield)
word processing Pue.R. (n phr) word
    processing

When Spain was under Moorish rule, Spanish absorbed and adapted Arabic terms including *aceite* (oil) and *aceituna* (olive), products of great importance to Moorish culture.

ABBREVIATIONS: Arg.=Argentina   Bol.=Bolivia   Chi.=Chile   Col.=Colombia
Cos.R.=Costa Rica Cub.=Cuba Dom.R.=Dominican Republic Ecu.=Ecuador ElS.=El
Salvador Gua.=Guatemala Hon.=Honduras Mex.=Mexico Pan.=Panama Per.=Peru
Pri.=Primary Term Pue.R.=Puerto Rico Spa.=Spain Uru.=Uruguay Venz.=Venezuela

X Y Z

xilófono (n) xylophone
yautía Dom.R. (n) taro
yerba Col. (n) marijuana
yerba Col., Pue.R. (n) hierba
yerba Cub., Dom.R. (n) lawn
yerba mala Pue.R. (n phr) weed
yugos Cub. (n) cufflinks
yunta Pue.R. (n) sickle
yuntas Pue.R., Venz. (n) cufflinks
yuyo Arg. (n) weed
zafar Col. (v) quit using drugs
zancos Chi. (n) clogs
zanja Pri. (n) ditch
zapalillas Cub. (n) slippers
zapallito Bol. (n) squash
zapallito italiano Chi. (n phr) zucchini
zapallo Bol., Chi., Pan. (n) pumpkin
zapallo Uru. (n) squash
zapapico Mex. (n) scythe
zapatera Pri. (n phr) shoe rack
zapatillas Arg., Chi., Pan. (n) shoes, tennis
zapatillas Arg., Chi., Pan., Per., Uru. (n) sneakers
zapatillas de casa Spa. (n phr) slippers
zapatillas de deporte Spa. (n phr) shoes, tennis
zapatillas de lona Spa. (n phr) sneakers
zapatos bajitos Dom.R. (n phr) loafers
zapatos de andar Pri. (n phr) loafers
zapatos de caminar Col. (n phr) shoes, hiking
zapatos de casa Mex. (n phr) loafers
zapatos de caucho Col. (n phr) rubbers (shoes)
zapatos de caucho Ecu. (n phr) sneakers
zapatos de charol Pri. (n phr) shoes, patent leather
zapatos de cuero barnizado Arg., Bol., Cos.R., Ecu., Per., Pue.R. (n phr) shoes, patent leather
zapatos de cuero Dom.R., Venz. (n phr) shoes, patent leather
zapatos de goma Chi., Uru. (n phr) rubbers (shoes)
zapatos de goma Venz. (n phr) shoes, tennis
zapatos de goma Venz. (n phr) sneakers
zapatos de lona con suela de hule ElS., Gua., Hon. (n phr) sneakers
zapatos de patente Venz. (n phr) shoes, patent leather
zapatos de piel Dom.R. (n phr) shoes, patent leather
zapatos de tenis Pri. (n) shoes, tennis
zapatos estilo mocasín ElS., Gua., Hon., Spa. (n phr) loafers
zapatos tenis Col. (n phr) shoes, tennis
zarcillos de presión Venz. (n phr) earrings, clip
zarcillos de tornillo Venz. (n phr) earrings, screw
zarcillos Venz. (n) earrings
zarcillos Venz. (n) earrings, pierced
zepelín Cub., Venz. (n) blimp
ziper Dom.R. (n) fly (pants)
zipper Pue.R. (n) fly (pants)
zobaco Dom.R. (n) armpit
zona comercial Col., Cub., Mex., Pue.R. (n phr) business district
zona de negocios Spa. (n phr) business district
zona residencial Pri. (n phr) residential area
zorra Pan. (n) fox

ABBREVIATIONS: Arg.=Argentina Bol.=Bolivia Chi.=Chile Col.=Colombia Cos.R.=Costa Rica Cub.=Cuba Dom.R.=Dominican Republic Ecu.=Ecuador ElS.=El Salvador Gua.=Guatemala Hon.=Honduras Mex.=Mexico Pan.=Panama Per.=Peru Pri.=Primary Term Pue.R.=Puerto Rico Spa.=Spain Uru.=Uruguay Venz.=Venezuela

zorro Pri. (n) fox
zuecos Col., Cub., Spa., Uru. (n) clogs
zumbido Pri. (n) hum

The vocative *che*, used to get people's attention—as in *¡Che, prestá atención!*—is characteristic of Argentina. It is believed to have come from the Canary Islands.

PART III: SUBJECT AREAS

Animals: Birds

blackbird (n) mirlo
   Pan. talingo
chicken (n) pollo
   Pan. gallina
cock (n) gallo
cockatoo (n) cacatúa
   Chi. cata
crow (n) cuervo
cuckoo (n) cuco
   Col., Venz. cuclillo
   Mex. cucú
dove (n) paloma
   Col. palomo, tórtola
   Pue.R. pichón
duck (n) pato
gander (n) ganso
hawk (n) halcón
   Bol. alcón
   Chi. peuco
hen (n) gallina
heron (n) garza
hummingbird (n) colibrí
   Arg., Col., Pan. picaflor
   Ecu. chupaflor
macaw (n) guacamayo
   ElS., Gua., Mex. guacamaya
nightingale (n) ruiseñor
ostrich (n) avestruz
   Col. ñandú
owl (n) búho

Arg., Col., Cub., Dom.R. lechuza
   Chi. chuncho
parakeet (n) perico
   Spa. periquito
parrot (n) loro
   Col. cotorra, papagayo
   Dom.R. cotorra
partridge (n) perdiz
peacock (n) pavo real
penguin (n) pingüino
pheasant (n) faisán
pigeon (n) paloma
quail (n) codorniz
robin (n) petirrojo
rooster (n) gallo
seagull (n) gaviota
sparrow (n) gorrión
stork (n) cigüeña
swallow (n) golondrina
swan (n) cisne
turkey (n) pavo
   Cub. guanajo
   Mex. guajolote
turtledove (n) tórtola
vulture (n) buitre
   Chi. jote
   Cub. aura tiñosa
woodcock (n) chocha
   Col. gallineta
   ElS., Gua. gallina sorda, gallineta
   Venz. perdiz
woodpecker (n) pájaro carpintero

ABBREVIATIONS: Arg.=Argentina Bol.=Bolivia Chi.=Chile Col.=Colombia
Cos.R.=Costa Rica Cub.=Cuba Dom.R.=Dominican Republic Ecu.=Ecuador ElS.=El
Salvador Gua.=Guatemala Hon.=Honduras Mex.=Mexico Pan.=Panama Per.=Peru
Pri.=Primary Term Pue.R.=Puerto Rico Spa.=Spain Uru.=Uruguay Venz.=Venezuela

Animals: Insects & Bugs

bee (n) abeja
beetle (n) escarabajo
  Chi. cucaracha
  Dom.R. avejón
bug (n) bicho, chinche
  Col., Per., Pue.R. insecto
  Dom.R. insecto, pajarito
bumblebee (n) abejorro
  Pue.R. avejita
centipede (n) ciempiés
cicada (n) cigarra
  Chi., Pue.R., Venz. chicharra
cockroach (n) cucaracha
cricket (n) grillo
dragonfly (n) libélula
  Chi. matapiojos
  Cub. caballito del diablo
  Pan. caballito
firefly (n) luciérnaga
  Cub. cocuyo
  Pue.R. cucubano
flea (n) pulga
fly (n) mosca
grasshopper (n) saltamontes
hornet (n) avispón
horsefly, gadfly (n) tábano
  Col. moscardón
  Pue.R. caballito de San Pedro
insect (n) insecto
ladybug (n) mariquita
  Arg. vaquita de San Antonio
  Chi. chinita
  Mex. catarina
  Venz. coquito
louse (n) piojo
moth (n) polilla
praying mantis (n phr) manta religiosa
  Pan. maría palito
  Pue.R. mantilla
  Spa. mantis religiosa
scorpion (n) alacrán
  Arg., Chi., Col., Cos.R., Pan.,
  Spa., Uru., Venz. escorpión
spider (n) araña
  Dom.R. cacata
termite (n) termita
  Cos.R., Cub., Dom.R., Pan.,
  Pue.R. comején
  Chi. polilla
  Ecu., ElS., Gua., Hon. comején
wasp (n) avispa
  Pan. abejorro
yellow jacket (n phr) avispa con pintas
  amarillas
  Cub., Pan. abispa

Animals: Mammals

bull (n) toro
calf (n) ternero/a
  Col., Spa. becerro
caribou (n) caribú
cat (n) gato
colt (n) potro
  Chi. potrillo
cow (n) vaca
deer (n) venado
  Arg., Bol., Cos.R., ElS., Gua.,
  Hon., Spa., Uru. ciervo
dolphin (n) delfín
ewe (n) oveja
flock (n) rebaño
  Arg. bandada
  Chi. piño
  Col. manada
foal (n) potro

ABBREVIATIONS: Arg.=Argentina Bol.=Bolivia Chi.=Chile Col.=Colombia
Cos.R.=Costa Rica Cub.=Cuba Dom.R.=Dominican Republic Ecu.=Ecuador ElS.=El
Salvador Gua.=Guatemala Hon.=Honduras Mex.=Mexico Pan.=Panama Per.=Peru
Pri.=Primary Term Pue.R.=Puerto Rico Spa.=Spain Uru.=Uruguay Venz.=Venezuela

Col., Venz. potrillo
fox (n) zorro
Pan. zorra
goat (n) cabra (male), chivo (female)
hare (n) liebre
Pue.R. conejo
horse (n) caballo
mare (n) yegua
mole (n) topo
monkey (n) mono
Col. mico
Mex. chango
moose (n) anta
Chi. ante
Col., Mex. alce, ante
Arg., Spa., Venz. alce
mouse (n) ratón
Chi. laucha
mustang (n) mustango
Arg. potro
ox (n) buey
pig (n) puerco
Per. cerdo, chancho
Bol. chancho, cuchi
Arg., Chi., Ecu., Uru. chancho
Col. cerdo, marrano
Cos.R. chancho, cochino
Cub., Venz. cerdo, cochino
ElS., Gua., Hon. coche, marrano
Mex. cochino, marrano
Pan. marrano
Dom.R., Pue.R., Spa. cerdo
pony (n) jaca
Col., Dom.R., Mex., Pan. pony
Cub., Ecu. caballito
Pue.R., Venz. caballito, pony
Arg., Spa. poni
Uru. poney
porcupine (n) puerco espín
porpoise (n) marsopa

Chi., Ecu. delfín
rabbit (n) conejo
rat (n) rata
reindeer (n) reno
Dom.R. cervatillo
seal (n) foca
sheep (n) oveja
Mex. borrego
squirrel (n) ardilla
stallion (n) padrillo
Arg., Col., Dom.R., Spa., Venz. semental
Chi. garañón
Gua. garañón, semental
walrus (n) morsa
Dom.R. foca marina
wapiti (n) ciervo canadiense
wolf (n) lobo

Animals: Mollusks & Crustaceans

clam (n) almeja
cockle (n) berberecho
crab (n) cangrejo
Chi. jaiba, pancora
crayfish (n) cangrejo de río
Chi. camarón de agua dulce
Col., Dom.R. jaiba
Pue.R. juey
lobster (n) langosta
mussel (n) mejillón
Chi. choro
octopus (n) pulpo
oyster (n) ostra
Mex. ostión
prawn (n) gamba
Arg., camarón, langostino
Chi. camarón gigante

Col., Cub., Mex., Pan., Spa.
langostino
Ecu., Uru. camarón
scallop (n) venera
Arg., Venz. vieira
Chi. ostión
ElS., Gua. concha, escalope
Pan. conchuela
Spa. concha
shrimp (n) camarón
Chi. langostino
Spa. gamba
snail (n) caracol
Dom.R. babosa
squid (n) calamar
Chi. jibia

Animals: Reptiles, Amphibians & Fish

anchovy (n) anchoa
Chi. anchoveta
Cos.R., Dom.R., Pue.R.,
boquerón
Per. anchoveta, boquerón
bass (n) róbalo
bluefish (n) pomátomo
Mex. anjova, pez azul
carp (n) carpa
catfish (n) bagre
Spa. barbo
cod (n) bacalao
eel (n) anguila
flounder (n) lenguado, platija
Gua. róbalo
herring (n) arenque
lizard (n) lagartija (small lizard), lagarto
(large lizard)
mackerel (n) caballa

perch (n) perca
pike (n) lucio
pompano (n) pámpano
salmon (n) salmón
sardine (n) sardina
smelt (n) eperlano
Chi. pejerrey
snake (n) culebra
Arg., Bol., Mex., Uru. víbora
Chi., Cub. serpiente
snapper (n) pargo
Dom.R., Pue.R. chillo
Mex. guachinango, huachinango
sole (n) lenguado
sturgeon (n) esturión
swordfish (n) pez espada
Chi. albacora
trout (n) trucha
tuna (n) atún
Cub., Pue.R. tuna

Indians present in the Dominican Republic before the thirteenth century lent Dominican Spanish terms such as *batey*, which originally meant a small village plaza usually used as a playing field. Today it refers to an open space in the sugar cane fields surrounded by houses.

Common Adjectives

amazing (adj) asombroso
  Arg., Chi., Dom.R. increíble
  Col. estupendo, fenomenal
angry (adj) enojado
  Col., Cub., Venz. bravo
  Dom.R. furioso
  Ecu. enfurecido
  Pue.R. enfogono, molesto
awful (adj) horrible
  Arg., Chi., Col. espantoso
  Dom.R. terrible
bad (adj) malo
beautiful (adj) bonito, hermoso
  Arg. lindo, precioso
  Chi., Cos.R., Cub., Dom.R. bello
  Col. bello, lindo, precioso
  Ecu., Pue.R., Venz. lindo
best (adj) el mejor
better (adj) mejor que
big (adj) grande
boring (adj) aburrido
  Col. harto, tedioso
bothersome (adj) molesto
  Col. incómodo, inoportuno
  Venz. molestoso
brave (adj) valiente
  Col. valeroso
  Dom.R. guapo
cheap (adj) barato
  Col. asequible, ganga
  Pan. runcho
closed (adj) cerrado
cold (adj) frío
cute (adj) mono
  Arg. divino
  Bol. amoroso
  Chi. simpático

Col. primoroso
Cub. guapo, lindo
Dom.R., Ecu., Pan. gracioso
Mex. chulo
ElS., Gua., Hon., Per., Venz. chulo, lindo
Pue.R. bonito, chulito
dark (adj) oscuro
delicious (adj) delicioso
  Arg., Pue.R. rico
  Per. exquisito
delightful (adj) divino
  Chi. agradable
  Col. agradable, deleitable, encantador, exquisito
  ElS., Gua., Hon. muy agradable
  Venz. rico
difficult (adj) difícil
  Col. dificultoso, peliagudo, trabajoso
early (adj) temprano
easy (adj) fácil, sencillo
empty (adj) vacío
evil (adj) malvado
  Arg. maldito, malo
  Chi., Dom.R. malo
  Col. maligno, malo
  Venz. maligno
exciting (adj) emocionante
  Col. conmovedor, impresionante
  Pue.R. excitante
expensive (adj) caro, costoso
far (adj) lejos
friendly (adj) amistoso
  Col., Mex., Pue.R. amigable
  Cub. simpático
full (adj) lleno
fun (adj) divertido, entretenido
funny (adj) divertido, gracioso

Chi. simpático
Col., Dom.R., Ecu., Pan. chistoso
gloomy (person) (adj) lúgubre
Col. sombrío
Cub. melancólico
Dom.R. de mal humor
Mex. triste
Venz. deprimido
good (adj) bueno
grumpy (adj) malhumorado
Chi. andar de malas pulgas
Col. gruñón, protestón,
refunfuñón, rezongón
Pue.R. de mal humor
Venz. cascarrabias
hairy (adj) velloso
Arg., Chi., Pue.R., Spa., Venz.
peludo
Bol., Dom.R., Ecu., Pan., Uru.
velludo
Col. mechudo, peludo
handsome (adj) guapo
Arg. buen mozo
Bol. churro
Chi., Dom.R. buenmozo
Col. bien parecido, buenmozo,
churro, majo
Venz. bien parecido
heavy (adj) pesado
impolite (adj) descortés, mal educado
Col. desatento, grosero, ramplón
Spa. maleducado
impressive (adj) impresionante
Col. emocionante
intelligent (adj) inteligente
interesting (adj) interesante
late (adj) tarde
lazy (adj) perezoso
Arg., Cub. vago
Bol., Chi., Venz. flojo

Col., Uru. haragán
Dom.R. haragán, vago
Mex. flojo, holgazán
light (color) (adj) claro
light (weight) (adj) ligero
Arg., Chi. liviano
loud (noise) (adj) ruidoso
Chi. fuerte
magnificent (adj) magnífico
naughty (adj) travieso
Arg. liero
Chi. malvado
Col. juguetón, retozón
Cub. pillo
Dom.R. bellaco
Pue.R. necio
near (adj) cerca
new (adj) nuevo
nice (adj) simpático
Col. agradable, amable, amigable
Cub., Spa. amable
Dom.R. chulo
Pue.R. chévere
Venz. agradable
occupied (adj) ocupado
open (adj) abierto
outgoing (adj) extrovertido
Arg. dado
Cub. sociable
overwhelming (adj) abrumador
Chi., Col. agobiante
polite (adj) cortés, educado
Col. atento, culto
Mex. caballeroso
pretty (adj) guapa
Arg., Cub., Pue.R. linda
Chi. bonita, preciosa
Col. bella, bonita, linda
Dom.R., Ecu., ElS., Gua., Pan.,
Uru. bonita

ABBREVIATIONS: Arg.=Argentina Bol.=Bolivia Chi.=Chile Col.=Colombia
Cos.R.=Costa Rica Cub.=Cuba Dom.R.=Dominican Republic Ecu.=Ecuador ElS.=El
Salvador Gua.=Guatemala Hon.=Honduras Mex.=Mexico Pan.=Panama Per.=Peru
Pri.=Primary Term Pue.R.=Puerto Rico Spa.=Spain Uru.=Uruguay Venz.=Venezuela

quick (adj) rápido
  Chi. veloz
  Col. presto, raudo, veloz
quiet (adj) silencioso
  Chi., Col., Venz. callado
  Dom.R., Pan. tranquilo
right (adj) correcto
rotten (food) (adj) podrido
  Mex. hechado a perder
round (adj) redondo
sad (adj) triste
scared (adj) asustado
  Col. atemorizado
sexy (adj) sexy
short (adj) pequeño
  Arg., Per., Spa. bajo
  Chi., Pan., Pue.R. corto
  Col., Dom.R. bajito
  Mex. bajo, chaparro, corto
shy (adj) tímido
  Cub., Pan. penoso
sleepy (adj) soñoliento
  Dom.R. asueñado
  Mex. adormilado
small (adj) chiquito, pequeño
  Arg., Chi. chico
  Col. chico, corto, menudo
sour (adj) agrio
  Col. ácido, acre
  Pan. ácido
spoiled (child) (adj) mimado
  Arg., Cub., Pan., Pue.R.
  malcriado
  Chi. regalón
  Col. consentido,
  malacostumbrado, malcriado
  Cos.R. chineado
  Dom.R. ñoño
  Ecu. consentido
  Mex. chiqueado, consentido

  Per. engreído
square (adj) cuadrado
superb (adj) magnífico
sweet (adj) dulce
talkative (adj) hablador, locuaz
  Arg. charlatán
  Col. charlatán, dicharachero,
  garlador
  Pan. conversador
tall (adj) alto
tasty (adj) sabroso
  Arg., Cub., Spa. rico
terrible (adj) terrible
terrifying (adj) aterrador
  Bol. miedoso
  Col. aterrorizante, horripilante,
  temible, terrorífico
tremendous (adj) imponente
  Arg., Chi., Cub., Mex., Venz.
  tremendo
  Col. asombroso, formidable
vacant (adj) libre
  Col. desocupado
  Dom.R. vacante
  Mex., Venz. vacío
warm (adj) tibio
worse (adj) peor que
worst (adj) el peor
wrong (adj) equivocado
  Col. erróneo
  Pue.R., Spa. incorrecto
young (adj) joven

Peru's native *cóndor* gets its name from the Quechuan *kuntur*.

Drug Culture

addicted (adj) adicto
Col. narcómano
addiction (n) dependencia
Col. adicción, hábito
Cos.R., Dom.R., Mex., Pan.,
Pue.R. adicción
alcoholic (n) alcohólico
alcoholic beverage (n phr) bebida
alcohólica
Chi. trago
become intoxicated (v phr) intoxicarse
Chi. embriagarse
Cub., Mex., Pan. emborracharse
Spa. estar bajo la influencia del
alcohol o de las drogas
cocaine (n) cocaína
Col. coca
cocaine spoon (n phr) cuchara de
cocaína
Col. cuchara para la cocaína
Mex. grapas de cocaína
Spa. cuchara para cocaína
deal (drugs) (v phr) vender
Col., ElS., Gua. traficar con
Mex., Venz. traficar
Pue.R. distribuir
drug abuse (n phr) toxicomanía
Col., Cub., Dom.R., Pue.R.
abuso de drogas
drug addict (n phr) drogadicto
Col. narcómano
drug addiction (n phr) drogadicción
Col. narcomanía
Pue.R. adicción a las drogas
drug deal (n phr) transacción de drogas
Col., Dom.R., Gua., Spa., Uru.
tráfico de drogas

Ecu., Venz. negocio de drogas
Pue.R. negociación
drug dealer (n phr) traficante de drogas
Bol., Cos.R., Cub., Venz.
narcotraficante
drug habit (n phr) drogadicción
Col. narcomanía
Cub. vicio de drogas
drug paraphernalia (n phr) parafernalia
de drogas
drug runner (n phr) narcotraficante
drug squad (n phr) brigada anti-drogas
drug test (n phr) prueba anti-doping
Col., Uru., Venz. prueba anti-
drogas
Cub., Mex., Pue.R. prueba de
drogas
Pan. prueba para drogas
drug user (n phr) consumidor de
drogas
Pue.R. usuario de drogas
drunk (adj) borracho
Col. bebido
drunkard (n) borracho
Col. beodo, borrachín
Dom.R. borrachón
get high (drugs) (v phr) colocarse
Bol., Per. volar
Chi. volarse
Col. entrar en onda, sollarse,
soltarse, volar
Cub. cojer nota
Dom.R. darse un viaje, ponerse
high
Mex. tocarse, traer un alucine
Pue.R. elevarse, tripear
Venz. meterse un viaje
habit (n) vicio
Col. hábito
hard drugs (n phr) drogas duras

ABBREVIATIONS: Arg.=Argentina Bol.=Bolivia Chi.=Chile Col.=Colombia
Cos.R.=Costa Rica Cub.=Cuba Dom.R.=Dominican Republic Ecu.=Ecuador ElS.=El
Salvador Gua.=Guatemala Hon.=Honduras Mex.=Mexico Pan.=Panama Per.=Peru
Pri.=Primary Term Pue.R.=Puerto Rico Spa.=Spain Uru.=Uruguay Venz.=Venezuela

Col. drogas fuertes
hard liquor (n phr) licor espiritoso
Bol., Dom.R., Venz. licor fuerte
Col. licor de alto contenido
alcohólico
ElS., Pan. licor
Mex. bebidas fuertes
Spa. bebida alcohólica fuerte
Uru. bebida alcohólica
heroin (n) heroína
inhale (drugs) (v) aspirar
Arg., Col., Mex., Pue.R. inhalar
Cub., Dom.R. oler
inject (drugs) (v phr) inyectar(se)
intoxicated (adj) borracho, embriagado
Spa. bajo la influencia
liquor (n) bebidas fuertes
Col., Cub., ElS., Gua., Hon.,
Mex., Pan., Venz. licor
Spa. bebida alcohólica fuerte
LSD (n) LSD
Cos.R., Cub. ácido
marijuana (n) marihuana
Col. yerba
Cos.R. monte, mota
marijuana cigarette (n phr) cigarrillo
de marihuana
Arg. porro
Chi. pito
Col. varillo
Cos.R. puro
Cub., Pue.R. pitillo de marihuana
Dom.R. joint, tabaco de
marihuana
marijuana pipe (n phr) pipa de
marihuana
quit using drugs (v phr) dejar las
drogas
Col. cortar con el vicio, zafar
sell drugs (v phr) vender drogas

Pue.R. tirar drogas
share needles (v phr) compartir agujas
Col. compartir jeringas
Mex. prestarse jeringas
Venz. compartir inyectadoras
soft drugs (n phr) drogas blandas
Col. drogas más suaves
Mex. drogas suaves
use drugs (v phr) drogarse
Col. consumir drogas, usar drogas
ElS., Gua. consumir drogas

A cousin to Russia's *piroshki* and Italy's *calzone*, Uruguay's *empanada* is a small pastry stuffed with meat, seafood, vegetables, or fruit.

Food: Breads & Pastries

bagel (n) rosca de pan
Bol., Col., Pue.R. bagel
baguette (n) baguette
Bol., Chi., Col., Dom.R., Venz.
pan francés
Pan. pan flauta, pan francés
Spa. barra de pan
bake (v) hornear
Spa. cocinar en el horno
batch (n) hornada
Chi. horneada
Col. tanda
Cos.R. lote
biscuit (n) bizcocho, galleta
Arg. galletita
Dom.R. bizcochito
Mex. bisquet
Pue.R. panecillo
bread, rye (n phr) pan negro
Arg., Col., Cub., Dom.R., Ecu.,
Spa., Venz. pan de centeno
Chi. pan centeno
bread, sliced (n phr) pan de molde
Arg. pan lactal
Col. pan tajado
Cos.R. pan cortado
Dom.R. pan de sandwich
Mex. pan de caja
Pue.R. pan especial
Venz. pan en rodajas
bread, white (n phr) pan blanco tajado
Cub. pan de molde
Pue.R. pan especial
Arg., Col., Dom.R., Mex., Spa.,
Venz. pan blanco
Uru. pan blanco rebanado
bun (n) panecillo

Arg., Uru. pancito
Bol., Spa. bollo
Col. pancillo, pan pequeño
Cos.R. bollito
Mex. pan para hamburgeusas, pan
para hot dogs
Pan. pan para hamburguesas
cake (n) pastel
Arg., Chi., Ecu., Uru., Venz. torta
Bol., Cos.R. queque
Col. ponqué, torta
Cub. cake
Dom.R., Pue.R. bizcocho
Pan. cake, dulce
Per. queque, torta
Spa. tarta
cookie (n) galleta
Arg. galletita, masita
Cos.R., Pue.R., Uru. galletita
Cub. galletica
ElS., Gua., Hon. galleta dulce
Per. galleta de dulce
Spa. pasta
cracker (n) galleta
Arg. galletita
Dom.R. galletica
Venz. galleta de soda
cream puff (n phr) repolla
Bol., ElS., Gua., Hon., Spa. bollo
de crema
Chi. repollito
Pan. ecler
Uru. bomba de crema
Venz. pastel de crema
croissant (n) croissant
Arg., Col. medialuna
Chi. media luna
Dom.R. cruasant, pan camarón
Mex. cuernito
Per. cachito

ABBREVIATIONS: Arg.=Argentina Bol.=Bolivia Chi.=Chile Col.=Colombia
Cos.R.=Costa Rica Cub.=Cuba Dom.R.=Dominican Republic Ecu.=Ecuador ElS.=El
Salvador Gua.=Guatemala Hon.=Honduras Mex.=Mexico Pan.=Panama Per.=Peru
Pri.=Primary Term Pue.R.=Puerto Rico Spa.=Spain Uru.=Uruguay Venz.=Venezuela

Danish (n) pastelillo de fruta y nueces
  Mex. pan dulce
  Pan. danesa
  Per. pastel
  Venz. pastel danés
dough (n) masa
doughnut (n) dónut
  Chi. rosca
  Col. dona, rosca
  ElS., Gua., Hon., Mex., Pan.,
  Pue.R. dona
hallah (Jewish) (n) hallah
knead (v) amasar
muffin (n) panecillo
  Arg., Col. muffin
  Bol. pancito
  Gua. mollete
  Mex. mufin, panqué, pastelito
  Per. quequito
  Spa. magdalena
pancake (n) panqueque
  Cub., Dom.R., Pan., Pue.R.
  pancake
  Mex. hotcake
  Venz. panqueca
pie (n) pastel, tarta
  Bol., Dom.R. pie
  Chi., Cos.R. torta
  Mex. pay
  Venz. tartaleta
puff pastry (n phr) hojaldre
  Chi. masa de mil hojas
  Venz. milhoja
rise (bread) (v) leudarse
  Bol., Chi., ElS., Gua., Hon.,
  Mex., Spa. levantarse
  Col. inflarse, levantarse
  Cos.R., Dom.R., Ecu., Pan.,
  Pue.R. crecer
roll (n) pancito

  Col., Pan. panecillo
  ElS., Gua., Spa. bollo
  Pue.R. pan
soufflé (n) soufflé
Swiss roll (n phr) rollo
  Spa. brazo de gitano
  Uru. rosca
  Venz. bollo de pan
tart (n) moldecito
  Bol., Chi., Pue.R., Uru., Venz.
  tarta
  Col. torta
  Dom.R. dulcito relleno
  Gua. pastelito
  Mex. tartaleta
  Spa. pastel de frutas
toast (n) tostada
  Mex., Pan. pan tostado
waffle (n) gofre
  Col. barquillo, waffle
  Gua. wafle
  Mex. waffle

Food: Fruits & Vegetables

almond (n) almendra
apple (n) manzana
apricot (n) albaricoque
  Arg., Chi., Uru. damasco
  Mex. chabacano
artichoke (n) alcachofa
  Arg., Uru. alcaucil
asparagus (n) espárrago
avocado (n) aguacate
  Arg., Bol., Chi., Per., Uru. palta
banana (n) plátano
  Arg., Uru. banana
  Col., Ecu. banano, guineo

Dom.R., Pan., Pue.R. guineo
Cos.R. banano
Venz. cambur
bean sprouts (n phr) germinados de
soja
Arg., Uru. brotes de soja
ElS., Gua. retoños de soya
Pan. frijol nacido
Pue.R. habichuelas de soya
beans (n) porotos
Col., Cub., Gua., Mex., Pan.
frijoles
Dom.R., Pue. R. habichuelas
Ecu. frejoles
Spa. alubias
Venz. caraotas
beans, black (n phr) frijoles
Arg., Uru. porotos negros
Col., Cub., ElS., Gua., Hon.,
Mex., Pan. frijoles negros
Pue.R. habichuelas negras
Spa. alubias negras
Venz. caraotas negras
beans, broad (n phr) habas
Arg., Uru. chauchas
Dom.R. guandules
beans, green (n phr) habichuelas
Arg., Uru. chauchas
Dom.R., Ecu., Per., Venz. vainitas
ElS., Gua., Hon., Mex. ejotes
Pue.R. habichuelas verdes
Spa. judías verdes
beans, kidney (n phr) habichuelas
Cub. frijoles colorados
Dom.R. habichuelas rojas
Spa. alubias rojas
beans, lima (n phr) frijoles de media
luna
Cub. habas limas
Spa. habas

beet (n) remolacha
Bol., Chi., Per. beterraga
Mex. betabel
berry (n) baya
Pue.R. cereza
black currant (n phr) casis
Col., Mex. grosella
Pan. pasita
blueberry (n) arándano
Mex. mora azul
Per. mora
Brazil nut (n phr) nuez de Brasil
Col. nuez del Brasil
broccoli (n) brócoli
Brussels sprouts (n phr) coles de
Bruselas
Arg., Uru. repollitos de Bruselas
Chi. repollitos italianos
cabbage, green (n phr) repollo verde
Cub., Ecu., Mex., Spa. col
Dom.R. lechuga repollada
cabbage, white (n phr) repollo
Cub., Spa. col
Mex. col blanca
cantaloupe (n) melón chino
Chi. melón calameño
Col. cantaloupe, melón
Cub. cantalupa
Pan., Per., Venz. melón
carrot (n) zanahoria
cashew (n) nuez de la India
Arg., Uru. castaña de cajú
Chi. castaña
Cub. anacardo
Dom.R. semilla de cajuil
Pan. pepita de marañón
Pue.R. avellana
cauliflower (n) coliflor
chard (n) acelga
cherry (n) cereza

ABBREVIATIONS: Arg.=Argentina Bol.=Bolivia Chi.=Chile Col.=Colombia
Cos.R.=Costa Rica Cub.=Cuba Dom.R.=Dominican Republic Ecu.=Ecuador ElS.=El
Salvador Gua.=Guatemala Hon.=Honduras Mex.=Mexico Pan.=Panama Per.=Peru
Pri.=Primary Term Pue.R.=Puerto Rico Spa.=Spain Uru.=Uruguay Venz.=Venezuela

chestnut (n) castaña
    Dom.R. pan de fruta
chickpeas (n) garbanzos
coconut (n) coco
corn (n) maíz
    Bol., Chi., Ecu., Per., Uru.
    choclo (choclo in Arg. is sweet
    corn)
    Cub. mazorca (on the cob)
    Mex. elote (on the cob)
cranberry (n) arándano agrio
    Mex. mora roja
    Pue.R. cranberry
    Venz. cereza agria
cucumber (n) pepino
    Pue.R. pepinillo
date (n) dátil
eggplant (n) berenjena
endive (n) escarola
    Arg., Col., Spa. endibia
    Col. endivia
fennel (n) hinojo
fig (n) higo
French fries (n phr) papas fritas
    Dom.R. papitas fritas
    Spa. patatas fritas
garlic (n) ajo
gooseberry (n) grosella silvestre
    Pue.R. grosella
grape (n) uva
grapefruit (n) toronja
    Arg., Chi., Spa., Uru. pomelo
guava (n) guayaba
hazelnut (n) avellana
    Dom.R. coquito
horseradish (n) rábano picante
huckleberry (n) mora
kiwi (n) kiwi
    Uru. quivi
kohlrabi (n) colinabo

leek (n) porro
    Arg., Col., Dom.R., Ecu., ElS.,
    Gua., Hon., Spa., Uru. puerro
    Mex., Per. poro
lemon (n) limón
lentils (n) lentejas
lettuce (n) lechuga
lime (n) lima
    Cub., Pan. limón
mandarine orange (n phr) mandarina
    Pue.R. china mandarina
melon (n) melón
mushroom (n) hongo
    Col., Mex. champiñón
    Spa. champiñón, seta
nectarine (n) ciruela de negra
    Chi. durazno pelado
    Col., Cub. nectarina
    Cos.R., Dom.R. ciruela
    ElS., Gua. nectarino
    Mex. nectarín
    Pan. ciruela negra
    Pue.R., Venz. nectarine
    Spa. briñón
    Uru. pelón
okra (n) quimbombó
    Dom.R. molondrón
    Mex. okra
olive (n) aceituna
    Cos.R. oliva
onion (n) cebolla
onion, pickling (n phr) cebollino
    Chi. cebollín
    Col. cebollina
    Mex. cebolla de cambray
    Spa. cebolleta
onion, red (Bermuda) (n phr) cebolla
roja
    Ecu. cebolla colorada
    Mex. cebolla morada

ABBREVIATIONS: Arg.=Argentina Bol.=Bolivia Chi.=Chile Col.=Colombia Cos.R.=Costa Rica Cub.=Cuba Dom.R.=Dominican Republic Ecu.=Ecuador ElS.=El Salvador Gua.=Guatemala Hon.=Honduras Mex.=Mexico Pan.=Panama Per.=Peru Pri.=Primary Term Pue.R.=Puerto Rico Spa.=Spain Uru.=Uruguay Venz.=Venezuela

onion, vidalia (n phr) vidalia
  Bol. cebolla
  Col. cebolla vidalia
orange (n) naranja
  Dom.R., Pue.R. china
papaya (n) papaya
  Cub. fruta bomba
  Dom.R., Pue.R. lechosa
  Venz. lechoso
parsnip (n) chiriva
  Col. chirivia, chirivía
  Gua. chiviría
  Uru. pastinaca
peach (n) durazno
  Cub., Dom.R., Para., Per.,
  Pue.R., Spa. melocotón
peanut (n) maní
  Mex. cacahuate
  Spa. cacahuete
pear (n) pera
peas, green (n phr) arvejas
  Cub. chícharos, petit pois
  Mex. chícharos
  Pan. petit pois
  Per. arvejitas
  Pue.R., Spa. guisantes
pecan (n) pacana
  Bol., ElS., Gua., Hon. pecana
  Mex. nuez
pepper, hot (n phr) chile
  Bol., Chi., Venz., Per. ají
  Col., Cub., Pan., Pue.R. ají
  picante
  Cos.R. chile picante
  Ecu. pimiento picante
  Spa. guindilla
pepper, sweet (n phr) pimiento morrón
  Col. pimentón rojo, pimentón
  verde
  Cos.R. chile dulce

Pan. ají dulce, pimentón
Per., Venz. pimentón
Spa. pimiento
pine nut (n phr) piñón
pineapple (n) piña
  Uru. ananá
pistachio (n) pistacho
  Mex. pistache
plum (n) ciruela
pomegranate (n) granada
  Cos.R. granadilla
potato (n) papa
  Cub., Spa. patata
pumpkin (n) calabaza
  Bol., Chi., Pan. zapallo
  Venz. ahuyama
quince (n) membrillo
radish (n) rábano
rhubarb (n) ruibarbo
rutabaga (n) nabo sueco
  Col. nabo de suecia, rutabaga
scallion (n) cebolla verde
  Bol. cebollita verde
  Col. cebolla larga
  ElS., Gua., Hon., Venz. cebollín
  Pan. cebollina
  Mex. cebollino
shallot (n) chalote
  Mex. cebollino, cebollita
soybeans (n) frijoles de soja
  Chi., Spa. soja
  Col., Gua. semillas de soya
  Cub., Venz. soya
  Uru. porotos de soja
spinach (n) espinaca
squash (n) chilacayote
  Bol. zapallito
  Col., Cos.R., Cub., Ecu., Spa.
  calabaza
  Dom.R., Venz. auyama

ABBREVIATIONS: Arg.=Argentina Bol.=Bolivia Chi.=Chile Col.=Colombia Cos.R.=Costa Rica Cub.=Cuba Dom.R.=Dominican Republic Ecu.=Ecuador ElS.=El Salvador Gua.=Guatemala Hon.=Honduras Mex.=Mexico Pan.=Panama Per.=Peru Pri.=Primary Term Pue.R.=Puerto Rico Spa.=Spain Uru.=Uruguay Venz.=Venezuela

Pan. chayote
Uru. zapallo
strawberry (n) fresa
Arg. frutilla
sweet potato (n phr) batata
Bol., Ecu., Gua., Mex., Pan.,
Per. camote
Chi. papa dulce
Cub., Uru. boniato
taro (n) taro
Cub. malanga
Dom.R. yautía
tomato (n) tomate
Mex. jitomate
turnip (n) nabo
watercress (n) berro
watermelon (n) sandía
Cub. melón de agua
yam (n) ñame
zucchini (n) calabacín
Chi. zapallito italiano
Mex. calabacita

Food: Kitchen & Meals

aluminum foil (n phr) papel de
aluminio
Chi., Pan. papel aluminio
Cos.R., ElS., Gua., Pan., Per.
lámina de aluminio
appetizer (n) aperitivo
Arg., Dom.R., Uru. entrada
Cos.R. bocas
Ecu. entrada, primer plato
Pan. abreboca
Per. bocaditos
Spa. tapa
Venz. entremés
baster (n) gotero

blender (n) licuadora
Cub., Dom.R., Spa., Venz.
batidora
bottle opener (n phr) destapador
Chi., Cos.R. abridor
Pan., Uru. abridor, saca corcho
Pue.R. abridor de botellas
Spa. abrebotellas
bowl (n) plato hondo
Chi. bol
Col. recipiente hondo, tazón,
vasija
Mex. tazón
Pan. vasija
Spa. cuenco
bowl, mixing (n phr) tazón para medir
Arg. bol
Col. vasija para mezclar
ElS., Gua., Venz. tazón para
mezclar
Mex. tazón para batir
Pan. platón, vasija
bowl, salad (n phr) ensaladera
Col., Pan. plato para ensalada
bowl, soup (n phr) tazón
Col., Venz. plato de sopa
Cub., Dom.R., Ecu. plato sopero
Pan. plato hondo, plato para sopa
Pue.R. sopera
bowl, sugar (n phr) azucarera
breakfast (n) desayuno
brunch (n) brunch
Mex. almuerzo
Uru. desayuno
Venz. desayuno-almuerzo
butcher block (n phr) bloque de
carnicero
Arg. tabla de cocina
Chi., Cub. tabla para cortar
Col. tabla para cortar, tabla

para picar
Pue.R. picador
can opener (n phr) abrelatas
Chi. abridor de latas
Cos.R. abridor
canned food (n phr) alimentos
enlatados
Chi. latas de conservas
Col., Cub., Dom.R., Pan. comida
enlatada
carving fork (n phr) trinche
Arg. tenedor
Col., ElS., Gua., Hon., Spa.
tenedor de trinchar
Pan., Pue.R. tenedor para servir
china (n) porcelana
Chi. loza
Col., Dom.R., Mex. vajilla
Pan. loza, vajilla fina
coffee maker (n phr) cafetera
Dom.R. greca
colander (n) colador
Bol., Col. coladera
Cos.R., Dom.R., Mex., Per.,
Spa., Uru. escurridor de verduras
condiments (n) condimentos
cookie cutters (n phr) cortadores de
galletas
Arg. moldes
Chi., Dom.R., Venz. moldes de
galletas
corkscrew (n) sacacorchos
Chi. destapador
counter (n) mostrador
Arg. mesada
Pue.R. counter
creamer (n) cremera
Arg. lechera
Spa. jarrita para leche
cup, coffee (n phr) taza para café

Arg. pocillo, taza de café
cutting board (n phr) tabla para cortar
Col. tabla de cortar
Pue.R. picador
decanter (n) licorera
Arg. jarra
Col., Spa. garrafa
demitasse (n) tacita de café
Arg. pocillo, taza de café
Col. tacita
Pue.R. pocillito de café
dessert (n) postre
dill (n) eneldo
dinner (n) cena
Arg., Col., Per., Pue.R. comida
dishes (n) platos
Pan. trastos, vajilla
dishwasher (n) lavaplatos
Arg. lavavajilla
Col., Cub., Pue.R. lavadora de
platos
Spa. lavavajillas
Uru. lava vajilla
disposer (n) triturador
draining spoon (n phr) cuchara para
escurrir
Col. cuchara de escurrir
Spa. espumadera
dryer (n) secadora
Arg. secarropas
Pue.R. secadora de ropa
egg beater (n phr) batidor manual
Chi., Pue.R. batidora
Ecu. batidor de mano
egg timer (n phr) minutero para huevos
freezer (n) congelador
Arg., Pue.R. freezer
Bol. refrigerador
funnel (n) embudo
garbage disposer (n phr) triturador de

basura
ginger (n) jengibre
glass (n) vaso
glassware (n) cristalería
goblet (n) copa
goblet, water (n phr) copa para agua
grater (n) rallador
   Col. rallo
   Dom.R. guallo
   Pue.R. guayo
gravy boat (n) salsera
griddle (n) asador eléctrico
   Col., Pan. sartén eléctrica
   Spa. plancha
grill (n) parrilla
ice bucket (n phr) balde de hielo
   Dom.R., Ecu., Gua., Mex.,
   Venz. hielera
   Pue.R. cubeta de hielo
icing syringe (n phr) jeringuilla de
   decoración
   Col. jeringuilla para decorar
   Venz. decorador para pasteleros
juicer (n) exprimidor
kettle (n) marmita
   Arg., Uru. pava
   Bol. caldera
   Chi., Col., Per., Spa. tetera
   Cub. caldero
   Ecu. cantina de agua
   Mex. olla grande
knife (n) cuchillo
knife sharpener (n phr) afilador de
   cuchillo
   Dom.R. amolador
knife, butter (n phr) cuchillo para
   mantequilla
   Arg. cuchillo para manteca
knife, electric (n phr) cuchillo eléctrico
knife, kitchen (n phr) cuchillo de

cocina
knife, steak (n phr) cuchillo para carne
ladle (n) cucharón
lunch (n) almuerzo
   Dom.R., Mex., Spa. comida
main course (nphr) plato principal
   Col. entrada
   Cub. plato fuerte
   Mex. platillo principal
measuring cups (n phr) tazas para
   medir
   Dom.R. tazas medidoras
measuring spoons (n phr) cucharas
   para medir
   Dom.R. cucharas medidoras
meat grinder (n phr) molino de carne
   Arg., Col., Dom.R. moledora de
   carne
   Cub. molidora
   Pan., Pue.R. moledor de carne
microwave (oven) (n) micro
   Arg., Col., Cub., Uru. microonda
   Chi., Mex., Pue.R., Spa., Venz.
   microondas
mixer (n) batidora
   Cub. mezclador
muffin pan (n phr) molde para
   panecillos
   Arg. molde para muffin
   Bol. molde para pancitos
   Mex. molde para mufin, molde
   para pastelitos
   Per. molde para quequitos
   Spa. molde para magdalenas
mug (n) jarro
   Arg. jarrita, jarrito
   Chi. jarra, tazón
   Cub. vaso
   ElS., Gua. pocillo
   Pue.R., Spa., Venz. jarra

ABBREVIATIONS: Arg.=Argentina Bol.=Bolivia Chi.=Chile Col.=Colombia
Cos.R.=Costa Rica Cub.=Cuba Dom.R.=Dominican Republic Ecu.=Ecuador ElS.=El
Salvador Gua.=Guatemala Hon.=Honduras Mex.=Mexico Pan.=Panama Per.=Peru
Pri.=Primary Term Pue.R.=Puerto Rico Spa.=Spain Uru.=Uruguay Venz.=Venezuela

mug, beer (n phr) jarra para cerveza
    Arg. porrón
    Mex. jarro de cerveza
    Pue.R., Spa., Venz. jarra de
    cerveza
mug, coffee (n phr) jarra para café
    Arg. jarrito, jarrita
    Cub. taza de café
    ElS., Gua. pocillo para café
    Mex. jarro para café
    Pue.R. tazón de café
    Venz. jarrita para café
nutcracker (n) cascanueces
nutmeg (n) nuez moscada
omelet (n) omelete
    Bol., Col., Cub., Per., Pue.R.,
    Spa., Venz. tortilla
    Dom.R. tortilla española
oregano (n) orégano
oven (n) horno
pan (n) sartén
parsley (n) perejil
pastry brush (n phr) pincel de
    repostería
    Col., Gua., ElS., Pan. brocha de
    repostería
pastry cutting wheel (n phr)
cortapastas
    Col. rodete para cortar masa
peeler (n) pelador
    Mex. pelapapas
pepper shaker (n phr) pimentera
    Arg., Col., Gua., Mex., Per.
    pimentero
    Pue.R. pimienta
    Venz. pimientero
pickle (n) pepino encurtido
    Cub. pepino
    Dom.R., Mex., Pue.R. pepinillo
    Spa. pepinillo en vinagre

    Venz. encurtido
pie pan (n phr) molde para pastel
    Arg. molde para tartas
    Chi. molde para pie
    Dom.R. molde de bizcocho
    Mex. molde para pay
pitcher (n) jarra
    Chi. jarrón
    Gua. pichel
platter (n) fuente de servir
    Col., Cub., Pan. bandeja
    Mex. platón
pot (n) olla
    Arg. cacerola
    Spa. puchero
potato masher (n phr) majador de
    papas
    Chi. moledor de papas
    Mex. prensapapas
    Per. machucador de papas
    Uru. triturador de papas
preserves (n) conserva (de alimentos)
    Chi., Col. conservas
    Dom.R. preservas
    Per., Spa. mermelada
refrigerator (n) refrigerador
    Arg. heladera
    Col., Dom.R., Pue.R., Venz.
    nevera
    Cos.R. refrí
    Ecu., nevera, refrigeradora
    Per. refrigeradora
    Spa. frigorífoco, nevera
roasting pan (n phr) sartén para asar
    Col. bandeja para hornear
    Spa. bandeja para el horno
    Venz. olla para hornear
rolling pin (n phr) rodillo
    Arg. palo de amasar
    Bol., Chi. fuslero

Per. amasador
rosemary (n) romero
salad (n) ensalada
salt shaker (n phr) salero
saucepan (n) cacerola
    Arg., Pue.R. olla
    Col. perol
    Spa. cazo
shot glass (n phr) copa de trago
    Chi. medida para bebida
    Col. copa de aguardiente, copita
    Dom.R. vaso de trago corto
    Mex. caballo (big), caballito
    (small), vaso tequilero
    Pue.R. vasito
    Spa. chupito
sieve (n) cedazo
    Arg., Spa. tamiz
    Chi., Cub., Venz. colador
    Col. coladera, tamiz
    Mex. coladera
silverware (n) cubiertos
    Col. platería
skimmer (n) espumadera
    Col. desnatadora
    Mex. desnatador
snack (n) merienda
    Col. bocadillo, refrigerio
    Dom.R. picadera
    Mex. botana
    Spa. snack
snifter (n) copa ancha de boca estrecha
    Chi. copa de cognac
soup tureen (n phr) sopera
spatula (n) espátula
stove (n) estufa
    Arg., Bol., Chi., Per., Spa., Uru.
    cocina
teapot (n) tetera
thyme (n) tomillo

toaster (n) tostador
    Chi., Col., Cub., Dom.R., Ecu.,
    Pue.R., Spa., Venz. tostadora
tongs (n) tenazas
    Arg., Col., Spa. pinzas
tumbler (n) vaso para whiskey
    Arg. vaso
turner (n) pala
    Pan. espátula
    Venz. paleta
vacuum cleaner (n phr) aspiradora
    Cub., Cos.R. aspirador

> The word *choclo,* used instead of *maíz* (corn) in some Spanish-speaking countries, comes from the Quechuan word *chokllo.*

ABBREVIATIONS: Arg.=Argentina Bol.=Bolivia Chi.=Chile Col.=Colombia
Cos.R.=Costa Rica Cub.=Cuba Dom.R.=Dominican Republic Ecu.=Ecuador ElS.=El
Salvador Gua.=Guatemala Hon.=Honduras Mex.=Mexico Pan.=Panama Per.=Peru
Pri.=Primary Term Pue.R.=Puerto Rico Spa.=Spain Uru.=Uruguay Venz.=Venezuela

Hobbies & Recreation:
Movies & Television

actor (n) actor
　Col. artista, galán
actress (n) actriz
　Col. artista
animation (n) animación
banned film (n phr) película prohibida
　Col., Dom.R. película censurada
broadcast (n) emisión televisiva
　Arg., Dom.R., Venz. programa
　de televisión
　Chi., Col., Cos.R., Gua.
　transmisión
　Cub. emisión
broadcast (v) emitir
　Col., Cos.R., ElS., Gua., Hon.,
　Venz. transmitir
cable television (n phr) televisión por
　cable
　Arg., Cub. cable
　Dom.R. telecable
　Mex. cable, cablevisión
cartoon (n) dibujo animado
　Col., Spa. dibujos animados
　Cub., Dom.R., Pue.R.
　muñequitos
　Mex. caricatura
　Pan. caricaturas
cast (show) (n) equipo artístico
　Chi., Pan.. Pue.R. elenco
　Col., Mex., Spa., Venz. reparto
channel (n) canal
　Spa. cadena
commercial (n) anuncio
　Arg. aviso, propaganda
　Chi., Ecu., Per. propaganda
　Col. anuncio comercial,

comercial, propaganda
　Dom.R., Mex. comercial
　Pan., Venz. comercial,
　propaganda
double feature (movies) (n phr)
　doble función
　Bol. película doble
　Col. doble
　Dom.R. doble presentación
　Mex. programa doble
　Spa. sesión de dos películas
　seguidas
　Uru. función doble
　Venz. cine continuado
drama (movies) (n) drama
drive-in (n) motocine
　Col., Pue.R. drive-in
　Dom.R. auto-cinema
　Mex. autocinema
　Pan., Per., Venz. autocine
dubbing (n) doblaje
film (n) película
　Arg., Cos.R., Ecu., Uru., Pan.
　filme
　Chi., Col., Cub. cinta
　Venz. film
film, dubbed (n phr) película doblada
film, silent (n phr) película muda
footage (n) metraje
frame (movie) (n phr) imagen
　Col. cuadro
game show (television) (n phr)
　programa concurso
　Arg. programa de
　entretenimientos
　Col. programa de concurso
　Cos.R. concurso televisivo
　Dom.R., Gua., Mex., Venz.
　programa de concursos
host (show) (n) presentador

Col. animador
Dom.R., Mex., Venz. anfitrión/a
Per. maestro de ceremonias
infomercial (n) comercial informativa
Col. anuncio informativo,
programa comercial para
promocionar algo
Cos.R. boletín informativo
Spa. telepromoción
Uru. información de interés
interview (n) entrevista
interview (v) entrevistar
interviewee (n) entrevistado/a
Arg., Cos.R., Cub., Ecu., ElS.,
Gua., Hon., Per., Pue.R.
encuestado/a
interviewer (n) entrevistador/a
Arg., Cos.R., Cub., Ecu., ElS.,
Gua., Hon., Per., Pue.R.
encuestador/a
live broadcast (n phr) transmisión en
directa
Arg. programa en vivo,
transmisión en directo
Bol., Col., ElS., Gua., Uru.
transmisión en directo
Chi., Per. transmisión en vivo y
en directo
Cos.R., Cub., Dom.R., Ecu.,
Pan., Spa., Venz. transmisión en
vivo
Mex. transmisión directa,
transmisión en vivo
movie (n) película
movie, action (n phr) película de
acción
movie, documentary (n phr) película
documental
movie, foreign (n phr) película
extranjera

movie, G-rated (n phr) película para
todo público
Mex. película para todo público
clasificación A
movie, horror (n phr) película de
miedo
Arg., Col., Cos.R., Dom.R.
película de terror
Mex., Uru. película de horror
Pue.R., Venz. película de horror,
película de terror
movie, PG-rated (n phr) película
para todo público
Mex. película para adolescentes
y adultos clasificación B
Pue.R. película público general
Spa. película apta para todos los
públicos
Venz. película censura B
movie, western (n phr) película de
vaqueros
Arg. película de cowboys
Spa. western
movie, x-rated (n phr) película para
adultos
Col. película clasificación X
Cub. película pornográfica
Mex. película sólo para adultos
clasificación C
Pue.R. película X
musical (movie) (n) película musical
Dom.R., Pue.R. músical
network (television) (n) cadena
Dom.R. telecadena
news brief (n phr) breves
Chi. breves informativos
Col. informativo breve
Cos.R. resúmen noticioso
Dom.R. titulares
Gua. resúmen de noticias

Mex. noticiero breve
Per., Venz. resúmen de noticias
newscast (n) telediario
Arg., Chi., Col., Ecu., Pan.
noticiero
Cos.R. telenoticiero
Cub. reporte
Dom.R. noticiero, telenoticiero
Mex. noticias, noticiero
Spa. noticiario
premiere (n) estreno
program (n) programa
Cub., Dom.R. show
props (n) accesorios
Col. ayudas de escenario, soporte
Mex. adornos
release (n) estreno
remote control (n phr) control remoto
Spa. mando a distancia
satellite television (n phr) televisión
por satélite
Spa. televisión vía satélite
screen (television) (n phr) pantalla
screenplay (n) guión cinematográfico
Bol. telón
Dom.R., ElS., Gua., Hon. libreto
Spa. argumento
script (n) guión
set (movie) (n) escenario
Chi. estudios
Col. decorado
Spa. plató
shoot (movie) (v) rodar
Venz. filmar
shooting (movie) (n) rodaje
Venz. filmación
show (movie) (v) proyectar
Arg. dar, pasar
Col. presentar
Dom.R. pasar

Venz. mostrar
sitcom, situation comedy (n phr)
comedia de situación
Chi., Col., Cub., Dom.R., Spa.
comedia
slow motion (n phr) cámara lenta
soap opera (n phr) telenovela
Arg., Cub. novela
sound effects (n phr) efectos sonoros
Arg., Col., Mex., Pan., Pue.R.,
Spa., Venz. efectos de sonido
sound track (n phr) banda sonora
Arg. banda de sonido
Mex., Pue.R. música
Venz. pista de sonido
stage (n) escenario
stunt (n) acrobática
Col., Mex. truco
Dom.R., Pue.R. doblaje
Spa., Venz. acrobacia
stuntman (n) acróbata
Arg. extra
Col. aquel que realiza los trucos
Dom.R., Mex., Pue.R. doble
Spa. doble, especialista
Venz. especialista en acrobacias
subtitles (n) subtítulos
Cub., Pan., Uru. leyendas
talk show (n phr) programa de
entrevistas
Col. programa de charlas
television set (n phr) televisor
Col., Mex., Spa. televisión
television viewer (n phr) televidente
Col. teleaudiencia
turn off (television) (v phr) apagar
turn on (television) (v phr) prender
Bol., Chi., Cub., Ecu., Gua.,
Spa., Uru. encender
videocamera (n) cámara de vídeo

ABBREVIATIONS: Arg.=Argentina Bol.=Bolivia Chi.=Chile Col.=Colombia
Cos.R.=Costa Rica Cub.=Cuba Dom.R.=Dominican Republic Ecu.=Ecuador ElS.=El
Salvador Gua.=Guatemala Hon.=Honduras Mex.=Mexico Pan.=Panama Per.=Peru
Pri.=Primary Term Pue.R.=Puerto Rico Spa.=Spain Uru.=Uruguay Venz.=Venezuela

videocassette (n) videocasete
  Col. casete para vídeo
  Dom.R. casette
  Spa. cinta de vídeo
videocassette recorder (VCR) (n phr)
  videograbadora
  Arg., Mex. videocasetera
  Chi. VCR
  Col. grabadora de vídeo, VCR
  Spa. vídeo
videogame (n) videojuego
  Col., Cos.R., Dom.R., Mex.,
  Venz. juego de vídeo
watch television (v phr) ver tele(visión)
  Col. mirar televisión
  Spa. ver la televisión
weather report (n phr) boletín
  meteorológico
  Arg. pronóstico del tiempo
  Col. reporte del estado del tiempo
  Venz. reporte del tiempo, reporte
  meteorológico
weather reporter (n phr)
  meteorólogo
  Venz. reportero del tiempo,
  reportero meteorológico

Hobbies & Recreation: Music

accordion (n) acordeón
alto (n) contralto
bagpipes (n) gaita
band (music) (n) banda
banjo (n) banjo
  Spa. banyo
bar (music) (n) compás
  Col. barra (entre compases)
bar rest (n phr) compás de espera

bass (stereo) (n) graves
  Col. bajo
bass (voice) (n) bajo
  Col. contrabajo
bass clef (n phr) clave de fa
bass drum (n phr) bombo
bassoon (n) fagot
beat (music) (n) ritmo
bongo drum (n phr) bongó
bow (n) arco
brass section (n phr) bronces
  Col. cobres, instrumentos
  metálicos de viento
  Mex. metales
  Spa. instrumentos de metal
bugle (n) clarín
  Col. corneta
  Spa. cornetín
castanets (n) castañuelas
celesta (n) celesta
  Col. celeste
chord (n) acorde
  Col. cuerda
chorus (people) (n) coro
chorus (refrain) (n) estribillo
clarinet (n) clarinete
classical music (n phr) música clásica
compact disk (n phr) disco compacto
  Arg., Col., Pan. CD
  Spa. CD, compact disk
compact disk player (n phr) tocadiscos
  Arg. equipo de música para CD
  Col. aparato de CD
  Cos.R. CD-player
  Cub. reproductor de compact-disc
  Dom.R. CD player, tocador de
  discos compactos
  ElS., Gua., Venz. reproductor de
  discos compactos
  Mex. tocadiscos para discos

compactos
Spa. reproductor de CD
concert (n) concierto
conduct (music) (v) dirigir
Col. conducir
conductor (n) director de orquesta
conga drum (n phr) conga
Cub. tumbadora
Venz. tambor de conga
contrabassoon (n) contrabajón
Mex. contrafagot
cornet (n) cornetín
Cub., Mex., Spa. corneta
cymbals (n) platillos
double bass (n phr) contrabajo
double reed (n phr) doble caña
drum (n) tambor
Dom.R. batería
drum major (n phr) tambor mayor
drum, tap (v) tamborilear
Col., Spa. tocar el tambor
drummer (n) tamborilero
Col. el que toca el tambor, tambor
Dom.R. baterista
duo (n) dúo
Col. dueto
electric guitar (n phr) guitarra eléctrica
English horn (n phr) corno inglés
Col. cuerno inglés
flute (n) flauta
flutist (n) flautista
four-four, common time (n phr)
compás mayor
Spa. compás de cuatro por cuatro
French horn (n phr) corno francés
Col. cuerno francés
Spa. trompa de pistones
fret (on guitar) (n) traste
gong (n) gong
group (music) (n) grupo musical

guitar (n) guitarra
guitar player (n phr) guitarrista
harmonica (n) armónica
harp (n) arpa
harpsichord (n) clavicordio
hit (song) (n) canción de moda
Col. éxito
Cos.R. éxito, hit
Cub., Dom.R. hit
hum (n) zumbido
Col. murmullo, susurro
hum (v) tararear
hymn (n) cántico
Bol., Col., Dom.R., Mex., Spa.,
Venz. himno
Pue.R. canción, himno
jam session (n phr) sesión de músicos
de jazz o rock que tocan por
placer propio
Chi. ensayo
Col. sesión de música
improvisado
Cub. descarga
Pue.R. jameo
Spa. jam session
jazz music (n phr) música jazz
Col. música de jazz
Dom.R., Spa. jazz
kettledrum (n) timbal
key (music) (n) tono
Col. tonalidad
key (n) tecla
keyboard (n) teclado
lip synch (v phr) doblar
Dom.R. hacer mímica
love song (n phr) canción de amor
Col., Pue.R. canción romántica
lyre (n) lira
lyrics (n) letra de una canción
Dom.R. letras de una canción

ABBREVIATIONS: Arg.=Argentina Bol.=Bolivia Chi.=Chile Col.=Colombia
Cos.R.=Costa Rica Cub.=Cuba Dom.R.=Dominican Republic Ecu.=Ecuador EIS.=El
Salvador Gua.=Guatemala Hon.=Honduras Mex.=Mexico Pan.=Panama Per.=Peru
Pri.=Primary Term Pue.R.=Puerto Rico Spa.=Spain Uru.=Uruguay Venz.=Venezuela

major chord (n phr) acorde mayor
mandolin (n) mandolina
   Chi. mandolín
maraca (n) maraca
metronome (n) metrónomo
minor chord (n phr) acorde menor
mouthpiece (n) boquilla
music stand (n phr) atril
neck (guitar) (n) mástil
   Chi. cuello
oboe (n) oboe
octave (n) octava
orchestra (n) orquesta
organ (n) órgano
panpipe (n) zampoña
percussion (n) percusión
percussionist (n) percusionista
performer (n) artista
   Col. intérprete
   Mex. intérprete, músico
piano (n) piano
piccolo (n) pícolo
   Col., Mex., Spa. flautín
pipe organ (n) órgano de tubos
play (instrument) (v) tocar
quartet (n) cuarteto
quintet (n) quinteto
record (music) (v) grabar
record album (n phr) álbum
   Col. disco
record player (n phr) tocadiscos
recorder (instrument) (n) flauta dulce
reed (n) caña
resonant (adj) sonoro
   Col. estruendoso, resonante
   Mex. resonante
rhythm (n) ritmo
rock music (n phr) música rock
   Col. música de rock
   Dom.R., Spa. rock

saxophone (n) saxofón
sextet (n) sexteto
sing (v) cantar
sing harmony (v phr) cantar en
   armonía
   Pue.R. cantar afinados
single reed (n phr) caña simple
sitar (n) sitar
   Venz. guitarra oriental
snare (of drum) (n) cuerdas
   Col. bordón, tirante
snare drum (n phr) tarola
   Col. tambor militar pequeño
   Cos.R. redoblante
song (n) canción
   Arg. tema
   Col. canto
songbook (n) cancionero
soprano (n) soprano
string (n) cuerda
string (v) encordar
string quartet (n phr) cuarteto de
   cuerdas
   Spa. cuarteto de cuerda
strum (v) guitarrear
   Col. rasgar, rasguear
   Cos.R. rasgar
   Spa. rasguear
strumming (n) guitarreo
   Col. rasgueo, rasgueado
   Cos.R. rasgueo
   Spa. rasgueado
symphony orchestra (n phr) orquesta
   sinfónica
synthesizer (n) sintetizador
tambour (n) tamborín
tambourine (n) pandero
   Chi., Col., Cub., Dom.R., Ecu.,
   Pue.R., Spa. pandereta
tape (cassette) (n) cinta

ABBREVIATIONS: Arg.=Argentina Bol.=Bolivia Chi.=Chile Col.=Colombia
Cos.R.=Costa Rica Cub.=Cuba Dom.R.=Dominican Republic Ecu.=Ecuador EIS.=El
Salvador Gua.=Guatemala Hon.=Honduras Mex.=Mexico Pan.=Panama Per.=Peru
Pri.=Primary Term Pue.R.=Puerto Rico Spa.=Spain Uru.=Uruguay Venz.=Venezuela

Arg., Col., Venz. casete
Cub., Dom.R., Mex. cassette
tenor (n) tenor
tenor drum (n phr) teno
   Col. tambor de tenor
   Spa. tenor
timpani (n) timbal
   Col., Cub. tímpanos
tom-tom (n) tam-tam
   Col. tantán
   Spa. tamtan
tone (n) sonoridad
   Col., Dom.R., Mex. tono
treble (stereo) (n) de agudos
   Col. tonos agudos
   Spa. agudos
treble clef (n phr) clave de sol
triangle (n) triángulo
trio (n) trío
trombone (n) trombón
trumpet (n) trompeta
trumpeter (n) trompetista
tuba (n) tuba
tuning fork (n phr) diapasón
tuning hammer (n phr) afinador
two-four time (n phr) compás menor,
   compasillo
   Spa. compás de dos por cuatro
upright piano (n phr) piano vertical
valve (trumpet) (n) pistón
   Mex. llave
viola (n) viola
violin (n) violín
violoncello (n) violoncelo
   Spa. violonchelo
voice (n) voz
xylophone (n) xilófono
   Cub. marimba
zither (n) cítara

Hobbies & Recreation: Sports

aerobics (n) aerobismo
   Col., Mex. aerobics
   Dom.R., ElS., Gua., Pan.,
   Pue.R., Uru. aeróbicos
   Spa. aerobic
amateur (n) amateur
   Col., Mex., Venz. aficionado
   Chi. amador
   Cub. no profesional
   Per. novato
athlete (n) atleta
   Pan. deportista
back (soccer) (n) defensa
   Spa. defensor
backstroke (swimming) (n) estilo
   espalda
   Cub. al revés
   Mex. dorso
ball (soccer) (n) pelota de fútbol
   Col. balón de fútbol
   Pue.R. bola de balompié
   Spa. balón
basket (basketball) (n) cesta
   Arg., Mex., Pan., Per., Uru.
   canasta
   Bol. cesto
   Dom.R., Pue.R. canasto
basketball (n) baloncesto
   Arg., Per., Uru. basketbol
   Mex., Pan. basketball
boat race (n phr) regata
boxer (n) boxeador
   Chi. pugilista
breaststroke (swimming) (n) estilo
   braza
   Arg. brazada

Chi., Col., Cub., Pue.R., Venz.
estilo pecho
Dom.R. brazado de pecho
ElS., Gua. brazada de pecho
Mex. pecho
broad jump (n phr) salto de longitud
Chi., ElS., Gua. salto largo
Col. salto ancho
Pue.R. salto a lo largo
butterfly (swimming) (n) estilo
mariposa
canoe (n) canoa
challenger (boxing) (n) contrincante
Col. contendor, retador
Dom.R., Mex. retador
Uru. aspirante
Venz. retador de boxeo
compete (v) competir
contestant (n) competidor
Chi. concursante
Cub., Pue.R. participante
court (tennis) (n) cancha
crawl (swimming) (n) crawl
Chi. estilo libre
Gua., Spa. estilo crol
Pue.R., Uru. brazada
discus throwing (n phr) lanzamiento
de disco
diver (n) buceador, buzo
Chi. hombre rana
Cub. clauadista
diving (n) bucear, buceo
forward (soccer) (n) delantero
freestyle (swimming) (n) estilo libre
goalie (n) portero
Arg., Chi., Per. arquero
Col. guarda-vallas
Cub. guardameta
Pan. goleador
Pue.R. porteador

Uru. golero
golf ball (n phr) pelota de golf
Col., Mex., Pue.R. bola de golf
golf club (n phr) palo de golf
Col. taco de golf
Pan. club de golf
golf course (n phr) campo de golf
Arg. cancha de golf
gymnastics (n) gimnasia
handball (n) handbol
ElS., Gua. balonmano
Uru. pelota de mano
high jump (n phr) salto de altura
Chi., Col., ElS., Gua., Hon. salto
alto
Pue.R. salto a lo alto
hole (golf) (n) hoyo
hole in one (n phr) hoyo en uno
Pue.R. bola en uno
horizontal bar (n phr) barra fija
Col., Pan., Pue.R., Venz. barra
horizontal
horseback riding (n phr) equitación
Col. montar a caballo
Cub. ir a caballo
hurdles race (n phr) vallas
Chi. obstáculos
Col. competencia de obstáculos
Cub., Dom.R., ElS., Gua.,
Hon., Venz. carrera de obstáculos
ice hockey (n phr) hockey sobre hielo
ice skating (n phr) patinaje sobre hielo
Chi., Cub. patinaje en hielo
Col. patinaje en el hielo
instructor (sports) (n) instructor de
deportes
Arg., Bol., Chi., Cub. entrenador
Col. instructor deportivo
Pue.R. maestro de educación
física

ABBREVIATIONS: Arg.=Argentina Bol.=Bolivia Chi.=Chile Col.=Colombia
Cos.R.=Costa Rica Cub.=Cuba Dom.R.=Dominican Republic Ecu.=Ecuador ElS.=El
Salvador Gua.=Guatemala Hon.=Honduras Mex.=Mexico Pan.=Panama Per.=Peru
Pri.=Primary Term Pue.R.=Puerto Rico Spa.=Spain Uru.=Uruguay Venz.=Venezuela

Venz. entrenador de deportes
javelin throwing (n phr) lanzamiento
de jabalina
jump (n) salto
kayak (n) kayac
manager (sports) (n) manager
deportivo
Col., Pan. administrador
deportivo
Mex. técnico
Venz. administrador deportivo,
gerente deportivo
marathon (n) maratón
motorcycle, motorbike (n)
motocicleta, moto
Pue.R. motora
offside (n) fuera de juego
Arg. offside
Col., ElS., Gua., Hon. de
posición adelantada
Mex. lateral
Pue.R. fuera de posición
parallel bars (n phr) barras paralelas
player (n) jugador
pole vault (n phr) salto con garrocha
Pue.R. salto con pértiga
Spa. salto de pértiga
Venz. salto de garrocha
racetrack (horse) (n) hipódromo
racetrack (runners or cars) (n) pista
record (sports) (n) récord deportivo
referee (n) árbitro
Arg. referee
Bol., Col., Ecu., Per. juez
Mex. refere
Pan. referí
relay (swimming) (n) relevo
ring (boxing) (n) ring de boxeo
Chi. cuadrilátero
Col., Pue.R., Uru. cuadrilátero

de boxeo
rowing (n) remo
runner (n) corredor
shot put (n phr) lanzamiento de peso
Pue.R. lanzamiento de pesa
ski jump (n phr) trampolín
Venz. salto en esquíes
skiing (n) esquí
soccer (n) fútbol
Pue.R. balompié
sprint (v) esprintar
Chi. picar
Col., Dom.R. correr a toda
velocidad
Cub. correr
stair machine (n phr) escaladora
Cos.R. máquina escalera
Dom.R. máquina de hacer
ejercicios
Mex. escalera
stationary bicycle (n phr) bicicleta
estacionaria
Mex. bicicleta fija
Pan. bicicleta estable
Spa. bicicleta estática
swimming (n) natación
swimming pool (n phr) piscina
Arg. pileta
Mex. alberca
team (n) equipo
tennis (n) tenis
track (n) pista
trainer (sports) (n) entrenador
treadmill (n) rueda de andar
Col. caminador
Cos.R. banda sin fin
Dom.R. máquina de caminar
Mex., Uru. caminadora
Pue.R. máquina de correr
triple jump (n phr) salto triple

Arg., Col. triple salto
umpire (baseball) (n) umpire
Cub., Ecu., Uru., Venz. árbitro
Mex. ampayer
water skiing (n phr) esquí acuático
Chi. ski acuático
Cos.R., Ecu., ElS., Gua., Per.,
Venz. esquí náutico
weight lifting (n phr) levantamiento de
pesas
Chi. alterofilismo
yacht (n) yate
yoga (n) yoga

Hobbies & Recreation: Workbench

anvil (n) yunque
awl (n) lezna
Bol., Col., Spa., Venz. punzón
Mex. berbiquí
ax (n) hacha
blowtorch (n) soplete
Pan., Pue.R. antorcha
brush (n) brocha, cepillo
bucket (n) balde
Col., Mex., Spa. cubeta
Cub. cubo
bucksaw (n) sierra de ballesta
Spa. sierra de bastidor
Uru. serrucho
chainsaw (n) serrucho eléctrico
Arg., Cos.R., Spa. motosierra
Chi., Uru. sierra eléctrica
Col., Mex., Pue.R. sierra de
cadena
chisel (for stone) (n) cincel
clamp (n) abrazadera
Col. grapa

Cos.R. prensa
Mex. pinzas
dowel (n) clavija
Gua. tarugo
Mex. espiga, pasador
drill bit (n phr) broca
Pue.R., Venz. barrena
drill, hand (n phr) taladro de mano
Arg., Ecu., Per., Spa., Uru.
taladradora de mano
Chi. taladro
Col., Mex. taladro manual
easel (n) caballete
Chi., Col., Spa. atril
file (n) lima
hacksaw (n) sierra de metal
Col. sierra para cortar metal
Cub. serrucho
Mex., Spa. sierra para metal
Pue.R. segueta
Venz. serrucho, sierra para metales
hatchet (n) hacha
Col. hachuela
hoe (n) azada
Bol. azador
Col., Pan. asadón
Dom.R., Gua. azadón
Mex. talacho
Venz. azadón, pico
hose, garden (n phr) manguera
ladder (n) escalera
lawn mower (n phr) cortacéspedes
Arg. máquina de cortar pasto
Bol. cortadora
Chi. cortapasto
Col. máquina para cortar el pasto
Cub. máquina de cortar yerba
ElS., Gua., Hon. cortagrama
Mex. podadora de pasto
Per. cortador de césped, cortador

---

del pasto
Pue.R. cortadora de grama
Spa. cortacésped
Venz. cortagrama, segadora
lawn rake (n phr) barredora
Arg., Chi., Col., Cub., Dom.R.,
Mex., Pan. rastrillo
level (n) nivel
Chi. nivelador
Uru. plomada
nut (n) tuerca
oil can (n phr) aceitera
Arg., Cub., Venz. lata de aceite
Col. tarro de aceite
pail (n) balde
Cub. cubo
Mex., Pue.R. cubeta
Venz. balde, tobo
paintbrush (n) brocha de pintar, pincel
painter's knife (n phr) navaja de pintor
Mex. espátula, raspa
pallet (n) paleta
Chi. palé
Mex. palet, tarima
Uru. plataforma
penknife (n) navaja
Chi., Spa., Venz. cortaplumas
Pue.R. cuchilla
pincers (n) tenazas
Col., Mex. pinzas
plane (carpentry) (n) plano
Arg., Col., Dom.R., Mex., Spa.,
Uru. cepillo
pliers (n) pinzas
Chi., Cos.R., Dom.R., Per.,
Pue.R., Venz. alicate
Col., Pan., Spa. alicates
Mex. alicatas
pruning shears (n phr) podadera
Arg., Dom.R., Spa. tijeras de

podar
Bol., Ecu., Pue.R. podadora
Col. tijeras para podar
Mex. podadoras
Venz. tijera podadora
rake (n) rastrillo
reamer (n) escariador
Mex. escariadora
Pue.R. arado
Spa. fresadora
Uru. escardador
rivet (n) remache
ruler (n) regla
saw (n) sierra
Arg., Cub., Per. serrucho
scraper (n) rascador
Chi. raspadora
Col. cuchilla raspadora
Mex. raspa
Pue.R. espátula
Venz. raspador
screwdriver (n) destornillador
Chi. llave
Mex., Per. desarmador
scythe (n) guadaña
Mex. zapapico
shovel (n) pala
Per. palana
sickle (n) hoz
Mex. pico
Pue.R. yunta
sledgehammer (n) almádena
Chi., Dom.R., Mex. mazo
Pue.R. marrón
spade (n) pala
Chi. pica
Venz. pico
spatula (n) espátula
sprinkler (n) rociador
Arg. regador

Cub. regadera
Mex. regilete
Spa. aspersor
stepladder (n) escalera de mano
stud (n) tachuela
Mex. espárrago, espiga, pasador,
viga vertical
tack (n) tachuela
Spa. chincheta
tape measure (n phr) metro
Arg., Col., Dom.R., Mex., Spa.
cinta métrica
Chi. huincha
Cub. centímetro
Pan. cinta de medir
toolbox (n) caja de herramientas
trowel (n) desplantador
Chi. paleta
Mex. palustre
Pue.R. palaustre
Venz. aplanadora
vise (n) prensa
Mex., Uru. torno
washer (n) arandela
Mex. rodana
watering can (n phr) regadera
Mex. regador de plantas
Venz. lata de regar
wheelbarrow (n) carretilla
wrench (n) llave inglesa

> Guatemala is called the "land of eternal spring" because the weather ranges between 13° to 27⁰ C. It is a country of sun, mountains, and volcanoes.

Nature: Vegetation & Landscape

acorn (n) bellota
annual (plant) (n) planta anual
bark (tree) (n) corteza
basin (n) cuenca
beach (n) playa
birch (tree) (n) abedul
bird of paradise (flower) (n) ave del
  Paraíso
bloom (v) florecer
  Col. dar flor
  Pue.R. retollar
branch (n) rama
bud (n) brote
  Col. botón, cogollo
  Spa. capullo
bulb (flower) (n) bulbo
bush (n) arbusto
  Cub. mata
  Pue.R. arbolito, palito
cactus (n) cacto
  Arg., Chi., Dom.R., Mex., Pan.,
  Pue.R., Spa. cactus
canyon (n) cañón
cape (n) cabo
carnation (n) clavel
cave (n) cueva
  Col. caverna
cedar (tree) (n) cedro
cliff (n) acantilado
  Cub., Pan. precipicio
  Cos.R. barranco
  Mex. barranca
  Pue.R. risco
climbing plant (n phr) trepadora
  Bol., Col., Cub., Mex., Pue.R.
  enredadera

clover (n) trébol
daisy (n) margarita
desert (n) desierto
earthquake (n) terremoto
  Chi., Mex. temblor
  Col. remezón, sacudida, sismo,
  temblor de tierra
  Dom.R., Pue.R. temblor de tierra
elm (tree) (n) olmo
fern (n) helecho
flower (n) flor
flower bed (n phr) macizo
  Arg. cantero
  Bol. macetero
  Gua. arriate de flores
  Mex. cama de flores
foliage (n) follaje
  Col. espesura, frondosidad
forest (n) bosque
fruit tree (n phr) árbol frutal
  Arg. frutal
  Pue.R. árbol de frutas
gardenia (n) gardenia
grass (n) hierba
  Chi. césped, pasto
  Col. pasto, yerba
  Mex., Per. pasto
  Pue.R. yerba
hedge (n) seto
  Col. matorral
  Mex. cercado de arbustos
hibiscus (n) hibisco
  Pan. papo
hill (n) colina
  Chi. cerro, loma
  Cub., Pan. loma
  Pue.R. cuesta
iceberg (n) iceberg
  Chi. témpano de hielo
iris (n) lirio

Venz. iris
island (n) isla
ivy (n) hiedra
jasmine (n) jazmín
jungle (n) selva
    Chi., Col., Dom.R., Pue.R., Venz.
    jungla
lagoon (n) laguna
lake (n) lago
landscape (n) paisaje
lawn (n) césped
    Arg., Bol., Mex., Per. pasto
    Col. hierba, manga, pasto, prado
    Cub., Dom.R. yerba
    Dom.R., ElS., Gua., Hon., Venz.
    grama
    Pue.R. grama, pasto
leaf (n) hoja
lily (n) lirio
maple (tree) (n) arce
    Gua., Mex. maple
moss (n) musgo
mountain (n) montaña
oak (tree) (n) roble
oasis (n) oasis
ocean (n) océano
orchard (n) huerto
    Pue.R. hortaliza
palm (tree) (n) palma
    Arg., Col., Mex. palmera
peak (mountain) (n) pico
    Chi. cima
perennial (plant) (n) perenne
    Pue.R. permanente
pine (tree) (n) pino
pine cone (n phr) piña
    Per. piñón
plain (topography) (n) llanura
    Col., Dom.R. llano
    Mex. esplanada, planicie

Pue.R. planicie
plateau (n) meseta
pond (n) charca
    Arg., Uru. charco
    Chi. charco, laguna
    Col., ElS., Gua., Hon., Mex.
    estanque
    Dom.R. laguna
    Venz. estanque, laguna
prairie (n) pradera
    Dom.R. valle
rain forest (n phr) selva tropical
    Col. bosque tropical
rainbow (n) arco iris
range (mountain) (n) sierra
    Chi. cordillera
    Col. cadena
reef (n) arrecife
river (n) río
riverbank (n) orilla del río
rose (n) rosa
rosebush (n) rosal
sand (n) arena
sand dune (n phr) duna de arena
sandbar (n) barra de arena
    Mex. banco de arena
sea (n) mar
seashore (n) orilla del mar
    Chi., Col., Pue.R. costa
seaweed (n) alga
seed (n) semilla
seedling (n) planta de semillero
    Chi. brote
    Col. planta de vivero
    Cos.R. almácigo
    Mex. plantita
shoreline (n) costa
    Col. litoral, orilla
shrub (n) arbusto
    Cub. mata

ABBREVIATIONS: Arg.=Argentina Bol.=Bolivia Chi.=Chile Col.=Colombia
Cos.R.=Costa Rica Cub.=Cuba Dom.R.=Dominican Republic Ecu.=Ecuador ElS.=El
Salvador Gua.=Guatemala Hon.=Honduras Mex.=Mexico Pan.=Panama Per.=Peru
Pri.=Primary Term Pue.R.=Puerto Rico Spa.=Spain Uru.=Uruguay Venz.=Venezuela

soil (n) tierra
stem (n) tallo
stream (n) arroyo
   Col. arroyuelo, riachuelo
   Dom.R., Pue.R. riachuelo
stump (n) tocón
   Dom.R. cabo
   Mex. parte del tronco
succulent (plant) (n) suculenta
   Mex. carnosa
swamp (n) marisma
   Chi. ciénaga, pantano
   Col., Dom.R., Ecu., Mex., Venz.
   pantano
   Uru. terreno pantanoso
thicket (n) matorral
thistle (n) cardo
thorn (n) espina
tree (n) árbol
   Dom.R. mata
trunk (n) tronco
tulip (n) tulipán
valley (n) valle
vegetable garden (n phr) huerto
   Arg. huerta, quinta
   Spa. huerta
vine (n) vid
violet (plant) (n) violeta
volcano (n) volcán
waterfall (n) cascada
   Dom.R. caída de agua
   Spa. catarata
weed (n) mala hierba
   Arg. maleza, yuyo
   Chi., Ecu. maleza
   Dom.R. maleza, pajón
   Mex. hierba silvestre
   Pue.R. yerba mala
wetlands (n) pantano
   Chi. marisma

Mex. terreno pantanoso
wooded (land) (adj) boscoso

Nature: Weather

cloud (n) nube
cloudy (adj) nublado
   Chi. tapado
   Col. cerrado, encapotado
   Cos.R., Cub., Gua. cubierto,
   nuboso
drizzle (n) llovizna
   Col. lluvia tenue
   Per. garúa
fog (n) niebla
   Arg., Cub., Dom.R., Mex., Per.
   neblina
   Chi. camanchaca
   Col. bruma, neblina
freezing rain (n phr) lluvia helada
frost (n) escarcha
hail (n) granizo
humid (n) húmedo
hurricane (n) huracán
   Dom.R. ciclón
lightning (n) rayo, relámpago
   Col. centella
mist (n) neblina
   Arg., Pue.R. niebla
   Col. bruma, llovizna, niebla
   Pan. bajareque
rain (n) lluvia
sandstorm (n) tormenta de arena
sleet (n) aguanieve
snow (n) nieve
storm (n) tormenta
thunder (n) trueno
tornado (n) tornado
wind (n) viento

Personal Life: Clothing & Accessories

bangle (n) brazalete tubular
bathing suit (n phr) traje de baño
  Arg. maya
  Col., Ecu., Pan. vestido de baño
  Cub. trusa
  Spa. bañador
bathrobe (n) bata de baño
  Bol. batón
  Spa. albornoz
belt (n) cinturón
  Col., Dom.R., Pan., Pue.R. correa
  Cos.R. faja
beret (n) boina
bifocals (n) lentes bifocales
  Arg. anteojos bifocales
  Cub., Pue.R. espejuelos bifocales
  Spa. gafas bifocales
bikini (n) bikini
bikini briefs (n phr) minitrusa
  Arg. bombacha
  Bol., Chi. bikini
  Col. calzoncillos
  Dom.R. tangas
  Ecu. calzón bikini
  Pan. calzoncillo corto
  Pue.R. panticitos del bikini
  Spa. braguita de bikini
  Venz. interiores bikini
blouse (n) blusa
blue jeans (n phr) jeans
  Arg., Cub., Uru. vaqueros
  Col., Venz. blue jeans
  Mex. pantalón de mezclilla
  Pue.R. mahones
  Spa. pantalones vaqueros, vaqueros

boots (n) botas
bow tie (n phr) corbata mariposa
  Arg. moñito
  Bol. corbata de gato
  Col. corbatín
  Cub., Spa. pajarita
  Dom.R. corbata de lacito
  Mex. corbata de moñito
  Pan. corbata de gatito
  Per. corbata michi
  Pue.R. lazo
  Uru., Venz. corbata de lazo
boxer shorts (n phr) calzoncillos
  Cub. calzones
  Dom.R. calzoncillos boxer
  Pan. calzoncillo largo
bra, brassiere (n) sostén
  Arg. corpiño
  Col. brassiere
  Cub. ajustador
  Dom.R., Pan. brasier
  Mex. brasiere
  Spa. sujetador
  Uru. soutien
bracelet (n) pulsera
  Cub. pulso
  Dom.R. guillo
bracelet, charm (n phr) pulsera de dijes
briefs (n) calzoncillos
  Col. trusa
  Dom.R. pantaloncillos
  Mex., Uru. calzones
  Venz. interiores
buckle (n) hebilla
buttonhole (n) ojal
cap (n) gorra
  Col., Dom.R. cachucha
cape (n) capa, capote
  Mex. chal, quisquemel
cardigan (n) cardigán

Arg. chaleco, saco de lana
Chi. sweater
Col. suéter abierto
Ecu., Venz. suéter
Mex. chamarra tejida, suéter
Spa. chaqueta de punto
casual clothes (n phr) ropa informal
Dom.R. ropa casual
cloak (n) capa
Col. manto
clogs (n) chanclos
Arg. ojotas
Chi. zancos
Col., Cub., Spa., Uru. zuecos
Dom.R., Mex., Pue.R. suecos
clothes (n) ropa
clothing articles (n phr) prendas de
vestir
coat (n) saco
Arg. tapado
Chi., Pue.R. chaqueta
Col., Cub., Mex., Pan., Spa.,
Venz. abrigo
coat, fur (n phr) saco de piel
Arg. tapado de piel
Chi., Col., Dom.R., Mex., Pan.,
Pue.R., Spa., Venz. abrigo de piel
Cub. abrigo de pieles
coat, mink (n phr) saco de visón
Arg. tapado de visón
Col., Mex., Pan., Pue.R. abrigo
de mink
Cub., Dom.R., Spa., Venz. abrigo
de visón
collar (n) cuello
crease (pants) (n) raya
Col. arruga, pliego
Cub., ElS., Gua., Hon. pliegue
Dom.R., Pue.R. filo
Pan. doblez

cuff (pants) (n) valenciana
Arg. botamanga
Bol. botapié
Col., Spa. doblez
Cub. dobladillo
Dom.R. doblado
Venz. ruedo doble
cuff (shirt) (n) puño
cufflinks (n) gemelos
Chi. colleras
Col., Ecu. mancornas
Cub. yugos
ElS., Gua., Hon., Mex.
mancuernillas
Pan. mancuernas
Pue.R., Venz. yuntas
dog tag (n phr) placa de identificación
Mex. etiqueta
dress (oneself) (v) vestirse
Col. ponerse la ropa
dress (woman's) (n) vestido
Arg., Col., Pan. traje
Bol. falda
Cos.R., Uru. pollera
Pue.R. traje de mujer
dress up (v phr) vestirse de etiqueta
Arg. arreglarse
Chi., Col. vestirse elegante
Dom.R. arreglarse, vestirse formal
Pue.R. engalanarse
earmuffs (n) orejeras
earrings (n) aretes
Arg. aros
Pue.R. pantallas
Spa. pendientes
Venz. zarcillos
earrings, clip (n phr) aretes de presión
Arg. aros de presión
Pue.R. pantallas de clips
Spa. pendientes de clip

Venz. zarcillos de presión
earrings, drop (n phr) pendientes
  Arg. aros colgantes
  Spa. pendientes largos
earrings, pierced (n phr) aretes de
  espiga
  Arg. aros de agujero
  Dom.R. aretes de hoyito
  Pue.R. pantallas de gancho
  Spa. pendientes de tornillo
  Venz. zarcillos
earrings, screw (n phr) aretes de
  tornillo
  Arg. aros de tornillo
  Spa. pendientes de tornillo
  Venz. zarcillos de tornillo
eyeglasses (n) anteojos
  Col. gafas, lentes
  Cub., Pue.R. espejuelos
  Dom.R., Ecu., Pan., Per., Venz.
  lentes
  Spa. gafas
fly (pants) (n) bragueta
  Chi. marrueco
  Cub. portañuela
  Dom.R. ziper
  Pue.R. zipper
formal wear (n phr) ropa formal
  Dom.R. ropa de vestir
  Mex. ropa de etiqueta
garment (n) vestido
  Arg. prenda
  Cub., ElS., Gua., Spa. prenda de
  vestir
  Mex. ropa, traje
girdle (n) faja
glasses, opera (n phr) gemelos de teatro
  Col. binoculares, binóculos
  Cub. anteojos de teatro
  Venz. lentes de ópera

glasses, safety (n phr) anteojos de
  camino
  Chi. anteojos de seguridad
  Mex. gafas de protección
  Pue.R. anteojos de protección
  Spa. gafas de seguridad
  Venz. lentes protectores
glove (n) guante
goggles, ski (n phr) anteojos para
  esquiar
  Arg. antiparras
  Mex. gogles para esquiar
  Spa. gafas de esquí
goggles, swimming (n phr) anteojos
  para nadar
  Arg. antiparras
  Mex. gogles
  Pue.R. goggles
  Spa. gafas de buceo
half-glasses (n) media luna
  Mex. lentes para leer
  Venz. medios-lentes
hat (n) sombrero
hat, straw (n phr) sombrero de paja
hat, top (n phr) sombrero de copa
  Arg. galera
heel (shoe) (n) taco
  Col., Cub., ElS., Gua., Hon.,
  Mex., Pan., Spa., Venz. tacón
heel, high (shoe) (n phr) taco alto
  Col., Cub., ElS., Gua., Hon.,
  Mex., Pan., Spa., Venz. tacón alto
hood (n) capucha
  Chi. capuchón
  Cub. caperuza
house robe (n phr) túnica
  Col. vestido casero
  Cub., Dom.R., Spa., Venz. bata
  de casa
  Pan. bata de estar en casa

jacket (n) chaqueta
  Arg. campera
  Dom.R., Pan. saco
  Mex. chamarra
  Per. casca
  Pue.R. blazer (women), gabán
  (men)
jersey (n) jersey
  Bol. saco
  Col. chompa
  Mex. playera de punto
  Venz. suéter
knit shirt (n phr) polo
  Dom.R., Pan. suéter
  Mex. playera
  Per. camiseta
lapel (n) solapa
leotard (n) leotardo
  Chi. malla
  Venz. mallas de ejercicio
lining (coat) (n) forro
loafers (n) zapatos de andar
  Chi., Col., Cub., Ecu., Venz.
  mocasines
  Dom.R. zapatos bajitos
  ElS., Gua., Spa. zapatos estilo
  mocasín
  Mex. zapatos de casa
locket (n) relicario
  Cub. guardapelo
  Dom.R. medallón
long johns (n phr) calzoncillos largos
miniskirt (n) minifalda
  Col., Pue.R. falda corta
necklace (n) collar
necklace, choker (n phr) gargantilla
necklace, pendant (n phr) collar con
  medallón
  Chi. medallón
  Dom.R. pendiente con medalla

  Mex. pendiente con cadena
  Spa. colgante con cadena
necktie (n) corbata
nightgown (n) camisón
  Chi., Col. camisa de dormir
  Cub., Pue.R. bata de dormir
  Ecu. camisa de noche
  Dom.R. pijama
outfit (n) conjunto
  Chi. traje
  Col. vestimenta
overalls (n) mono
  Arg., Dom.R., Pue.R. mameluco
  Chi., Col., Pan. overol
  Cub. guardapolvo
  Mex. overales, pantalones de peto
  Per. coverall
  Uru. entero
overcoat (n) abrigo
  Arg. sobretodo
pajamas (n) piyamas
  Col. pijama, piyama
  Dom.R., Pue.R. pijamas
  Spa. pijama
panties (n) calzones
  Arg., Uru. bombachas
  Cub., Pan. blúmer, pantis
  Dom.R., Pue.R. panties
  Mex. pantaleta
  Spa. bragas
  Venz. pantaletas
pantyhose (n) media pantalón
  Arg. medias largas
  Dom.R. media panty, pantyhose
  Mex. pantimedia
  Pan. pantihose
  Per. media nylon
  Pue.R. medias nylon
  Spa. panty
  Uru. pantimedias

Venz. medias panty
parka (n) parka
  Pue.R. capa
petticoat (n) combinación
  Chi. enagüa
  Cub. sayuela
  Dom.R. mediofondo, refajo
  Mex. enaguas
  Pan. peticote
  Pue.R. refajo
  Venz. enaguas, fondo
pince nez (n) quevedos
pocket (n) bolsillo
pocket, back (n phr) bolsillo trasero
  Dom.R. bolsillo de atrás
pocket, breast (n phr) bolsillo superior
  Dom.R. bolsillo de la camisa
pullover (n) pulóver
  Arg. sweater
  Bol. saco
  Mex. suéter cerrado
  Per. chompa
  Spa. jersey
  Venz. suéter
raincoat (n) impermeable
  Arg. piloto
  Col., Spa. gabardina
  Cub. capa de agua
  Pan. capote
  Pue.R. capa
ring (n) anillo
  Pan., Pue.R. sortija
ring, class (n phr) anillo de graduación
  Pue.R. sortija de graduación
ring, diamond (n phr) anillo de
  diamante
  Pue.R. sortija de diamante
  Spa. anillo de diamantes
ring, engagement (n phr) anillo de
  compromiso

ring, signet (n phr) sortija de sello
  Col. anillo de sello
  Spa. sello
ring, solitaire (n phr) solitario
ring, wedding (n phr) anillo de
  matrimonio
  Arg. alianza, anillo de casamiento
  Per., Pue.R. aro de matrimonio
robe (n) bata
rubbers (shoes) (n) chanclos de goma
  Arg. ojotas de goma
  Chi., Uru. zapatos de goma
  Col. zapatos de caucho
  Cub., Pue.R. chancletas de goma
  ElS., Gua., Hon. chanclas de hule
  Mex. chanclas de plástico,
  huaraches de plástico, sandalias de
  plástico
  Spa. chanclas
sandals (n) sandalias
  Cub., Pue.R. chancletas
scarf (n) bufanda
shirt (n) camisa
shirt, dressy (n phr) camisa formal
  Arg., Dom.R., Mex., Pan., Uru.,
  Venz. camisa de vestir
shirt, long-sleeved (n phr) camisa de
  manga larga
  Arg. remera de manga larga
shirt, short-sleeved (n phr) camisa de
  manga corta
  Arg. remera de manga corta
shoe rack (n phr) zapatera
  Col. repisa para zapatos
shoehorn (n phr) calzador
shoelace (n) cordón
  Mex. agujeta
  Pue.R. gabete
shoes (n) zapatos
shoes, hiking (n phr) botas

Chi. bototos
Col. zapatos de caminar
Mex. botas de alpinismo
Spa. botas de monte
shoes, patent leather (n phr) zapatos
de charol
Arg., Bol., Cos.R., Ecu., Per.,
Pue.R. zapatos de cuero barnizado
Dom.R. zapatos de cuero,
zapatos de piel
Venz. zapatos de cuero, zapatos
de patente
shoes, tennis (n phr) zapatos de tenis
Arg., Chi., Pan. zapatillas
Col. zapatos tenis
Cub., Dom.R., Mex. tenis
Spa. zapatillas de deporte
Venz. zapatos de goma
shorts (n) pantalones cortos
Arg., Chi., Col., Dom.R.,
Mex., Venz. shorts
Cub. bermudas
Pan. pantaloncitos cortos
Pue.R. pantalón corto
skirt (n) falda
Arg., Uru. pollera
Cub. saya
slip (n) combinación
Chi., Pue.R. enagüa
Cub. sayuela
Dom.R. mediofondo
Pan. peticote
Mex., Venz. fondo
slippers (n) pantuflas
Arg. chinelas
Col. babuchas
Cos.R., Pan. chancletas
Cub. zapalillas
Spa. zapatillas de casa
sneakers (n) snikers

Arg., Chi., Pan., Per., Uru.
zapatillas
Col., Cos.R., Dom.R., Pue.R.
tenis
Ecu. zapatos de caucho
ElS., Gua., Hon. zapatos de lona
con suela de hule
Mex. tenis de lona
Spa. zapatillas de lona
Venz. zapatos de goma
sock (n) calcetín
Arg., Uru. media (tres cuartos),
soquete
Col., Cub., Dom.R., Ecu., Pan.,
Pue.R., Venz. media
sole (shoe) (n) suela
spectacles (n) anteojos
Col. gafas, lentes
Cub., Venz. espejuelos
suit (n) traje
Bol., Per. terno
Col., Pan. vestido
suit, double-breasted (n phr) traje
cruzado
Gua. traje traslapado
suit, tailored (n phr) traje sastre
Col. vestido hecho a la medida
Pan. vestido sastre
Venz. traje a la medida
suit, three-piece (n phr) terno
Bol., Dom.R., Mex., Pue.R.,
Venz. traje de tres piezas
Pan. vestido de tres piezas
suspenders (n) ligas
Chi. suspensores
Cub., Gua., Pan., Spa., Venz.
tirantes
Dom.R. breteles
Mex. ligeros
sweater (n) suéter

Arg. pulover
Chi. chomba
Per. chompa
Spa. jersey
sweatshirt (n) camisa de trabajo
Arg. buzo
Chi., Col., Mex., Pue.R. sudadera
Dom.R. abrigo, sudadera
Gua. sudadero
Spa. jersey
tailcoat (n) frac
Venz. smoking
tights (n) leotardo
Chi. medias gruesas
Col. media pantalón
Mex., Venz. mallas
Pue.R. tights
Spa. leotardos, medias
trench coat (n phr) trinchera
Col., Spa. impermeable
Mex. gabardina
trifocals (n) trifocales
Spa. gafas trifocales
Venz. lentes trifocales
t-shirt (n) camiseta
Arg. remera
Chi. polera
Dom.R. polo-shirt
turban (n) turbante
turtleneck (n) cuello vuelto
Arg. polera
Chi. beatle
Col. buzo
Dom.R., Pan., Venz. cuello
tortuga
Mex., Pue.R. cuello de tortuga
Per. cuello Jorge Chavez
Spa. polo de cuello alto
Uru. rompeviento
tuxedo (n) smoking

Cub., Pue.R. tuxedo
Pan. toxido
underpants (n) calzoncillos
underwear (n) ropa interior
Cos.R., Bol., Uru. ropa blanca
Cub. ropa de interior
undress (v) desvestirse
Col., Venz. quitarse la ropa
vest (n) chaleco
Arg. camiseta, musculosa
vest (sweater) (n) chaleco
v-neck (n) cuello de pico
Arg., Chi., Col., Gua., Mex.,
Venz. cuello en V
Dom.R., Pan., Per., Pue.R. cuello
V
Uru. escote en V
wear (clothing) (v) llevar
Arg., Bol., Gua., Pan., Venz. usar
Chi. ponerse, vestir
Col. tener puesto
Cub. llevar puesto, tener puesto
Dom.R. llevar puesto, ponerse
Mex. ponerse

Personal Life: Greetings & Forms of Address

brat (n) mocoso
Col. niño/a malcriado/a
Cub., Pan. malcriado/a
Dom.R. carajito/a, muchachito/a
Pue.R. chiquillo/a
buddy, pal (n) compañero/a
Chi., Cub. compadre
Col. amigazo/a
Dom.R. compinche, pana
ElS., Gua., Hon. cuate
Mex. amigocho, amigote, cuate

Pan., Pue.R. amigo/a
Bye! (int) ¡Adiós!
  Arg. ¡Chau!
  Chi. ¡Chao!
  Col. ¡Ciao!, ¡Hasta luego!
  Dom.R. ¡Bye!
cheater (n) tramposo
  Col. embustero, estafador, pícaro
dear, darling, honey (n) querido/a
  Arg., Chi., ElS., Gua., Hon.
  mi amor
  Col. mi amor, amorcito, tesoro
  Cub. mi amor, mi cielo, mi vida
  Pan. cariño
  Pue.R. mi amor, mi vida
Good afternoon! (int phr) ¡Buenas
tardes!
Good evening! (int phr) ¡Buenas
tardes!
  Col., Ecu. ¡Buenas noches!
Good morning! (int phr) ¡Buenos días!
  Arg. ¡Buen día!
Good night! (int phr) ¡Buenas noches!
  Ecu. ¡Hasta mañana!
Goodbye! (int) ¡Adiós!
  Arg. ¡Chau!
  Chi. ¡Chao!
  Col. ¡Hasta luego!, ¡Hasta pronto!
  Dom.R. ¡Bye!
Hello! (int) ¡Hola!
Hello? (answering telephone) (int)
¿Dígame?
  Arg., Bol. ¿Hola?
  Cub. ¿Oigo?
  Col., Cos.R., Dom.R., Ecu.,
  ElS., Gua., Hon., Per., Venz.
  ¿Aló?
  Mex. ¿Bueno?
  Pan., Pue.R. ¿Haló?
  Uru. ¿Aló?, ¿Hola?

Hi! (int) ¡Hola!
How's it going? (phr) ¿Cómo te (le) va?
  Arg., Mex., Pue.R., Uru. ¿Qué tal?
  Bol. ¿Cómo estás?
  Dom.R. ¿Cómo tú estás?
  Ecu. ¿Qué ha habido?, ¿Qué tal?
liar (n) mentiroso
  Chi. chamullento
  Col. embustero
love, lovey (n) amor
  Chi. tesoro
  Col. amorcito, cariño
  Cos.R. amorcito
Ma'am, Madam (n) Señora
  Cos.R., Pan. Doña
Miss (n) Señorita
Mr. (n) Señor
Mrs. (n) Señora
pest (person) (n) machaca
  Bol. cargoso
  Chi. insoportable
  Col. apestoso, lagarto, peste
  Cub. chivón, ladilla
  Dom.R. pesta, plaga
  Ecu. necio/a
  ElS., Gua. tipo/a pesado/a
  Mex., Venz. fastidioso
  Pan. peste
  Pue.R. sabandija
  Spa. pelma, pelmazo
See you later! (int phr) ¡Hasta luego!
  Col. ¡Te veo luego!, ¡Te veo más
  tarde!, ¡Hasta pronto!
  Dom.R., ElS., Gua., Pan. ¡Nos
  vemos!
  Pue.R. ¡Hasta la vista!
Sir (n) Señor
snoop (n) fisgón
  Chi. intruso
  Col., Cub. entremetido, metiche,

ABBREVIATIONS: Arg.=Argentina Bol.=Bolivia Chi.=Chile Col.=Colombia
Cos.R.=Costa Rica Cub.=Cuba Dom.R.=Dominican Republic Ecu.=Ecuador ElS.=El
Salvador Gua.=Guatemala Hon.=Honduras Mex.=Mexico Pan.=Panama Per.=Peru
Pri.=Primary Term Pue.R.=Puerto Rico Spa.=Spain Uru.=Uruguay Venz.=Venezuela

metido
Dom.R. curioso, entrometido,
metiche
Ecu., Mex. metiche
Gua. entrometido, shute
Pan. vidajeno/a
Pue.R. ligón
Venz. averiguador
sweetheart (n) enamorado/a
Chi. pololo/a
Mex. corazón
Spa. cariño, querido
tattler (n) charlatán
Chi., Gua. chismoso/a
Cub. chismoso/a, chivato
Dom.R., Pue.R. sinvergüenza
Mex. hablador
Spa. chivato
What's up? (int phr) ¿Qué pasa?
Chi. ¿Qué hay?
Col. ¿En qué andas/an?, ¿Qué
hay?
Dom.R. ¿Qué hay de nuevo?
Pan. ¿Quiubo?

Personal Life: Human Body

abdomen (n) abdomen
Chi. guata
Col. región abdominal, vientre
Dom.R. vientre
Per. barriga
Adam's apple (n phr) manzana de Adán
Arg. nuez de Adán
Cub. nuez
Spa. nuez de la garganta
ankle (n) tobillo
anus (n) ano

aorta (n) aorta
appendix (n) apéndice
arm (n) brazo
armpit (n) axila
Dom.R. zobaco
Pan. sobaco
artery (n) arteria
back (n) espalda
bags (under eyes) (n) ojeras
Chi. chasquillas
Dom.R. bolsas
bangs (hair) (n) flequillo
Col. capul
Cos.R. pava
Cub., Ecu., Per. cerquillo
Dom.R., Venz. pollina
Mex. fleco
Pan. gallusa
beard (n) barba
belly (n) barriga
Arg., Cos.R., Dom.R., Mex., Uru.
panza
Chi. guata
Col. panza, pipa
Venz. estómago
belly button (n phr) ombligo
Chi. pupo
biceps (n) bíceps
Mex. conejos
big toe (n phr) dedo gordo
Arg., Dom.R., Spa., Venz. dedo
gordo del pie
big-nosed (adj) narizón
Arg., Bol., Chi., Uru. narigón
Dom.R. narizú
birthmark (n) marca de nacimiento
Cub., Ecu., Per., Venz. lunar
Dom.R., Spa. antojo
Mex. mancha de nacimiento
blister (n) ampolla

blond (hair) (adj) rubio
Col. mono
Mex. güero
Pan. fulo
Venz. catire
blond (person) (n) rubio/a
Col. mono/a
Cos.R. macho (person with light hair)
Mex. güero/a
Pan. fulo/a
Venz. catire/a
blood (n) sangre
blood vessel (n phr) vaso sanguíneo
blue (eyes) (adj) azul
Col. ojiazul
Cos.R. macho (person with light-colored eyes)
bone (n) hueso
braid (hair) (n) trenza
Pan. moño
Venz. crineja
brain (n) cerebro
breast (n) seno
Arg., Col., Cos.R., Uru. teta
Chi. pechuga
Dom.R., ElS., Gua., Spa. pecho
Mex. chiche, chichi, busto
Pan. pecho, teta
bridge of nose (n phr) caballete
Chi., Dom.R. tabique
Mex., Venz. puente de la nariz
brown (eyes) (adj) castaño
Arg., Col., Dom.R., Per., Spa. marrón
Bol., Chi., Cos.R., Mex. café
brown (hair) (adj) moreno
Arg., Mex., Spa. castaño
Col. marrón, pelicastaño
Cub., Dom.R. trigueño

Uru. morocho
bruise (n) cardenal
Arg., Bol., Chi., Mex., Pan. moretón
Col., Cub. morado
Cos.R. morete
Dom.R. hematoma, morado
ElS., Gua., Hon. magulladura
Spa. moratón
Venz. golpe, magulladura
brunette (person) (n) moreno/a
Arg., Uru. morocho/a
Col., Cub., Dom.R. trigueño/a
Spa. persona de pelo castaño
bun (hair) (n) moño
Chi. tomate
Mex. chongo
Pan. cebolla
butt (n) trasero
Arg. cola, traste
Chi. traste
Col. cola, culo
Cub. nalgas
Mex. asentaderas
Pan. nalga
Per. poto
Spa. culo
Uru. cola
buttock (n) nalga
Arg. cachete
Chi. poto
Mex. pompa, pompis
calf (leg) (n) pantorrilla
callus (n) callo
canine (tooth) (n) canino
Cos.R. premolar
Cub., Mex., Spa. colmillo
cartilage (n) cartílago
cheek (n) mejilla
Chi., Col., Dom.R., Mex., Pan.,

Per., Venz. cachete
Spa. carrillo
chest (n) pecho
Chi., Col. tórax
chin (n) barbilla
Arg. mentón, pera
Chi. pera
Col. mentón
Mex. barba
Per. quijada
cleft (chin) (n) hendidura
Chi. labio leporino
Cos.R. camanance
Dom.R. hoyito
Mex. barba partida
Per. barbida partida
Venz. barbilla hendida
collarbone (n) clavícula
colon (n) colon
cornea (n) córnea
curly (hair) (adj) rizado
Arg., Pan. enrulado
Bol., Chi., Venz. ondulado
Col. crespo, ondulado
Dom.R. duro, malo
Mex. chino
Per. crespo
diaphragm (n) diafragma
dimple (n) hoyuelo
Bol. hoyo
Chi., Dom.R., Mex. hoyito
Cos.R., ElS., Gua., Hon.
camanance
double chin (n phr) papada
Chi. doble pera
Dom.R. doble barbilla
duct (n) conducto
ear (n) oreja
ear drum (n phr) tímpano
elbow (n) codo

epiglottis (n) epiglotis
esophagus (n) esófago
eye (n) ojo
eyeball (n) globo ocular
eyebrow (n) ceja
eyelash (n) pestaña
eyelid (n) párpado
face (n) cara, rostro
finger (n) dedo
fingernail (n) uña
follicle (n) folículo
foot (n) pie
forearm (n) antebrazo
forehead (n) frente
freckle (n) peca
gallbladder (n) vesícula biliar
gland (n) glándula
goatee (n) barbas de chivo
Col. chivera
Cub. chivo
Dom.R. chiva, chivita
Ecu. chivita
Spa. perilla
Venz. chiva
gray (hair) (adj) canoso
Col. cano
Spa. blanco
green (eyes) (adj) verde
Col. ojiverde
Cos.R. gato
groin (n) ingle
gum (n) encía
hair (n) cabello, pelo
Arg. vello
Col. cabellera, melena
hand (n) mano
head (n) cabeza
heart (n) corazón
heel (n) talón
hip (n) cadera

incisor (n) incisivo
index finger (n phr) dedo índice
intestine (n) intestino
iris (n) iris
jaw (n) mandíbula
  Col. quijada
joint (n) articulación
  Dom.R., Spa. coyuntura
kidney (n) riñón
knee (n) rodilla
knee cap (n phr) rótula
larynx (n) laringe
leg (n) pierna
lens (eye) (n) cristalino
lip (n) labio
liver (n) hígado
lobe (ear) (n) lóbulo
lung (n) pulmón
middle finger (n phr) dedo del
  corazón
  Arg. medio
  Col. dedo corazón
  Cub., Dom.R., Venz. dedo del
  medio
  Mex., Uru. dedo medio
molar (n) muela
  Col. molar
mole (skin) (n) lunar
mouth (n) boca
muscle (n) músculo
mustache (n) bigote
nape (n) nuca
  Col. cogote
navel (n) ombligo
  Arg., Chi. pupo
neck (n) cuello
nerve (n) nervio
nipple (n) pezón
  Col. tetilla
nose (n) nariz

nostril (n) ventanilla
  Chi. narina
  Cub. ventana de la nariz
  Dom.R. hoyo de la nariz
  Mex. poro de la nariz
  Pue.R. roto de la nariz
  Venz. orificio nasal
palate (n) paladar
palm (hand) (n) palma de la mano
pancreas (n) páncreas
part (hair) (n) raya
  Chi., Pan. partidura
  Dom.R., Mex., Venz. partido
pelvis (n) pelvis
pharynx (n) faringe
pigtail (n) trenza
  Bol., Cos.R. cola
  Chi. colita, moño
  Col., Dom.R., Mex., Venz. colita
  Per. cachito
  Spa., Uru. coleta
pimple (n) grano
  Chi., Cos.R., Dom.R., Spa.
  espinilla
  Col., Venz. barro, espinilla
  Mex. barro
  Per. barrito
pinkie finger (n phr) dedo meñique
  Cub. dedo chiquito
plantar arch (foot) (n phr) arco plantar
  Arg., Mex., Venz. arco del pie
  Col. arco de la planta del pie
  Dom.R. puente
ponytail (hair) (n) cola de caballo
  Arg. cola, colita
  Pue.R. rabo de caballo
  Spa. coleta
pore (n) poro
pubic hair (n phr) vello pubiano
  Col., Cos.R., ElS., Gua., Mex.,

ABBREVIATIONS: Arg.=Argentina Bol.=Bolivia Chi.=Chile Col.=Colombia
Cos.R.=Costa Rica Cub.=Cuba Dom.R.=Dominican Republic Ecu.=Ecuador ElS.=El
Salvador Gua.=Guatemala Hon.=Honduras Mex.=Mexico Pan.=Panama Per.=Peru
Pri.=Primary Term Pue.R.=Puerto Rico Spa.=Spain Uru.=Uruguay Venz.=Venezuela

Venz. vello púbico
Dom.R. vello
Uru. vello del pubis
pubis (n) pubis
pupil (n) pupila
rectum (n) recto
red (hair) (adj) pelirrojo
redhead (n) pelirrojo/a
retina (n) retina
rib (n) costilla
ring finger (n phr) dedo anular
root (hair) (n) raíz
   Dom.R. crecimeinto
scab (n) costra
   Cub., Dom.R. postilla
scalp (n) cuero cabelludo
scar (n) cicatriz
shin (n) espinilla
   Chi. canilla
short (person) (adj) pequeño
   Arg., Uru. bajito, petiso
   Col. bajito, bajo
   Dom.R. bajito
   Mex. de estatura baja, chaparro
   Venz. bajo
shoulder (n) hombro
shoulder blade (n phr) omóplato
sideburn (n) patilla
sinus (n) seno
   Mex., Spa. seno nasal
   Venz. cavidad
skeleton (n) esqueleto
   Col. osamenta
   Mex. calaca
skin (n) piel
skull (n) cráneo
   Col., Cos.R., Mex. calavera
sole (foot) (n) planta del pie
spine (n) columna vertebral
   Col. espinazo

Ecu. espina dorsal, espinaso
Gua. espina dorsal
spleen (n) bazo
stomach (n) estómago
straight (hair) (adj) lacio
   Chi., Col., Spa., Venz. liso
   Dom.R. bueno
tall (adj) alto
tan (v) broncearse
   Arg., Chi., Cub., Dom.R.
   quemarse
   Col. dorarse al sol
tan (skin) (adj) bronceado
   Arg., Chi., Cub., Dom.R.
   quemado
   Col. tostado
taste bud (n phr) papila gustativa
teeth (n) dientes
   Col. dentadura
temple (n) sien
tendon (n) tendón
thigh (n) muslo
thorax (n) tórax
throat (n) garganta
thumb (n) pulgar
   Arg. dedo gordo
tip of nose (n phr) lóbulo
   Chi., Col., Mex., Spa., Venz.
   punta de la nariz
tissue (n) tejido
toe (n) dedo del pie
toenail (n) uña del pie
tongue (n) lengua
tonsil (n) amígdala
   Mex. angina
trachea (n) tráquea
triceps (n) tríceps
trunk (n) tronco
urinary bladder (n phr) vejiga
vein (n) vena

vocal cord (n phr) cuerda vocal
waist (n) cintura
  Col. cinto, talle
wart (n) verruga
  Mex. mezquino
  Per. callo
wavy (hair) (adj) ondulado
  Venz. crespo
wrist (n) muñeca

Personal Life: Personal Articles

antiperspirant (n) desodorante
  Gua., Mex., Pue.R.
  antiperspirante
ashtray (n) cenicero
attaché case (n) maletín
  Arg. portafolios
  Mex. portafolio
backpack (n) mochila
barrette (n) broche para el pelo
  Arg., Bol., Col., Cub., Pue.R.
  hebilla
  Chi. traba
  Dom.R., Pan., Per., Spa. gancho
  para el pelo
  Venz. ganchito de pelo
briefcase (n) portafolios
  Bol. cartera, portafolio
  Col., Cub., Per., Pue.R. maletín
cigar (n) cigarro, puro
  Cub. tabaco
cigarette (n) cigarrillo
  Chi. pucho
  Mex. cigarro
coin purse (n phr) monedero
  Dom.R. portamonedas
comb (n) peine

  Chi. peineta
  Col., Ecu., Pan., Pue.R. peinilla
cream (for skin) (n) crema
curling iron (n phr) tenazas
dental floss (n phr) hilo dental
deodorant (n) desodorante
eyeliner (n) delineador
eyeshadow (n) sombra de ojos
hair dryer (n phr) secadora manual
  Arg. secador
  Chi., Spa., Venz. secador de pelo
  Cub. secadora de pelo
  Dom.R., Pue.R. blower
  Mex. pistola de pelo, secadora de pelo
hair gel (n phr) gel para el pelo
  Dom.R., ElS., Gua. gelatina para el pelo
  Ecu. gel fijador
  Mex. jalea
  Spa. gomina para el pelo
hair mousse (n phr) mousse para el pelo
  Dom.R. mus para el pelo
  ElS., Gua., Spa. espuma para el pelo
  Mex. mouse para el pelo
hair rollers (n phr) ruleros
  Chi. ondulines
  Col., Spa. rulos
  Cub., Pue.R. rolos
  ElS., Gua., Mex. tubos
  Pan., Venz. rollos
hairbrush (n) cepillo de pelo
hairspray (n) laca para el pelo
  Cub. espray de pelo
  Dom.R., Mex., Pan. spray para el pelo
  Pue.R. spray de pelo
handbag (n) cartera

Col., Cos.R., Gua., Mex., Pan.
bolsa de mano
Dom.R. bolso
Spa., Venz. bolso de mano
keychain (n) llavero
lighter (n) encendedor
Cub. fosforera
lipstick (n) lápiz labial
Arg., Bol., Chi. rouge
Col., Cub., Dom.R. pintalabios
Mex. bilé
Pan. lipstick
Pue.R. lipstic
Spa., Uru. lápiz de labios
makeup kit (n phr) estuche de
maquillaje
Col. juego de maquillaje
Pue.R. cartera de maquillaje
mascara (n) rímel
matchstick (n) cerilla, fósforo
Mex. cerillo
nail clippers (n phr) cortauñas
nail polish (n phr) esmalte de uñas
Chi. cutex
Col., Spa. pintauñas
Cub., Venz. pintura de uñas
Dom.R. cuté
pipe (n) pipa
pocket watch (n phr) reloj de bolsillo
razor (n) rasuradora
Arg., Chi. gillette
Col. máquina de afeitar
Cub., Spa. cuchilla de afeitar
Dom.R., Pue.R. afeitadora
Mex. rastrillo
Pan. navaja
Venz. hojilla de afeitar
shampoo (n) champú
Arg. shampoo
shaving brush (n phr) brocha de

afeitar
shaving cream (n) crema de afeitar
soap (n) jabón
sunscreen (n) loción solar
Arg. pantalla solar, protector
Chi., Cos.R. protector solar
Dom.R. bloqueador solar
Mex., Per. bronceador
Spa. crema de protección solar
Venz. protector de sol
toothbrush (n) cepillo de dientes
toothpaste (n) dentífrico, pasta de
dientes
Col. crema dental
Per., Pue.R. pasta dental
tweezers (n) pinzas
umbrella (n) paraguas, sombrilla
walking stick (n phr) bastón
wallet (n) billetera, cartera
Dom.R. cartera de hombre
watch (n) reloj

Personal Life: Relationships

adopt (a child) (v) adoptar
adult (n) adulto
Col. persona mayor
aunt (n) tía
baby (n) bebé
Arg., Uru. beba, bebe
Chi. guagua
babysit (v) hacer de niñero/a
Arg., Uru. cuidar a un/a beba/
bebe/chico/chica/nene/nena
Chi., Col., Ecu., Per., Pue.R.,
Venz. cuidar niños
Mex. cuidar a un bebé/niño/niña
babysitter (n) niñero/a

Arg. babysitter
Chi. niñera, nodriza
Mex. nana
Per., Venz. cuidador/a de niños
boy (n) niño
Arg., Pue.R., Uru. nene
Col. chino
Dom.R. muchachito
Mex. chamaco
boyfriend (n) novio
Chi. pololo
Col. pretendiente
Ecu., Per. enamorado
break up (relationship) (v phr) romper
Arg., Dom.R. cortar
Chi., Mex. cortar, terminar
Col. separarse
Cub. pelearse
Ecu., ElS., Gua., Hon., Venz.
terminar
bridal shower (n phr) despedida de
soltera
Col. shower
bride (n) novia
brother (n) hermano
brother-in-law (n) cuñado
burial (n) entierro
Chi., Mex. sepelio
Col. exequias, sepelio
child (n) niño/a
Arg. chico/a
christen (v) bautizar
christening (n) bautizo
Arg., Col. bautismo
cousin (female) (n) prima
cousin (male) (n) primo
date (v) tener una cita
Arg. estar de novio
Col. tener compromiso
Dom.R., Gua., Mex., Venz. salir

con
daughter (n) hija
daughter-in-law (n) nuera
divorce (v) divorciarse
Col. apartarse, desunirse,
separarse
divorced (adj) divorciado
Col. separado
family (n) familia
family member (n phr) familiar
Arg., Chi., Ecu., Mex., Pue.R.,
Venz. pariente
Col. miembro de la familia
father (n) padre
father-in-law (n) suegro
fiancé (male) (n) novio
Col., Cos.R., Dom.R., Pan.
prometido
Mex. comprometido
fiancée (female) (n) novia
Col., Cos.R., Dom.R., Pan.
prometida
Mex. comprometida
first cousin (n phr) primo hermano/
prima hermana
friend (female) (n) amiga
friend (male) (n) amigo
girl (n) niña
Arg., Uru. chica, nena
Dom.R. muchachita
Mex. chamaca
girlfriend (n) novia
Chi. polola
Ecu., Per. enamorada
give birth (v phr) dar a luz
Arg. tener un/a beba/bebe/bebé/
hijo/hija
Col. alumbrar, parir
Cos.R., Dom.R., Pan. parir
goddaughter (n) ahijada

godfather (n) padrino
godmother (n) madrina
godson (n) ahijado
granddaughter (n) nieta
grandfather (n) abuelo
grandmother (n) abuela
grandson (n) nieto
great aunt (n phr) tía abuela
great uncle (n phr) tío abuelo
great-granddaughter (n) bisnieta
great-grandfather (n) bisabuelo
great-grandmother (n) bisabuela
great-grandson (n) bisnieto
great-great-granddaughter (n)
    tataranieta
great-great-grandfather (n) tatarabuelo
great-great-grandmother (n)
    tatarabuela
great-great-grandson (n) tataranieto
groom (n) novio
grow up (v phr) crecer
    Col. madurar
guardian (n) tutor
    Col., Pan., Venz. guardián
guy (n) muchacho, tipo
    Arg. pibe
    Chi. cabro
    Cos.R. mae, fulano/a
    Cub., Pue.R. chico
    Mex., Pan. fulano/a
guys (dual gender plural) (n)
    muchachos, tipos
    Arg., Ecu. chicos
    Chi. cabros, chiquillos
infant (n) niño/a
    Arg., Uru. chico/a, nene/a
    Col. criatura, infante, menor
    Cub., Mex., Spa. bebé
    Gua. criatura
kid (n) chico/a

Cub. chiquito/a
Col., Venz. niño/a
Dom.R. muchacho/a
lover (n) amante
married (n) casado
mistress (n) amante
    Cub., Spa. querida
    Mex. concubina
    Pue.R. chilla
mother (n) madre
mother-in-law (n) suegra
nanny (n) niñera
    Chi., Col., Mex., Venz. nana
nephew (n) sobrino
niece (n) sobrina
parents (n) padres
pregnant (adj) embarazada
    Col. encinta, esperando,
    preñada
    Pan., Per. encinta
    Venz. en estado
relative (n) pariente
second cousin (n phr) primo/a
    segundo/a
sister (n) hermana
sister-in-law (n) cuñada
son (n) hijo
son-in-law (n) yerno
stepbrother (n) hermanastro
stepdaughter (n) hijastra
stepfather (n) padrastro
stepmother (n) madrastra
stepsister (n) hermanastra
stepson (n) hijastro
teenager (n) adolescente
    Dom.R. teenager
toddler (n) pequeñito/a
    Arg. beba, bebe, bebé
    Col. niño/a chiquito/a
    ElS., Gua., Hon. niño/a que

empieza a andar
Mex. niño/a de edad pre-escolar,
niño/a que empieza a andar
Spa. niño/a
Venz. niñito/a
uncle (n) tío
wake (n) velorio
Col. velación
Cos.R. vela
Dom.R. funeral
Spa. velatorio
widow (n) viuda
widower (n) viudo
young (adj) joven

Friends in Venezuela are sometimes called *panas*. Very loyal friends earn the name *panadería*, which literally means "bakery."

ABBREVIATIONS: Arg.=Argentina Bol.=Bolivia Chi.=Chile Col.=Colombia
Cos.R.=Costa Rica Cub.=Cuba Dom.R.=Dominican Republic Ecu.=Ecuador ElS.=El
Salvador Gua.=Guatemala Hon.=Honduras Mex.=Mexico Pan.=Panama Per.=Peru
Pri.=Primary Term Pue.R.=Puerto Rico Spa.=Spain Uru.=Uruguay Venz.=Venezuela

Shelter & Daily Life: Furnishings

armchair (n) silla de brazos
  Arg., Chi., Spa., Uru. sillón
  Cub., Pue.R. butaca
  Dom.R. butaca, sillón
  Mex. silla con coderas
bed (n) cama
bed, double (n phr) cama doble
  Gua., Mex. cama matrimonial
  Spa. cama de matrimonio
bed, king-sized (n phr) cama grande
  Arg. cama camera
  Col., Dom.R. cama king size
  Mex. cama king-size
  Pan., Venz. cama king
bed, queen-sized (n phr) cama doble
  Arg. cama camera
  Dom.R. cama queen size
  Mex. cama queen-size
  Pan. cama matrimonial
  Venz. cama queen
bed, single (n phr) cama
  Chi. cama de soltero
  Col., Ecu., Pue.R. cama sencilla
  Gua. cama imperial
  Pan. cama tres cuartos
  Mex., Venz. cama individual
bench (n) banco
  Arg. banca
  Spa. banqueta
berth (n) litera
  Chi. camarote
blanket (n) cobija
  Arg., Bol., Col., Cub., Uru. frazada
  Ecu. colcha
  Pue.R. frisa

  Spa. manta
blinds (n) persianas
  Col. cortinas
box spring (n phr) colchón de resortes
  Chi. catre
  Dom.R., Mex., Venz. box spring
  Pan. esprín
  Spa. somier
buffet (n) aparador
  Col. mostrador
  Dom.R. despensa
  Gua. bufetera
  Mex. mesa de buffet
  Pue.R. chinero
bunkbed (n) litera
  Chi. camarote
  Col., Dom.R., Pan. cama camarote
  Cub. cama litera
chair (n) silla
chair, director's (n phr) silla de director, silla plegable
  Mex. silla ejecutiva, sillón ejecutivo
chair, folding (n phr) silla plegable
  Dom.R. silla plegadiza
chair, lounging (n phr) catre, chaise
  Chi. asiento, poltrona
  Col. silla de extensión
  Mex. sillón reclinable
  Pue.R. silla reclinable
  Spa. hamaca
chair, rocking (n phr) mecedora
  Arg. silla hamaca
  Col. mecedor
  Cub., Pue.R. sillón
chair, step (n phr) banco-escalera
  Venz. silla con escalón
closet (clothes) (n) clóset
  Arg. placard

Bol., Chi., Cos.R., Ecu., Uru.
ropero
Pan. estante
Spa. armario
closet (general) (n) armario
Chi. guardarropa
Col., Cos.R., Cub., Mex., Pan.,
Per. clóset
cradle, crib (n) cuna
Dom.R. catre
curtains (n) cortinas
desk (n) escritorio
display cabinet (n phr) vitrina
Arg. aparador
Pue.R. chinero
drawer (n) gaveta
Arg., Chi., Col., Ecu., Mex., Per.,
Spa., Uru. cajón
drawer knob (n phr) perilla
Col. botón, pomo
Dom. R. manubrio
Pan. agarrador
Venz. manilla
dresser (n) ropero
Arg., Chi., Col., Cub., Per.
cómoda
Venz. gavetero
Pue.R., Spa. tocador
footboard (n) pie de la cama
hammock (n) hamaca
Venz. chinchorro
headboard (n) cabecera
Ecu. espaldar
Pue.R. espaldal
love seat (n phr) confidente
Arg. silloncito
Col., ElS., Gua., Venz. sofá para
dos personas
Dom.R., Mex. love seat
Pue.R., Spa. sofá

mattress (n) colchón
Pue.R. matres
ottoman (n) otomana
Mex. taburete
Pan. banquillo
Pue.R. banquillo, ottomán
pillow (n) almohada
pillowcase (n) funda
Gua. sobrefunda
sheet, bed (n phr) sábana
sheet, contour (n phr) sábana de cajón
Arg. sábana de elástico
Col. sábana de forro
Spa. sábana bajera ajustable
Venz. sábana de esquinera
shutters (n) postigos
Col., Ecu., Gua. persianas
Mex. contraventanas
sofa (n) sofá
stool (n) banco
Chi. piso
Dom.R. banqueta, banquito
table (n) mesa
table leaf (n phr) tablero
Chi. tabla
Col. hoja, lámina
Mex. tablón de extensión
table leg (n phr) pata
table, drop-leaf (n phr) mesa plegable
table, kitchen (n phr) mesa de cocina
Pan. mesita de cocina
table, night (n phr) mesilla de noche
Arg. mesa de luz, mesita de luz
Bol. mesita de noche, velador
Chi. velador
Col., ElS., Gua., Hon., Pue.R.,
Venz. mesa de noche
Cub., Dom.R., Pan. mesita de
noche
table, ping pong (n phr) mesa de

ping pong
table, pool (n phr) mesa de billar
table, round (n phr) mesa redonda
table, serving (n phr) mesita de
servicio
Arg. mesita rodante
Col. mesa de servicio
Venz. mesa de servir

Shelter & Daily Living: Housing

apartment (n) apartamento
Arg., Bol., Chi., Mex.
departamento
Spa. piso
apartment building (n phr) edificio de
apartamentos
Arg., Bol., Mex. edificio de
departamentos
Chi., Col. edificio
Dom.R. torre de apartamentos
Spa. edificio de pisos
Uru. propiedad horizontal
balcony (n) balcón
Chi. terraza
Col. balaustrada, balconcillo
barracks (n) cuartel
Pan. barracas
Pue.R. barraca
bathroom (n) cuarto de baño
Bol., Chi., Cos.R., Cub., Ecu.,
Spa., Uru., Venz. baño
bedroom (n) dormitorio
Arg., Col., Cub., Pue.R. cuarto
Dom.R. aposento, cuarto
Mex. cuarto, recámara
Pan. habitación
boathouse (n) caseta de botes

Col. cobertizo para las lanchas,
garaje para botes
Dom.R. casa-botes
Gua. cobertizo de lanchas
bungalow (n) casa independiente
Arg., Uru. bungalow
Bol. cabañita
Chi. cabaña, chalet
Col. bungaló, cabaña, casita
campestre, casita playera
Dom.R. bungaloo
ElS., Gua., Hon. casa campestre,
casa de playa
Mex. búngalo
Pan. bungalu
Spa. bungaló
Venz. casa de campo
cabin (n) cabaña, choza
Chi. refugio
church (n) iglesia
condominium (n) condominios
Cub., ElS., Gua., Pue.R., Spa.
condominio
cottage (n) casa de campo
Arg. casa, casa-quinta, quinta
Chi. cabaña, chalet
Col. casita de campo
courtyard (n) patio
dining room (n phr) comedor
doghouse (n) perrera
Arg. cucha
Chi., Venz. casa de perro
duplex (n) dúplex
Chi. casa pareada
Dom.R., Pue.R. casa dúplex
fireplace (n) chimenea
Arg. estufa, hogar
garage (storage) (n) garaje
Dom.R. marquesina
ground floor (n phr) planta baja

ABBREVIATIONS: Arg.=Argentina Bol.=Bolivia Chi.=Chile Col.=Colombia
Cos.R.=Costa Rica Cub.=Cuba Dom.R.=Dominican Republic Ecu.=Ecuador ElS.=El
Salvador Gua.=Guatemala Hon.=Honduras Mex.=Mexico Pan.=Panama Per.=Peru
Pri.=Primary Term Pue.R.=Puerto Rico Spa.=Spain Uru.=Uruguay Venz.=Venezuela

Col. piso de abajo, primer piso
Dom.R. primer piso
hallway (n) pasillo, corredor
hangar (n) hangar
hut (n) choza
  Arg. albergue, cabaña, casilla
  Dom.R. casita de paja
kitchen (n) cocina
living room (n phr) cuarto de estar,
  sala
  Arg. living
main entrance (n phr) entrada principal
mansion (n) mansión
move (v) mudarse
  Bol. trasladarse
  Col. cambiarse de casa
pantry (n) despensa
  Bol., Mex. alacena
  Dom.R. pantry
  ElS., Gua., Hon. comedor
  auxiliar, pantry
  Pue.R. gabinete
porch (n) pórtico
  Cub. porche
  Dom.R. galería
  Gua. terraza cubierta
  Pan. porch
rent (housing) (v) alquilar
  Chi., Col. arrendar
  Mex., Pue.R. rentar
shed (n) cobertizo
  Chi. galpón
  Pue.R. casita de herramientas
side entrance (n phr) puerta lateral
  Arg. puerta de servicio
  Col. entrada lateral
  Cub. puerta del costado
  Mex. puerta del lado
study (n) estudio
tent (n) carpa

Chi., Cos.R., Dom.R., Mex.,
  Spa., Venz. tienda de campaña
  Pan. tolda
townhouse (n) casa en hilera
  Bol., Uru. casa pegada
  Col. casa de ciudad, casa
  particular en la ciudad
  Dom.R., Pue.R. townhouse
  Gua. casa particular en complejos
  residenciales
  Mex. dúplex horizontal
  Spa. casa adosada
upper floor (n phr) planta alta
  Col. piso superior
  Dom.R. piso de arriba
  Spa. planta superior
villa (n) villa

Shelter & Daily Living: Town & City

bakery (n) panadería
  Chi., Col. pastelería
  Pue.R. repostería
bank (n) banco
bar (n) bar
  Col. taberna
  Mex., Pan. cantina
billboard (n) anuncio panorámico
  Chi., Cub. cartelera
  Col. cartelera, valla
  Cos.R. rótulo
  Dom.R. valla
  Mex. anuncio
  Pue.R. billboard
bookstore (n) librería
  Pue.R. tienda de libros
building (n) edificio
  Col. construcción, edificación

ABBREVIATIONS: Arg.=Argentina Bol.=Bolivia Chi.=Chile Col.=Colombia Cos.R.=Costa Rica Cub.=Cuba Dom.R.=Dominican Republic Ecu.=Ecuador ElS.=El Salvador Gua.=Guatemala Hon.=Honduras Mex.=Mexico Pan.=Panama Per.=Peru Pri.=Primary Term Pue.R.=Puerto Rico Spa.=Spain Uru.=Uruguay Venz.=Venezuela

business district (n phr) barrio
comercial
Col., Cub., Mex., Pue.R. zona
comercial
Dom.R. centro de negocios
Spa. zona de negocios
cathedral (n) catedral
cemetery (n) cementerio
Chi., Col. campo santo
Mex. panteón
city (n) ciudad
Col. metrópoli, urbe
city hall (n phr) ayuntamiento
Bol., Pue.R. alcaldía
Chi., Col., ElS., Gua., Hon.
municipalidad
Ecu. alcaldía, municipalidad
Uru. intendencia
clinic (n) clínica
coffee bar (n phr) café
Col., Pue.R., Spa. cafetería
Cos.R. café bar
coffee plantation (n phr) cafetal
courthouse (n) tribunal de justicia
Col. edificio de los tribunales
Cub., Mex., Pue.R. corte
Dom.R. palacio de justicia
Spa. juzgado, palacio de justicia
daycare center (n phr) guardería
infantil
Arg., Dom.R. guardería
Col. jardín de infantes
Pue.R. nursery
department store (n phr) grandes
almacenes
Cub. tienda
Col. almacén grande
Cos.R. tienda de departamentos
Dom.R., ElS., Gua., Hon.,
Pue.R., Venz. tienda por

departamentos
Mex. tienda departamental
Pan. almacén
docks (n) muelle
doctor's office (n phr) consultorio
médico
Pue.R. oficina del médico, oficina
del doctor
downtown (n) centro de la ciudad
Pue.R. centro del pueblo,
pueblo
drug store (n phr) farmacia
Col. botica, droguería
Ecu., Per. botica
dump (n) basurero
entrance fee (n phr) entrada
Col. precio de la entrada
Pue.R., Venz. precio de entrada
factory (n) fábrica
Col. empresa, industria
Dom.R., Pue.R. factoría
fairground (n) parque de atracciones
Col. terreno para ferias, terreno
para circos
Dom.R., Ecu. parque de
diversiones
Mex. feria
Pue.R. feria, parque de diversiones
fire station (n phr) estación de
bomberos
Bol., Cos.R., Ecu., Spa., Uru.
parque de bomberos
Mex. departamento de bomberos
florist's shop (n phr) florista
Col., Dom.R., Pan., Pue.R.,
Venz. floristería
Cub. florería
fountain (n) fuente
free admission (n phr) entrada libre
Chi., Cub., Dom.R., ElS., Gua.,

Pan., Pue.R. entrada gratis
Spa. entrada gratuita
fruit stand (n phr) puesto de frutas
Pue.R. frutería
funeral home (n phr) funeraria
Spa. tanatorio
grocery (n) tienda de comestibles
Arg., Uru. almacén
Col. mercado
Cos.R. compras
Cub., Per. bodega
Dom.R. bodega, supercolmado, víveres
ElS. pulpería
Gua. tienda
Mex. super, tienda de abarrotes
Pan. abarrotería, tienda
Pue.R. colmado
Spa. supermercado
Venz. abastos, supermercado
hairdresser's shop (n phr) peluquería
Dom.R., Mex., Pan. salón de belleza
Pue.R. beauty parlor, salón de belleza
harbor (n) puerto
herbalist's shop (n) botánica
Col. tienda botánica
Mex. tienda naturista
Spa. tienda de botánica
Uru. herbolario
hospital (n) hospital
Col. clínica
hotel (n) hotel
ice cream parlor (n phr) heladería
Mex. nevería
laundry (n) lavandería
Arg. lavadero
lawyer's office (n phr) bufete de abogados

Arg. estudio de abogados
Col., Pue.R. oficina de abogados
Ecu. estudio juridico
library (n) biblioteca
liquor store (n phr) tienda de bebidas alcohólicas
Bol., Col., Mex. licorería
Dom.R., Pue.R. liquor store
Pan. bodega
market (n) mercado
mosque (n) mezquita
museum (n) museo
neighborhood (n) vecindad
Arg., Ecu., Pan., Uru. barrio
Bol., Gua., Pue.R., Venz. vecindario
Col., Dom.R., Per., Spa. barrio, vecindario
neon sign (n phr) anuncio de neón
Arg. cartel de néon
Col. aviso con luz de neón
Dom.R. letrero de néon
newsstand (n) puesto de periódicos
Arg. puesto de diarios
Col. puesto de periódicos y de revistas
nursery (plants) (n) semillero
Arg., Col., Dom.R. vivero
Mex. invernadero
park (n) parque
Arg. plaza
pet shop (n phr) pajarería
Col. almacén de mascotas
Dom.R. pet shop, tienda de mascotas
ElS., Gua. tienda de mascotes
Mex. tienda de animales domésticos, veterinaria
Pue.R. pet shop, tienda de animales

Spa. tienda de animales
police station (n phr) comisaría
Col., Cub., Gua., Pan., Pue.R.
estación de policía
Dom.R. destacamento policial
polls (voting) (n) urnas
pollution (n) contaminación
Col. polución
post office (n phr) oficina de correos
Arg., Cub. correo
Col. oficina postal
print shop (n phr) imprenta
Col. taller tipográfico, talleres
gráficos
residencial area (n phr) zona
residencial
Arg. barrio residencial
Col. área residencial
Pue.R. área residencial, sector
residencial
restaurant (n) restaurante
retirement home (n phr) hogar de
ancianos
Arg. asilo de ancianos
Col. ancianato
Mex. asilo
Pan. retiro para ancianos
school (n) escuela
Arg., Col., Gua. colegio
shop sign (n phr) letrero comercial
Arg. cartel
Col. anuncio de almacén
shop window (n phr) vitrina
Arg. vidriera
Cos.R., Cub., Per., Spa. escaparate
Mex. aparador
shopping center (n phr) centro
comercial
skyscraper (n) rascacielos
square (city) (n) plaza

stadium (n) estadio
Pue.R. parque
street lamp (n phr) farol
Dom.R. palo de luz
Pan. poste de luz
Spa. farola
suburb (n) barrio
Col. barrio en las afueras,
suburbio
Cub., Dom.R., Gua. suburbio
Mex. colonia, fraccionamiento
supermarket (n) supermercado
synagogue (n) sinagoga
telephone booth (n phr) cabina
telefónica
Mex. teléfono público
theater (n) teatro
university (n) universidad
uptown (n) distrito residencial
Dom.R. área residencial
village (n) aldea
Arg. pueblo
Col. población
Cub. pueblecito
Dom.R. pueblito
vote (v) votar
wine shop (n phr) bodega
Col. taberna
Dom.R. tienda de vinos
Ecu. tienda de licores
Mex., Pue.R. vinatería
Uru. vinería
zoo (n) zoológico

> *Adobe*—sun-baked bricks used
> for building houses—has its
> roots in the Quechuan term
> *adobi.*

ABBREVIATIONS: Arg.=Argentina Bol.=Bolivia Chi.=Chile Col.=Colombia
Cos.R.=Costa Rica Cub.=Cuba Dom.R.=Dominican Republic Ecu.=Ecuador ElS.=El
Salvador Gua.=Guatemala Hon.=Honduras Mex.=Mexico Pan.=Panama Per.=Peru
Pri.=Primary Term Pue.R.=Puerto Rico Spa.=Spain Uru.=Uruguay Venz.=Venezuela

Transportation: Bicycle

bell (bicycle) (n) timbre
  Arg., Chi., Dom.R., Uru. bocina
  Bol. campanilla
bicycle (n) bicicleta
bike, hybrid (n phr) bicicleta híbrida
bike, mountain (n phr) montañera
  Arg. bicicleta todo terreno
  Chi., Col., Venz. bicicleta de
  montaña
  Dom.R., Pue.R. mountain bike
  ElS., Gua. bicicleta montañesa
  Mex. bicicleta de campotraviesa
  Spa. bicicleta de montaña,
  mountain bike
bike, road (n phr) bicicleta de camino
  Arg., Cub., Uru. bicicleta
  Col. bicicleta de ruta, bicicleta
  para carretera
  Dom.R. bicicleta de carrera
  Mex. bicicleta turismo
  Spa. bicicleta de carreras
bike, tandem (n phr) bicicleta para dos
  personas
  Col. bicicleta de dos personas,
  bicicleta doble, tándem
  Mex. bicicleta doble
  Pue.R. doblecleta
  Spa. tándem
chain (bicycle) (n) cadena
flat tire (n phr) llanta reventada
  Arg., Dom.R. goma pinchada
  Bol. llanta pinchada
  Chi. pneumático pinchado
  Col. llanta desinflada, llanta
  pinchada
  Cos.R., Per. llanta desinflada
  Cub. goma ponchada

  Ecu. tubo bajo
  Gua. llanta pache, llanta pinchada
  Mex. llanta pinchada, llanta
  ponchada
  Pan. flat
  Pue.R. goma vacía
  Spa. neumático pinchado, rueda
  pinchada
  Uru. llanta desinflada, neumático
  desinflado
  Venz. caucho pinchado
handlebar grips (bicycle) (n phr) puños
  Col. manillas
  Gua., Venz. agarraderas del
  manubrio
  Per. mangos
handlebars (bicycle) (n) guía
  Arg., Bol., Chi., Col., Mex.,
  Pue.R., Venz. manubrio
  Cub., Dom.R., Pan. timón
  Ecu. manubrios
  Gua. manubrio, timón
  Spa., Uru. manillar
inner tube (bicycle tire) (n phr) tubo
  Chi., Spa. cámara
  Cos.R. neumático
  Venz. tripa del caucho
pedal (n) pedal
pedal (v) pedalear
reflector (bicycle) (n) reflector
  Arg. faro, luz
ride (bicycle) (v phr) montar en
  bicicleta
  Arg., Chi., Cos.R., Mex. andar
  en bicicleta
  Pue.R. correr bicicleta
rim (bicycle wheel) (n) llanta
  Chi., Col., Cos.R. aro
  Mex. rin
  Venz. rueda

ABBREVIATIONS: Arg.=Argentina Bol.=Bolivia Chi.=Chile Col.=Colombia
Cos.R.=Costa Rica Cub.=Cuba Dom.R.=Dominican Republic Ecu.=Ecuador ElS.=El
Salvador Gua.=Guatemala Hon.=Honduras Mex.=Mexico Pan.=Panama Per.=Peru
Pri.=Primary Term Pue.R.=Puerto Rico Spa.=Spain Uru.=Uruguay Venz.=Venezuela

seat (bicycle) (n) asiento
  Bol., Col. silla
  Chi., Dom.R., Ecu., Pue.R.,
  Spa., Uru. sillín
spoke (bicycle wheel) (n) faro
  Arg., Cub., Gua., Mex. rayo
  Col. radio, rayo
  Spa., Venz. radio
tire (bicycle) (n) neumático
  Arg., Dom.R., Pue.R. goma
  Bol., Col., Cos.R., Gua., Mex.,
  Pan., Per. llanta
  Cub. rueda
  Venz. caucho

Transportation: Car & Traffic

alley (n) callejón
  Col. callejuela, pasadizo
  Per. pasaje
automatic transmission (n phr)
  transmisión automática
  Spa. cambio automático
back seat (n phr) asiento trasero
battery (n) batería
bend (in road) (n) curva
blinker (light) (n) intermitente, luz
  intermitente
  Arg. guiño
  Bol. guiñador
  Pan. luz direccional
  Venz. luz de cruce
brake (n) freno
brake (v) frenar
brights (headlights) (n) luces fuertes
  Arg., Chi., Dom.R., Mex., Pan.,
  Venz. luces altas
  Col. plenas

  Cub., Pue.R., Spa. luces largas
  Ecu. faros intensos
bump (road) (n) bache
  Chi. lomo de toro
  Dom.R. hoyo
  Mex. tope
bumper (n) parachoques
  Arg. paragolpes
  Col. amortiguador
  Dom.R., Pan., Pue.R. bumper
  Mex. defensa
car (n) carro
  Arg., Chi., Col. auto, coche
  Mex. auto, coche, automóvil
  Spa. coche, automóvil
  Uru. coche
car body (n phr) carrocería
  Pan. chasis
car jack (crime) (v phr) sequestrar en
  auto
  Bol. raptar
  Col. asaltar
  Cub. robarse un carro
  Mex. asaltar con violencia
  Pue.R. car jack
  Spa. robar un vehículo con
  alguien dentro
  Uru. atracar un coche
  Venz. robar un carro
car, private (n phr) carro privado
  Arg. auto particular
  Chi., Ecu. carro particular
  Spa., Uru. coche particular
carburetor (n) carburador
chassis (n) chasis
  Dom.R., Pue.R. chassis
  Ecu., Pan., Per. bastidor
city block (n phr) manzana
  Dom.R., Ecu., Pan. cuadra
  Pue.R. bloque

cloverleaf junction (n phr) trébol
  Col. confluencia, empalme,
  entronque en forma de trébol
  Mex. paso a desnivel
convertible (n) convertible
  Spa. descapotable
crash (vehicle) (v) chocar
  Col. estrellar
crosswalk (n) paso de peatones
  Col. cruce peatonal
  Cub. acera
  Dom.R. cruce de peatones
curve (in road) (n) curva
decelerate (v) disminuir la velocidad
  Chi., Dom.R., Pue.R., Spa.
  reducir la velocidad
  Col., Cub. desacelerar
detour (n) desvío
  Mex. desviación
dipstick (n) indicador del nivel de
  aceite
  Col. varilla para medir el aceite
  Pue.R. varilla de aceite
  Venz. indicador de medir el aceite
ditch (n) zanja
  Col., Spa. cuneta
  Cos.R. sanja
  Uru. pozo
drive (car) (v) manejar
  Chi., Col., Pan., Spa. conducir
  Pue.R. guiar
driver's seat (n phr) asiento del
  conductor
  Chi. asiento del chofer, asiento
  del piloto
  Cub. asiento del chofer
drive drunk (v phr) manejar borracho
  Arg., Pue.R. conducir en estado
  de embriaguez
  Chi. manejar en estado de

ebriedad
  Col. manejar embriagado
  Cos.R. manejar tomado
  Dom.R. manejar en estado de
  embriaguez
  Spa. conducir borracho,
  conducir ebrio
emergency lights (n phr) luces de
  emergencia
  Arg. balizas
  Ecu. faros de emergencia
  Pue.R. luces intermitentes
engine (n) motor
exhaust pipe (n phr) tubo de escape
  Arg. caño de escape
  Col. exosto
  Mex. escape
expressway (n) autopista
  Mex. vía rápida
  Spa. carretera
fan belt (n phr) correa del ventilador
  Mex. banda del ventilador
fender (n) ala
  Arg. paragolpes
  Col. guardabarro, guardafango
  Cub., Ecu., ElS., Gua., Venz.
  guardafango
  Mex. defensa
  Pue.R. fender
  Spa. guardabarro
flat tire (n phr) llanta reventada
  Arg., Dom.R. goma pinchada
  Bol. llanta pinchada
  Chi. pneumático pinchado
  Col. llanta desinflada, llanta
  pinchada
  Cos.R., Per. llanta desinflada
  Cub. goma ponchada
  Ecu. tubo bajo
  ElS., Gua. llanta pache, llanta

ABBREVIATIONS: Arg.=Argentina Bol.=Bolivia Chi.=Chile Col.=Colombia
Cos.R.=Costa Rica Cub.=Cuba Dom.R.=Dominican Republic Ecu.=Ecuador ElS.=El
Salvador Gua.=Guatemala Hon.=Honduras Mex.=Mexico Pan.=Panama Per.=Peru
Pri.=Primary Term Pue.R.=Puerto Rico Spa.=Spain Uru.=Uruguay Venz.=Venezuela

pinchada
Mex. llanta pinchada, llanta
ponchada
Pan. flat
Pue.R. goma vacía
Spa. neumático pinchado, rueda
pinchada
Venz. caucho pinchado
Uru. llanta desinflada, neumático
desinflado
four-wheel drive (n phr) propulsión
total
Arg., Chi., Col., Gua., Mex.
tracción en las cuatro ruedas
Cub., Venz. tracción de cuatro
ruedas
Dom.R. cuatro tracciónes
Spa. tracción a las cuatro ruedas
garage (repairs) (n) garaje
Arg. taller mecánico
Col. taller
gas (vehicle) (n) gasolina
Arg. nafta
gas pedal (n phr) acelerador
Pue.R. pedal de la gasolina
Venz. pedal de gasolina
gas tank (n phr) tanque de gasolina
Arg. tanque de nafta
Spa. depósito de gasolina
gearbox (n) caja de cambios
ElS., Gua., Mex. caja de
velocidades
Pue.R. transmisión
gears (n) velocidades
Arg., Chi., Cub., Dom.R., Pan.,
Pue.R., Uru., Venz. cambios
Cos.R. marchas
headlights (n) faros
Arg., Cub. focos, luces
Chi., Pan., Pue.R. luces

Col. faroles delanteros
Dom.R., Mex., Venz. luces
delanteras
head-on collision (n phr) choque de
frente
Col. colisión frente a frente
Per. choque frente a frente
Spa., Uru. choque frontal
hubcap (n) tapacubos
Chi. taparuedas
Col. copa de la rueda
Cub. tambora
Ecu., Spa. tabacubo
Mex. tapón
Pan. rin
Pue.R. tapabocina
Uru. embellecedor
Venz. taza del caucho
ice cream truck (n phr) heladero
Col. camión del helado, carrito
de helados
Mex. carro de helados
Spa. camión del helado
jack (car) (n) gato
Bol., Chi., Per. gata
Gua. triquet
lane (n) carril
Cub. línea
Venz. canal
limousine (n) limosina
lubrication (n) engrase
Chi. lubrificación
Col., Dom.R., Gua., Pan.
lubricación
Mex. engrasado
median (n) centro de la calle
Col. isla de tráfico, separador
Pue.R. carril del centro
Spa. mediana
Venz. isla

muffler (n) mofle
  Arg., Col., Ecu., Spa., Uru.
  silenciador
  Dom.R. muffler
  Mex. mufler
  Venz. amortiguador
park (v) estacionar
  Bol., Col., Cos.R., Cub.,
  Dom.R., ElS., Gua., Hon., Pan.
  parquear
  Spa. aparcar
parking lot (n phr) estacionamiento
  Arg. playa de estacionamiento
  Bol., Cos.R., Cub., Dom.R.
  ElS., Gua., Hon. parqueo
  Col., Pan. parqueadero
  Pue.R. parking
  Spa. parking, aparcamiento
pass (traffic) (v) pasar
  Chi. ultrapasar
  Cos.R. adelantarse
  Dom.R., Mex. rebasar
  Spa. adelantar
pedestrian (n) peatón
pickup truck (n phr) camioneta
  Cos.R., ElS., Gua., Hon., Pan.,
  Per. pickup
  Mex., Venz. camioneta pickup
pothole (n) pozo
  Arg., Cub., Gua., Mex., Spa.
  bache
  Chi., Dom.R. hoyo
  Col., Cos.R., Ecu., Pan. hueco
racecar (n) coche de carrera
  Arg., Chi. auto de carrera
  Cub., ElS., Gua., Hon., Pan.,
  Pue.R. carro de carrera
  Col., Per., Venz. carro de carreras
  Dom.R. auto de carrera, carro
  de carrera

  Spa. coche de carreras
radar (traffic) (n) radar
radiator (n) radiador
radiator grill (n phr) rejilla del
  radiador
  Arg., Col. parrilla del radiador
rear window (n phr) ventana trasera
  Arg. luneta
  Col. ventanilla trasera
  Pue.R. cristal trasero
rear-view mirror (n phr) espejo
  retrovisor
  Uru. espejo trasero
recreational vehicle (n phr) vehículo
  de recreo
  Bol. vagoneta
  Chi. casa rodante
  Mex. camper
  Pue.R. RV
  Spa. caravana
  Venz. vehículo recreacional
reverse (n) marcha atrás
  Col. reversa, reverso
  Dom.R., Mex., Pan. reversa
  Pue.R. riversa
  Venz. retroceso
right of way (n phr) prioridad
  Arg., Cub., Pue.R. derecho de
  paso
  Chi., Mex. paso
  Col. derecho a la vía
  Dom.R., Ecu., Spa. preferencia
  ElS., Gua., Pan. derecho de vía
  Venz. prioridad de circulación
road (n) calle, carretera
road shoulder (n phr) lomo
  Arg. banquina
  Col. breda, orilla de la carretera
  Cos.R. orilla de la carretera
  ElS., Gua. borde de la carretera

ABBREVIATIONS: Arg.=Argentina Bol.=Bolivia Chi.=Chile Col.=Colombia
Cos.R.=Costa Rica Cub.=Cuba Dom.R.=Dominican Republic Ecu.=Ecuador ElS.=El
Salvador Gua.=Guatemala Hon.=Honduras Mex.=Mexico Pan.=Panama Per.=Peru
Pri.=Primary Term Pue.R.=Puerto Rico Spa.=Spain Uru.=Uruguay Venz.=Venezuela

Pue.R. paseo
Spa., Uru. arcén
Venz. hombrillo
road sign (n phr) letrero de carretera
  Arg. cartel
  Chi. señalización en la carretera
  Col. aviso vial
  Dom.R., Spa., Uru. señal de
  tráfico
  Per. señal del camino
  Venz. señal de tránsito
road works (n phr) obras
  Arg., Pue.R. construcción
  Col. arreglos en la vía
  Venz. mantenimiento de calles
road, country (n phr) camino rural
rush hour (n phr) hora pico
  Arg. rush hour
  Cub., Mex. hora de tráfico
  Per. hora de entrada o salida a los
  trabajos
  Pue.R. hora del tapón
  Spa. hora punta
sedan (n) sedán
  Spa. turismo
shift gear (v phr) cambiar la velocidad
  Arg. hacer un cambio
  Chi. pasar la marcha, reducir la
  marcha
  Col. meter un cambio
  Pue.R. cambiar de cambios
  Spa. cambiar la marcha
side mirror (n) espejo lateral
sidewalk (n) acera
  Arg., Chi., Cos.R., Ecu., Per.,
  Uru. vereda
  Col. andén
  Mex. banqueta
spare parts (n phr) repuestos
  Cub., Spa. piezas de repuesto

Mex. refacciones
Pue.R. repuestas
spare tire (n phr) rueda de repuesto
  Arg. goma de auxilio, rueda de
  auxilio
  Bol., Ecu., Gua., Pan. llanta de
  repuesto
  Cub., Dom.R. goma de repuesto
  Mex. llanta de refacción
  Pue.R. goma de repuesta
  Venz. caucho de repuesto
spark plug (n phr) bujía
speed limit (n phr) límite de velocidad
  Mex., Pue.R. velocidad máxima
speedometer (n) velocímetro
  Chi. cuenta kilómetros
  Cub. cuentakilómetro
sports car (n phr) carro deportivo
  Arg., Chi. auto deportivo
  Bol. coche sport
  Cub. carro de deporte
  Spa., Uru. coche deportivo
stall (car) (v) calar
  Arg., Cub., Ecu., Mex., Pan. parar
  Chi. pararse
  Col. vararse
  Cos.R. quedar varado
  Pue.R. inundar
  Spa. calarse
  Venz. apagarse el carro
start (car) (v) arrancar
  Chi., Dom.R. encender, prender
  Col. poner en marcha
  Pue.R. prender
starter (n) arranque
  Chi. salir
  Cos.R., Mex. arrancador
  Cub., Spa. motor de arranque
  Pue.R. estarter
station wagon (n phr) camioneta

Cos.R., Ecu., Per., Spa.
combinable
Bol. vagoneta
Cub. pisicorre
Dom.R. station, van
Pue.R. guagüita
steering wheel (n phr) volante
Chi. manubrio
Col., Cub., Gua., Pan. timón
Dom.R., Pue.R. guía
stick shift (n phr) palanca de cambios
Arg. cambio
Cos.R. marcha
Mex. palanca de velocidades
Spa. cambio manual
stop (sign) (int) alto
Arg., Chi., Col., Pue.R. pare
Spa. stop
street (n) calle
street, cobblestone (n phr) calle de
guijarro
Arg., Bol., Col., Ecu., Venz. calle
empedrada
Chi. calle de adoquines, calle de
paralelepípedos
Gua. calle de adoquín
Mex. calle adoquinada
Pan. calle de ladrillo
Per. calle de piedras
Pue.R., Spa., Uru. calle de
adoquines
street, dead-end (n phr) calle sin salida
Col., Mex. calle cerrada
Dom.R. cul de sac
Venz. calle ciega
street, one-way (n phr) calle de una
mano
Chi. vía única
Col., Mex., Per. calle de un solo
sentido

Cos.R., Dom.R., Pue.R., Venz.
calle de una vía
Ecu. calle de una sola dirección
ElS., Gua., Hon. calle de una
sola vía
Pan. calle de una vía, one way
Spa. calle de dirección única
sunroof (n) sunroof
Chi., Spa. techo solar
Col. techo corredizo
Mex. quemacocos
Venz. techo corredizo, techo
descapotable
ticket, speeding (n phr) multa por
exceso de velocidad
Mex. infracción por exceso de
velocidad
Pan. boleta por velocidad
ticket, traffic (n phr) multa
Mex. infracción
Pan. boleta
tire (car) (n) llanta
Arg., Cub. goma, rueda
Chi., Col. pneumático
Dom.R., Pue.R. goma
Spa. rueda
Venz. caucho
traffic (n) tráfico
Chi., Cos.R., Dom.R. tránsito
traffic island (n phr) isleta
Arg., Col., Venz. isla
traffic jam (n phr)
congestionamiento
Arg., Per., Uru. embotellamiento
Chi. atascamiento, congestión,
taco
Col. trancón
Cos.R. atasco, presa
Cub. tráfico, tranque
Dom.R., Pue.R. tapón

ABBREVIATIONS: Arg.=Argentina Bol.=Bolivia Chi.=Chile Col.=Colombia
Cos.R.=Costa Rica Cub.=Cuba Dom.R.=Dominican Republic Ecu.=Ecuador ElS.=El
Salvador Gua.=Guatemala Hon.=Honduras Mex.=Mexico Pan.=Panama Per.=Peru
Pri.=Primary Term Pue.R.=Puerto Rico Spa.=Spain Uru.=Uruguay Venz.=Venezuela

Pan. tranque
Spa. atasco
traffic light (n phr) semáforo
trailer (n) remolque
Chi., Cos.R., Cub., Dom.R., Pan.
trailer
tread (tire) (n) ranuras
Mex. dibujo de llanta
Spa. cubierta
Venz. huella del caucho
truck (n) camión
trunk (car) (n) baúl
Bol., Per. maletera
Chi. porta equipaje
Cub., Pan., Spa. maletero
Mex. cajuela
Venz. maleta
tune up (v phr) revisar
Cub. reglar
Dom.R. arreglar
Gua., Mex. afinar
Venz. entonar
turn right, left (v phr) doblar a la
derecha, izquierda
Cos.R. virar a la derecha,
izquierda
Mex. dar vuelta a la derecha,
izquierda
Spa. torcer a la derecha, izquierda
turning light (n phr) luz direccional
Arg. guiño
Chi. luz del indicador
Col. luz para doblar
Cub., Spa. intermitente
Dom.R. luz de doblar
Gua. pidevías
Mex. dirreccional
Per. luz para voltear
Uru. señal intermitente
Venz. señal de cruce

underpass (n) paso subterráneo
Chi. paso nivel
Col. pasadizo subterráneo
Spa. paso inferior
valve (n) válvula
van (n) camión
Arg., Chi., Cub., Dom.R., Pue.R.
van
Col., Uru. furgón
Cos.R., Mex. camioneta
Ecu. buseta
Pan. busito, van
Per. microbus
Spa. furgoneta
Venz. camioneta, furgoneta
windshield (n) parabrisas
wipers (windshield) (n)
limpiaparabrisas
Col. limpiabrisas
Cub., Per. parabrisas
Dom.R. limpiavidrios
Pue.R. wipers
Venz. limpia-parabrisas

Transportation: Public Transport

airfare (n) precio del pasaje
Arg., Ecu. tarifa
Col. tarifa aérea
Mex. tarifa de vuelo
Spa. precio del billete de avión
Venz. precio del boleto
airline (n) aerolínea
Col. compañía de aviación, línea
aérea
Dom.R. línea aérea
airplane (n) avión
Col. aeronave

airport (n) aeropuerto
arrival (n) llegada
   Chi. desembarque
baggage (n) equipaje
   Cos.R. maletas
blimp (n) dirigible no rígido
   Col., Spa. dirigible
   Cub., Venz. zepelín
board (v) embarcarse
   Chi., Col., Dom.R., Mex. abordar
   Spa., Venz. embarcar
boat (n) barco
   Cub., Venz. bote
bumper car (n phr) carro loco
   Arg. autito chocador
   Dom.R. carrito chocón
   Mex., Per., Venz. carro chocón
   Spa. auto de choque
bus (n) autobús
   Arg. bus, ómnibus
   Col., Pan. bus
   Bol. colectivo
   Chi. micro
   Col. bus, buseta, colectivo
   Cos.R. bus, lata
   Cub., Dom.R., Pue.R. guagua
   ElS., Gua. camioneta
   Mex. camión
   Per., Uru. ómnibus
bus stop (n phr) parada de autobús
   Arg., Per., Uru. parada del
   ómnibus
   Bol. parada del colectivo
   Chi. parada del micro
   Col., Pan. parada de bus
   Cos.R. parada de lata, parada de
   bus
   Cub., Dom.R., Pue.R. parada de
   guagua
business trip (n phr) viaje de negocios

carousel (with horses) (n) caballitos
   Arg., Uru. calesita
   Chi., Col., Ecu., ElS., Gua.,
   Hon., Pan., Venz. carrusel
carpool (v) compartir coches
   Arg. hacer pool
   Col. compartir viajes en carro
   Gua. compartir carros
   Mex. turnarse alternando coches
   Venz. ir juntos en un carro
change (train) (v) transbordar
   Arg. hacer una conexión
   Col., Cub. cambiar de tren
   Venz. hacer un transbordo de
   trenes
check in (baggage) (v phr) registrar el
   equipaje
   Chi. despachar
   Dom.R., Venz. chequear el
   equipaje
commute (v) viajar a diario al trabajo
delay (n) retraso
   Arg. demora
   Chi. atraso
   Col. atraso, demora, retardo
departure (n) salida
   Chi. embarque
dining car (train) (n phr) coche
   comedor
   Col. vagón-restaurante
   Spa. coche restaurante
   Venz. carro comedor
driver's license (n phr) licencia de
   conducir
   Arg. carnet de conductor,
   permiso de conductor
   Chi. carnet de chofer
   Col. pase para conducir
   Cub., Venz. licencia de manejar
   Spa. carnet de conducir

ABBREVIATIONS: Arg.=Argentina Bol.=Bolivia Chi.=Chile Col.=Colombia
Cos.R.=Costa Rica Cub.=Cuba Dom.R.=Dominican Republic Ecu.=Ecuador ElS.=El
Salvador Gua.=Guatemala Hon.=Honduras Mex.=Mexico Pan.=Panama Per.=Peru
Pri.=Primary Term Pue.R.=Puerto Rico Spa.=Spain Uru.=Uruguay Venz.=Venezuela

elevator (n) ascensor
Cub., Mex., Pan., Pue.R. elevador
escalator (n) escalera mecánica
Col. escalera automática
Dom.R., Mex. escalera eléctrica
fare (n) precio, tarifa
ferris wheel (n phr) noria
Chi. rueda gigante
Col. rueda de Chicago, rueda
giratoria gigante
Cub., Dom.R., Pan. estrella
Ecu. rueda muscovita
Mex. rueda de la fortuna
Venz. rueda
ferry (n) transbordador
Col., Cos.R., Dom.R., Spa.,
Venz. ferry
Cub. lancha
first class (adj phr) primera clase
Arg. primera
flight (n) vuelo
float (parade) (n) carroza
Chi. carro alegórico
flotilla (n) flotilla
funicular (n) funicular
Mex., Venz. teleférico
get off (bus) (v phr) bajarse
Bol., Cos.R., Dom.R., Per., Uru.
apearse
get on (bus) (v phr) subirse
Col. montarse
helicopter (n) helicóptero
hitchhike (v) hacer autostop
Arg., Chi. hacer dedo
Col. echar dedo
Cos.R. pedir ride
Dom.R. pedir bola
ElS., Gua., Hon. pedir jalón a
dedo
Per. tirar dedo

Pue.R. pedir pon
Venz. pedir cola
hot air balloon (n phr) globo
aerostático
Chi., Col. globo
Venz. globo de aire caliente
hydrofoil boat (n phr) hidroala
Chi. hidroavión
Col. aereodeslizador
Mex. hidrofoil
jet (n) jet
Chi. avión a chorro
jet-lag, to have (v phr) tener jet lag
Dom.R. estar desorientado por
desfase de horarios
Mex. sentirse mal por la altura,
sentirse mal por el vuelo
Spa. tener desfase horario
landing (n) aterrizaje
local train (n phr) tren local
Mex. metro
Spa. tren de cercanías
ocean liner (n phr) transatlántico
one-way ticket (n phr) billete sencillo
Arg. boleto de ida, pasaje de ida
Bol. billete de ida, billete de una
sola vía
Chi., Mex., Pan., Venz. boleto de
ida
Col. tiquete de una sola vía
Cos.R., Dom.R. pasaje de ida
Ecu., Spa. billete de ida
Per. boleto en un solo sentido
platform (train) (n) andén
Col., Cub., Per. plataforma
porter (n) maletero
Bol. maletera
Col., Cub. portero
Spa. mozo
Venz. cargador de maletas

ABBREVIATIONS: Arg.=Argentina Bol.=Bolivia Chi.=Chile Col.=Colombia
Cos.R.=Costa Rica Cub.=Cuba Dom.R.=Dominican Republic Ecu.=Ecuador ElS.=El
Salvador Gua.=Guatemala Hon.=Honduras Mex.=Mexico Pan.=Panama Per.=Peru
Pri.=Primary Term Pue.R.=Puerto Rico Spa.=Spain Uru.=Uruguay Venz.=Venezuela

request stop (bus) (n phr) parada
  facultativa
  Col. solicitud para hacer detener
  el bus
  Mex. parada solicitada
  Spa. parada discrecional
  Venz. parada pedida
rocket (n) cohete
roller coaster (n phr) montaña rusa
round trip ticket (n phr) billete de ida
  y vuelta
  Arg. boleto de ida y vuelta, pasaje
  de ida y vuelta
  Chi., Pan., Per., Venz. boleto de
  ida y vuelta
  Col. tiquete de ida y vuelta
  Cos.R., Dom.R. pasaje de ida y
  vuelta
  Mex. boleto de ida y vuelta,
  boleto de viaje redondo
sail (v) navegar
sailboat (n) barco de vela
  Col. bote de vela
  Dom.R. velero
second class (n phr) segunda clase
  Arg. segunda
  Dom.R. clase económica
ship (n) buque
  Arg., Cos.R., Pan., Uru., Venz.
  barco
  Chi. barco, navío
  Col. barco, embarcación
sleeping car (train) (n phr) coche cama
  Col. litera
space shuttle (n phr) transbordador
  espacial
submarine (n) submarino
suitcase (n) maleta
  Arg. valija
takeoff (n) despegue

taxi (n) taxi
  Venz. libre
taxi stand (n phr) parada de taxi
  Venz. parada de libres, parada de
  taxis
through train (n phr) tren directo
  Venz. tren expreso
ticket (n) billete
  Arg., Cub. boleto, pasaje
  Chi., Mex., Pan., Per., Pue.R.
  boleto
  Col. tiquete
  Cos.R. pasaje
  Dom.R. pasaje, ticket
  Venz. boleto, ticket
ticket collector (n phr) revisor
  Chi., Ecu. conductor
  Col. recolector de tiquetes
  Mex. persona que recoge los
  boletos
  Per. boletero
  Venz. chequeador de boletos,
  chequeador de tickets
timetable (n) horario
  Col. itinerario
train station (n phr) estación de tren
travel (n) viajar
trolley (n) tranvía
  Chi. trole
  Dom.R. carrito
  Mex. trolebús
wagon (n) carreta
  Bol., Ecu., Gua., Spa. vagón

> The Spanish word *izquierda* (left) is a variation of the Basque *ezkerra*.

ABBREVIATIONS: Arg.=Argentina Bol.=Bolivia Chi.=Chile Col.=Colombia Cos.R.=Costa Rica Cub.=Cuba Dom.R.=Dominican Republic Ecu.=Ecuador ElS.=El Salvador Gua.=Guatemala Hon.=Honduras Mex.=Mexico Pan.=Panama Per.=Peru Pri.=Primary Term Pue.R.=Puerto Rico Spa.=Spain Uru.=Uruguay Venz.=Venezuela

Workplace: Computer

buffer storage (n phr) memoria
intermediaria
Col. memoria intermedia,
memoria temporal
Mex. búfer
Pue.R. buffer storage
Venz. memoria de reserva,
memoria intermedia, memoria
temporal
click (computer) (v) hacer clic
Cub. pulsar
Pue.R. apretar
computer (n) computadora
Col. computador
Spa. ordenador
data (n) datos
Col. información
debug (computer) (v) depurar
Dom.R. desinfectar
Pue.R., Venz. limpiar
delete (v) borrar, eliminar
Arg. deletear
directory (computer) (n) directorio
DOS (disc operating system) (n phr)
DOS (sistema operativo de disco)
drive (computer) (n) unidad de disco
Dom. R., Pue.R. drive
e-mail (n) correo electrónico
Arg., Dom.R., Mex., Pue.R., Spa.
e-mail
encrypt (computer) (v) ocultar
Col., Mex., Spa. encriptar
Uru. cifrar
Venz. cifrar, codificar
file (computer) (n) archivo
hard drive (n phr) disco duro
Pue.R. hard drive

hardware (n) hardware
icon (computer) (n) icono
Cub. símbolo gráfico
Pue.R. icon
keyboard (computer) (n) teclado
Pue.R. keyboard
LAN (local area network) (n phr) LAN
Mex. red local LAN
Spa., Venz. red de área local
monitor (computer) (n) monitor
Arg., Chi. pantalla
motherboard (n) placa madre
Col., Spa. tarjeta madre
Mex. tarjeta principal
Pan. mother board
Venz. placa base
network (computer) (n) red
PC (n) PC
Arg., Gua., Mex., Venz.
computadora personal
Bol. computador personal
Spa. ordenador personal (OP)
printer (computer) (n) impresora
Pue.R. printer
scanner, optical (n phr) explorador
óptico
Arg., Dom.R., Pue.R. scanner
Chi., Cub., Mex., Pan., Spa.
escáner
Venz. copiador óptico
scroll (computer) (v) desplazar
Pan. mover
Pue.R. scroll
software (n) software
Spa. programas
store (computer data) (v) almacenar
Arg. grabar, guardar
Dom.R. archivar
Mex., Pan. guardar
Venz. guarder

subdirectory (computer) (n)
subdirectorio
surf the net (v phr) surfear la Internet
   Arg. navegar la red
   Bol., Ecu. navegar en el Internet
   Chi., Gua. navegar por la Internet
   Col. navegar la red, navegar por
   Internet
   Cub., Spa., Uru. navegar por la
   red
   Dom.R. surfear en el Internet
   Mex. accesar a la red, buscar en
   la red, usar la red
   Venz. explorar el Internet
virus (computer) (n) virus
WAN (wide area network) (n phr)
   WAN
   Col. red de área extendida
   Cub., Mex., Spa. red de área
   amplia
   Uru. red de área ancha
   Venz. red de área extensa
website (n) sitio web
   Arg. página principal
   Dom.R., Pue.R. web-site
   Gua. sitio de la red
   Venz. lugar del Web, página del
   Web
word processing (n phr)
   procesamiento de palabras
   Arg., Mex. procesamiento de
   textos
   Cub., Ecu. procesamiento de
   texto
   Pue.R. word processing

Workplace: Occupations

architect (n) arquitecto
artist (n) artista
attorney (n) abogado
baker (n) panadero
barber (n) barbero
   Arg., Ecu., Mex., Per. peluquero
bartender (n) barman
   Col., Ecu., ElS., Gua., Hon.,
   Mex., Pan., Pue.R. cantinero
   Cub., Dom.R. bartender
bookkeeper (n) contador
   Cub. tenedor de libros
   Spa. contable
boss (n) jefe
   Col. patrón
bus driver (n phr) conductor de
   autobús
   Arg. chofer de colectivo, chofer
   de micro
   Chi. chofer
   Col. chofer de bus
   Cub. guagüero
   Dom.R., Pue.R. chofer de guagua
   Mex. camionero
   Pan. busero
businessman (n) hombre de negocios
   Arg., Chi. empresario
   Col. ejecutivo
   Pan. hombre profesional
businesswoman (n) mujer de negocios
   Arg., Chi., Cos.R. empresaria
   Col. ejecutiva
   Pan. mujer profesional
butcher (n) carnicero
carpenter (n) carpintero
cashier (n) cajero/a
certified public accountant (CPA) (n

---

phr) contador público certificado
Chi. contador
Cos.R. contador público
autorizado
Dom.R. contable, contador, CPA
Pan. contador público autorizado,
CPA
Spa. contable
chef (n) chef
Col. cocinero, jefe de cocina
Per. jefe de cocina
Spa. cocinero
chief executive officer (CEO) (n phr)
jefe ejecutivo principal
Arg. presidente
Chi. gerente ejecutivo
Col. gerente general
Cos.R. director general, gerente
general
Dom.R. director ejecutivo
Gua. personero ejecutivo de más
alto rango
Mex. director general
Venz. oficial ejecutivo jefe
coal miner (n phr) minero del carbón
comptroller (n) controlador
Cos.R. auditor
Dom.R. contralor
Venz. interventor
consultant (n) consejero
Arg., Col., Mex., Pan., Spa. asesor
Chi., Cos.R., Cub., Dom.R.,
Ecu., Per. consultor
Venz. asesor, consultor
counselor (n) consejero
Ecu., Mex., Spa. asesor
craftsperson (n) artesano
dentist (n) dentista
doctor (n) médico
Arg., Col., Chi. doctor

door-to-door salesperson (n phr)
vendedor a domicilio
Col. vendedor puerta a puerta
Cos.R. representante de ventas
dry cleaner (n phr) tintorero
editor (n) redactor
Col., Pue.R., Spa., Venz. editor
electrician (n) electricista
executive (n) ejecutivo
farmer (n) agricultor
Chi. ganadero
Col. campesino
Per. granjero
fire (v) despedir
Arg. echar
Col. destituir, echar
Cub., Dom.R botar
firefighter (n) bombero
flight attendant (n phr) auxiliar de
vuelo, azafata
Col. cabinera
Cub., Mex., Pan., Venz.
aeromozo/a
florist (n) florista
fringe benefit (n phr) incentivo
Col. beneficio adicional,
beneficio suplementario
Cos.R. beneficio laborable
ElS., Gua. prestación
complementaria
full-time (work) (adj) de jornada
completa
Arg. de horario completo
Col., Mex. de tiempo completo
Cub., Dom.R., Venz. a tiempo
completo
garbage collector (n phr) basurero
Col., Venz. recogedor de basura
gardener (n) jardinero
grocer (n) tendero

Arg., Uru. almacenero
Col. comerciante, vendedor
Cub. bodeguero
Dom.R. dependiente de colmado/
supermercado/tienda
Ecu., Mex. abarrotero
hairdresser (n) peluquero/a
Col. barbero
Mex., Pan. estilista
healer (n) curandero
hire (v) contratar, emplear
holiday (n) día feriado
Arg. feriado
Col., Spa. día festivo
Mex. día de fiesta, día de
vacaciones
inmate (n) preso
Col. encarcelado, prisionero,
recluso
Pan. reo
interpreter (n) intérprete
interview (n) entrevista
janitor (n) conserje
Chi. limpiador
Col. portero
Cub. barrendero
judge (n) juez
jury (n) jurado
lawyer (n) abogado
Col. jurista
librarian (n) bibliotecario/a
Dom.R. bibliotecólogo
mail carrier (n phr) cartero
manicurist (n) manicuro/a
Chi. manicure
Dom.R., Ecu., Mex., Pan., Per.,
Venz. manicurista
mayor (n) alcalde/sa
Chi. prefecto
Dom.R. síndico

Mex. presidente municipal
Uru. intendente
midwife (n) partera
Col., Dom.R., ElS., Gua., Hon.,
Spa. comadrona
musician (n) músico
nurse (n) enfermero/a
office manager (n phr) jefe de oficina
Col. administrador, gerente
Cub., Mex., Pue.R., Venz. gerente
de oficina
part-time (work) (adj) por parte de la
jornada
Cub., Per., Spa. a tiempo parcial
Mex. de medio tiempo, parte de
tiempo
Pue.R. part-time
patient (n) paciente
Arg., Bol., Cub., Cos.R., Ecu.,
Gua., Uru. enfermo/a
Col. doliente
pharmacist (n) farmacéutico
Col. boticario, farmaceuta
Venz. farmaceuta
pilot (n) piloto
Col. aviador
pimp (n) chulo
Chi. cafiche
ElS., Gua., Hon. alcahuete
plumber (n) plomero
Chi. gáfiter [from "gas fitter"]
Ecu. gasfitero
Spa. fontanero
police detective (n) agente
Chi., Cub., Mex., Pan., Venz.
detective
Col. agente de policía, detective
policíaco
Dom.R. detective policial
ElS., Gua., Hon. detective de la

policía
Spa. investigador
police officer (n phr) policía
Chi. carabinero
Col., Spa. agente de policía
Dom.R. agente policial
Venz. oficial de policía
prisoner (n) preso
Chi. reo
Col. encarcelado, prisionero,
recluso
Pan. prisionero
private detective (n phr) detective
privado
psychiatrist (n) psiquiatra
psychotherapist (n) psicoterapeuta
publisher (n) editor/a
rabbi (n) rabino
Spa. rabí
realtor (n) corredor de bienes raíces
Arg. inmobiliario
receptionist (n) recepcionista
salary (n) sueldo
Col. honorarios, paga, salario
Mex., Pan. salario
salesperson (n) dependiente
Chi. promotor/a, vendedor/a
Col. empleado/a, vendedor/a
Dom.R., Ecu., ElS., Gua., Hon.,
Mex., Venz. vendedor/a
school day (n phr) día lectivo
Col. día de colegio
Dom.R., Per. día de clases
Mex., Venz. día de escuela
Pue.R. día de clase
scientist (n) científico
seamstress (n) costurera
Arg., Chi., Col., Pan., Spa.
modista
secretary (n) secretario/a

sick leave (n phr) permiso de
convalecencia
Arg., Bol., ElS., Gua., Hon.
permiso por enfermedad
Col., Dom.R. licencia por
enfermedad
Cub. días de enfermedad
Venz. permiso de convalescencia
superviser (n) supervisor
tailor (n) sastre
Col. costurero, modisto
Spa. costurero
taxi driver (n phr) conductor de taxi
Arg., Cub., Dom.R., Gua.,
Mex., Per., Spa. taxista
Chi., Col., Cos.R. chofer de taxi
Venz. conductor de libre
technician (n) técnico
teller (bank) (n) cajero/a
temporary worker (n phr) temporero
Bol. temporal
Chi. jornalero
Col., Cos.R., Gua., Venz.
empleado/a temporal
Mex. trabajador eventual
Uru. temporario
train (for job) (v) capacitar
Col., Cub., Dom.R., Ecu., Pan.,
Venz. entrenar
translator (n) traductor/a
travel agent (n phr) agente de viajes
veterinarian (n) veterinario
waiter (n) camarero
Arg., Bol., Cos.R., Dom.R.,
Uru. mozo
Chi. garzón, mesero, mozo
Col., Cub., Dom.R., ElS., Gua.,
Mex., Pan., Pue.R. mesero
Venz. mesonero
warden (prison) (n) director/a de la

cárcel
Col. carcelero, guarda
Venz. carcelero, guardián de la
cárcel
weekday (n) día de entre semana
Arg., Col., Dom.R., Pue.R.,
Venz. día de semana
Cub., Gua., Spa. día entre semana
work day (n phr) día hábil
Col. día laborable, día de trabajo
Cub., Per., Pue.R. día de trabajo
Dom.R., Spa. día laborable

Workplace: Office

air conditioning (n phr) aire
acondicionado
Cos.R. airecondicionado
coffee maker (n phr) cafetera
Dom.R. greca
copier (n) copiadora
Spa. fotocopiadora
desk (n) escritorio
envelope (n) sobre
fax machine (n phr) màquina de fax
file (v) archivar
file cabinet (n phr) archivo
Chi. archivador
Mex. archivero
folder (n) carpeta de archivo
Bol. archivador
Dom.R., Mex., Pan., Pue.R.
folder
Spa. archivadora, carpeta
heating (n) calefacción
index card (n phr) ficha
Col., Pue.R. tarjeta
label (n) etiqueta
Dom.R., Pue.R. label

label, adhesive (n phr) etiqueta
adhesiva
Dom.R., Pue.R. label adhesiva
loading dock (n phr) plataforma de
carga
Col. muelle de carga
lobby (n) foyer
Arg. hall de entrada, lobby,
recepción
Chi. hall de entrada, recepción
Col. pasillo, vestíbulo
Cub., ElS., Gua., Spa. vestíbulo
Dom.R., Mex., Pue.R. lobby
Pan. loby
Venz. sala de espera, vestíbulo
mail room (n phr) cuarto de correos,
sala de correos
Spa. cuarto del correo
marker (n) marcador
Cub., Mex. plumón
Spa. rotulador
modular office (n phr) oficina
modular
Dom.R. módulo
notebook (n) cuaderno
Cub. carpeta
Dom.R. libreta, mascota
Pue.R. libreta
office building (n phr) edificio de
oficinas
office cubicle (n phr) recinto
Bol. oficina
Col., Dom.R., Gua., Mex., Pan.,
Pue.R., Venz. cubículo
office divider (n phr) partidor
Bol., Ecu. divisor
Col. divisor, separador
Dom.R. división
Mex. biombo separador
office hours (n phr) horas de oficina

Cub. horas de trabajo
office suite (n phr) oficina
Venz. suite de oficinas
office supplies (n phr) artículos de
oficina
Cub. materiales de oficina
Ecu. útiles de oficina
pad (paper) (n) cuaderno
Arg., Mex., Per. bloc
Bol., Cub., Pan., Pue.R., Venz.
libreta
Col. bloc, cuaderno de notas,
libreta
Spa. bloc de notas
pad, legal (n phr) cuaderno legal
Arg., Chi. bloc
Bol. libreta legal
Dom.R., Pan., Pue.R., Venz.
libreta tamaño legal
Mex. bloc tamaño oficio
Spa. bloc tamaño legal
pad, writing (n phr) cuaderno
Arg., Chi. bloc
Col., Cub., Dom.R., Pue.R.,
Venz. libreta
Mex. bloc tamaño carta
Spa. bloc de notas
pad, yellow (n phr) cuaderno amarillo
Arg., Chi. bloc
Bol., Col. Dom.R. libreta amarilla
Mex., Spa. bloc amarillo
Pue.R., Venz. libreta de papel
amarilla
paperclip (n) clip
Arg., Uru. ganchito
Bol., Cos.R., Cub., ElS., Gua.,
Hon. sujetapapel
Col. grapa, sujetador
pen (n) pluma
Arg., Chi., Uru. lapicera

Per. lapicero
Spa. bolígrafo
pen, ball-point (n phr) bolígrafo,
pluma
Bol. punta bola
Chi. lapicera de pasta
Col. esfero
Per. lapicero
pen, fountain (n phr) pluma de fuente
Arg. lapicera fuente
Bol., Mex., Pue.R., Venz. pluma
fuente
Chi. lapicera a fuente
Per. lapicero de tinta
Spa. pluma, pluma estilográfica
Uru. estilográfica
post office box (n phr) apartado postal
Bol. casilla
Chi. casilla postal
Col. buzón postal
Spa. apartado de correos
résumé (work history) (n) currículum
(vitae)
Col. hoja de vida
Mex. currículo
Pue.R. resumé
rolodex (n) fichero giratorio
Pue.R. rolodex
rubber band (n phr) cinta elástica
Arg., Dom.R., Pue.R. gomita
Bol., Chi. elástico
Col. caucho
Cub., Mex., Pan., Per., Venz. liga
ElS., Gua., Hon. hule
Spa., Uru. goma elástica
shredder (n) trituradora
Mex. picadora de papel
staple (n) grapa
Arg. ganchito
Chi. corchete

ABBREVIATIONS: Arg.=Argentina Bol.=Bolivia Chi.=Chile Col.=Colombia
Cos.R.=Costa Rica Cub.=Cuba Dom.R.=Dominican Republic Ecu.=Ecuador ElS.=El
Salvador Gua.=Guatemala Hon.=Honduras Mex.=Mexico Pan.=Panama Per.=Peru
Pri.=Primary Term Pue.R.=Puerto Rico Spa.=Spain Uru.=Uruguay Venz.=Venezuela

Cub. presilla
Per. grampa
staple remover (n phr) uñas
  Bol., Ecu., ElS., Gua., Hon.
  sacagrapas
  Chi. saca corchetes
  Col. removedor de grapas
  Dom. R. uñas saca grapas
  Mex. uña quitagrapas
  Spa. quitagrapas
  Venz. saca-grapas
stapler (n) engrapadora
  Arg. abrochadora
  Chi. corchetera
  Cub. presilladora
  Per. engrampador
  Pue.R., Spa. grapadora
storage room (n phr) almacenaje
  Arg., Col. depósito
  Bol., Dom.R., Pue.R., Spa.
  almacén
  Chi. despensa
  Cos.R., Ecu., Gua. bodega
  Mex. almacén, bodega
swivel chair (n phr) silla giratoria
tape (n) cinta adhesiva
  Ecu. cinta pegante
  Mex. durex
  Pue.R. tape
  Spa. celo
tape dispenser (n phr) carrete de cinta
  Col. dispensador de cinta pegante
  Dom.R. rollo de tape
  Mex. dispensador de durex,
  portarrollo
  Spa. carrete de celo
  Venz. dispensador de cinta
  adhesiva
three-ring binder (n phr) carpeta de
  argollas

Arg. carpeta con ganchos
Chi. archivador
Col. folder de argollas
Dom.R. carpeta de tres hoyos
Pan. portafolio
Spa. carpeta de tres anillos
toner (n) tinta
  Dom. R. toner
  Mex. tonificador
toner cartridge (n phr) cartucho de
  tinta
  Dom.R. cartucho del toner
  Mex. cartucho tonificador
water fountain (n phr) fuente de agua
  Arg., Chi., Mex., Venz. bebedero
  Dom.R. neverita

ABBREVIATIONS: Arg.=Argentina Bol.=Bolivia Chi.=Chile Col.=Colombia
Cos.R.=Costa Rica Cub.=Cuba Dom.R.=Dominican Republic Ecu.=Ecuador ElS.=El
Salvador Gua.=Guatemala Hon.=Honduras Mex.=Mexico Pan.=Panama Per.=Peru
Pri.=Primary Term Pue.R.=Puerto Rico Spa.=Spain Uru.=Uruguay Venz.=Venezuela

ALSO FROM SCHREIBER PUBLISHING . . .

Schreiber's Translator Self-Training Program
Includes workbooks with "real-life" assignments in subjects which are most often translated throughout the US, offering practical suggestions and insights on how to translate them accurately and in a timely manner.

The Translator's Handbook
Everything a translator needs to know, from dictionaries to education to developing work contacts.

Translation UPDATE Newsletter
Our bimonthly newsletter to help you keep up with the latest and best in the field.

21st Century American English Compendium
The "ins and outs" of American English.

Phone orders: in Maryland (301) 424-7737 Toll-free 1-(800)-822-3213
Fax: (301) 424-2336 e-mail: spbooks@aol.com
website: www.schreiberNet.com

Schreiber Publishing / P.O.Box 4193 / Rockville, MD 20849

ORDER FORM

Please send me a program for the following language (circle one):

Spanish French German Russian Japanese Italian Portuguese
Chinese Arabic Hebrew

☐ *Translator Self-Training Program,* including two Self-Training Workbooks
(from and into English) Qty. ____ @$69.00, total $_____

☐ *The Translator's Handbook.* Qty. ____ @$24.95, total $_____
In Canada ____ @$32.50, total $ _____

☐ *21ˢᵗ Century English Compendium* Qty.____ @$19.95, total $____ ____
In Canada ____ @$24.95, total $_____

☐ One-year subscription to *Update* newsletter only
Qty.___@$18.00, total $ _____

TOTAL PURCHASE: $_____

☐ Enclosed is my check or money order for the above amount
☐ Please charge my:
☐ VISA ☐ MC. Acct #_____ ____
Exp._____

Name_____ __ __

Address_____

City/State/Zip_____

Phone (   ) _____

Additional postage will be assessed for overseas orders.
Maryland residents add 5% sales tax.

Phone orders: in Maryland (301) 424-7737 Toll-free 1-(800)-822-3213
Fax: (301) 424-2336 e-mail: spbooks@aol.com
website: www.schreiberNet.com

Schreiber Publishing / P.O.Box 4193 / Rockville, MD 20849